Anna Seward's Life of
ERASMUS
DARWIN

Erasmus Darwin Bas-Relief Medallion produced by Josiah Wedgwood. This medallion passed through generations of the Darwin Family, and has now been placed on loan in the Erasmus Darwin House Library by Jeremy Barlow upon the death of his father, Dr Erasmus Darwin Barlow. Photography used with permission of Jeremy Barlow.

Anna Seward's Life of
ERASMUS DARWIN

Philip K. Wilson,
Elizabeth A. Dolan,
& Malcolm Dick

BREWIN BOOKS

First published by
Brewin Books Ltd, 56 Alcester Road,
Studley, Warwickshire B80 7LG in 2010
www.brewinbooks.com

ISBN: 978-1-85858-452-2 (Hardback)
ISBN: 978-1-85858-453-9 (Paperback)

A Cataloguing in Publication Record
for this title is available from the British Library.

Typeset in Bembo
Printed in Great Britain by
Hobbs the Printers Ltd

Contents

Foreword

Since 1994, a number of individuals, mostly volunteers, have worked to reclaim the Lichfield home of its once notable tenant, Dr Erasmus Darwin. At the forefront of this effort, Canon Tony Barnard, Dr Denis Gibbs, and Dr Gordon Cook, coupled with support from the Dean and Chapter of Lichfield Cathedral and from Erasmus Darwin Barlow, led the efforts which have renewed this important "artifact" of Erasmus Darwin for a new generation. The preservation and opening of Erasmus Darwin House to the public means that individuals can walk through and learn within the actual surrounds in which Darwin and members of his family lived and worked for a quarter of a century. The support offered by volunteers and members of the Friends of The Erasmus Darwin House and the Erasmus Darwin Foundation complements the staff – currently led by the Curator, Alison Wallis – in opening new vistas of Dr Darwin and his contemporaries for the many who turn to this house for a multitude of purposes.

Readers will encounter many of Dr Darwin's contemporaries in this volume. Above all, we find Miss Anna Seward. For many years, Darwin and Seward were the poets of Lichfield. Lichfield contributed in important ways to the literary and intellectual life of England's West Midlands as well as to the transitional era between the Enlightenment and the Romantic Period. The introductory essay attempts to provide at least some of this context from which both Seward and Darwin may be better understood.

Our efforts in bringing out a new version of Dr Darwin's first biography – a work written by Anna Seward – complements continuing efforts to reintroduce both luminaries to a new generation. Although Seward's biography is not the most accurate, particularly in comparison to later accounts whose authors had the benefit of hindsight, her work has the unique strength of being the only life story written by one of Darwin's contemporaries. Moreover, unlike later biographies of Dr Darwin, Seward's account purposefully records a broad view of the city in which he lived, practiced medicine, and wrote at least the first drafts of many of his major works.

As editors, we have benefitted from the contributions of many individuals. To paraphrase the twelfth-century scholastic translator, Bernard of Chartres, if this annotated commentary extends the utility of its original printing, it is only because we are privileged to stand upon the shoulders of those who have contributed to scholarly investigation of Darwin, Seward, and the West Midlands over the past two centuries. Their names are recorded in the text and footnotes which follow.

One of us (PKW) was privileged to spend a sabbatical year in Lichfield during 2006–2007 as the first Scholar-in-Residence at Erasmus Darwin House. It was during that year that the seed of this project was planted with another editor (MMD). Soon thereafter, we realized the need of remediating our deficiencies by adding a scholar of Romantic

Period English literature (EAD) to our editorial team. A number of key individuals have, in their respective ways, helped nurture the generation of this life history. Within the Lichfield community, Alison Wallis, David (and the late Joan) Tucker, Peter and Marie Gilbert, Madeleine Budgen, Jenny and David Arthur, Ishbel Curr and John Lane, Dr Chris and Lynneth Lockwood, Stephen Sanders, Ian S. Clark, Canon Tony and Anne Barnard, Dr Hazel Baker, Professor John and Kate Chapple, Kathy Simmons, Canon Pete, Dr Cathy, Jonathan and Tom Wilcox, Dr Bill and Mary Hassell, Gwyneth and Dr Gerald Boyle, Dean Adrian and Caroline Dorber, and Bishop Jonathan and Dr Jane Gledhill – in addition to many members of the Friends and Foundation of Erasmus Darwin as well as many members of the Dean and Chapter of Lichfield Cathedral – have contributed to the stability that life requires for laboured investigation into our subject. Pat Bancroft of the Cathedral Library in Lichfield, staff of the Samuel Johnson Birthplace Museum library, the Lichfield Record Office and the Lichfield Library provided exemplary assistance.

Beyond Lichfield, this work has benefitted from advice provided by Marion Roberts, who is completing a University of Birmingham Postgraduate degree on Anna Seward as a provincial cultural figure. Similarly, Desmond King-Hele has helped cast Dr Darwin in a more accurate light than we may have done otherwise. When we had questions that pushed us beyond his definitive biography of Dr Darwin, he helped to document several points in our footnotes. Stuart Harris, who is currently working with King-Hele to bring long-overlooked poems of Darwin to light once again, has enlightened our project with his own writings and continual support. Romantic-era literary scholars Aishah Al-Shatti, Deidre Lynch, Jeanne Moskal, Alan Rauch, and especially Mary Waters provided helpful information on the late-eighteenth-century memoir writing tradition.

Dr Denis and Rachel Gibbs continue to provide a nurturing environment within which to explore further the intricacies of history. As a treasure trove of Lichfieldiana and of medical history, Denis proved an ideal companion with which one of us (PKW) explored and published on the life of Dr Darwin's medical predecessor, Sir John Floyer. The success of our joint effort prompted this further jointly-prepared expansion into Lichfield's history and literary output.

This work adds further visibility to the Revolutionary Players website, www.revolutionary players.org.uk which is devoted to the history of the West Midlands in the eighteenth and nineteenth centuries which one of us (MMD) developed. Kate Iles, who also contributed to the development of Revolutionary Players, has offered assistance in piecing together part of our account by adding novel insights that she has unearthed regarding the lives of Darwin and Seward's contemporaries, Thomas Day and Sabrina Sidney Bicknell. Professor Ruth Watts, Professor C.U.M. Smith and Professor Bob Arnott have continued, enthusiastically, to support this and other efforts to expand investigations into Dr Darwin.

Members of the Darwin family, including Jeremy Barlow, Christopher and Heather Darwin, and Rosemary Bonham-Smith have shown a special interest in perpetuating the memory of their ancestor.

Further afield, Martina Higgins Stacey welcomed one of us (PKW) into the home of Darwin's fellow Lunar Society colleague, Richard Lovell Edgeworth. This home, in Edgeworthstown, County Longford, Ireland, currently serves its community as Our Lady's

Manor Nursing Home, for which Stacey is Director of Nursing. Stacey, and Edgeworthstown local historian, Matt Farrell, provided a personalized and unforgettable historical exploration though many nearby Edgeworth-related sites.

As this work has truly been a trans-Atlantic project, a number of individuals in the USA must also be acknowledged. Dr Joseph Priestley, known personally to both Darwin and Seward, emigrated from Birmingham to Northumberland, Pennsylvania in 1794. It is the Priestley connection, particularly through the support of the Friends of Joseph Priestley House, its Board of Directors, Brooke Dearman, and especially Andrea Bashore who help perpetuate Dr Darwin's memory in the United States.

Despite their ever-changing architecture and infrastructure, libraries remain essential to scholarly endeavours. The staff of the Paterno Library, the Pattee Library, the George Harrell College of Medicine Library of Penn State University (especially Esther Dell), Birmingham Central Library Archive and Heritage Service, The University of Birmingham, The American Philosophical Society Library (especially Roy Goodman), and the Lichfield Record Office (especially Andrew George) deserve special mention.

Jeanne Brandt of the Humanities Department at Penn State's College of Medicine has been a linchpin in ensuring that an historian's scholarly needs are fulfilled through inter-library loans. Deborah Tomazin of the same department has helpfully provided some scanned illustrations from original sources. Lehigh University English graduate students Christine Tucker and Elizabeth Vogtsberger proofread the text of the *Memoir* in record time and with impressive accuracy. We thank them both for their work.

Having a "personal librarian" is an exceptional privilege. For twenty years Janice Wilson has – among so many other things – offered her unflagging support to one of our (PKW) historical pursuits. She has worked with Erasmus Darwin-related material since her days assisting the late Professor Roy Porter at the then Wellcome Institute for the History of Medicine in London. Within the current project, she assembled the working text of Seward's *Life of Dr Darwin*, proofread sections, and provided a user-friendly and complete index.

Several young, yet engaging minds have shown great patience as their parents have delved into seemingly obscure subject matter. They must, at times, feel that their mom or dad pursues quite a different line of work from that of the "normal" parents of their schoolmates. For their patience – and for believing in us – we affectionately thank you, James, Doug, and Emma.

We also extend our gratitude to the following organizations for their assistance in various aspects of our research and in the preparation of this work. Penn State University, Lehigh University, The University of Birmingham, and The John Templeton Foundation. We are especially grateful to the Henry Gipson Institute for Eighteenth-Century Studies at Lehigh University for a grant funding the fees associated with including illustrations.

Many of the illustrations reproduced in this work were obtained, with permission, from the website of Revolutionary Players, a project focusing on the history of the Industrial Revolution in the West Midlands in Britain between the years 1700 and 1830. A number of additional illustrations were photographed by Dr Chris Lockwood using the Erasmus Darwin House Library collection. Dr Lockwood has long maintained a caring and compassionate general practice in Lichfield, somewhat following Dr Darwin's footsteps. We are grateful for his expertise with the camera – a skill that one of England's founders of photography, Thomas Wedgwood, would have admired. We are most appreciative of the staff of Erasmus Darwin House for allowing us to utilize their collections as a resource for many of our images.

The text of Anna Seward's that we have reproduced here includes the insertion of the twelve items of errata that she had listed in later printings of the 1804 edition which were published that same year. In reproducing this text, we have retained Seward's spelling and punctuation, though we have modernized her capitalization. Except when we concurred with Seward's emphasis, we have omitted her wide and scattered use of italics throughout, though we have followed the modern form of italicising the genus and species of scientific names of plants and animals. Where possible, we have indicated instances in which passages that Seward quotes deviate from those in the original sources available to us.

To preserve as much of the flow as possible in Seward's text, we have placed a Biographical Register near the end of the book where readers may find more extensive information about the life of individuals who are discussed with some regularity throughout Seward's text. At times sources disagree regarding basic biographical facts such as birth and death dates. If such dates were available in the *Oxford Dictionary of National Biography* or *Encyclopaedia Britannica*, then these were used. Others are included in this Register who, though not frequently mentioned, made significant contributions to the lives or the thinking of those living in Lichfield during the time of Seward and Darwin. The biographical information in this Register is not meant to be comprehensive but rather directed specifically to themes which Seward introduced. Further direction toward scholarship pertinent to these individuals is provided, particularly to that which illuminates the individuals as referenced within the text.

Alan and Alistair Brewin have provided helpful assistance at multiple stages of this project. We are grateful for their dedication to perpetuate deeper explorations into the history of the West Midlands through their publications. Their efforts – and those of all listed above – have helped make our book more accurate. Any lapses in accuracy, however, remain the sole responsibility of the editors.

List of Illustrations

Erasmus Darwin – Anna Seward
Selective Time Line

Erasmus Darwin	Date	Anna Seward
Born at Elston Hall	1731	
	1742	Born in Eyam, Derbyshire
	1749	Moves with family to Lichfield
Admitted to St. John's College, Cambridge	1750	
First published poem, "Death of Prince Frederick"	1751	Can recite the first three books of *Paradise Lost*
Travels to Edinburgh Medical School	1753	
	1754	Moves with family to Bishop's Palace, Lichfield
Takes M.B. degree at Cambridge	1755	Honora Sneyd taken into Seward household
Arrives at Lichfield as local physician; Meets Anna Seward	1756	Meets Dr Darwin
Paper on 'Ascent of Vapour' published in *Philosophical Transactions of Royal Society;* Marries Mary (Polly) Howard	1757	
First son Charles born; Acquires house near Cathedral Close	1758	

Erasmus Darwin	Date	Anna Seward
Second son, Erasmus Jr., born	1759	
Elected Fellow of the Royal Society	1761	
Daughter Elizabeth born (dies March 1764)	1763	
	1764	Sister Sarah dies, having recently been engaged to Joseph Porter, step-son of Samuel Johnson
Meets Josiah Wedgwood; they become involved in Grand Trunk Canal promotion; Dr William Small settles in Birmingham; Lunar Society developed	1765	
Son Robert born; First signs of wife Polly's illness; Meets Richard Lovell Edgeworth	1766	
Son William Alvey born (dies in August); Meets James Watt	1767	
Carriage accident, breaks patella; Meets Thomas Day	1768	Breaks patella in a fall
	1769	Meets John André in Buxton
Polly dies; Dr Darwin's portrait painted by Joseph Wright of Derby; Begins writing *Zoonomia*	1770	
Initiates liaison with Mary Parker	1771	
Susanna Parker born	1772	Seward-Saville scandal erupts; Seward meets Lady Miller at Batheaston
	1773	Honora Sneyd marries Richard Lovell Edgeworth in Lichfield Cathedral

Erasmus Darwin	Date	Anna Seward
Mary Parker born; Forms Lichfield literary circle, with Anna Seward and Sir Brooke Boothby	1774	
Dr Small dies	1775	
Begins developing a botanic garden at Abnalls, Lichfield; Begins compiling "Commonplace Book"	1776	
Son Charles dies	1778	
Completes Lichfield botanic garden; Forms Lichfield Botanical Society	1779	
	1780	Mother dies; Father has first stroke; *Elegy on Captain Cook* published; Honora (Sneyd) Edgeworth dies
Marries Elizabeth Pole; Leaves Lichfield for Radburn Hall, near Derby	1781	*Monody on the Death of Major André* published
Son Edward born; Son Erasmus Jr. becomes solicitor in Derby	1782	*Poem to the Memory of Lady Miller* published
Daughter Violetta born; Forms Derby Philosophical Society	1783	
Daughter Emma born	1784	Novel *Louisa* published; Samuel Johnson dies
Translation of Linnaeas' *System of Vegetables* published	1785	Boswell visits Lichfield
Son Francis born; Son Robert begins medical practice in Shrewsbury	1786	'Benvolio' letters to *Gentleman's Magazine*.
Son John born	1787	*Ode on General Eliott's Return from Gibraltar* published

Erasmus Darwin	Date	Anna Seward
	1788	Becomes patron to Thomas Lister and Henry Francis Cary
The Loves of The Plants (Part II of *The Botanic Garden*) published; Son Henry born (dies 1790); Thomas Day dies; Josiah Wedgwood sends Dr Darwin copy of the Portland Vase	1789	
Daughter Harriet born	1790	Father dies
Birmingham riots; Priestley to America; Lunar Society declines	1791	
The Economy of Vegetation: (Part I of *The Botanic Garden*) published; Recognized as England's leading poet.	1792	
Second portrait by Wright completed	1793	Contest with Boswell in *Gentleman's Magazine*
Zoonomia, Vol.1 published; Susanna and Mary Parker start girls' boarding school at Ashbourne; Josiah Wedgwood dies	1794	
	1795	Visits The Ladies of Llangollen
Zoonomia, Vol.2 published; Regarded as a leading medical writer	1796	*Llangollen Vale* published
Female Education in Boarding Schools published; Joseph Wright dies	1797	
Son Erasmus Jr. drowns in River Derwent	1798	Initiates correspondence with Walter Scott

Erasmus Darwin	Date	Anna Seward
	1799	*Original Sonnets on Various Subjects* published
Phytologia; or, The Philosophy of Agriculture and Gardening published	1800	
Dies at Breadsall Priory, aged 70	1802	
The Temple of Nature; or, The Origin of Society published	1803	John Saville dies
	1804	*Memoirs of the Life of Dr Darwin* published
	1805	Miss Fern comes to Bishop's Palace as companion
	1807	Negotiates with Archibald Constable for posthumous publication of her Letters and Writings; Walter Scott visits Seward in Lichfield
	1809	Dies at Bishop's Palace, Lichfield
	1810	*The Poetical Works of Anna Seward; With Extracts From Her Literary Correspondence* published
	1811	*Letters of Anna Seward: Written Between the Years 1784 and 1807* published

About the Editors

Philip K. Wilson, Ph.D., an historian of medicine and science with an interest in British history of the Enlightenment and Romantic periods, is Professor of Medical Humanities at Penn State Hershey College of Medicine and Science, Technology, and Society at Penn State University Park campus. He also serves as Director of the Doctors Kienle Center for Humanistic Medicine at Penn State Hershey. Wilson was previously the Biomedical and Health Editor for *Encyclopaedia Britannica*, has contributed writings on Dr Darwin to a number of works, including C. Smith and R. Arnot (eds) *The Genius of Erasmus Darwin* (2005), and in 2006–2007, served as Scholar-in-Residence at the Erasmus Darwin House in Lichfield, England.

Elizabeth A. Dolan, Ph.D., Associate Professor of English and Director of the Health, Medicine, and Society program at Lehigh University, Bethlehem, Pennsylvania, USA, is the author of *Seeing Suffering in Women's Literature of the Romantic Era* (2008), which examines writings by Mary Wollstonecraft, Charlotte Smith, and Mary Shelley. Committed to recovering Romantic-era women's texts, she also edited Charlotte Smith's first three children's works, volume 12 of *The Works of Charlotte Smith* (2007).

Malcolm McKinnon Dick, Ph.D. is Director of the Centre for West Midlands History at the University of Birmingham. He was manager of the Revolutionary Players Project between 2002 and 2004, which created a website of the history of the West Midlands www.revolutionaryplayers.org.uk. In 2005, Dick edited and contributed to *Joseph Priestley and Birmingham* and wrote *Birmingham: a History of the City and its People*, and in 2009, edited *Matthew Boulton – A Revolutionary Player*.

Introduction

For 75 years, Anna Seward's *Memoirs of the Life of Dr Darwin, Chiefly During his Residence in Lichfield; with Anecdotes of his Friends, and Criticisms of his Writings* (1804) remained the chief source of biographical information about her subject.[1] Although much of the world beyond Lichfield knew of Darwin (1731–1802) through his poetic and scientific writings, and may have learned more of his life through obituary accounts in the *Monthly Magazine* and in *Gentleman's Magazine*, the major source of information about Darwin's life for his generation and the next was Anna Seward's *Memoir*.[2] Indeed, it was not until Charles Darwin's 1879 biography, a work often misattributed to Ernst Krause with whose writings it was appended, that another full-length biographical account was offered *(Figure 1)*. That work has only been published in a full, unabridged version as recently as 2003.[3] Privileged as we are to have had a number of later writers illuminating the life of Darwin, we easily forget just how prominent – if only by its mere singularity – Seward's biography was for three quarters of a century.[4] Thus, it seems fitting in the year of Darwin celebrations across the globe to tease out some of the story behind this biography of early and, in many ways, lasting significance.

At the time of Erasmus Darwin's death – a moment that Seward (pronounced See-ward) posited as "a bright luminary" having "recently shot from this sphere, with awful and deplored suddenness" – we learn from Seward (1742–1809) that she received a letter from Erasmus' son, Robert.[5] At that time, Robert was a "successful, prosperous, and admired" physician practicing in Shrewsbury.[6] He had married Susannah Wedgwood in 1796, and by the time Seward's biography of Erasmus appeared in 1804, they had four children.[7] This Dr Darwin asked Seward to "supply him with such anecdotes of his father's early life", as "intimacy with him, during that period", had enabled her to obtain, and "which might assist in forming a biographical sketch, to be prefixed to his writings at some future time".[8] It seems that Erasmus Darwin's "utter dislike to all personal questions" had left his son, Robert, "almost entirely in the dark respecting the earlier part of" his father's life. The early death of

Figure 1: Title page of work in which Charles Darwin's biography of his grandfather, Dr Erasmus Darwin first appeared (1880). This was the first major biography of Dr Darwin to follow that by Seward.

Robert's mother had "closed upon him the best source of information" about Darwin's time in Lichfield.[9] Thus, Seward appeared to be the next best, and only available source for reliable information.

Whether or not Robert was actually planning to write this work himself, an acquaintance of his and of his father's, Dewhurst Bilsborrow, a physician at Derbyshire General Infirmary, was gathering information for a full-length "life and letters" biographical account. Bilsborrow was, in many ways, well placed to prepare such a work.[10] Once a pupil, and later a friend of Erasmus Darwin, Bilsborrow had, while studying medicine at Trinity College Cambridge, composed a poem summarizing the virtues he saw in *Zoonomia*, a work Darwin published between 1794–1796.[11]

"In purposed obedience" to Robert Darwin, Seward initially began to record her thoughts, but as she continued, her inclinations rapidly changed. In particular, she found that her anecdotes became "too extended to form only materials for another person's composition" and "too impartial to pass with propriety through the filial channel".[12] Seward remained worried that she was only a "limited biographer" – limited in the sense that she was "qualified to present no more than a merely general view" of his later life in Derby.[13] However, with Bilsborrow she had an ally, for he was limited, too. Since Bilsborrow was "scarcely in existence when his illustrious friend ... changed his sphere of existence" from Lichfield to Derby, he must, Seward continued, "find himself as much a stranger to the particulars of [Darwin's] Lichfield residence, as I am of those ... he passed at Derby". But "[b]etween us" she concluded "all will probably be known that can now with accuracy be traced to Dr Darwin".[14] She began writing the *Life of Dr Darwin* in 1802 and it appeared in 1804.

Before turning to the scenes of a life that Seward created, it may be helpful to establish a contextual background along several lines. To do so, we first present a brief introduction to life in England's Midlands, and specifically Lichfield, during the late eighteenth century, a period that included significant changes as the result of what is commonly, if sometimes over simply, called the Industrial Revolution. Therefore, we also lay down some general insights into the industrialization of this region during this period.

Seward, a poet and literary critic, wrote not only in the midst of these cultural shifts in the Midlands, but also during a time of proliferation and increasing acceptance of women's published work.[15] Thus, establishing the context within which Seward was noticed for her writing is also important. In addition we attempt to shed a bit more light upon Seward's own life than is otherwise raised through this text, including what is known of Seward's process of creating Darwin's biography. Such a glimpse provides us with a bit more insight into why she may have teased out the particulars that she did of the man whose image she posthumously perpetuated.

As in all life-story writing, biographers must be selective as to the parts of a life they wish to unfold. Although Seward offers insights into many areas of Darwin's adventure-filled life, some aspects are only touched upon in brief. For example, during the twenty-five years that Darwin resided in Lichfield – and it is only this period of his life that Seward attempts to recount – he was chiefly known by many of his associates for his prowess as a physician. Since Seward skims over the surface of this aspect in order to train her critical eye on the details of his poetry, we have added a few more glimpses into Darwin's medical thinking and practice as well as into his work with the noted scientifically minded natural philosophers in the Midlands.

Finally, although Seward's biography was the only substantial work on her subject for three-quarters of a century, other biographies of Erasmus Darwin appeared over time. The extent to which the later biographers relied upon Seward's account will be addressed. These views, together with those of contemporaries known to both Seward and Darwin, will bring our introductory essay to a close.

England's West Midlands & Lichfield

Erasmus Darwin lived in the West Midlands, the eighteenth-century equivalent of California's Silicon Valley in the twentieth century. The region was a centre for industrial expansion and technological innovation and, through the activities of philosophers such as Darwin and Joseph Priestley (1733–1804), a location for intellectual exploration as well. The term West Midlands was unknown to eighteenth-century Englishmen and women, but looking at the area from the perspective of an historian, it was developing a set of characteristics which marked it out as an area of special significance in the history of industrial and intellectual development.[16]

Industrially, the West Midlands witnessed the emergence of coke smelting for the production of pig iron and the development of new uses for iron in Coalbrookdale and the Ironbridge Gorge. The iron bridge of 1779, an early industrial tourist attraction, was the most famous example of the cast-iron artifacts which were made in the Gorge.[17] Seward wrote critically about its desolated industrial landscape, a consequence of the economic exploitation of this part of the Severn Valley, when she visited the area in the 1780s.[18] The Potteries district of North Staffordshire, where the modern city of Stoke-on-Trent is located, was a centre for innovation in the production of ceramics. Josiah Wedgwood (1730–1795), a friend of both Darwin and Seward was an exponent of new forms of pottery manufacture and design.[19] The coal and metal producing areas of South Staffordshire, known as the Black Country, were expanding rapidly, not only as the result of the development of iron and coal mines, but through growth of a glass industry in Stourbridge, nailmaking in Cradley Heath and Halesowen, lockmaking in Willenhall and Wolverhampton and enamel manufacture in Bilston. John Wilkinson (1728–1808), was the best-known of the Black Country iron manufacturers, but his metallurgical kingdom extended over other parts of the West Midlands and Wales. He supplied the precision-made cylinders for the first steam engines of Matthew Boulton (1728–1809) and James Watt (1736–1819) and drew attention to his pioneering entrepreneurship through the production of token coinage which celebrated his might as a manufacturer.[20] Most significantly, there was the town of Birmingham, which grew from, possibly, 7,000 people in 1700 to over 73,000 in 1801. Birmingham was, with Sheffield, the most rapidly growing large town in England in the eighteenth century. The breadth of its industrial base, which included brass, swords, guns, buttons and the production of 'toys' or small metal goods such as buckles, was extended by the late eighteenth century to include high-quality silver goods, steam-engine manufacture and coins. Raw materials were sucked into Birmingham from the coal and iron-ore mines of South Staffordshire and, in the case of other products such as silver, copper, pearls and tortoiseshell, further afield. Finished products were

XVIII

To Mathew Boulton Esq. this S.W. View of SOHO, is inscribed by his obliged Servt. S. Shaw

Figure 2: Matthew Boulton's Soho Works, Iron Foundry and House at Soho near Birmingham (1801). Courtesy of Archives and Heritage, Birmingham Central Library.

distributed regionally and nationally via roads, rivers, especially the Trent and Severn and, from the 1760s, canals.[21] Matthew Boulton was the best-known Birmingham manufacturer, who created what was purportedly the largest factory in the world at Soho *(Figure 2)*, just over the Birmingham border in Handsworth, Staffordshire, in the 1760s.[22] As early examples of modern manufacturers, both Wedgwood and Boulton exploited mass-production techniques, the division of labour, and effective marketing.[23]

The expansion of the West Midlands, unlike, perhaps, other parts of the industrial British economy, such as the Lancashire cotton industry or the woollen industry in Yorkshire was underpinned by a high degree of scientific thought and innovation. In their different ways, Robert E. Schofield and Jenny Uglow have drawn attention to the relationships between provincial science and industrial activity amongst the entrepreneurs, inventors, innovators and educationalists, who lived in the region and were associated with the Lunar Society from the 1760s until the early 1800s. These men included, as well as Darwin, Priestley, Wedgwood, Boulton and Watt, Thomas Day (1748–1789), Richard Lovell Edgeworth (1744–1817), Samuel Galton junior (1753–1832), James Keir (1735–1820), William Small (1734–1775), John Whitehurst (1713–1788) and William Withering (1741–1799). These individuals were simply the best-known Midlands gentlemen who operated within a regional, national and international network of correspondents, visitors, artisans and artists who had connections with the Lunar circle, or 'Lunaticks', as Darwin called them. This wider circle included Benjamin Franklin, Thomas Jefferson, Daniel Solander, Joseph Banks, William Herschel, William Murdock and Joseph Wright.[24]

Industrialisation created wealth and stimulated, together with agricultural improvement, the development of an expanding communication network for people and goods along turnpiked roads and, a new transport system in the late eighteenth century, canals. They linked the West Midlands manufacturing industries with supplies of raw materials and the export markets in Europe, North America, Africa and Asia via the ports of Hull, Liverpool, Bristol and London.[25] Lichfield was located on a principal crossroads of England. The large number of surviving coaching inns is an indication of Lichfield's importance on a number of passenger routes between north and south. The region, however, was not only an economic powerhouse; it was also a centre for genteel culture and exploratory thought. The generation of ideas could take place in a number of places, the dining and drawing rooms of the rich, newspapers, taverns, coffee houses, clubs, books, bookshops and places of work, for example.[26] There was no university in the eighteenth-century Midlands and only a few grammar schools, but this did not matter, as speculation, experimentation and discussion could take place elsewhere. The City of Lichfield was one place where intellectual activity was prominent. It contained a wealthy and leisured élite of clerics, doctors and members of the gentry and upper-middle classes.[27] The literary figure Samuel Johnson, a native of Lichfield, was recorded by James Boswell (1740–1795) as saying: 'Sir, we are a city of philosophers; we work with our heads and make the boobies of Birmingham work for us with their hands.'[28] Whatever the accuracy of Johnson's remarks, it does indicate the status that Lichfield, the home of Darwin and Seward, had acquired by the end of the eighteenth century as a place of intellectual and cultural exchange.

For Darwin, Lichfield *(Figure 3)* provided the spark that ignited his professional calling. He did not see this city, as is incorporated in the coat of arms and corporation seal, as a "lic" field – a *cadaverum campus* – a field of dead bodies, but rather as a "lician" field – an agreeable or pleasant field.[29] In so doing, Darwin corroborated what John André, a frequent visitor to Seward's Lichfield residence – the Bishop's Palace – nostalgically expressed,

> Lichfield! Ah! Of what magic letters is that little word
> compos'd! – How grateful it looks when it is written! – Let
> nobody talk to me of its original meaning, "The Field of
> Dead Bodies!" Oh! No such thing! It is the field of joy.
> "The beautiful city that lifts her fair head in the valley,
> and says, I *am*, and there is none beside me!"[30]

An early Lichfield historian, John Britton, argued similarly, that Lichfield represented one of those "certain spots of the earth" that held "the power of exciting particular reflections and sentiments" – an invisible power whose effects became more visible as Lichfield gained renown during the eighteenth century as "the birth-place of genius and the asylum of talent".[31] Lichfield, as both Seward's admirers and critics note, is the chief focus of her *Life of*

Figure 3: Lichfield, Staffordshire.

Dr Darwin. In that way, her account stands as more than just biography, but also as an informative tale of one city and its cathedral community life that places it alongside those other enduring early nineteenth-century works of Lichfield written by The Revd. Thomas Harwood (1767–1842), John Jackson, John Britton, and T.G. Lomax (1783–1873).[32]

Cathedral cities, as E.V. Lucas noted, have a way of conserving their antiquity. The "rhythm of chimes floating over the countryside; the chant of ritual and the music of men's singing voices" remains constant over time.[33] Darwin and Seward experienced the Cathedral Close, that Mary Alden Hopkins helps us recall: "Against the dignity of the red sandstone Cathedral, among Tudor houses and Georgian mansions with flowering gardens strode somber clergy in black knee-breeches, black wool stockings, voluminous robes, full-bottomed, powdered wigs and round, low-crowned, broad-rimmed felt hats. Hooped-skirted ladies in bright silks strolled the shaded Dean's Walk". The Close embodied the "more learned section" of Lichfield. There were sentiments in Latin, Hebrew, and Greek expressed throughout the Close. People of the Close "tended to look down on [those in] the City, because the ecclesiastical families were in general of a higher social rank than the City folk". From the historical standpoint, we "know much more about the people who lived in the Close" – people including Seward and Darwin – than we do "about those who lived in the City", for the people of the Close "wrote more letters, histories, and biographies" than did their City counterparts.[34]

British Women Writers of the late 18th Century

Seward's *Memoirs of the Life of Dr Darwin* was published both within a rich, multi-generic context of female-authored texts and also within a developing genre for women writers: the critical memoir. Seward's fellow author, Mary Robinson (1756/57–1801) includes "Miss

Seward" in a list of 40 esteemed "British Female Literary Characters Living in the Eighteenth Century" appended to her *Letter to the Women of England, on the Injustice of Mental Subordination* (1799).[35] The list serves as a useful contemporary index of significant women authors of Seward's immediate generation. Women on Robinson's list who, like Seward and Robinson, were born between 1740 and 1770 and published in the last two decades of the eighteenth century include: Hester Lynch Piozzi (1741–1821), Anna Letitia Barbauld (1743–1825), Hannah Cowley (1743–1809), Hannah More (1745–1833), Charlotte Smith (1749–1806), Sophia Lee (1750–1824), Frances Burney, Madame d'Arblay (1752–1840), Ann Yearsley (1752–1806), Elizabeth Inchbald (1753–1821), Harriet Lee (1757–1851), Jane West (1758–1852), Mary Wollstonecraft (1759–1797), Mary Hays (1759–1843), Helen Maria Williams (1761–1827), Ann Radcliffe (1764–1823) and Maria Edgeworth (1767–1849). Seward corresponded with and commented critically on the works of many of these authors, and of course, she knew Honora Sneyd's step daughter Edgeworth personally. Like many of the women catalogued by Robinson, then, Seward straddles what we think of as the Bluestocking era and the early Romantic era, and her writing exhibits characteristics attributed to the work of women authors in both periods. As Stuart Curran noted in 1993, "there were not merely dozens, nor even hundreds, but actually thousands, of women whose writing was published in Great Britain in the half century between 1780 and 1830 that subsumes the Romantic period; and … until recently we have known very little about it".[36] Since 1993, scholars have discovered a great deal about these writers and that information has considerably altered the chronological and generic boundaries of "the Romantic era", a period conventionally thought to begin with the publication of William Wordsworth's and Samuel Taylor Coleridge's *Lyrical Ballads* (1798), and assumed to be dominated by six male poets who were admired primarily for their innovations in poetic form including the sonnet, the ode, the lyric poem, and the ballad. However, it is now known that eighteenth-century women writing well before the publication of *Lyrical Ballads* not only produced influential experiments in poetic form, but also published quite successfully in many other genres.

Emblematic of these achievements, Smith's *Elegiac Sonnets* (1784–97) are now credited with reviving the sonnet in the Romantic era. Robinson's sonnet sequence *Sappho and Phaon* (1796) and Seward's *Original Sonnets on Various Subjects* (1799) contributed to the sonnet revival and helped shape an animated critical discussion about the relative value of the illegitimate sonnet (Shakespearean) and the legitimate sonnet (Petrarchan). While Smith's collection was the most enduring and influential of the three, Daniel Robinson identifies Seward as "the first serious writer of sonnets who was also a woman", because she published individual sonnets as early as 1773, before Smith's collection appeared.[37] In addition to these poetic innovators, women writers such as Burney, the Lee sisters, Inchbald, Wollstonecraft, Smith, Radcliffe, and Hays experimented with the genre of the novel, producing sentimental, gothic, historical, and Jacobin forms. Seward's *Louisa: A Poetical Novel, in Four Epistles* (1784) uniquely mixes the genres of novel and poetry in a manner unequaled until Elizabeth Barrett Browning's *Aurora Leigh* (1857), but resonates with other women's writing in its emphasis on the explication of the characters' sensibility and intellect rather than the development of the plot. In addition to novels, women produced plays: Cowley, Inchbald, Smith, the Lee sisters, and Robinson all wrote for the stage (Inchbald and

Robinson were also actresses). Although Seward did not compose plays, she achieved a fine reputation for her recitations of poetry and drama (particularly Shakespearean drama) at social gatherings, and commented regularly on the Lichfield theatrical scene in her letters.[38] Women writers such as Barbauld, West, Edgeworth, Smith, Wollstonecraft, and More also published children's literature, a relatively lucrative genre dominated by women in the Romantic period.

Curran explains that "in the 1770s and 1780s women had moved to the forefront of the publishing world", and there was no real backlash or attempt to limit their increased cultural power until the late 1790s.[39] Perhaps not coincidentally, the 1790s in Britain witnessed "the first concerted expression of feminist thought in modern European culture", in which authors primarily challenged assumptions about "female intellectual inferiority and women's essential role in the family".[40] Although Seward did not contribute to this discussion with a major pamphlet such as Wollstonecraft's *Vindication of the Rights of Woman* (1792), Hays's anonymous *An Appeal to the Men of Great Britain in Behalf of Women* (1798), or Robinson's pseudonymous *Letter to the Women of England on the Injustice of Mental Subordination* (1799), her life itself challenged these stereotypes quite directly. She published an impressive body of literature, participated vigorously in literary debates of her era, appeared to have romantic relationships with the men and women she loved, and deftly avoided the legal constraints of marriage and the attendant professional limitations inherent in a conventional domestic life, all while maintaining her social respectability.[41] This independence was no small achievement, though one must acknowledge how significantly her class standing and financial security supported her choices.

In addition to engaging in political writing, women contributed valuable literary criticism in an effort to establish a British national canon that included current as well as historical writers. Mary A. Waters charts the "rise of the professional woman literary critic" between 1789 and 1832, distinguishing these women from earlier Bluestockings, such as Elizabeth Carter and Elizabeth Montague, who published literary criticism, but who did not present themselves as professional critics.[42] In contrast, Waters argues, Romantic-era women critics "saw themselves as professionals and as authorities on a crucial topic, the nation's literature".[43] According to Waters, this criticism took the form of critical prefaces to books and anonymous reviews in periodicals. Barbauld and Inchbald wrote influential critical prefaces on the novel and on theater, respectively. Wollstonecraft's and Hays's many anonymous literary reviews published in the *Analytical Review* helped shape the nation's taste for experimental Romantic-era literature. Likewise, Barbauld and Elizabeth Moody guided the literary choices of a dedicated readership in their regular reviews for the *Monthly Review*. Like these women, Seward took her role as critic quite seriously, implicitly comparing herself to fellow Lichfield native Samuel Johnson: "Many excel me in the power of writing verse; perhaps scarcely one … in the ability to estimate its claims – arising from a fifty years sedulous and discriminating study of the best English poets, and of the best translations from the Greek, Roman, and Italian".[44] This confidence in her own opinion along with her class standing and independence seemed to free her to debate publicly with male writers of the time. Seward secured her reputation as a literary critic not by writing anonymous reviews, but rather by publishing signed letters to the *Gentleman's Magazine* (discussed below). As

Norma Clarke argues, Seward built her reputation on the success of her poems, but it rested on "her powers as a literary critic".[45]

The three genres most relevant for contextualizing the literary resonance of Seward's *Life of Dr Darwin*, then, are poetry, criticism, and, most obviously, the memoir. An increasing interest in subjective experience in the Romantic era ignited the popularity of memoirs. If the number of memoirs included in the Eighteenth-Century Collection On-line database is any indication, booksellers' shelves overflowed with memoirs of actresses and of military men in the last two decades of the century. In a characteristically curmudgeonly tone, Johnson captures the century's enthusiasm for life stories, noting Joseph Addison's adage that the "Grubstreet biographers" of the day "watch for the death of a great man, like so many undertakers, on purpose to make a penny of him".[46] And yet in his *Lives of the Poets* (1779–1781), Johnson displayed a curiosity about the "distinct mannerisms, eccentricities, and particularities" of his chosen subjects in a manner that "allowed an outsider to see the human being within the vestments and achievements of a personality".[47] He warned, however, that if one "professes to write *A Life* he must represent it really as it was".[48] Two biographies of Johnson – Piozzi's *Anecdotes of the Late Samuel Johnson* (1788) and Boswell's *Life of Johnson* (1791) – are major milestones in the history of biography.[49] Significantly, Piozzi and Boswell both approached Seward for personal letters and anecdotes regarding the writer. Seward acknowledged the "arduous task of presenting to the world the portrait of Johnson's mind and manners", and added the cautionary forecast to Boswell that "If faithful", this biography will be "brilliant in its lights, but deep [in] its shades".[50] Such comments reflect those of Seward's own biographer, Walter Scott, who claimed that biography "loses all its interest … when the shades and light of the principal character are not accurately and faithfully detailed".[51] In the end, Seward found Boswell's approach to Johnson's life to be sycophantic and much preferred Piozzi's more ambivalent representation of the writer.

Like Piozzi, other women writers composed well-received memoirs or biographies of male authors. Published the same year as Piozzi's *Anecdotes of Johnson*, the French author Germaine de Stael's laudatory account of Rousseau, *Letters sur les Ouvrages et le Caractere de J.-J. Rousseau* (1788) was translated the following year into English. The poet, children's writer, educator, and essayist, Barbauld, like Seward, commingled the genres of criticism and memoir.[52] Barbauld began her foray into critical biography by writing introductions to Mark Akenside's *The Pleasures of the Imagination* (1795) and William Collins's *Poetical Works* (1797), both of which offer a detailed critical discussion of the poetry alongside biographical observations. Most similar to Seward's *Life of Dr Darwin*, Barbauld's 200-page critical introduction and memoir of Samuel Richardson in *The Correspondence of Samuel Richardson* (1804), is the first substantial biography of the novelist. Barbauld also composed a significant critical memoir of Joseph Addison in the introduction to her edition of *Selections from Spectator, Tatler, Guardian, and Freeholder* (1805), and memoirs of various lengths and detail in her separate introductions to the fifty-volume series *The British Novelists* (1810).

If the pleasures of life writing were evident in the late eighteenth century, so were the hazards. Famously, William Godwin's *Memoir of the Author of the Vindication of the Rights of Woman* (1798), written to memorialize his deceased and much admired wife, instead sunk

Wollstonecraft's reputation for over a century. Hays's six volume *Female Biography: or Memoirs of Illustrious and Celebrated Women of All Ages and Countries* (1803) includes 290 biographies of women authors both current and historical, yet omits her friend Wollstonecraft, perhaps due to the scandal ignited by Godwin's *Memoir*. As we will see, Seward's *Life of Dr Darwin* created its own controversy.

Anna Seward

Even as the industrial and literary scene underwent massive shifts, Seward's own life was remarkably stable. Her father, the Reverend Thomas Seward *(Figure 4)*, Rector of Eyam in the Derbyshire Hills when she was born, became Prebendary of Salisbury and Canon Residentiary in Lichfield in 1749/50, when Anna – frequently called Nancy – was seven. Although she lived her early childhood in Eyam, Seward spent the rest of her life in Lichfield, and from the age of thirteen until her death, in one house – the Bishop's Palace *(Figure 5)* in the Cathedral Close. Lichfield was, according to Seward's later correspondent and literary executor, Walter Scott, comprised of a "body of learned and well-educated clergy attached to its cathedral" and a city which had "been long distinguished by its classical pretensions".[53] Biographer Margaret Ashmun notes that "Eminent Lichfieldians vied with visitors from the great world, who were drawn unerringly to the Canon's *salon*".[54] The Canon's "urbanity" appears to have "put him at ease with persons of title and [of] ecclesiastical rank", and his "friendliness" made him "agreeable to the less distinguished".[55] As his contemporary, the educator and Lunar Man, Richard Lovell Edgeworth relates, Canon Seward was "the resort of every person in that neighbourhood, who had any taste for letters".[56] Not surprisingly, former Lichfield native and unhappy student of the Canon's father-in-law, Samuel Johnson "despised" Canon Seward as "a provincial dilettante".[57] A "versifying man"[58] known for publishing minor poems and a co-edited annotated edition of Beaumont and Fletcher's plays, the Canon was actually "a man of learning and taste; he was fond of conversation, in which he bore a considerable part, good natured, and indulgent to the little foibles of others: he scarcely seemed to notice any animadversions, that were made upon his own [foibles]". Surprisingly, his "naïveté" in this matter "was beyond what could easily be believed of a man of such talents, or of one who has seen any thing of the world", as he certainly had done in accompanying Lord Charles Fitzroy on a Grand Tour in the late 1730s.[59] Significantly, Seward's father also published "The Female Right to Literature, in a Letter to a Young Lady from Florence" (1748), in which he

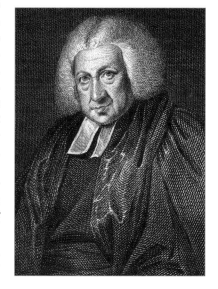

Figure 4 Canon Thomas Seward (1708-1790). Robert Hartley Cromek's engraving based upon Joseph Wright of Derby's original portrait (early 1780s). This image was used as the frontispiece to the second volume of the published Letters of Anna Seward *(1811).*

Figure 5: Bishop's Palace, Lichfield. Anna Seward's Home. Photograph by W. Morrison in Margaret Ashmun, The Singing Swan: An Account of Anna Seward and her Acquaintance with Dr Johnson, Boswell & Others of Their Time (1931).

recommended that girls be educated in all disciplines, without regard for traditional notions of women's intellectual limitations.[60] Seward's mother Elizabeth Hunter (*d.*1780), the daughter of the headmaster of the Lichfield Grammar School, was also quite well read.

Seward, then, grew up in an intellectually and socially vibrant household. Her father read Milton and Shakespeare to her beginning at age three, and she was known for reciting the first three books of Milton's *Paradise Lost* by age nine. In addition, she had free access to a "substantial library of English poetry and drama, history, essays and sermons, as well as fiction", and current publications such as the *Gentleman's Magazine* and Johnson's *Rambler*.[61] In addition to her father, the major influence on her education and writing was Darwin. Bearing a letter of introduction to Canon Seward when he arrived in Lichfield, Darwin became close to the young Seward. She referred to him as her "bright luminary" in the poetic art.[62] Darwin had encouraged Seward's early entrée into poetry, and she viewed him as her "poetic praeceptor" for the rest of her life.[63] Seward's verse reveals her admiration for Darwin's "highly picturesque descriptions of mechanic construction, and process of various arts, and of mythological marvels" as well as for his depiction of landscapes, his ornamental diction, and his "instructive" notes.[64] They seemed to have "enjoyed each other's poetry and projects", although Darwin was "often impatient with her romantic susceptibility", whereas Seward "resented his corrosive sarcasms".[65] Nonetheless, Seward claimed that when Darwin lived in Lichfield, "we two were the poets of the place".[66] Another important mentor, Lady Anna Miller also encouraged the young poet to share her verse at the social gatherings held in Miller's Batheaston villa from 1775–1781, and published Seward's first poems in her annual volume of poetry.

Seward, her sister Sarah (1744–1762), and foster sister Honora Sneyd (1752–1780), who came to live with the family when Sneyd was five and Seward was fourteen, formed a close trio for the five years before Sarah's death. Seward became even more closely attached to Sneyd following her sister's passing, serving as her teacher and developing what many scholars now describe as a "romantic friendship". After fourteen years, Sneyd left the Seward household, shortly after married Richard Lovell Edgeworth, and then died of consumption seven years later. Seward mourned Sneyd in her poetry and in her letters throughout her life.

In 1780, Seward's mother Elizabeth died, and her father "began to show that decay of the mental faculties which settled year by year into" what was termed, "complete imbecility".[67] Seward was close to her father, and cared for him, her "aged nurseling", during what must have appeared a rather long decade.[68] However, while she cared for her ailing father, Seward was not without a companion. She maintained a close, probably romantic, relationship with her former harpsichord teacher, the concert singer and Vicar Choral, John Saville, with whom she enjoyed reading, singing, and gardening. Saville and Seward met in the mid 1750s, when he was nineteen and she was thirteen, and their friendship deepened over the decades. They shared enormous enthusiasm for the music of Handel, and Seward referred to Saville as her beloved "Giovanni".[69] Though he married and had two children during their acquaintance, he appears to have made the Bishop's Palace, where the Sewards resided, his second home and Seward herself his daily companion until his death in 1803.[70]

Seward did receive criticism for her unconventional relationship with Saville, including an order from her father in 1771 to stop seeing him after Mrs Saville complained about the impropriety of the connection. Seward, however, not only persisted in her friendship with Saville, she also maintained her social ascendancy in Lichfield. Mary Martha Butt (1775–1851), later Mrs Henry Sherwood, came to know Seward in Lichfield during her youth, and commented on both the scandal and Seward's social appeal. She noted that Seward:

> had that peculiar sort of beauty which consists in the most brilliant eyes, glowing complexion, and rich dark hair. She was tall and majestic, and was unrivalled in the power of expressing herself. She was at the same time exceedingly greedy of the admiration of the other sex; and though capable of individual attachment, as she manifested in after-life much to her cost, yet [she was] not very nice as to the person by whom the homage of flattery was rendered at her shrine.

Seward was, "in a word, such a woman as we read of in romances; and, had she lived in some dark age of the past, she might have been charged with sorcery, for even in advanced life she often bore away the palm of admiration from the young and beautiful, and many even were fascinated who wholly condemned her conduct".[71] In Lichfield, Mrs Sherwood continues:

> all gathered round Miss Seward, as a sort of centre, enacting many a romance of real life, and forming the basis for several deep tragedies, thus proving that human happiness is not prompted by mere cultivation of intellect, and that the assumption of genius, unless controlled by religion, only adds strength to the passions, and acuteness to the inevitable trials and afflictions of life.[72]

Seward defied this type of criticism, insisting on her autonomy and her prerogative as a woman in her mid-thirties to "think, judge, and act for herself", not only in managing her literary life with authority, but also in handling her private relationships as she thought best.[73]

Seward experienced a series of emotional and physical setbacks in the second half of her life, for which she travelled to spas, the seaside, and idyllic landscapes for restoration. In addition to a permanent limp resulting from a patella broken in 1768, Seward also suffered from both rheumatic and severe respiratory conditions.[74] She undertook annual visits to Buxton, Matlock, Harrowgate, and the coast for relief. After her sister's death in 1764 and her father's death in 1791, she took refuge in the home of Mrs Mompesson at Mansfield Woodhouse, within the ancient Sherwood Forest. Later in life, looking for alternative healthy and beautiful environments with breathable air, Seward visited the famed ladies of Llangollen Vale in Wales: Lady Eleanor Butler and Sarah Ponsonby.[75] After Butler and Ponsonby "eloped" in 1778, the couple lived together in a beautiful house outside of Llangollen for fifty years.[76] Seward praised them for having "converted a cottage, in two acres and a half of turnip ground, to a fairy-palace, amid the bowers of Calypso".[77] Revealing how deeply Seward admired their home and garden, Seward's letters also describe her gift to them of a print of Romney's Serena, an image that reminded her of her own beloved Sneyd.[78]

Realizing that her health was declining, Seward asked Scott to serve as the executor of her poetry. Scott published a three volume edition of her verse with a prefatory biography in 1810. Seward began collecting her literary correspondence in 1784, when her "fame as a writer was at its height".[79] Clarke observes: "Unlike other letter collections assembled after an author's death, these were written and rewritten with a view to publication, selected and ordered by the writer to provide a portrait of herself and enshrine her views about matters she considered of particular importance".[80] The letters are, in short, "both manifesto and monument".[81] The transcribed letters filled twelve volumes by the time of Seward's death in 1807. She bequeathed the letters to Edinburgh publisher Archibald Constable, requesting that he bring them out in two volumes a year. Instead, Constable selected about half the letters for inclusion in a six volume set that he published in 1811 *(Figure 6)*.[82]

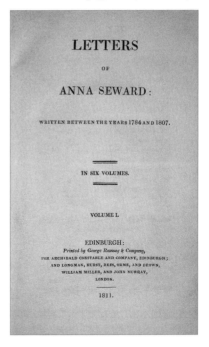

Figure 6: Title page of Letters of Anna Seward written between the years 1784 and 1807 *(1811).*

Anna Seward as a Poet and Critic

By the time that Seward embarked upon her critical memoir of Darwin in 1802, she was well known as a poet and literary critic. And indeed, as Elizabeth Fay suggests, Seward was "perhaps the one woman of the Romantic Period who saw her place in literary history, particularly in the production of poetry, as rivaling any of her male counterparts".[83] Her title, the "Swan of Lichfield" carried not only her own acclaim, but that of Lichfield, far beyond the city's borders. Scott claimed that "for many years" Seward "held a high rank in the annals of British literature".[84] William Bagshaw Stevens, when passing through Lichfield, commented upon Seward's talent in a verse which he left behind at the George Inn:

> And here the flower of England's virgin train,
> Boast of our isle, Lichfield's peculiar pride,
> Here Seward caught the dew-drops of her strain,
> From Grief and Fancy's magic-mingled tide.[85]

Adding to this admiration from her contemporaries, recent scholars value Seward's verse for its contribution to the elegy, the verse novel, environmental poetry, the sonnet tradition, and the poetry of romantic friendship.

Seward's initial acclaim was derived from her *Elegy on Captain Cook*, written in 1780, soon after learning of his death at the hands of the Sandwich Islanders. Darwin later boasted that Seward had "invented this epic [form of an] elegy, in which a form of narrative was combined with lamentation".[86] Ashmun refers readers to earlier contributors of this form, but acknowledges that Seward was heavily influenced by this style as it "allowed scope for the lofty language which she loved, and for the emotional fervours and lyrical license which fulfilled her notion of poetic diction".[87] Ashmun further claimed that Seward's monodies, such as her famed *Monody on Major André* (1781), "brought her into public notice, secured for her the real boon of many agreeable friendships, and opened the way for that exchange of letters which was the chief pride and diversion of her later years".[88]

If she came into public notice with her elegiac monodies, Seward achieved more widespread popularity with her unique verse novel, *Louisa* (1784), which went into four English editions within a year and one American edition the following year. Like Wollstonecraft's first novel *Mary* (1787), Seward's *Louisa* represents feelings and ideas rather than events. Seward characterizes the work as "a description rather of passions than of incidents".[89] With similar language, Wollstonecraft introduces *Mary*: "In an artless tale, without episodes, the mind of a woman who has thinking powers is displayed".[90] Both authors seek to revise decadent representations of sensibility, exploring instead the moral grounding of refined feeling. Hybridizing the epistolary novel and the heroic epistle, Seward revises Alexander Pope's "Eloisa to Abelard" (1717) and Jean-Jacques Rousseau's *Julie, ou la nouvelle Héloïse* (1761) by inserting a female friend, Emma, to whom the main female character may write to "clarify her feelings" and "safeguard her private emotions from public display".[91] Louisa filters her romantic feelings through a friend, rather than directly expressing them to a lover, and thus maintains her purity; likewise, Seward "elevates" the epistolary novel "from moral turpitude to refined sensibility through poetry".[92]

The female friendship evident in *Louisa* is a feature of Seward's poetry that modern critics have sought to understand, primarily through an analysis of her poetic tributes to the Ladies of Llangollen and to Honora Sneyd. Seward's volume of verse *Llangollen Vale, with Other Poems* (1796), the title poem of which is dedicated to Butler and Ponsonby, went through three editions in 1796. The poem praises the couple's relationship, as well as their cultivation and feminisation of the "rude and remote valley" in which their house stood.[93] Seward began writing tributes to Sneyd in 1769 and continued to honor her in verse through Sneyd's marriage, death, and well after.[94] Several of these poems, including "To Time Past, Written Dec. 1772" were published in *Llangollen Vale*. One of the most significant poetic eulogiums of Sneyd, "Lichfield, An Elegy. Written May 1781", describes the physical and social environs of Lichfield in six pages of verse and then suddenly concludes with a visit to Sneyd's grave and an expression of deep regret that the loss of Sneyd tempers Seward's enjoyment of Lichfield. Curran notes that of the sonnets included in Seward's *Original Sonnets* (1799), many of the finest are "addressed to Sneyd within the traditional complex of platonic love", in which "Sneyd functions with curious propriety as the Muse whose afflatus impels Seward into verse".[95] Although it would be impossible to label Seward's sexuality using current terminology, it seems clear that her deep friendships with women provided inspiration for some of her most moving verse.[96]

As her poems on Llangollen Vale/the Ladies of Llangollen, and Lichfield/Sneyd suggest, a major characteristic of Seward's poetry is its depiction of the sympathy between the natural world and human emotion. Thus, she revises Darwin's playful "habit of assigning emotions and sensations to plants", suggesting instead that plants and humans have corresponding feelings.[97] As a result, in the first decade of the twenty-first century, Seward is discussed as an environmental writer of some importance. She expressed a different view on industrialization than did Darwin, particularly in their responses to the discovery of petroleum at Coalbrookdale in 1786. In her sonnet "To Colebrook [sic] Dale" (written *c*.1785–87, published 1799), in the longer poem "Coalbrook [sic] Dale" (written *c*.1785–90, published 1810) and in a letter to William Hayley, Seward laments "the ways in which the natural beauty of Coalbrookdale has been spoiled by the industrial process", whereas Darwin, in both a letter to Thomas Beddoes and in an extended footnote note on coal in the second canto of "The Economy of Vegetation" in *The Botanic Garden* "celebrate[s] the potential of science and technology to capitalize on the natural resources found in the dale".[98] Although Seward does not choose to comment on Darwin's praise for Coalbrookdale in her *Life of Dr Darwin*, in her own poetry she, unlike Darwin, objected in strong terms to the air, water, and noise pollution in "violated Coalbrook".[99] Seward, Sharon Setzer argues, makes "a significant intervention in the masculine loco-descriptive tradition" by translating "mythic images of sexual violation from narratives of providential or progressive history into an implicit argument against the industrial degradation of Colebrook Dale".[100] As in her poems about Llangollen Vale, Seward depicts tension between the feminine beauty of a place and the masculine threat of violence.

Seward wrote about her historical moment by focusing in on the people and landscape around her. She memorialized important contemporary military figures in her monodies, responded to the literature of sensibility that dominated her cultural moment in *Louisa*, honored women's friendships and the cultivation of beautiful landscapes in *Llangollen Vale*, lamented the loss of close relationships in her sonnets, and commented on the local effects of burgeoning industrialization in the Coalbrooke Dale poems. She was, in short, a writer dedicated both to describing the world and people around her and also to making her own voice heard.

In addition to poetry, Seward gained recognition as a literary critic. Turning what might be considered a deficiency in her education into an advantage, Seward argued that unlike male intellectuals who devoted so much of their education to learning Latin, she was free to read deeply in the English tradition, and was thus better equipped to help establish a British national literature.[101] She contributed to several extended literary discussions in the *Gentleman's Magazine*. For example, between 1789 and 1791, she and Joseph Weston began a public debate in the periodical about the relative merits of the poetry of Dryden and of Pope. Seward strongly defended Pope's supremacy. Gretchen Foster notes that the controversy "lasted two years and drew letters from seventeen correspondents in addition to herself and Joseph Weston … In all, the debate ran to some 30,000 words of reasoning and opinion, quotation and counter quotation, and heated attack, rebuttal, and re-rebuttal".[102] Seward quarreled with Boswell in the *Gentleman's Magazine* after he published corrections to his *Life of Johnson* and noted that she had supplied him with inaccurate information.[103] Seward responded publicly in the magazine, firing the second shot in a "paper war" that the two writers conducted between 1793 and 1794.[104] Like other women writers of her day, Seward also commented on the literature of her age in her prefaces. In the preface to her *Original Sonnets*, she challenges the popularity of Charlotte Smith's use of the Shakespearean sonnet in her highly praised and popular *Elegiac Sonnets* as "illegitimate". Seward chose to write Petrarchan sonnets, claiming that the English language was just as versatile and powerful as the Italian. Seward composed the sonnet "To Mr Henry Cary, on the Publication of his Sonnets" (1788), in reaction to Smith's experimentation with the Shakespearean form.[105] In a series of letters to the poet William Hayley, Seward's and Smith's mutual friend, Seward blasts Smith's sonnets and blames the public's bad taste for their popularity.[106] As this example suggests, Seward's letters are another rich, and largely un-mined, source of her literary criticism.

Given her spirited, indefatigable critical judgments, her poetic friendship with Darwin, and her love of poetry, it is not surprising that Seward devotes more than half the pages of her *Life of Dr Darwin* to a close analysis of *The Botanic Garden*. While these two chapters may be somewhat tiresome to modern readers, they are worth our attention for at least three primary reasons. First, in her enthusiasm for and detailed attention to *The Botanic Garden*, Seward both reflected and perhaps to some extent inspired the interest of Romantic-era poets in Darwin's poem. Although his poetic style and the use of the heroic couplet evoke the neo-classical more than the Romantic tradition, Darwin's representation of natural science in "imaginative terms" influenced both male and female Romantic-era poets.[107] For many years, scholars have noted the indelible traces of Darwin's influence in the poetry of William Blake,[108] Coleridge,[109] Wordsworth,[110] The Shelleys,[111] and Byron.[112] More recently, Ann B. Shtier has contextualized women writers' interest in Darwin's poetry within their general fascination with botany.[113] Judith Pascoe identifies Darwin as the "model" of the "curious practice" of augmenting "poetry with extensive scientific notation", a phenomenon she analyzes particularly in Charlotte Smith's poetry, including her final poem "Beachy Head".[114] Pascoe notes that *The Botanic Garden* "became an object of particular fascination for women [writers]".[115]

Furthermore, Seward's commentary on Darwin's poetry enacts her contemporaries' ways of reading *The Botanic Garden*, a second reason to attend to her detailed criticism. In fact, it is perhaps most enjoyable to read chapters five and six of Seward's *Life of Dr Darwin* with a copy of Darwin's *The Botanic Garden* at hand. Slowing down to read the two books together, one enters into conversation with Seward about Darwin's poem. Seward becomes a kind of literary tour guide, pointing out moments of great beauty, and evaluating Darwin's imagery, metaphors, and word choice by comparing specific examples to lines by poets such as Shakespeare, Milton, Cowper, Pope, and Collins. She sometimes finds that Darwin exceeds these models. The description of Venus, for example, is "incomparably more elegant in the verse of Darwin than in the translation of Cowper or even of Pope". Characteristically, she supports this claim by quoting all three examples.[116] Even when she suggests, for example, that Milton has used alliteration with more finesse, she implicitly situates Darwin's poetry among the great English writers.[117] Aileen Douglas's discovery of Seward's annotated copy of Godwin's *Caleb Williams* reveals that Seward's reading practices were just as she represents them in her discussion of *The Botanic Garden*: "One realizes that for Anna Seward reading was a formal debate with the text, and that annotation was a solemn duty".[118] "To annotate", Douglas notes, "is to instruct through particulars … It is refreshing to come across an 18th-century woman so certain that her private reading will be transformed into a source of general instruction".[119] It is absolutely this spirit that motivates Seward's extensive discussion of Darwin's technique.

Finally, Seward's literary criticism is worthy of our attention because it evokes a deeply relational mode of analytical thought and creative work not always associated with late eighteenth-century literature. Seward's relentless, specific comparisons between Darwin's verses and those of other poets demonstrates that she read works of literature always in relation to the books that already filled her library shelves and her memory. The many comparisons also remind readers that poets wrote in communities and were shaped by their literary inheritances as well as by their historical moments, a sharp contrast to the image of the solitary Romantic poet writing original literature in isolation. Seward's approach to biography is similar to her literary criticism. Promising a discussion of Darwin's life in Lichfield, she repeatedly swerves into the lives of those in the community around Darwin, such as Thomas Day or Richard Lovell Edgeworth. In the first chapter of her *Life of Dr Darwin*, for example, Seward devotes 11 of 15 total pages to Day, noting that "The circumstances of Mr Day's disposition, habits, and destiny were so peculiar, as to justify digression from the principal subject of these pages". And, although she begins Chapter II noting that "It is now perhaps more than time to resume the recollected circumstances of Dr Darwin's life", she dives instead into a two paragraph account of his friend Sir Brooke Boothby.[120] If we come to understand the value of Darwin's literature by comparisons to that of his fellow writers, we will come to know Darwin, Seward suggests, by the company that he keeps.

Dr Erasmus Darwin

Seward presented too many aspects of Darwin to be considered in this introductory essay.[121] As an overview, Seward talks briefly of his multitude of skills and successes as a physician. "Extreme was his skepticism to human truth", she reveals. Though perhaps not the best of humanitarian traits, it may well have aided his attempt to discern the underlying truth in the tales his patients told. Seward never questions Darwin's abilities in his professional calling. Upon Darwin's "extinction", Seward noted that disease could "no longer turn the eye of hope upon his rescuing and restoring skill", that philosophical science would be wanting "an ingenious and daring dictator", and that the medicinal art would suffer in its loss of "a pillar of transcendent strength".[122] Seward was familiar with Darwin's concern that gaining notice for his "highly poetic imagination" was not necessarily beneficial to his reputation among the theoretical-minded leaders of the medical profession. The Scottish physician and poet, John Armstrong, in response to his *The Art of Preserving Health* (1744),[123] and the "English Pindar", Akenside, for his *The Pleasures of Imagination* (1744)[124] suffered professionally from a natural philosopher's quest into poetry. Carrying forth this concern, Seward argued that Darwin pursued the practice of physic "with the wisdom of Ulysses", binding himself "to the medical mast", so that he "might not follow those delusive sirens, the muses, or be considered as their avowed votary".[125] Still, the first editions of all of Darwin's works that appeared during his lifetime which contained a substantial amount of poetry were published anonymously.

According to a brochure for visitors to Erasmus Darwin House, it has "often been said, so far without contradiction, that no one since [Erasmus] Darwin's day has achieved so much in so many different fields of endeavour".[126] Walking from this House through its herb and flower garden, one finds his accomplishments memorialized on individual stone pavements reading Humanitarian, Poet, Evolutionist, Inventor, Scientist and Doctor.

Visitors to the house are reminded of many of these particular attributes. For example, as a keen mechanical inventor, he devised the steering system used in modern cars, produced a speaking-machine that astonished his friends, and constructed a copying machine (the "Bi-grapher", *Figure 7*) which produced documents that were indistinguishable from the originals. In addition, he contributed to the designs of a horizontal windmill, a canal lift for barges, an artesian well, and a variety of weather monitoring devices. Visitors may also marvel at being in the very rooms in which his inventive and scientific-minded friends met on occasion as part of what became known as the Lunar Society of Birmingham.

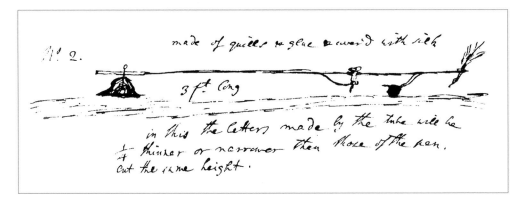

Figure 7: One of Dr Darwin's "Bi-Graphers" with which he produced a duplicate of each letter written. From the Commonplace Book *(1777), used with permission of Erasmus Darwin House.*

Although the text of this volume provides considerable insight into Darwin's poetic endeavours, it seems appropriate to briefly explore a few of his notable contributions to the field of natural philosophy (i.e., what we have come to know as science) as well as a glimpse into his medical thinking and practice.

Darwin as Evolutionist

Although it is typically that other Darwin, Erasmus's grandson Charles, who is credited with ideas about evolution, Erasmus did contribute to the ongoing discussion in his own day.[127] Some have depicted Darwin as the first individual since the Roman era to express ideas about progressive evolution as thoroughly as Lucretius (*c*.99–*c*.55 B.C.) had done in his major didactic poem, *De Rerum Naturae*. For Darwin, evolution appears to have been an "extension of the normal process" of reproductive generation. He envisioned every living organism having embryonically originated as a simple "living filament" upon which are imparted "some acquired habits or propensities [to it that are] peculiar to the parent".[128] Once becoming excited into action, this filament can absorb nutrition, alter its shape, form new organs – each of which follows its respective "propensity" to meet its own needs. As such, the living filament is ultimately transformed into an entire living organism.

Darwin accepted the theory current in his day of the inheritance of acquired characteristics. Accordingly, variations in a parent's experiences might "exercise" altered forms of directed development in their offspring which, over time, could alter the physical form of an entire species.[129] By hypothesizing that the characteristics which an individual acquired over a lifetime were heritable, Darwin anticipated what Jean-Baptiste Lamarck (1744–1829) later claimed about the passage of acquired characteristics.[130] The progressive developments during embryonic development were carried forth to the next generation, or in other words, inherited. It might be said, giving priority to who published first, though contrary to the usual phrasing, that Lamarck was actually Darwinian in his thinking.

Darwin, one of the "prophets of progress" of his age, theorized that transferring an organism's acquired transformations to the next generation was a way to retain the more progressive or desirable hereditary traits. Allowing for influences from the environment as well as from heredity, he viewed a human's form as "the product of either its own historical development or that of its ancestor".[131] To ensure progressive development, the "strongest and most active animal should propagate the species, which should thence become improved". Furthering this idea he adds, "Would it be too bold to imagine, that in the great length of time since the earth began to exist … that all warm-blooded animals having arisen from one living filament … possessing the faculty of continuing to improve by its own inherent activity" might have "deliver[ed] down those improvements by generation to its posterity, world without end!"[132]

Some, such as King-Hele, have asserted that it was not "until Erasmus Darwin appeared that the truth [about evolution] emerged. He bypassed the concocted stories and specified a natural progression of life from submicroscopic specks in primaeval waters, through stages now scientifically established, to the humanimals".[133] Turning to a form of expression of which Darwin was fond, we find that Alfred Noyes recapped Darwin's evolutionary thought nicely in poesy:

He saw the multitudinous hosts of life,
All creatures of the sea and earth and air,
Ascending from one living spiral thread,
Through tracts of time, unreckonable in years.
He saw them varying as the plastic clay
Under the Sculptor's hands.

He saw them flowing
From one Eternal Fount beyond our world,
The inscrutable and indwelling Primal Power,
His only *vera causa*; by whose will
There was no gulf between the first and last,
There was no break in that long line of law
Between the first life drifting in the sea,
And man, proud man, the crowning form of earth,
Man whose own spine, the framework of his pride,
The fern-stem of his life, trunk of his tree,
Sleeps in the fish, the reptile, and the orang,
As all those lives in his own embryo sleep.

What deeper revolution, then, must shake
Those proud ancestral dynasties of earth?
What little man-made temples must go down?
And what august new temple must arise,
One vast cathedral, gargoyled with strange life,
Surging through darkness, up to the unknown end?[134]

Although Darwin was quite public about his views of the origin of life, these views were not accepted by the church. In response to Darwin displaying the motto "All Things from Shell Fish" under his family coat of arms on his carriage, Canon Seward published an invective against Darwin's apparently irreligious view of organic life in *Gentleman's Magazine*:

Some modern minute Philosophers lately furbished up an
old Heathen System of this World being originally covered
with water, and stored only with aquatic animals: that earthquakes
in a few millions of millions of ages [ago] raised continents
and mountains, and that men and all the terrestrial tribes sprung
from fish, or their exuviae, and that hence such numbers of fossils
are found even on the highest mountains; and all this they eagerly
swallowed, to get rid of the belief of Noah's flood. A Doctor of the
above sect, therefore, put as the motto of his family arms, which
were three scallop shells, "*Omniae e Conchis*", "All things from shell fish".

The Canon then addressed this act of his neighbour, Dr Darwin:

From atoms, in confusion hurl'd,
Old Epicurus built a World;
Maintain'd that all was accidental.
Whether corporeal pow'rs, or mental;
That neither hands, head, heart, or mind,
By any foresight were design'd;
That feet were not devis'd for walking;
For eating, teeth; or tongues for talking;
That Chance each casual texture made –

Then every member found its trade;
And in this whirlpool of stark nonsense,
He buried virtue, truth, and conscience.
For this he spent much studious toil,
And oft consum'd the midnight oil;
Each year produc'd long labour'd volumes,
Which cover'd half the Attic columns:[135]
And thus his sect spread far around,
In Asia, Greece, and Rome renown'd;
For all the bad receiv'd with glee
This hodge-podge of iniquity.
Celsus [136] at length resolves to lift
Under this grand cosmogenist;
He too renounces his Creator,
And forms all sense from senseless matter;
Makes men start up from dead fish-bones,
As old Deucalion did from stones;
Great wizard he, by magic spells
Can build a world of cockle-shells,
And all things frame, while eye-lid twinkles,
From lobsters, crabs, and periwinkles. –
O Doctor! Change thy foolish motto,
Or keep it for some lady's grotto,
Else they poor patients well may quake,
If thou no more canst *mend*, than *make*.

Canon Thomas Seward

Reluctantly, Darwin painted over the motto displayed on his carriage in 1770, but from that time forward, he had no kind words for the Canon.[137] Anna Seward, however, does not address this aspect of Darwin's life directly in the *Life of Dr Darwin*. When it is mentioned, rather than commenting first hand, Seward offers a few passages from contemporary letters.

One is from Robert Fellowes, who at the time of Darwin's biography was editor of the *Critical Review* and had become well known for his religious writings that were "tinged with the ideas of practical philanthropy".[138] Fellowes, a professional critic, practiced this trade on Darwin's writings, noting that although he "was acquainted with more links in the chain of *second* [earthly] causes than had probably been known to any individual … before him", but that "he dwelt so … *exclusively* on second causes, that he … generally seems to have forgotten that there is a first [heavenly cause]".[139] Elsewhere, in a letter to the Manchester physician and father of medical ethics writing, Thomas Percival, Seward explains that she "disliked invective in religious opinions" as she thought it "ungenerous, intolerant, and contrary to the very spirit of the New Testament".[140] In her biographical writing, Seward followed these leanings, and she omitted direct reference to Darwin's religion.

Darwin as Physician and Medical Author

Throughout his time in Lichfield, Darwin served the medical needs of the community – both those living in the city and those living in the Cathedral Close.[141] In addition, he travelled extensively – some have estimated 10,000 miles per year – in his horse and carriage or on his horse, "Doctor", throughout the Midlands. His carriage was equipped with hampers whose contents kept him well nourished as well as a writing table and a specially devised bookshelf which provided him the necessities from which he produced early drafts of many of his publications. Throughout these travels, he served as physician to, among others, the Wedgwood family, James Brindley, James Watt and Joseph Wright. Others came from afar to seek his expertise, including Dr Richard Warren who travelled from London for Darwin to treat his grievous medical needs. Darwin also received repeated invitations from George III to move to London to become his physician. Overall, however, the provinces seemed to suit Darwin much better. It may likely have been as much for his unorthodox religious leanings as for his professional inclinations that Darwin remained at a distance from the Anglican stronghold of London.

Seward called Darwin the "great system monger".[142] Building upon the Enlightenment projects of ordering and classifying information into new knowledge, as Darwin prepared his major medical writing, he envisioned his *Zoonomia; or, The Laws of Organic Life* as a Linnaean classification for disease *(Figure 8)*.[143] "There is need of a theory in the medical profession", he argued, "a theory founded upon nature, that should bind together the scattered facts of medical knowledge and converge into one point of view the laws of organic life".[144] Darwin's nosology was consistent with his view of society in that he viewed diseases in dynamic, evolving terms.[145] Within a short time, this work made him, in the view of King-Hele, the "leading medical author in the world".[146]

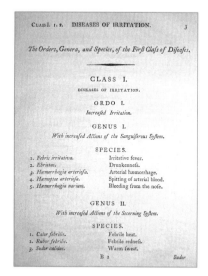

Figure 8: Sample of Dr Darwin's classification scheme of disease. Zoonomia; or, The Laws of Organic Life (1794-1796).

Disease was not, to the industrial-minded deist Darwin, an entity that invaded the body nor was it predestined. Rather, he viewed disease more as the result of a "malfunction" of the healthy motions within the body. Similar to habits, characteristics and physical constitutions, diseases were believed to be subject to alteration over time. The physician's role, therefore, was "to apply remedies which would restore ... [the body's] normal functioning", or even better, to prevent any malfunction in the first place.[147] Following the nonconformist's practice of working to improve one's earthly existence, he worked to overcome or to prevent the diseases to which one might be hereditarily predisposed. To achieve these aims, he argued with true industrial revolution zeal that one must learn how best to exert power over nature.

Much of what we know of Darwin's medical practice is derived from the handwritten cases he included in his *Commonplace Book*. Though considerably less than half of this book is devoted to medicine, it offers an otherwise inaccessible view into his professional life. The medical disorders described range from treating symptoms including headache, sore throat, and angina pectoris to diseases including asthma, dropsy, gout, smallpox, hydrophobia, and diabetes, as well as the complications surrounding childbirth. The detail of his discussion surrounding maternal/child care supports Sheena Mason's view, based upon her exemplary historical work on the Boulton family, that Darwin was "well ahead of his time in his ideas on childcare".[148] Devoting attention to such a wide variety of disorders strongly suggests that he assumed the role of what we would call a general practitioner.

Some of the entries in this book are merely transcriptions of other's medical writings which Darwin deemed to be helpful enough to record in his own hand. At times, these transcribed writings are expounded upon with details of Darwin's course of treating his own patients. Overall, they corroborate claims that as a physician, Darwin became "renowned for his acumen in cross-examining the patient until a satisfactory clinical judgment was arrived at".[149] He was "a good doctor by the standards of his profession in the period" who "believed in making notes, in comparing his observations with those of other doctors, and in ceaseless experimentation".[150] A sampling of these case studies offers keen insight into the experimental-mindedness underlying Darwin's medical thinking and practice.

Following a pleurisy and inflammation of the diaphragm, one female patient developed pain in the middle of her breast bone and, more problematically, a "lock'd jaw". After "having in vain indeavour'd to inject a fluid into her [locked] mouth far enough to be swallow'd, by means of a syringe introduced between two teeth", Darwin "roll'd up five grains of opium into a long cylinder, introduced it into the interstice between the teeth, & push'd it forwards towards the throat by means of a thin crow-quill". In "about two hours the spasm ceas'd, & she talked & drank as usual, but was left with great thirst & vomiting, as is usual after so large a dose of opium".[151]

Darwin treated an infant "a week old" who was "seized with difficulty breathing" whose sternum remained "seemingly without motion", but around which "great cavities [were] made at the time of inspiration". He "observed" that the child's "hands were cold & yet its stomach was much distended with air". He administered ipecac, calomel, opium and asafoetida – noting "I thought [the opium] of most use" – still, the child "died on the third day". He further queried, "Did the air in the stomach prevent the action of the diaphragm

... like a broken winded horse?"[152] These two cases corroborate King-Hele's summation that Darwin had no magic potion for his patients; indeed, he said that nearly all the 'boasted nostrums' were useless, and opium was the only one that could be relied upon".[153]

Among the most devastating diseases of Darwin's day was smallpox. He describes having seen "a child who by taking a grain or two of calomel ... after inoculation" experienced "violent vomiting & purging, & had the disease afterwards of the confluent kind, with blackheads to several of the pocks". This child "escape[d]" falling fatally ill "by having four drops of Laudanum twice a day before and during the secondary fever, which evidently supported it's strength, & thence prevented the increase of what are term'd putrid symptoms".[154]

In another case, he describes a "coachman, about 40, [who] seem's an habitual drinker" to have been inflicted with "the confluent smallpox to the greatest degree". Darwin "saw him on the 5th day of the eruption, [when] he had one pock on the back of each hand about two inches diameter, & his cheeks were also [marked with] one pock each. He was quite full [of marks] all over ... [many with] dark spots in the center of them. I directed him 5 grains of calomel each evening, & a purge of infusion of Sena every morning for five successive nights, of the last ... he also [took] about a grain of opium". Darwin continued, "what I depended much upon was that I directed his face & hands to be cover'd with plaister of the emplastrum adhesionum spread on linned [sic] & afterwards on London brown paper. These were renew'd night & morning, & I was astonish'd to see the quantity of a white purulent matter [that] was discharged with each dressing. He was kept airy, & rather cool, has as much small beer as he chose & towards the eleventh day had one sixth of ale mixed with it". Ultimately, he "recover'd beyond my most sanguine expectation in respect to every symptom".[155]

In a case describing the treatment of jaundice, Darwin steers our attention elsewhere. This patient, "a woman very yellow with the jaundice" also "suckled a child" and produced milk that was "quite white, or what is term'd blue". Wondering about the mechanics underlying milk production, he postulates, "Now as the pectoral arteries are very small, and milk is affected with all purgatives (except perhaps brimstone) I suspect [milk] is made by a retrograde motion of the chyle". He concluded, "This subject is worth the attention of anatomy".[156]

In treating the jaundice of another patient, Darwin had "pretty potent electric shocks pass'd through the body", especially "about the region of the gall bladder", after which the patient "began to mend the next day, & on continuing the electricity", the patient "recover'd fast".[157]

Darwin describes many cases of ascarides (intestinal nematode roundworms). Apart from recording his successes in treating these patients, he also talks of his experiments with worms. Among the more telling tales, Darwin describes treating one of the children of his Midland's Lunar Society colleague, Josiah Wedgwood. In May 1780, Wedgwood showed him the ascarides that one of his children had "just voided". On "taking them in a cold teaspoon, they became instantly lifeless", though when placed "in a warm one they beat themselves with great quickness", but on "putting one [of these] on a cold glass, it instantly ... [ceased] to move".[158] He continued to examine them, noting that under "the microscope the tail was not visible with too much light, it was so transparent", and when "they lay on the glass the opake [sic] part or bowels seem'd to retain some life, & had some circulation & sometimes parted oddly [sic] in places, or nearly parted & joined again". These observations contributed to his empirical medicinal art, in that he conjectured that "As cold so soon destroys them, I proposed to put some salt in cold water, & give [it] as an injection immediately – or ice-water with salt".[159]

Elsewhere, we get a glimpse into Darwin's own physical sufferings – especially in regard to gout. In a case dated 10 August 1779, Darwin informs us that "yesterday on walking about the town I felt a pain with a tension about the joint of the great toe of my right foot which continued [the] most part of the day. A day or two before I had felt a fullness about my stomach or liver, & a degree of sickness on eating hastily. This morning about three I waked with much pain, & tumour, & redness about the joint of the toe. I bled immediately to about 10 or 12 ounces, my pulse was not much quicken'd nor much less'd. About 4 I took calomel … at six this [purgative] operated, at seven I was very faint & had a slight chillness, & 3 or 4 nice stools. At 8 I put aether repeatedly on the tumor'd & red part, & kept it from evaporating by a piece of oil'd silk. The pain became less. At 9 [I] set out for Burton, with difficulty got into the chaise. At 11 was easier. Went on to Aston. At 4 or 6 p.m. was quite easy. Took a grain of opium at night. [The gout] had not return[ed], the swelling in two days subsided & the skin peel'd off".[160]

Given Darwin's penchant for verse, we close this reflection upon his medical thinking and practice with an extract from a number of his "occasional poems" which are included in his *Commonplace Book*.

> *A Parody on Pope*

> Doctors themselves must die, like those they kill
> Sunk the quick pulse, the brazen Pestil still,
> E'en he whose hand the potion'd cup extends
> Shall shortly want the cordial draught he sends,
> Then from his opening hand the fee shall part,
> And the last pang shall tear it from his heart,
> His idle business at one gasp be o'er,
> The bill forgot and patient's drench'd no more.[161]

Seward's Creation of *The Memoirs of the Life of Dr Darwin*

Although Seward may not have detailed Darwin's work as a physician in her *Life of Dr Darwin*, she was committed to writing a full, if not wholly flattering, account of his personality. This work would not be in the form of an apotheosis – attaining the highest level of praise – as she had formed for Cook and André. She considered her efforts were to be but a "memoir", for "from its shortness", it was not "worthy to be called a life".[162] Furthermore, she considered it to be a "defecit" in that she was able to draw upon insights only into that portion of Darwin's life that he lived in Lichfield – the years in which she knew him well. Seward created the memoir drawing upon accounts from a variety of living people, from previous letters, and from her own memory. Even then she had shortcomings, claiming that her memoir did not "form a regular detail of biographical circumstances, even in that moiety of his professional existence formed by his residence at Lichfield" for she knew only some aspects of Darwin's life.[163]

Seward noted that Darwin had "frequent[ly] remark[ed], that literary fame invariably suffers by the publication of every thing which is below the level of that celebrity which it has already gained". She was, after all, quite familiar with his letter writing habits in those that he composed for others. On at least a few occasions, as in the case of writing to Benjamin Franklin, Darwin asked Seward to compose such important letters herself, after which he copied them in his own hand. Overall, Seward remarked that Darwin's letters "though professionally numerous, were short from necessity, and by his choice compressed". Darwin himself had admitted that he "had not the talent of elegant letter writing", and Seward believed "there would be no kindness to his memory in obtruding them upon the public".[164]

Still, noting her own particular position, she attempted to persuade readers that "of those years in which the talents and social virtues" of Darwin "shed their lustre over … [Lichfield], no historian remains, who, with vicinity of habitation, and domestic intercourse with Darwin, took equal interest with myself in all that marked … that period … and which engaged my attention from my very earliest youth". She further remarks that only "few of his contemporaries in this town yet remain; but not one who could be induced to publish what their observations may have traced, and their memory treasured".[165]

Warning abounded for Seward to consider whether she should undertake such a depiction of a life. Her acquaintance, the poet Robert Southey, decried that biography should "never be written, unless the whole truth is told, and the whole truth ought never be told, while any good feelings can be wounded, or any evil ones gratified by divulging it. It is well that the heart of every remarkable man should be laid open to posterity; but it is not well, that his friends and his enemies should be invited to the dissection".[166] Richard Lovell Edgeworth, held similar views, particularly in regard to any biography of Darwin. He viewed that "in writing the life of a person, even [if done by] the closest of friends, nothing of importance should be concealed, even details that might be distasteful". Given that "many of Darwin's intimate friends were alive", Edgeworth eschewed composing Darwin's biography, fearing that presenting a full life exposé at this time would appear distasteful and hurtful to many individuals.[167]

Seward expressed concern about achieving truthfulness in the writing of life stories. In defence of her own approach, Seward claimed that biography "very seldom" yielded "characteristic trust" when it was written by "near relations, … obliged or partial friends, or by editors, who consider it highly conducive to their own profits" such that the biographical subject must be portrayed to "possess the unqualified esteem and admiration" of readers.[168] Too many biographies, she exclaimed, were written by a cherished friend who in attempt to relay "gratitude and affection" actually "render [them] blindly partial" and who become "influenced by a desire of gratifying, with a description of all-excelling endowment and angelic excellence" in order to please the surviving family members.[169] This type of life writer is, in Seward's terms, attempting to "draw a picture without shades".[170]

Yet, not acting at such a time also presented problems. For, as the biographer of another one of Seward's acquaintances, Thomas Day, argued, the "best picture" of an individual comes from "comparing and balancing the impressions recorded by people of varying types who had known" the biographical subject. He added further prohibitions about using only one's letters to build an account. For letters may, he argued, "appear cruelly cold or scandalously affectionate", concluding that "very few of our friends could be visualized from what they write".[171] Including limited material about Darwin's pre- and post-Lichfield life might draw criticism from their contemporaries, but Seward viewed drawing first-hand information from the few remaining individuals who once knew the man as the best way of rendering an accurate life story.

References to the fine art of painting were not unusual in commentary on the art of biography. The eighteenth-century artist, Jonathan Richardson (1667–1745), had previously noted that portraiture was but a form of depicting a life. "A Portrait", Richardson claimed, is "a sort of General History of Life of the Person it represents".[172] To sit for one's portrait was to have "an Abstract of one's Life written and published, and ourselves consign'd over to Honour, or Infamy".[173] Indeed, for Richardson, portraiture was actually "another sort of writing" – one destined to overshadow literary biography.[174] A portraitist represented his subject's life "more expressly, and particularly" than his literary counterpart. For in "making a portrait", although the "Complexion and each particular feature may have been Carefully Observ'd and Imitated … what is Most Important remains; the Air, the Mind, the Grace, the Dignity, the Capacity, the Vertue, Goodness, &c" if precisely and accurately detailed.[175]

Seward's *Life of Dr Darwin* is as much panorama as it is portrait. Important for later readers, not only was Seward able to shed at least some light on Darwin's Lichfield life, but also on the life of Lichfield during that remarkable period. John Brewer claims that her *Life of Dr Darwin* "incidentally memorialized the cultural circles of Lichfield where [Seward] played such an important part".[176] When Seward "wanted to publicize Lichfield's culture she shrewdly chose to write a biographical memoir of its most illustrious figure. She knew that she owed Darwin a great deal. His presence in Lichfield had enormously increased her circle of acquaintance and, when he left … [Seward] inherited his mantle as the most conspicuous of its writers".[177] Overall, Seward's work was something akin to the biographer and historian of biography, Ian Hamilton's depiction of a biographer as someone who provides "a glimpse both into a past society via its individuals, and possible insights into the very *nature of individuality* [Hamilton's italics] … one moment in a culture's history".[178]

Seward approached her own account of Darwin by "draw[ing] aside the domestic curtain" so that we learn much more truth about how a person really lived than is often revealed in biographies. "Every man has his errors", she noted, and "the errors of public characters are too well known not to expose unfounded eulogium to the distaste of all who prefer truth to enthusiasm". Returning to that image of an artist, Seward recalls that a "portrait painter might as well omit each appropriate distinction of feature, countenance, and form, because it may not be elegant … as the historian [of a life] conceal the faults, foibles, and weaknesses of the individual whom he delineates".[179] Indeed, she argues, it is "this fidelity of representation which makes Mrs Piozzi's *Memoirs of Dr Johnson*, and Mr Boswell's *Tour*, and his *Life* of [Johnson] … so valuable to those who wish not for an idol to worship, instead of a great man to contemplate, as nature, passion, and habit, compounded his character".[180]

For Seward, "just biographic record" touched upon the "failings of the good and the eminent with tenderness" and need not "spread over them a veil of suppression" nor invest their subject with "unrivalled genius and super-human virtue".[181] Rather, she attempted, using the "best of [her power], to "be the recorder of [Darwin's] vanished genius", all the while recalling the "sacred duties" of biography and criticism to serve the deceased and the public in a way that precludes "on one hand, unjust depreciation, [and] on the other, over-valuing partiality".[182]

In the preface of *Life of Dr Darwin*, Seward explains that her focus is on "the person, the mind, the temper of Dr Darwin; his powers as a Physician, Philosopher, and Poet; the peculiar traits of his manners; his excellencies and faults; the Petrarchan attachment of his middle life more happy in its result than was that of the Bard of Vaucluse; the beautific poetic testimonies of its fervour, while yet, it remained hopeless; an investigation of the consistent excellencies and defects of his magnificent poem, the *Botanic Garden*; remarks upon his philosophic prose writings; the characteristics and talents of those who formed the circle of his friends while he resided in Lichfield; and the very singular and interesting history of one of them [Lunar Man, Thomas Day], well-known in the lettered world, whose domestic history, remarkable as it is, has been unaccountably omitted by the gentleman [Lunar Man, John Keir] who wrote his life".[183]

In addition, we find that Seward's *Life of Dr Darwin* also provided her with a final venue to voice in print her vehemence against Darwin for having borrowed lines of poetry she had once composed and having published them as his own. Like so many accounts about Seward and Darwin, this story has a romantic beginning. In revitalizing what was once Sir John Floyer's Cold Bath and garden, which had become a "mere morass, till drained, cultivated, and formed into a picturesque garden of botanic science", Darwin's "forming hand" had "clear[ed] the underbrush with discretion" and "set out many varieties of trees, shrubs, and other plants".[184] Overall, he "widened the brook into pools that reflected the surrounding loveliness". Once "all was prepared", Darwin invited Seward in July 1778 "for a formal inspection" of this garden. But, "at the last moment", he was "called to a sickroom and Seward went on ahead".[185] She was "enchanted" by the beauty of this botanic garden in which she sat down and composed a panegyric to the water nymph, that began as follows:

O, come not here, ye Proud, whose breasts infold
Th'insatiate wish of glory or of gold;
O come not ye, whose branded foreheads wear
Th'eternal frown of envy or of care.

Darwin appears to have been elated with Seward's lines in a literary display of his garden, and, in due course, his friend, the Reverend William Stevens, a poet and headmaster of Repton School, sent the verses to *Gentleman's Magazine* where they were published in 1783 under her name.[186] When they appeared, Seward realized, to her annoyance, that Darwin had replaced the last six lines of the poem with eight of his own.[187] The common practice of "tinkering with verses" frequently "confused ownership....The genteel practice of publishing anonymously, the weakness of the copyright law, pirating by publishers, and the fact that the magazines seldom paid for the verses they accepted, all added to the confusion" over authorship.[188] In time, her annoyance was to be fueled even further.

Over the next ten years, while traveling in his chaise between patients, Darwin worked on his "compendium of [botanical] science and imagination", what would become his two-volume epic poem, *The Botanic Garden*. Seward's initial letters to Darwin about this epic were filled with praise. Even in her *Life of Dr Darwin*, she encourages future readers to explore it thoroughly: "Every skillful Botanist, every mere Tyro in the science, would wish to possess it for the sake of the notes, though [these readers be] insensible … to the charms of the poetry; while every reader awakened to them, must be ambitious to see such a constellation of poetic stars in his library".[189] Seward concluded by judging *The Botanic Garden* as "one of the richest effusions of the poetic mind, that has shed luster over Europe in the eighteenth century".[190] Her enthusiasm remained strong as witnessed by the devotion of nearly half of her 430-page *Life of Dr Darwin* towards an effusive and positive critical analysis of the poem which, according to King-Hele, remains the "best full critique that has been written" on the subject.[191]

Though the memoir's devotion to literary analysis suggests Seward's enthusiasm for this poem, overall, she was far from pleased with part of this work. Darwin had used the original verses she had compiled in his actual botanic garden, altered only slightly with some of his own lines interwoven, as the exordium — the very introduction — to this epic scientific poem. Unfortunately, for Seward, he included these lines without acknowledging their true author.[192] In admonishing Darwin, she retorted in 1792 that the "disingenuousness of making no mention that the scenic description, with which he opens his poem, was the work of another" leads one to imagine that "a charge of plagiarism must rest somewhere".[193]

Nine years later we find her opinion unchanged:

I disavow all partiality to Darwin. His conduct to me has not been calculated to inspire it. … His taking the landscape of the valley he cultivated near Lichfield, written and published in my name, … without the least acknowledgement [to me], could have no tendency to produce in me an exaggerating spirit concerning his talents. But treatment, this unhandsome, shall not induce me to suppress the fervour of my testimony in their favour, when they appear to me unjustly arraigned.[194]

Scott claimed that the "disingenuous suppression of the aid of which [Darwin] availed himself, must remain a considerable stain upon the character of the poet of Flora".[195] It seems of little surprise that when Seward encountered the great popularity of George Canning's parody of Darwin's *Botanic Garden* entitled *The Loves of the Triangles*, Seward retorted, "If Dr Darwin had been a fair and generous decider on the literary claims of others", she would have "sympathize[d] with the mortification he is likely to feel".[196]

Curiously, in a letter to Maria Edgeworth, Seward's literary executor noted "I do not think the verses very much worth struggling about".[197] Such a statement could be read in several ways. On one level, they could convey his dislike of these lines, on another, he may have been suggesting that as she had written much accomplished poetry of her own, why quibble about these few lines? Support for the latter argument is strengthened when we find Scott positioning Seward in "a higher rank among the poets of Britain than the judges of literature are … inclined to allow [Darwin]", thus bringing to question who was the true "poetical praeceptor".[198]

Seward remained perturbed about this issue throughout her life, even after Darwin's death. Beyond the plagiarism issue alone, she was among that generation of female poets and authors to break through the age-old practice of publishing primarily male authors. In order to voice their own opinions, women had previously resorted to publishing their own work under the name of their husband, father, brother or a male pseudonym. One later critic claimed that as Darwin "did not acknowledge this high-handed borrowing", his "oversight seems disingenuous, to say the least. The rights of women to recognition for their personal achievements were", the critic continues, "somewhat misty to the gentlemen of the period".[199]

Stuart Harris urges us to see Darwin's "adoption of Seward's lines … in a collaborative context". This collaboration, he continues, provided Darwin "a real female voice analogous to the female voice of the Goddess of Botany who later takes charge of the discourse throughout the poem".[200] As to Seward's action about Darwin's borrowing, even King-Hele claims it "a compliment … [that] Seward took … as an insult".[201] Regardless of how Darwin may have envisioned his lack of crediting Seward's significant contribution to *The Botanic Garden*, it weighed heavily upon her mind, tormenting the very one who ultimately devoted considerable time toward crafting Darwin's life story.

Publication and Reception of Seward's *Life of Dr Darwin*

Seward lamented, in an 1802 letter to Bilsborrow, that her "attempt [to complete the *Life of Dr Darwin*] ought long since to have been finished, but ill-health frequently preclude[d] my use of the pen". In addition, her "perpetual claims of social engagements", a "ten weeks absence from home", and "the incessant and unavoidable business of answering letters from literary strangers, have retarded the progress of my little Darwiniana".[202]

In May 1803, Seward sent the manuscript of her *Life of Dr Darwin* to London under the care of her cousin, Henry White (1761–1836). The publisher Joseph Johnson (1738–1809) quickly offered her "a handsome price", but then "delay ensued". Delay was, to Seward's way of thinking, particularly "unfavourable to biographic composition". For in this genre, [a]bove all other species of writings", it is "expedient that it should 'catch the *aura popularis*' which curiosity breathes, ere it wastes and sinks in expectation".[203] This delay arose from the publisher's concern that "some of the remarks in the book might cause offense to Darwin's friends and their families". Johnson "insisted on expurgations and changes" or her publishing contract would be dissolved.[204] Though Seward claimed such "facts" to be "unexaggerated" and "which all the world knew [to be true] at the time they happened", after careful deliberation – and "a good deal of demur and haggling", she "attempted that softened colouring" of the facts that Johnson demanded.[205]

Throughout the remainder of 1803, Seward proofread portions of the book that Johnson's "press-corrector" had revised and sent to her in Lichfield. However, it was during this time that she also suffered "under the heavy shadow of grief". John Saville died in August, and it was said that Seward's grief was "terrible" – more "that of a widow … than [that of] a friend". She did not leave the Bishop's Palace for weeks, and "never [fully] recovered from the blow of her bereavement".[206] The overbearing nature of her loss occupied her mind "too much … to take pleasure in any plaudits" which might have come her way after its publication in early January 1804.[207] Such plaudits, however, were few, at least in published critical reviews.[208]

Scott noted that Darwin "could not have wished his fame and character entrusted to a pen more capable of doing them ample and … discriminating justice".[209] But Seward had conceived her *Life of Dr Darwin* as much more than mere biography. In addition to fixing her place in the Lichfield circle, she saw it as a means to secure further her status as a critic. However, notwithstanding Scott's praise, one of Seward's biographers claimed that "on the whole" this work "did not bring much glory or happiness to the author".[210]

Critics seemed appalled by Seward's unconventional style of assembling a biography. At the time of its publication, this book "proved problematic to the literary establishment".[211] Readers noticed at the outset that the book broke from standard biographical format. The work lacked the traditional chronological order. Additionally, it did not retell the life of Darwin in an adulatory yet standard "Great Man" approach. Though critics characterize such works as hagiography, these forms of writings remained among the most popular selling books of the period. Some critics raised the issue that Seward was not "sufficiently competent either to appreciate or to express the scientific qualities" of the life of her subject.[212] But it was not the medical and natural philosophical side of Darwin's life that Seward intended to recreate. Indeed, she had acknowledged before the book's publication that she "had not science … [nor] sufficient knowledge of [Darwin's] philosophical correspondence" to "make any such pretention" of relaying details about those parts of his life.[213] Rather, she was intensely interested in drawing upon the "emotional and personal traits" that were evidenced in his poetry. In addition, she employed her talents at the analytic reading of poetry in the critique upon Darwin's botanic poetry. After all, as Teresa Barnard has noted, Seward had a very close connection with the epic poem, *The Botanic Garden*. Seward had "inspired its inception, written the opening lines, proof read the manuscripts and suggested alterations, some of which Darwin implemented".[214] Even Scott, who applauded the way she had "preserved … [many] curious and interesting literary anecdotes", noted that her *Life of Dr Darwin* was "written upon a desultory plan, and in a style disfigured by the use of frequent inversions and compounded epithets".[215]

Seward had anticipated that her memoir of Darwin would receive some criticism, particularly due to there being two extreme camps in regards to Darwin's poetry. The "world of letters" was equally divided between those who considered him "the first genius of his age" in terms of both his "poetic system" and his "execution" of writing and those critics who "so injuriously avowed" all such "Pursuits of Literature".[216] The "same extremes of opinion prevail", Seward continued, "among his acquaintance[s] respecting his moral character". Half "exalt him as having been almost superior to human frailty" whereas others "stigmatize him as an empiric in medicine, a Jacobin in politics, deceitful to those who trusted him, covetous of gain, and an alien to his God".[217]

Some critics did, indeed, challenge Darwin's poetry, but not quite for the reasons Seward had anticipated. For example, Lee Phillips of Mayfield questioned whether mere coincidence or unacknowledged borrowing had intervened. In particular, he argued that once the "sexes of plants" had been discovered, it appears that the "idea of writing a poem upon the subject" looked promising to more than one poet. In an attempt to disavow Darwin's originality in the underlying theme of *The Botanic Garden*, Phillips noted a particular poetical work that had been attached to the Tübingen physician and botanist, Rudolf Jakob Camerarii's (1666–1721) *De Sexu Plantarum Epistole* (Tübingen: Le Drük, 1694). John Martyn (1699–1768) translated this poem into English as "An Ode formerly Dedicated to Camerarius", and it had been published in Patrick Blair's *Botanick Essays* (1720).[218] Darwin may, indeed, have come across this work. However, as Seward replied, the "very basic idea of the sexes of plants" is the "only affinity between [Camerarius's] mere skeleton, and Darwin's extended and complicated work".[219] Far beyond the work of Camerarius, Darwin's "extended and complicated work" expounded upon "not merely … plants and flowers, but of all the elemental properties, branching out into allusive ramifications of classic fable, history, ancient and modern and of many of the remarkable events of more recent periods".[220]

More difficult challenges lay ahead. In reading a review of her work in the *Edinburgh Review* (See Appendix IV), Seward found that it was her characterization of Darwin more than his poetry which raised the most ire. There, tucked between reviews of works by the utilitarian philosopher Jeremy Bentham, the chemist Thomas Thompson, and the impostor Thomas Chatterton, Seward's credentials, abilities, and intentions were seriously questioned.

> After perusing … [the] table of contents, the reader will have himself alone to blame if he expect in this volume any exact or orderly deduction of the facts of Dr Darwin's life. Miss Seward apparently spurns the fetters of vulgar, chronological narration … After having followed her with patience through her eccentric and capricious evolutions, we are unable to say that our progress has been rendered more pleasing by this irregular variety, or that it has afforded us any tolerable compensation for the want of a distinct and intelligible narrative.[221]

Seward replied that "ignorance and envy are the only possible parents of such criticisms …. In putting them forth, their author is baser than a thief, since to blight the early sale of an eminent work by unjust criticism is to rob the bard of his remuneration, while the arrested progress of his fame inflict severer mortification".[222]

Though Seward's reply to the editor went virtually unnoticed, her *Life of Dr Darwin* had "aroused a storm".[223] Aspects of Darwin's life were "revealed that had never been remotely hinted at before".[224] As one of Thomas Day's biographers, Peter Rowland, argued, the "world at large was partly stunned, and partly fascinated, by Anna Seward's lurid Book of Revelations".[225] In addition to revealing a prejudiced characterization of Darwin, Rowland noted that Seward's memoir showed that she had "been revolted … by the deluge of praise heaped upon" one of Darwin's contemporaries, Thomas Day, after his own demise. Beyond her unrelenting attacks upon Darwin's use of her poetry, Seward also sought to "settle a few old scores and to work off some ancient grudges" that she held against Day. According to Rowland, Day, a close friend of Edgeworth, "positively urge[d] him on in his fiendish conquest of Honora [Sneyd]", an act for which Seward apparently never forgave either Edgeworth or Day.[226]

More notable to contemporaries was Seward's depiction of Darwin following the death of his son, Erasmus, Junior. Seward had reported that in December 1799, Erasmus, Junior –

a "victim of melancholia, aggravated by worry over some unimportant accounts" – "threw himself into the river Derwent, which flowed at the lower end of the garden" of his father's Derby home. She continued, arguing that "the younger Erasmus was a sensitive and retiring person, who wished to enter the Church and avoid the harsh contacts of the world; that he was wounded by the rough irony of his father, and morbidly conscious of being the butt of paternal ridicule". Moreover, in words that infuriated Robert Darwin in particular, Seward asserted that Erasmus Darwin "showed hard and unfeeling spirit" at the time of Erasmus, Junior's death; that he "spoke contemptuously of the dead man's cowardice, and after the funeral never referred to the lost son again".[227]

The editor of the *Edinburgh Review* had been in touch with the Darwin family, and at Robert's demand, Seward was forced to publish a retraction. When her attempt at rewording this statement failed to meet the family's expectations, Robert wrote much of it himself. The retraction was published along with the review. In it, we read that Seward's depiction of Darwin following Erasmus, Junior's death "is entirely without foundation, and that the Doctor, on that melancholy event, gave amongst his own family proofs of strong sensibility at the time, and of succeeding regard to the memory of his son, which he seems to have a pride in concealing from the world". In "justice to his memory", Seward "is desirous to correct this misinformation she had received" and is "obliged to the Editor of the *Edinburgh Review*" for appending it to the review of her work, since, unless a second edition should be called for, she has no [other] means … of counteracting the mistake".[228]

Robert Darwin's concerns garnered support from several of the Lunar Society members. Josiah Wedgwood, Jr. despised the "gross, coarse, and cruel" lingering image of his friend Darwin in Seward's account, but he implored Robert to forget the situation. From Wedgwood's view, Seward had inflicted indelible damage upon Darwin's reputation.[229] Edgeworth, who had personally experienced Seward's scorn following the death of Honora, received a letter from Robert Darwin's half-sister, Emma, stating that there is "nothing else of such infinite consequence as [Seward's] daring publicity to accuse my dear papa of want of affection and feeling towards his son. How can this be contradicted?", she asked. "I want to scratch a pen over all the lies and send the book back to Miss Seward, but Mamma won't allow this".[230] Robert Darwin closed the matter stating, in a letter to Seward, that "[w]ere I to publish my father's papers in illustration of his conduct, some circumstances must unavoidably have appeared which would have been as unpleasant for you to read as for me to publish".[231]

Seward confided to Dr Thomas Percival, that "I see" that the Darwin family "wanted to have only the lights of his character shewn, and all its shades omitted". Yet, as she claims, some of "my friends murmur[ed]" that "I have not … sufficiently stigmatized his irreligion; at least his long insinuated contempt of the revelation, and of what appeared to him the improbability of the mediatorial sacrifice".[232]

During the twentieth century, Seward's *Life of Dr Darwin* received mixed reviews. E.V. Lucas argued, in *A Swan and Her Friends* (1907), that for a biography, Miss Seward's book could not be … worse; and it is dull too. Everything great in the Doctor's character is omitted; while such trifling as he occasionally condescended to … is turned into silliness".[233] Stapleton Martin declared, in 1909, that this work "is, nowadays, considered but a poor piece of writing".[234]

Hesketh Pearson *(Figure 9)*, who drew much from the work of others for his many popular biographies, merely acknowledged that Seward's work was one "on which a biographer must draw pretty extensively".[235] James Venable Logan argued that Seward's biography was "not marked by unfriendly bias". If it appeared that the author did not "always draw a favorable picture of her subject" it was merely that Seward did not want to appear as a "dazzled idolater" of Darwin. Seward worked to preserve Darwin's "generosity and charm" as well as his "wit and genius", though he acknowledged that for a life depiction, some would see it as "endowed with too much of ... [that] charming but sometime dangerous gift" – imagination. Most importantly, however, Logan elevated Seward's *Life of Dr Darwin* over later accounts in that Seward's had the advantage of being composed by someone who had "the freshness of personal contact".[236] The British philosopher and critic Elizabeth Sewell rated Seward's memoir as "a minor classic in its own right, fascinatingly florid in style, frequently irrelevant, but never dull, exhibiting from time to time unmistakable and enjoyable feminine malice, unreliable in its facts, but containing shrewd critical judgment of Darwin's literary work".[237]

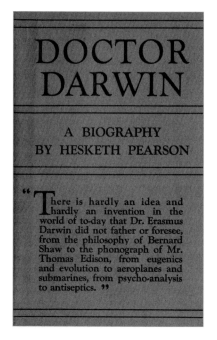

DOCTOR DARWIN

A BIOGRAPHY
BY HESKETH PEARSON

" There is hardly an idea and hardly an invention in the world of to-day that Dr. Erasmus Darwin did not father or foresee, from the philosophy of Bernard Shaw to the phonograph of Mr. Thomas Edison, from eugenics and evolution to aeroplanes and submarines, from psycho-analysis to antiseptics. "

Figure 9: Dust jacket cover of Hesketh Pearson's Doctor Darwin: A Biography *(1930).*

Not all of the late-twentieth-century accounts were so positive. Before Jenny Uglow's *The Lunar Men*, Robert Schofield's 1963 account of *The Lunar Society of Birmingham* was the most frequently referenced history of that group of men. Schofield found Seward's *Life of Dr Darwin* "an almost libelous biography ... which discusses, in absurdly stilted language, the trivial activities and interests of Darwin's life" in a way that shows Seward's "lack of taste by its fulsome praise of his poetry, and ignores his important accomplishments".[238]

Maureen McNeil, in her representation of Darwin's revolutionary efforts in pursuing knowledge, *Under the Banner of Science*, notes that Seward, though "coloured by the stormy history of her personal relations with Doctor Darwin", "tells the story of his life through a series of anecdotes which emphasize his wit and joviality, and which have been replicated in various forms in subsequent studies".[239]

Over time, Desmond King-Hele, Erasmus Darwin's best-known biographer of recent years, appears to have modified his view of Seward's biography of Darwin. In 1963, King-Hele acknowledged that Seward's biography served as "the chief source for our knowledge of Darwin at Lichfield, and a mine of quaintly phrased stories, some of which may be mythical".[240] By 1968, he viewed it as "generous yet also malicious, and quite inimitable in its stilted phraseology".[241] By 1977, though finding Seward to be "amazingly prolix in style and often unreliable", he acknowledged that her *Life of Dr Darwin* remains "indispensable to a biographer of Erasmus [Darwin]". Still, the author herself was "a little waspish and ambivalent about her famous neighbour in the close, whom she admired and yet also sometimes detested".[242] By 1986, he rendered the work to be "rather scathing about Darwin as a man", but "her tribute to [the] power of his poem [*The Botanic Garden*] was both discerning and magnanimous".[243] Finally, in his definitive 1999 biographical account of Darwin, King-Hele repeats several of the above views, concluding that Seward's work remains "essential to later biographers".[244]

So we still find mixed views of Seward's *Life of Dr Darwin*. Just what should biography be? We can allow Erasmus Darwin the last word. In *The Loves of the Plants* (Volume II of *The Botanic Garden*, 1789), Darwin turns to what for him was a most unexpected and unfrequented venue – Lichfield Cathedral. He recounts that:

> In the fourth aisle of the cathedral church at Lichfield,
> there is an ancient monument of a recumbent figure;
> the head and neck of which lie on a roll of matting in a
> kind of niche or cavern in the wall; and about
> five feet distant horizontally in another opening or cavern in
> the wall are seen the feet and ankles, with some folds
> of garment, lying also on a mat; and through the intermediate
> space in a solid stone-wall, yet the imagination supplies
> the deficiency, and the whole figure seems to exist before
> our eyes. Does not this resemble one of the arts both of
> the painter and the poet?

Could not this also be said of the biographer? Indeed, it is up to the biographer to craft that middle ground between the beginning and end of a life. For over two centuries, Darwin's biographers have filled in bits and pieces of that middle ground, choosing to depict him as "Grandfather of Meteorology"; "Champion of Oxygen Treatment"; "Chronicler of Lustful Plants"; "Master of Many Crafts"; "Master of Interdisciplinary Science"; "A Man of Ideas and Inventor of Words"; "Doctor of Revolution"; and the "Chief Scientific Source for the Romantic Poets". Stuart Harris has shown the breadth of Darwin's thinking by describing how Darwin's three epic poems [*The Loves of the Plants* (1789); *The Economy of Vegetation* (1791); and *The Temple of Nature* (1803)] cover such a vast "cosmic sweep", tying together so many important themes common to all times: love and sympathy, sexuality and fertility, health and happiness; beauty and utility; personal and social improvement; climatology and environmental management; and the study of natural law that "underpins all of them".[245] But despite many criticisms, whether just or unjust, Seward's *Life of Dr Darwin* portrays the essence of the individual that King-Hele has captured in the subtitle of his last full-length biography – *A Life of Unequalled Achievement*.

Chapter Summary
The variety of topics and modes of writing contained in Seward's *Life of Dr Darwin* invites a brief summary of its chapters to guide the reader. Chapter One describes Darwin's distinctive physical characteristics and mannerisms, as well as the major events of his early years in

Lichfield (1756-1772), including his marriage to Polly Darwin, which ended with her death in 1770. Seward paints detailed portraits of Darwin's circle of Lichfield friends from this period, including members of the Lunar Society such as Small, Boulton, Edgeworth, and Day. She lingers longest on the fascinating character and life choices of Day. Describing in sympathetic terms his attempted education of the two foundling girls that he named Lucretia and Sabrina, Seward also details the girls' lives after Day determined them to be unsuitable as spouses. Seward further chronicles Day's search for love, which happily culminated in his marriage to Esther Milnes in 1780.

Chapter Two offers brief sketches of Darwin's Lichfield friends in the 1770s, including the poet, botanist, and politician, Sir Brooke Boothby (1744-1824). Focusing a bit more on Darwin himself in this chapter, Seward offers an anecdote about his broken patella, amusing examples of his satiric wit, an account of the singular instance in which he publicly violated his own commitment to sobriety, as well as a history of the mutual dislike between Darwin and Dr Johnson. She proceeds to defend members of the Lichfield literati, including her own father, against "the arrogant Johnson['s]" "depreciating estimate of Lichfield talent".[246]

In the following chapter, Seward supports her defense of Lichfield's writers with a discussion of the controversy around and contributions of Darwin's *Zoonomia* (1794-96), which he began composing in 1770-71. She describes the Botanical Society that Darwin founded in Lichfield and introduces the Sneyd family and Elizabeth Pole, who was first a patient and later the second wife of Darwin. The chapter includes a fascinating account of a blood transfusion that Darwin nearly gave to the Countess of Northesk, with Seward offering to serve as the donor. Seward reprints her own poem celebrating Darwin's ingenious cultivation of his garden. These lines, which Darwin revised and included without acknowledgement in *The Botanic Garden*, were a subsequent source of tension between the two poets. The chapter offers reprints of several of Darwin's shorter lyrics, as well as a series of playful letters that Darwin and Seward exchanged in 1780 in the voices of their cats.

In Chapter Four, Seward recounts Darwin's successful courtship of Elizabeth Pole, following Colonel Pole's death. The marriage of Elizabeth Pole's second daughter to John Gisborne inspires an extended digression on the merits of Gisborne's verse. Seward concludes the chapter with an overview of the composition, publication history, and major strengths of Darwin's *The Botanic Garden*.

In the lengthy and detailed Chapters Five and Six, Seward displays her considerable talent as a literary critic in a close reading and comparative discussion of *The Botanic Garden*. With Chapter Five focused on *Part I: "The Economy of Vegetation"*, and Chapter Six taking up *Part II: "Loves of the Plants"*, Darwin's fellow poet assesses his achievement from the standpoint of craft—down to issues of meter and sound. Displaying her own impressive command of the emerging British canon, Seward discusses Darwin's poetic choices—canto by canto, and stanza by stanza—in comparison to poetry by both British and classical poets.

The final chapter of Seward's *Life of Dr Darwin* recounts William Cowper's and Richard Polwhele's praise for *The Botanic Garden*. Incorporating an overview of Darwin's life after he left Lichfield for Derby in 1781, the chapter mentions Darwin's later publications, including *A Plan for the Conduct of Female Education in Boarding Schools* (1797), three short poems reprinted in this chapter, *Phytologia, or the Philosophy of Agriculture and Gardening* (1800), and

The Temple of Nature (1803). The chapter also features Seward's controversial account of Darwin's reaction to the likely suicide of his son Erasmus, Junior in 1799. Seward concludes the memoir by describing the days' activities preceding Darwin's own death in 1802.

Notes

1   Anna Seward, *Memoirs of the Life of Dr Darwin, Chiefly During his Residence in Lichfield; With Anecdotes of his Friends, and Criticisms of his Writings* (London: For J[oseph] Johnson, by T. Bensley, 1804). Joseph Johnson (1738–1809), who H.R. Tedder describes as the "father of the book trade" in London, had also published works by Erasmus Darwin, Joseph Priestley, Mary Wollstonecraft, and Maria Edgeworth. "Joseph Johnson", *Dictionary of National Biography* (London: Smith, Elder, and Co, 1892), Vol.30, p.22. See also Gerald P. Tyson, *Joseph Johnson: A Liberal Publisher* (Iowa City: University of Iowa Press, 1979).

2   In the definitive *Erasmus Darwin: A Life of Unequalled Achievement* (London: De la Mare, 1999), pp.343–344, Desmond King-Hele claims that Erasmus Darwin's "most important obituary" appeared, perhaps under the authorship of the magazine's editor, John Aiken, who disliked Darwin, in *Monthly Magazine* 13 (1802): 457–463. Richard Lovell Edgeworth contributed a more friendly obituary that appeared in the same magazine, 14 (1802): 115–116, whereas the "most widely-read" of Darwin's obituaries appeared in *Gentleman's Magazine* 72 (1802): 473–474.

3   Desmond King-Hele (ed) *Charles Darwin's The Life of Erasmus Darwin* (Cambridge: Cambridge University Press, 2003).

4   Apart from King-Hele's masterful work, see also the work of Erasmus' great-great-great grandson, Hesketh Pearson, *Doctor Darwin* (London: J.M. Dent, 1930), Maureen McNeil, *Under the Banner of Science: Erasmus Darwin and His Age* (Manchester: Manchester University Press, 1987), and the many biographical insights included in C.U.M. Smith and Robert Arnott (eds) *The Genius of Erasmus Darwin* (Aldershot, Hampshire: Ashgate, 2005). The physician John Dowson also prepared a life of Dr Darwin which was initially delivered as a lecture in 1860 in Whitby, and published as *Erasmus Darwin, Philosopher, Poet and Physician* (Whitby [London?], 1861). The scarcity of this work puts into question its influence and readership. Maureen McNeill also prepared the Erasmus Darwin entry for the *Oxford Dictionary of National Biography*, Oxford: Oxford University Press, 2004 (*www.oxforddnb.com/view/article/7177, accessed 31 Oct 2008*).

5   Anna Seward to Walter Scott, 29 April 1802, *Letters of Anna Seward*, Letter 3, Vol.6, p.20.

6   Margaret Ashmun, *The Singing Swan: An Account of Anna Seward and her Acquaintance with Dr Johnson, Boswell and Others of Their Time* (New Haven, Connecticut: Yale University Press, 1931), pp.234–235.

7   Their children: Marianne (*b.*1798), Caroline (*b.*1799), Susan (*b.*1803), and Erasmus (*b.*1804). Charles would not come along until 1809, with Emily following a year later.

8   Seward, *Life of Dr Darwin*, p.54, pagination based upon this 2010 annotated version.

9   Anna Seward to Thomas Whalley, 12 May 1802, as reprinted in Revd. Hill Wickham (ed) *Journals and Correspondence of Thomas Sedgewick Whalley, D.D.* (London: Richard Bentley, 1836), Vol.2, p.221. In this important letter, Anna begins to recapture the image of Dr Darwin as well as conveying her view on the construction of biography. All of these aspects are later polished in her *Life of Dr Darwin*.

10   Paul Elliott briefly mentions Bilsborrow and his Infirmary connection in "The Derbyshire 'Darwins': The Persistence of Erasmus Darwin's Influence on a British Provincial Literary and Scientific Community, *c.*1780–1850", in Smith and Arnott (eds) *Genius of Erasmus Darwin*, p.187.

11   One passage of Bilsborrow's poem, "On Erasmus Darwin's work entitled *Zoonomia*" (1794), which discusses the formation of life itself seems particularly fitting to include in that we are discussing how the creations of stories are also a manner of forming a life.

Erewhile, emerging from its liquid bed,

It lifts in gelid air its nodding head;

The lights first dawn with trembling eyelid hails,

With lungs untaught arrests the balmy gales;

Tries its new tongue in tones unknown, and hears

The strange vibrations with unpractised ears;

Seeks with spread hands the bosom's velvet orbs.

With closing lips the milky fount absorbs;

And, as compress'd the dulcet streams distil,

Drinks warmth and fragrance from the living rill; –

Eyes with mute rapture every waving line,

Prints with adoring kiss the Paphian shrine,

And learns erelong, the perfect form confess'd,

Ideal Beauty from its mother's breast.

12 Seward, *Life of Dr Darwin*, p.54.

13 Seward, *Life of Dr Darwin*, pp.125, 52.

14 Seward, *Life of Dr Darwin*, p.54.

15 Among the many recent overviews of Anna Seward's contribution to the literature of her age, see Norma Clarke, "Anna Seward, Bluestocking", Chapter 1 of her *The Rise and Fall of the Woman of Letters* (London: Pimlico, 2004), pp.13–52, Jennifer Kelly (ed) *Anna Seward* in Gary Kelly (ed) *Bluestocking Feminism: Writings of the Bluestocking Circle 1738–1785*, Vol.4. (London: Pickering & Chatto, 1999), and Teresa Barnard, *Anna Seward: A Constructed Life* (Farnham, Surrey: Ashgate, 2009).

16 The history of the West Midlands is the subject of a major new publication: Peter Jones, *Industrial Enlightenment in Birmingham and the West Midlands, 1760–1820: Science, Technology and Culture* (Manchester: Manchester University Press, 2008).

17 Barrie Trinder, *The Industrial Revolution in Shropshire* (Chichester: Phillimore, 2000); Barry Trinder and Neil Cossons, *The Iron Bridge: Symbol of the Industrial Revolution* (Chichester: Phillimore, 2002); and Barrie Trinder (ed), *The Most Extraordinary District in the World: Ironbridge and Coalbrookdale* (Chichester: Phillimore, 2007).

18 Malcolm Dick, "Discourses for the New Industrial World: Industrialisation and the Education of the Public in Late Eighteenth-Century Britain", *History of Education* 37 (2008): 577–582. Several scholars have begun to explore the industrial revolution's influence upon Seward's poetry: Donna Coffey in her "Protecting the Botanic Garden: Seward, Darwin, and Coalbrookdale", *Women's Studies* 31 (2002): 141–64; Silvia Bowerbank's chapter on Seward in her *Speaking for Nature: Women and Ecologies of Early Modern England* (Baltimore: Johns Hopkins University Press, 2004), pp.161–87; Sharon Setzer, "'Ponderous Engines' in 'Outraged Groves': The Environmental Argument of Anna Seward's 'Colebrook Dale,'" *European Romantic Review* 18 (2007): 69–82; and Timothy Webb in "Listing the Busy Sounds: Anna Seward, Mary Robinson and the Poetic Challenge of the City" in Lilla Maria Crisafulli and Cecilia Pietropoli (eds) *Romantic Women Poets: Genre and Gender* (Amsterdam: Rodopi, 2007), esp. pp.83–96. On industrial themes, Anna Seward's "Colebrook Dale" and Doctor Darwin's "The Power of Steam" appeared in juxtaposition to each other in Jeremy Warburg (ed) *The Industrial Muse: The Industrial Revolution in English Poetry* (Oxford: Oxford University Press, 1958), pp.3–8.

19 Robin Reilly, "Wedgwood, Josiah (1730–1795)", *Oxford Dictionary of National Biography,* Oxford University Press, 2004 *(www.oxforddnb.com/view/article/28966, accessed 19 Oct 2008)* and Robin Reilly, *Josiah Wedgwood, 1730–1795* (London: Macmillan, 1992).

20   J. R. Harris, "Wilkinson, John (1728–1808)", *Oxford Dictionary of National Biography,* Oxford University Press, 2004 *(www.oxforddnb.com/view/article/29428, accessed 19 Oct 2008);* Norbert C. Soldon, *John Wilkinson (1728–1808), English Ironmaster and Inventor, Studies in British History,* Vol.49, (Lewiston, New York: Edwin Mellen Press, 1998).

21   Eric Hopkins, *The Rise of the Manufacturing Town: Birmingham and the Industrial Revolution* (Stroud: Sutton Publishing, 1998), pp.20–21, 73–74, and 118.

22   Jennifer Tann, "Boulton, Matthew (1728–1809)", *Oxford Dictionary of National Biography,* Oxford University Press, Sept 2004; online edn, May 2007 *(www.oxforddnb.com/view/article/2983, accessed 19 Oct 2008);* Malcolm Dick (ed) *Matthew Boulton – A Revolutionary Player* (Studley: Brewin Books, 2009).

23   Neil McKendrick, "The Commercialization of Fashion" and "Josiah Wedgwood and the Commercialization of the Potteries" in Neil McKendrick, John Brewer and J. H. Plumb, *The Birth of a Consumer Society: the Commercialization of Eighteenth-Century England* (London: Hutchinson, 1983), pp.69–77 and 100–145; Maxine Berg, *Luxury and Pleasure in Eighteenth-Century Britain* (Oxford: Oxford University Press, 2007).

24   Robert E. Schofield, *The Lunar Society of Birmingham* (Oxford: Clarendon Press, 1963); Jenny Uglow, *The Lunar Men* (London: Faber & Faber, 2002); www.revolutionaryplayers.org.uk

25   Marie B. Rowlands, *The West Midlands from AD 1000* (London and New York: Longman, 1987), pp.228–251.

26   John Money, *Experience and Identity: Birmingham and the West Midlands 1760–1800* (Manchester: Manchester University Press, 1977).

27   Chris Upton, *A History of Lichfield* (Chichester: Phillimore, 2001); and Malcolm Dick, "Eighteenth–Century England: Cultural Capital of the Midlands" in www.search.revolutionaryplayers.org.uk/engine/resource/exhibition/standard/default.asp?resource=3533 (accessed 18 October, 2008).

28   James Boswell, *The Life of Samuel Johnson* (London: J Richardson and Co., 1823), Vol.II, p.462.

29   John Britton, *The History and Antiquities of the See and Cathedral Church of Lichfield* (London: Longman, Hurst, Rees, Orme, Brown, Britton, and J. Taylor, 1820), p.10. An "escutcheon or landscape of three slain kings, or martyrs" dismembered "in diverse manners" forms part of these arms and seal. Revd. Stebbing Shaw, *The History and Antiquities of Staffordshire* (London: J. Nicols, 1798), Vol.1, p.343. As poetically captured:

>   The ground when watered with their holy blood
>
>   Who died for Christ, shall be accounted good;
>
>   The name of Lichfield to the place they gave,
>
>   The field of bodies or the martyr's grave.

Reproduced in Charles Edward Stringer, *A Short Account of the Ancient and Modern State of the City and Close of Lichfield* (Lichfield: T.G. Lomax, 1819), p.6.

30   Copied in Stebbing Shaw, *History and Antiquities of Staffordshire,* Vol.1, p.343.

31   Britton, *History and Antiquities of Lichfield,* p.8.

32   Thomas Harwood, *The History and Antiquities of the Church and City of Lichfield* (Gloucester: Cadel and Davies, 1806), John Jackson, *History of the City and County of Lichfield* (Lichfield: John Jackson, 1795), and John Jackson, *History of the City and Cathedral of Lichfield* (London: Nichols for C. Rivington and J. Jackson, 1805), John Britton, *History and Antiquities of Lichfield,* and T. G. Lomax, *Short Account of the Ancient and Modern State of the City and Close of Lichfield* (Lichfield: T.G. Lomax, 1819).

33   E.V. Lucas, *A Swan and Her Friends* (London: Methuen, 1907), p.9.

34   Mary Alden Hopkins, *Dr Johnson's Lichfield* (London: Peter Owen, 1956), pp.22–23.

35   Perhaps because of her own infamy as the former mistress of the Prince of Wales, Robinson published this work under the pseudonym Anne Frances Randall. *Letter to the Women of England, on the Injustice of Mental Subordination* (London: T.N. Longman, and O. Rees, 1799).

36 Stuart Curran, "Women Readers, Women Writers", *The Cambridge Companion to British Romanticism* (Cambridge: Cambridge University Press, 1993), p.179.

37 Daniel Robinson, "Reviving the Sonnet: Women Romantic Poets and the Sonnet Claim", *European Romantic Review* 6 (1995): 101.

38 See especially her letters to Penelope Sophia Weston Pennington (1752?–1827), written in 1784 and held in the Houghton Library, Harvard University.

39 Curran, "Women Readers", p.184.

40 Curran, "Women Readers", p.185.

41 See Clarke, "Anna Seward, Bluestocking", pp.33–45 for an extended discussion of non-marriage in Seward's life.

42 Mary A. Waters, *British Women Authors and the Profession of Literary Criticism* (Houndmills, Basingstoke: Palgrave Macmillan, 2004), p.3. It is worth noting, however, that Robinson includes both Carter and Montague on her list of important eighteenth-century British women writers, suggesting less of a distinction between Bluestocking and Romantic writers than we now assume, though they were born some 30 years earlier. For further insight, see Stephen C. Behrendt, *British Women Poets and the Romantic Writing Community* (Baltimore: The Johns Hopkins University Press, 2008).

43 Waters, *British Women Authors*, p.2.

44 Seward, *Poetical Works*, Vol.1, "Biographical Preface", p.xiii. For more on her competition with and criticism of Johnson, see Clarke, "Anna Seward, Bluestocking", pp.20–24.

45 Clarke, "Anna Seward, Bluestocking", p.18.

46 Joseph Addison, *The Freeholder*, as cited by Nigel Hamilton in *Biography: A Brief History* (Cambridge: Harvard University Press, 2007), pp.85–86.

47 Nigel Hamilton's assessment of Johnson as biographer in *Biography*, p.90. The Roman biographical essayist, Plutarch (46–120), viewed his own contributions not as writing histories, but rather, like a portrait painter, that of designing lives. By dwelling "upon those actions which illuminate the working of the soul", he found himself able to "create a portrait of a man's life". (Plutarch, *Life of Alexander*, as cited by Hamilton, *Biography*, p.21). Seward argued that it was from the publication of Johnson's *Life of the Poets* that she "date[s] the downfall of just poetic taste in this kingdom". Seward to Thomas Whalley, 22 November 1781, *Journals and Correspondence of Thomas Sedgewick Whalley*, Vol.1, p.348.

48 Samuel Johnson, *The Rambler* 60 (13 October 1750), as cited by Hamilton, *Biography*, p.87.

49 See James D. Woolley, "Johnson as Despot: Anna Seward's Rejected Contribution to Boswell's *Life*", *Modern Philology* 70 (1972): 140–45; and Donna Heiland, "Swan Songs: The Correspondence of Anna Seward and James Boswell", *Modern Philology* 90 (1993): pp.381–91.

50 Stapleton Martin, *Anna Seward and Classic Lichfield* (Worcester: Deighton and Co., 1909), pp.26–27.

51 Walter Scott to Anna Seward (no date), as reprinted in J.G. Lockhart (ed) *Memoirs of Walter Scott* (Edinburgh: Adam and Charles Black, 1882), Vol.2, p.123. Scott's biographical sketch of Anna Seward was appended to the beginning of the first volume of his edited *The Poetical Works of Anna Seward; With Extracts from Her Literary Correspondence*, (Edinburgh: J. Ballantyne and Co., 1810), and it was reprinted in Scott's *Biographical Memoirs* (Paris: A. and W. Galignani, 1830), Vol.1, pp.211–243.

52 See Waters, *British Women Authors*, pp.28–56, for a detailed discussion of Barbauld's introductions.

53 Walter Scott, "Biographical Preface", Scott (ed) *The Poetical Works of Anna Seward*, Vol.1, p.vi.

54 Ashmun, *Singing Swan*, p.15. For a thorough, albeit brief, biographical overview, see Sylvia Bowerbank, "Anna Seward", in H.C.G. Matthew and Brian Harris (eds) *Oxford Dictionary of National Biography* (Oxford: Oxford University Press, 2004), Vol.49, pp.827–830.

55 Ashmun, *The Singing Swan*, p.190. Marion Roberts further reviews Seward's literary life in "Anna Seward – 'The Queen Muse of Britain'", *The Female Spectator* 9 (2005):1–4.

56   *Memoirs of Richard Lovell Edgeworth* (London: R. Hunter, 1820), vol. 1, p.232.

57   King-Hele, *Erasmus Darwin: A Life of Unequalled Achievement*, p.72.

58   Ashmun, *The Singing Swan*, p.12.

59   *Memoirs of Richard Lovell Edgeworth*, Vol.1, p.237. Seward had served as private chaplain to Charles FitzRoy, 2nd Duke of Grafton (1683–1757). Lord Charles Fitzroy (1718–1739), the Duke of Grafton's fifth son, died in Italy while on his Grand Tour.

60   Clarke, "Anna Seward, Bluestocking", p.26.

61   Clarke, "Anna Seward, Bluestocking", p.26.

62   Martin, *Anna Seward and Classical Lichfield*, p.19.

63   Desmond King-Hele, *The Collected Letters of Erasmus Darwin* (Cambridge: Cambridge University Press, 2006), Snow Grimalkin to Miss Pussy, Letter 80–5, fn, p.179.

64   Gioia Angeletti noted this in "Women Re-Writing Men: The Examples of Anna Seward and Lacy Caroline Lamb", in Lilla Maria Crisafulli and Cecilia Pietropoli (eds) *Romantic Women Poets: Genre and Gender* (Amsterdam: Rodopi, 2007), esp. pp.244–247.

65   Hopkins, *Dr Johnson's Lichfield*, p.191.

66   Seward to Thomas Whalley, 22 November 1781, *Journals and Correspondence of Thomas Sedgewick Whalley*, Vol.1, p.342.

67   Ashmun, *Singing Swan*, p.88.

68   Ashmun, *Singing Swan*, p.144.

69   For an excellent discussion of the influence of Seward's love of Handel on her poetry, see Gillen D'Arcy Wood, "The Female Penseroso: Anna Seward, Sociable Poetry, and the Handelian Consensus", *Modern Language Quarterly* 67 (2006): 451–77.

70   For further discussion of the relationship between Seward and Saville, see Ashmun, *Singing Swan*, pp.178–187, Marion Roberts, "Anna Seward (1742–1809) – The Virgin Muse?", *BMI Insight*, 6 (2005): 12–14; and Clarke, "Anna Seward, Bluestocking", pp.33–45. For a period of years, John Saville (1736–1803) and his wife lived separately, he in No. 6 Vicars' Close, while his wife lived in No. 7. Anna was a frequent visitor to No. 6 where, together with John, they enjoyed time in the private walled garden.

71   Mary Sherwood (née Butt) (1775–1851), in Sophia Kelly (ed) *The Life of Mrs Sherwood, Chiefly Autobiographical with extracts from Mr Sherwood's Journal during His Imprisonment in France and Residence in India* (London: Darton and Co., 1857), p.11.

72   Mary Sherwood (née Butt), in F.J. Harvey Darton (ed) *The Life and Times of Mrs Sherwood (1775–1851). From the Diaries of Captain and Mrs Sherwood* (London: Wells, Gardner, Darton & Co, 1910), pp.10–11.

73   Clarke, "Anna Seward, Bluestocking", p.46.

74   For a full account of Seward's health problems, see Sylvia Bowerbank, *Speaking for Nature: Women and Ecologies of Early Modern England* (Baltimore: The Johns Hopkins University Press, 2004), pp.180–187.

75   Bowerbank, *Speaking for Nature*, pp.184–87.

76   Stuart Curran, "Anna Seward and the Dynamics of Female Friendship" in Lilla Maria Crisafulli and Cecelia Pietropoli (eds) *Romantic Women Poets: Genre and Gender* (Amsterdam: Rodopi Press, 2007), p.12.

77   *Letters of Anna Seward: Written Between the Years 1784 and 1807*, A. Constable (ed), Vol.6 (Edinburgh: A. Constable and Company, 1811), p.499.

78   Bowerbank, *Speaking for Nature*, p.186.

79   Clarke, "Anna Seward, Bluestocking", p.47.

80   Clarke, "Anna Seward, Bluestocking", p.51.

81   Clarke, "Anna Seward, Bluestocking", p.51.

82 Clarke, "Anna Seward, Bluestocking", pp.13–15.

83 Elizabeth Fay, *Romanticism: A Feminist Introduction* (Oxford: Blackwell, 1998), p.180.

84 Scott, "Biographical Preface", *Poetical Works of Anna Seward*, vol. 1, p.iii. Scott was presented with, and accepted, a Baronetcy in 1818, after which he was titled, Sir Walter Scott. Anna Seward, who died in 1809, never knew him as Sir Walter. Thus, by omitting his title in this work, we are merely referring to him as Seward would have known him and in no way mean any disrespect to the Scottish Bard.

85 This poem gained a wide reading as it was published in *Gentleman's Magazine* 53 (1783): 784. Stebbing Shaw copied it again in his *History and Antiquities of Staffordshire*, Vol.1, p.347, and E.V. Lucas copied it in *A Swan and Her Friends* (London: Methuen, 1907), p.xi, though in this format, the last line was changed to read "From grief, and pity's intermingled tide". William Bagshaw Stevens (1756–1800) published two collections of his work, *Poems, Consisting of Indian Odes and Miscellaneous Pieces* (Oxford: J. and J. Fletcher and S. Palmer, London: J. Brew, 1775), and *Poems* (London: A. Portal, R. Faulder, and G. Kearsley, 1782).

86 Ashmun, *The Singing Swan*, pp.87–88. At her death, Seward left unfinished a verse translation of François de Fénelon's (1651–1715) *Les Adventures de Télémaque* (1699), as Adeline Johns-Putra discusses in "Gendering Telemachus: Anna Seward and the Epic Rewriting of Fénelon's *Télémaque*" in Bernard Schweizer (ed) *Approaches to the Anglo and American Female Epic, 1621–1982* (Aldershot, Hampshire: Ashgate, 2006), pp.85–97.

87 Ashmun, *The Singing Swan*, pp.87–88.

88 Ashmun, *The Singing Swan*, p.88. Ashmun claims that Seward was particularly influenced by Lord Lyttleton's "Lucy" Monody (1747). For a more complete contextualization of the forms of Seward's writings, see Jacqueline M. Labbe, "Every Poet Her Own Drawing Master: Charlotte Smith, Anna Seward and *ut pictura poesis*", Thomas Woodman (ed) *Early Romantics: Perspectives in British Poetry from Pope to Wordsworth* (London: Macmillan and New York: St Martin's, 1998), 200–214; Harriet Guest, "Britain Mourns: Anna Seward's Patriotic Elegies" chapter in her *Small Change: Women, Learning, Patriotism, 1750–1810* (Chicago: University of Chicago Press, 2000), pp 252–267; Paula R. Backsheider, *Eighteenth-Century Women Poets and their Poetry: Inventing Agency, Inventing Genre* (Baltimore: The Johns Hopkins University Press, 2005), esp. pp.291–313; and Bill Overton, *The Eighteenth-Century British Verse Epistle* (London: Palgrave, 2007).

89 *The Poetical Works of Anna Seward*, Vol.2, p.219.

90 Mary Wollstonecraft, "Preface" in Gary Kelly (ed) *Mary, and the Wrongs of Woman* (Oxford: Oxford University Press, 1976), p.xxx.

91 Elizabeth Fay, "Anna Seward, the Swan of Lichfield: Reading *Louisa*", *Approaches to Teaching British Women Poets of the Romantic Period* (New York: The Modern Language Association, 1997), p.130.

92 Daniel Robinson, "Forging the Poetical Novel: The Elision of Form in Anna Seward's *Louisa*", *The Wordsworth Circle* 27 (1996): 28.

93 Curran, "Anna Seward", p.13.

94 For a discussion of the individual poems written to Sneyd and of the romantic friendship, see Stuart Curran, "Dynamics of Female Friendship in the Later Eighteenth Century", *Nineteenth-Century Contexts* 23 (2001): 221–239.

95 Curran "Dynamics", pp.230, 231.

96 Two unpublished poems from Seward to Honora Sneyd, discovered in the British Library, are described in Sandro Jung in "Two New Poems by Anna Seward", *ANQ: A Quarterly Journal of Short Articles, Notes, and Reviews* 16 (2003): 19–21.

97 Gioia Angeletti, "Women Re-writing Men: The Examples of Anna Seward and Lady Caroline Lamb", in Lilla Maria Crisafulli and Cecelia Pietropoli (eds) *Romantic Women Poets: Genre and Gender* (Amsterdam: Rodopi Press, 2007), p.246.

98 Donna Coffey, "Protecting the Botanic Garden: Seward, Darwin, and Coalbrookdale", *Women's Studies* 31 (2002): 142.

99 Setzer, "'Ponderous Engines' in 'Outraged Groves'", p.70.

100 Setzer, "'Ponderous Engines' in 'Outraged Groves'", pp.69–70.

101 Clarke, "Anna Seward, Bluestocking", p.19.

102 Gretchen M. Foster, *Pope Versus Dryden: A Controversy in Letters to the 'Gentleman's Magazine', 1789–1791* (Victoria, B.C.: English Literary Studies, 1989), p.10.

103 Heiland, "Swan Songs", p.381.

104 Heiland, "Swan Songs", p.381.

105 Daniel Robinson, "Reviving", p.111.

106 Daniel Robinson, "Reviving", p.112.

107 Michael Page, "The Darwin Before Darwin: Erasmus Darwin, Visionary Science, and Romantic Poetry", *Papers on Language and Literature* 41 (2005): 149.

108 See, for example, David Worrall, "William Blake and Erasmus Darwin's *Botanic Garden*", *Bulletin of the New York Public Library* 79 (1975): 397–417; David Charles Leonard, "Erasmus Darwin and William Blake", *Eighteenth Century Life* 4 (1978): 79–81.

109 See, for example, Tim Fulford, "Coleridge, Darwin, Linneaus: The Sexual Politics of Botany", *The Wordsworth Circle* 28 (1997): 124–30; David W. Ullrich, "Distinctions in Poetic and Intellectual Influence: Coleridge's Use of Erasmus Darwin", *The Wordsworth Circle* 15 (1984): 74–80.

110 See, for example, Nicola Trott, "Wordsworth's Loves of the Plants" in Nicola Trott and Seamus Perry (eds) *1800: The New Lyrical Ballads* (Basingstoke: Palgrave, 2001), pp.141–68; Richard Matlak, "Wordsworth's Reading of *Zoonomia* in Early Spring", *The Wordsworth Circle* 21 (1990): 76–81; and Kent Beyette, "Wordsworth's Medical Muse: Erasmus Darwin and Psychology in 'Strange Fits of Passion Have I Known'", *Literature and Psychology* 23 (1973): 93–101.

111 Alan Richardson, "Erasmus Darwin and the Fungus School", *The Wordsworth Circle* 33 (2002): 113–16; Desmond King-Hele, "Shelley and Erasmus Darwin" in Kelvin Everest (ed) *Shelley Re-evaluated* (Totowa, NJ: Barnes and Noble, 1983), pp.129–46.

112 Donald M. Hassler, "Byron and Erasmus Darwin", *Forum* 20 (1979): 75–80.

113 Ann B. Shtier, *Cultivating Women, Cultivating Science: Flora's Daughters and Botany in England 1760–1860* (Baltimore: Johns Hopkins University Press, 1996).

114 Judith Pascoe, "Female Botanists and the Poetry of Charlotte Smith", in Carol Shiner Wilson and Joel Haefner (eds) *Re-visioning Romanticism: British Women Writers, 1776–1837* (Philadelphia: University of Pennsylvania Press, 1994), p.199.

115 Pascoe, "Female Botanists and the Poetry of Charlotte Smith", p.199.

116 Seward, *Life of Dr Darwin*, p.159.

117 Seward, *Life of Dr Darwin*, p.198.

118 Aileen Douglas, "Anna Seward's Annotated Copy of *Caleb Williams*", *The Princeton University Library Chronicle* 49 (1987): 75.

119 Douglas, "Anna Seward's Annotated Copy of *Caleb Williams*", p.75.

120 Seward, *Life of Dr Darwin*, pp.65, 84.

121 Apart from many fine written accounts, particulars of Darwin's Lichfield life are easily learned and enjoyed through the splendid displays in Erasmus Darwin House.

122 Anna Seward to Revd. T.S. Whalley, 15 May 1802, *Letters of Anna Seward*, Letter 4, Vol. 6, p.23.

123 *The Art of Preserving Health: A Poem* (London: A. Millar, 1744).

124 *The Pleasures of Imagination: A Poem, In Three Books* (London: R. Dodsley, 1744).

125 Seward, *Life of Darwin*, p.58.

126 *Erasmus Darwin: Physician, Scientist, Inventor, Poet & Philosopher* (Lichfield: Lichfield District Council, nd), "His Achievements" section.

127 Dr Darwin's evolutionary theorizing has been discussed in some key earlier works as well as in several recent popular academic works on evolution. Among these works, see Edward Clodd, *Pioneers of Evolution: From Thales to Huxley* (London: Cassell and Co, 1907), esp. pp.102–105; Henry Fairfield Osborn, *From the Greeks to Darwin: An Outline of the Development of the Evolution Idea* (New York: Macmillan and Co., 1908), pp.152–157, and 167–181; Carl Grabo, *A Newton Among Poets: Shelley's Use of Science in Prometheus Unbound* (Chapel Hill, NC: The University of North Carolina Press, 1930), pp.61–79; John C. Greene's classical, *The Death of Adam* (Ames, IA: Iowa State University Press, 1959), pp.166–169; Francis C. Haber, "Fossils and the Idea of a Process of Time in Natural History", in Bentley Glass, Owsei Temkin, and William L. Strauss, Jr. (eds) *Forerunners of Darwin 1745–1859* (Baltimore: The Johns Hopkins University Press, 1968 edition), pp.250–251; James Harrison, "Erasmus Darwin's Views of Evolution", *Journal of the History of Ideas* 32 (1971): 247–264; Peter J. Bowler, *Evolution: History of an Idea* (Berkeley: University of California Press, 1984), in a chapter on "Erasmus Darwin and Lamarck", pp.76–84; Roy Porter, "Erasmus Darwin: Doctor of Evolution?", in James R. Moore (ed) *History, Humanity and Evolution: Essays for John C. Greene* (Cambridge: Cambridge University Press, 1989), pp.39–69; Robert J. Richards, *The Meaning of Evolution: The Morphological Construction and Ideological Reconstruction of Darwin's Theory* (Chicago: University of Chicago Press, 1992), esp. pp.92–94; Steven J. Gould, *Dinosaur in a Haystack: Reflection in Natural History* (New York: Harmony, 1995), esp. pp.427–457; Michael Ruse, *Monad to Man: The Conquest of Progress in Evolutionary Biology* (Cambridge: Harvard University Press, 1996), pp.55–64; Michael Ruse, *Mystery of Mysteries: Is Evolution a Social Construction?* (Harvard: Harvard University Press, 1999), an entire chapter on "Erasmus Darwin: From Fish to Philosopher", pp.37–53; Michael Ruse, *Darwin and Design: Does Evolution have a Purpose?* (Harvard: Harvard University Press, 2003) in a section on "Erasmus Darwin Embraces Evolutionary Progress", pp.54–58; and David Young, *The Discovery of Evolution* (Cambridge: Cambridge University Press, 2007), pp.73–75. For a comparison between the evolutionary thinking of Dr Darwin and that of his grandson, Charles, see, among others, Ralph Colp, "The Relationship of Charles Darwin to the Ideas of his Grandfather, Dr Erasmus Darwin", *Biography* 9 (1986): 1–24.

128 Erasmus Darwin, *Zoonomia; or, The Laws of Organic Life* (London: J. Johnson, 1794–1796), Vol.1, p.377.

129 David Burbridge nicely summarized this in "William Paley Confronts Erasmus Darwin: Natural Theology and Evolutionism in the Eighteenth Century", *Science and Christian Belief* 10 (1998): 61–63.

130 In his *Philosophie Zoologique* (1806), Lamarck provided considerably more evidence drawn from nature than did Dr Darwin. Moreover, he argued for a directional development that Darwin had not done. Still, Darwin's argument made similar claims to his wide reading audience a decade prior to Lamarck. Ernst Krause made a similar comparison, rightly noting that it is "more proper" to view Lamarck as "a Darwinian of the older school" than to characterize Dr Darwin as a Lamarckian. See Ernst Krause, *The Scientific Works of Erasmus Darwin*, translated by W.S. Dallas (London: John Murray, 1879), p.133.

131 McNeil, *Under the Banner of Science*, p.105.

132 Darwin, *Zoonomia*, Vol.1, pp.507–509.

133 King-Hele, "Prologue: Catching Up with Erasmus Darwin in the New Century" in Smith and Arnott (eds) *Genius of Erasmus Darwin*, p.29. It should be noted that King-Hele first identified Dr Darwin's evolutionary theories for a major scientific audience in "Dr Erasmus Darwin and the Theory of Evolution" *Nature* 200 (1963): 304–306.

134 From the close of Alfred Noyes's "An English Interlude: Erasmus Darwin", in *The Torch-Bearers Vol. II. The Book of Earth* (Edinburgh and London: William Blackwood & Sons, 1934), pp.234–235.

135 As Canon Seward footnoted for his readers, "It was customary for the Athenian and Roman booksellers to hang a volume of each book they had to sell upon pillars of temples, the forum, etc". Attic columns, also known as Corinthian, which were the most ornate of the Roman architectural columns whose capitals were decorated with acanthus leaves and rosettes.

136 Again, according to the Canon notes, Celsus was "the name both of an eminent Roman physician and of an eminent writer against the primitive Christians", and he further commented that "both characters [were] applicable". Dr Darwin was most familiar with Celsus (25BC – 50AD), the Roman physician and encyclopaedist, known through his sole surviving encyclopaedic work, *De Medicina.*

137 According to Darwin's definitive biographer, King-Hele (*Erasmus Darwin: A Life of Unequalled Achievement*, p 72), Seward, Johnson, and Darwin represented a "mutually repellant triumvirate".

138 The Revd. Alexander Gordon, "Robert Fellowes", *Dictionary of National Biography* (London: Smith, Elder, and Co, 1889), Vol.18, pp.300–301. Ashley Marshall added a brief discussion of Dr Darwin's religious views in "Erasmus Darwin *contra* David Hume", *British Journal for Eighteenth-Century Studies* 30 (2007): 89–111.

139 Seward, *Life of Erasmus Darwin*, pp.96-97.

140 Anna Seward to Thomas Percival, 28 March 1804, *Letters of Anna Seward*, Letter 24, Vol.6, p.137.

141 Dr Darwin treated Lichfield's Cathedral community without charge. Despite little surviving information, Tim Carter has convincingly argued that Darwin likely took care of workers and tradesmen of the industrial Midlands as part of his philanthropic service to the region. See his "Erasmus Darwin, Work and Health" in Smith and Arnott (eds) *Genius of Erasmus Darwin*, pp.289–301. With a different take, Roy Porter also used industrial imagery in a chapter that prominently featured Dr Darwin entitled "Industrial Bodies", in his posthumously published *Flesh in the Age of Reason* (New York: Norton, 2003), pp.374–397.

142 Anna Seward to H. Cary, 9 March 1793, *Letters of Anna Seward*, Vol.3, p.211.

143 Dr Darwin began writing this work in Lichfield in 1770–1771, soon after Polly Darwin's death. Jenny Uglow depicted ordering and classifying as among the key projects of the Enlightenment in *The Lunar Men*, p.266.

144 E. Darwin, *Zoonomia*, vol 1, p.viii.

145 See, for example, Peter Bowler, "Evolutionism in the Enlightenment", *History of Science* 12 (1974):166–179, and McNeil, *Under the Banner of Science*, pp.86–124.

146 King-Hele, "Prologue", p.16.

147 Ralph B. Crum, *Scientific Thought in Poetry* (New York: Columbia University Press, 1931), p.124.

148 Sheena Mason, *The Hardware Man's Daughter: Matthew Boulton and his 'Dear Girl'* (Chichester, West Essex: Phillimore, 2005), p.19.

149 Roy Porter, as quoted by Malcolm Nicolson in "The Art of Diagnosis: Medicine and the Five Senses", in W.F. Bynum and Roy Porter (eds) *Companion Encyclopedia of the History of Medicine* (London: Routledge, 1993), Vol.2, p.809.

150 Marilyn Butler, *Maria Edgeworth: A Literary Biography* (Oxford: Clarendon Press, 1972), p.32.

151 Erasmus Darwin, *Commonplace Book*, manuscript, Erasmus Darwin House, p.16.

152 Erasmus Darwin, *Commonplace Book*, p.86.

153 King-Hele, "Prologue", p.15.

154 Erasmus Darwin, *Commonplace Book*, p.18.

155 Erasmus Darwin, *Commonplace Book*, pp.19 and 54.

156 Erasmus Darwin, *Commonplace Book*, p.149.

157 Erasmus Darwin, *Commonplace Book*, p.27.

158 Erasmus Darwin, *Commonplace Book*, p.96. The movements described here are somewhat reminiscent of those that Mary Shelley attributes to Dr Darwin in *Frankenstein*. In the very opening lines of the preface for the premier (1818) publication of this work, Shelley notes that "[t]he event upon which this fiction is founded, has been supposed, by Dr Darwin, and some of the physiological writers of Germany, as not of impossible occurrence". In the preface of the third edition of *Frankenstein* (1831), Shelley explicitly recalls "talk about Erasmus Darwin (I speak not of what the Doctor really did, or said that he did, but, as more to my purpose, of what was then spoken of as having been done by him), who preserved a piece of vermicelli in a glass case, till by some extraordinary means it began to move with voluntary motion". The "extraordinary means" she referred to was the introduction of electricity, one of the new tools of nature that Darwin and his Lunar Society colleagues had harnessed to assist with their demonstrations and discoveries. In *Frankenstein*, Dr Darwin gets brief mention, alongside Humphry Davy and Luigi Galvani as having directly influenced Mary Shelley's "thought-experiment". Among the many authors who have referenced the Shelley-Darwin connection, see Anne K. Mellor, "Making a Monster: An Introduction to *Frankenstein*", in Esther Schor (ed) *The Cambridge Companion to Mary Shelley* (Cambridge: Cambridge University Press, 2003), p.17, and Desmond King-Hele, *Erasmus Darwin and the Romantic Poets* (Basingstoke, Hampshire: Macmillan, 1986), pp.259-260. See also Susan Lederer, *Frankenstein: Penetrating the Secrets of Nature* (Rutgers University Press, 2002), which is the book accompanying a recent National Library of Medicine exhibition. Myriad other historical works examine natural philosophers of Dr Frankenstein's era who investigated restoring or creating life. Among them, see in particular Stanley Finger and Mark B. Law, "Karl August Weinhold and His 'Science' in the Era of Mary Shelley's *Frankenstein*: Experiments on Electricity and the Restoration of Life", *Journal of the History of Medicine* 53 (1998): 161-180, and James A. Secord, "Extraordinary Experiment: Electricity and the Creation of Life in Victorian England", in David Gooding, Trevor Pinch, and Simon Schaffer (eds) *The Use of Experiment: Studies in the Natural Sciences* (Cambridge: Cambridge University Press, 1989), pp.337-383, and C.U.M. Smith, "A Strand of Vermicelli: Dr Darwin's Part in the Creation of Frankenstein's Monster", *Interdisciplinary Science Reviews* 32 (2007): 45-53. In passing, it should be noted that Dr Darwin may have been that "English philosopher" referred to late in the text. As Dr Frankenstein relates, "I found that I could not compose a female without again devoting several months to profound study and laborious disquisition. I had heard of some discoveries having been made by an English philosopher, the knowledge of which was material to my success, and I sometimes thought of obtaining my father's consent to visit England for this purpose; but I clung to every pretence of delay, and shrunk from taking the first step in an undertaking whose immediate necessity began to appear less absolute to me", *Frankenstein* (London: Colburn and Bentley, 1831), Chapter 18, p.131.

159 Erasmus Darwin, *Commonplace Book*, p.96.

160 Erasmus Darwin, *Commonplace Book*, p.89. For further insight into Dr Darwin and gout, see Philip K. Wilson, "Erasmus Darwin and the 'Noble' Disease (Gout): Conceptualizing Heredity and Disease in Enlightenment England", in S. Müller-Willie and H-J. Rheinberger (eds) *Heredity Produced: At the Crossroads of Biology, Politics and Culture 1500–1870* (Cambridge, MA: MIT Press, 2007), 133–154.

161 Erasmus Darwin, *Commonplace Book*, p.164.

162 Anna Seward to Revd. Dewhurst Bilsboro [sic], 9 October 1802, in *Letters of Anna Seward*, Vol.6, p.54.

163 Seward, *Life of Dr Darwin*, p.52.

164 Of historiographical note, Seward claimed that she "had but few of … [his letters] myself, and those perfectly inconsequential". Furthermore, she expended "no effort … to obtain them from others" (Seward, *Life of Dr Darwin*, p.48).

165 Seward, *Life of Dr Darwin*, p.54.

166 Robert Southey, *Specimens of the Later English Poets* (London: Longman, Hurst, Rees and Orme, 1807), Vol.3, p.308.

167 As recounted by Desmond Clarke in *The Ingenious Mr Edgeworth* (London: Oldbourne, 1965), p.186.

168 Anna Seward to Revd. T.S. Whalley, 15 May 1802, *Letters of Anna Seward*, Letter 4, Vol.6, p.25.

169 Seward, *Life of Dr Darwin*, p.53.

170 Seward, *Life of Dr Darwin*, p.53.

171 Sir S. H. Scott, *The Exemplary Mr Day 1748–1789* (London: Faber and Faber, 1935), p.8.

172 Jonathan Richardson, *The Connoisseur: An Essay on the Whole Art of Criticism, as it Relates to Painting,* in J. Richardson, *Two Discourses* (London: W. Churchill, 1719), p.45.

173 Jonathan Richardson, *An Essay on the Theory of Painting*, 2nd ed (Menston, Yorkshire: Scholar Press, 1971, 1725), pp.13–14.

174 J. Richardson, *Essay of the Theory of Painting*, pp.13–14. Richardson fully appreciated the task of biography and discussed the peculiar relationship that it held with portraiture. See Richard Wendorf's "*Ut Pictura Biograhia*: Biography and Portrait Painting as Sister Arts", in R. Wendorf (ed) *Articulate Images: The Sister Arts from Hogarth to Tennyson* (Minneapolis: University of Minnesota Press, 1983), pp.98–124. For a general discussion of the social utility of contemporary portraiture, see Shearer West, "Patronage and Power: The Role of the Portrait in Eighteenth-Century England" in J. Black and J. Gregory (eds) *Culture, Politics and Society in Britain, 1660–1800* (Manchester: Manchester University Press, 1991), 131–153, and Marcia Pointon, *Hanging the Head: Portraiture and Social Formation in Eighteenth-Century England* (New Haven, Yale University Press, 1993).

175 Wendorf, "*Ut Pictura Biograhia*", p.144.

176 John Brewer, *The Pleasures of the Imagination: English Culture in the Eighteenth Century* (New York: Farrar Straus Giroux, 1997), p.574.

177 J. Brewer, *Pleasures of the Imagination*, p.593.

178 Hamilton, *Biography*, p.11.

179 Seward, *Life of Dr Darwin*, p.53.

180 Seward, *Life of Dr Darwin*, p.53. Hester Lynch Piozzi, *Anecdotes of the Late Samuel Johnson, LL.D., During the Last Twenty Years of His Life* (London: T. Cadell, 1786), and *Letters to and from Samuel Johnson, LL.D.* (London: A. Strahan and T. Cadell, 1788). James Boswell, *The Life of Samuel Johnson* (London: H. Baldwin for C. Dilly, 1791), and *The Journey of a Tour to the Hebrides with Samuel Johnson, D.D.* (London: H. Baldwin for C. Dilly, 1785).

181 Seward, *Life of Dr Darwin*, p.53.

182 Seward, *Life of Dr Darwin*, p.54.

183 Seward, *Life of Dr Darwin*, p.52.

184 Anna Seward to H. Repton, Esq., 15 July 1789, *Letters of Anna Seward*, Letter 77, Vol.2, p.311. Jenny Uglow nicely summarizes this Botanic Garden experience in her highly readable, *The Lunar Men*, pp.274–275.

185 Hopkins, *Dr Johnson's Lichfield*, p.191.

186 Ashmun introduces William Stevens as the messenger in her *Singing Swan*, p.67. Anna's poem also appeared in the *Annual Register.*

187 Hopkins, *Dr Johnson's Lichfield*, p.192.

188 Hopkins, *Dr Johnson's Lichfield*, p.244.

189 Seward, *Life of Dr Darwin*, p.131.

190 Seward, *Life of Dr Darwin*, p.221.

191 Desmond King-Hele, *Doctor of the Revolution* (London: Faber and Faber, 1977), p.197.

192 The specific lines in question are footnoted within the text of Seward's *Life of Dr Darwin.*

193 Anna Seward to Mrs Jackson, 3 August 1792, *Letters of Anna Seward*, Letter 47, Vol.3, p.155.

194   Anna Seward to Thomas Park, Esq., 5 January 1801, *Letters of Anna Seward*, Letter 59, Vol.5, pp.333–334.

195   Scott, Biographical Preface, *Poetical Works of Anna Seward*, Vol.1, p.xxi,

196   Cited by Pearson in *Doctor Darwin*, pp, 208–209.

197   Cited by Pearson in *Doctor Darwin*, p, 208, note.

198   Scott, Biographical Preface, *Poetical Works of Anna Seward*, vol.1, p.xxv.

199   Ashmun, *Singing Swan*, p.68.

200   Stuart Harris, *Erasmus Darwin's Enlightenment Epic* (Sheffield: Stuart Harris, 2002), pp.13–14.

201   King-Hele, *Doctor of the Revolution*, p.112.

202   Anna Sward to Dewhurst Bilsbury [sic], 9 October 1802, *Letters of Anna Seward*, Letter 10, Vol.6, p.55.

203   Anna Seward to Robert Fellowes, 14 June 1803, *Letters of Anna Seward*, Letter 13, Vol.6, p.78.

204   Ashmun, *Singing Swan*, pp.234–235.

205   Ashmun, *Singing Swan*, pp.234–235.

206   Ashmun, *Singing Swan*, pp.236, 239.

207   Ashmun, *Singing Swan*, p.236.

208   Reviews other than those cited in this essay include *Monthly Magazine* 17 (1804): 378, and *Monthly Review* 43 (1804): 113–127.

209   Martin, *Anna Seward and Classical Lichfield*, p.20.

210   Ashmun, *Singing Swan*, p.238.

211   Teresa Barnard, "Anna Seward and the Battle for Authorship", *CW3 Journal: Corvey Women Writers on the Web*, item 31. (www2.shu.ac.uk/corvey/CW3journal/Issue%20one/barnard.html, accessed 4 February 2007).

212   T. Barnard, "Anna Seward and the Battle for Authorship", item 4.

213   Anna Seward to Walter Scott, 29 July 1809, *Letters of Anna Seward*, Vol.6, p.94.

214   T. Barnard, "Anna Seward and the Battle for Authorship", item 30.

215   Scott, Biographical Preface, *Poetical Works of Anna Seward*, Vol.1, p.xx.

216   Anna Seward to William Halley, 7 March 1803, in *Letters of Anna Seward*, Vol.6, p.73.

217   Anna Seward to William Halley, 7 March 1803, in *Letters of Anna Seward*, Vol.6, pp.73–74.

218   Patrick Blair (*c.*1680–1728), a Scottish physician and botanist, prepared *Botanick Essay in Two parts: The First Containing, The Structure of the Flowers and the Fructification of the Plants, with their Various Distributions into Method; and the Second, the Generation of Plants, with their Sexes, and Manner of Impregnating the Seed; Also Concerning the "Animalcula in Semine Masculino". Together with the Nourishment of Plant and Circulation of the Sap in all Seasons, Analogous to that of the Blood in Animals* (London: William and John Innys, 1720). In it, pp.326–329, Blair appended Martyn's translation entitled, "An Ode formerly Dedicated to Camerarius".

219   Anna Seward to Lee Phillips, 1 June 1804, in *Letters of Anna Seward*, Vol.6, pp.179–180. To validate Seward's claim yourself, see Martyn's translation in Appendix III.

220   Anna Seward to Lee Phillips, 1 June 1804, in *Letters of Anna Seward*, Vol.6, p.180.

221   *The Edinburgh Review, or Critical Journal* 4 (April 1804): 231.

222   Anna Seward to Walter Scott, 20 June 1806, as printed in *Archibald Constable and His Literary Correspondents: A Memorial by His Son, Thomas Constable*, cited by Ashmun, *Singing Swan*, p.237.

223   Clarke's characterization in *The Ingenious Mr Edgeworth*, p.187.

224   Peter Rowland's characterization in *The Life and Times of Thomas Day, 1748–1789: English Philanthropist and Author, Virtue Almost Personified* (Lewiston: E. Mellen Press, 1996), p.xi.

225   P. Rowland, *Life and Times of Thomas Day*, p.350.

226 P. Rowland, *Life and Times of Thomas Day*, pp.338, 349. Stuart Curran discussed Seward's intimate female friendship with Honora in "Anna Seward and the Dynamics of Female Friendship", pp.11–21.

227 As cited in Ashmun, *Singing Swan*, p.234. Another paper, the eight-page manuscript dated 1812 which the Revd. Richard George Robinson prepared as a critique of Seward's *Life of Dr Darwin* was in the hands of Mary Alden Hopkins when she was writing *Dr Johnson's Lichfield* (see p.251). Although it would likely add further insight into the range of contemporary responses to this work, its current whereabouts remain unknown to this volume's editors.

228 Ashmun, *Singing Swan*, p.238. Seward did send Johnson, her publisher, "changes … to be made for the advantage" of her *Life of Dr Darwin* in case he "permits my book … [the] credit" of a second edition. Though there were "not many" changes, she acknowledged that since Johnson had "purchased the copyright, he must do with it as he pleases. Wealthy, procrastinating, and now become the most fashionable bookseller, while new works are crowding into his press, he may not think it worth his while to re-admit mine" for another edition (Anna Seward to Thomas Whalley, 27 July 1804, *Journals and Correspondence of Thomas Whalley*, Vol.2, p.252). Alas, he did not.

229 Barbara and Hensleigh Wedgwood, *The Wedgwood Circle 1730–1897: Four Generations of a Family and Their Friends* (London: Studio Vista, 1980), p.136.

230 Cited by Clarke, *The Ingenious Mr Edgeworth*, p.187.

231 Robert Darwin to Anna Seward, 5 October 1804, as cited in King-Hele (ed) *Charles Darwin's Life of Erasmus Darwin*, p.76.

232 Anna Seward to Thomas Percival, 28 March 1804, in *Letters of Anna Seward*, Vol.6, p.136.

233 Lucas, *A Swan and Her Friends*, pp.105–106.

234 Martin, *Anna Seward and Classical Lichfield*, p.20.

235 Pearson, *Doctor Darwin*, p.8.

236 James Venable Logan, *The Poetry and Aesthetics of Erasmus Darwin* (Princeton: Princeton University Press, 1936), pp.1–3.

237 Elizabeth Sewell, *The Orphic Voice: Poetry and National History* (New Haven, CT: Yale University Press, 1960), p.223.

238 Schofield, *The Lunar Society of Birmingham*, p.56.

239 M. McNeil, *Under the Banner of Science*, p.4.

240 Desmond King-Hele, *Erasmus Darwin* (London: Macmillan, 1963), p.15.

241 Desmond King-Hele, *Essential Writings of Erasmus Darwin* (London: MacGibbin and Kee, 1968), p.15.

242 King-Hele, *Doctor of the Revolution*, pp.38, 46.

243 King-Hele, *Erasmus Darwin and the Romantic Poets*, p.155.

244 King-Hele, *Erasmus Darwin: A Life of Unequalled Achievement*, p.26.

245 Stuart Harris introduced this theme in his lecture, "Millennial Hope that the Rehabilitation of Erasmus Darwin's epic poetry is Possible in the 21st Century", typescript, p.3, Erasmus Darwin House, Lichfield, England. Harris elaborated upon this theme in his introduction to his edited work of Erasmus Darwin's writings, *Cosmologia: A Sequence of Epic Poems in Three Parts* (Sheffield: Stuart Harris, 2002), pp.viii–x.

246 Seward, *Life of Dr Darwin*, pp.87, 89.

MEMOIRS OF THE LIFE OF
DR DARWIN,
CHIEFLY DURING HIS RESIDENCE AT LICHFIELD,
WITH
ANECDOTES OF HIS FRIENDS,
AND CRITICISMS
ON HIS WRITINGS[1]

By Anna Seward.

London:

Printed for J. Johnson, St Paul's Church-Yard,
By T. Bensley, Bolt Court, 1804

To The Right Honorable
The Earl of Carlisle[2]

My Lord,

Where hereditary honours, splendid fortune, and personal graces, have secured, from the first dawn of youth, the external respect and gratifying attention of the world, it is seldom found that their possessor has emulously and sedulously distilled the sweetness from the classic fountains. There is no flattery in observing, that of those rare instances your Lordship is conspicuously one. Such energetic industry involves a superior claim to estimation than where it has appeared the only means by which native talent and laudable ambition could have pierced the mists of obscurity.

You, Sir, have nobly chosen to adorn your rank, instead of indolently leaning upon its inherent distinction, or even satisfying yourself with the acquirement of senatorial eloquence. Professedly a disciple of the Muses, and on public proof an highly-favoured disciple, you must be interested in the life and character of one of the most eminent of your poetic contemporaries.[3]

Hence, my Lord, do I presume to lay these *Memoirs of Dr Darwin* at your feet. From all I hear of Lord Carlisle's virtues, as from all I know of his genius, it is one of my first wishes for this little Tract, that it may interest and amuse a transient hour of his leisure, and obtain that approbation from him which must reward biographic integrity, while literary reputation brightens in his smile.

I have the honour to be, with the most perfect respect and esteem,

My Lord,
Your Lordship's faithful and obedient servant,

Anna Seward

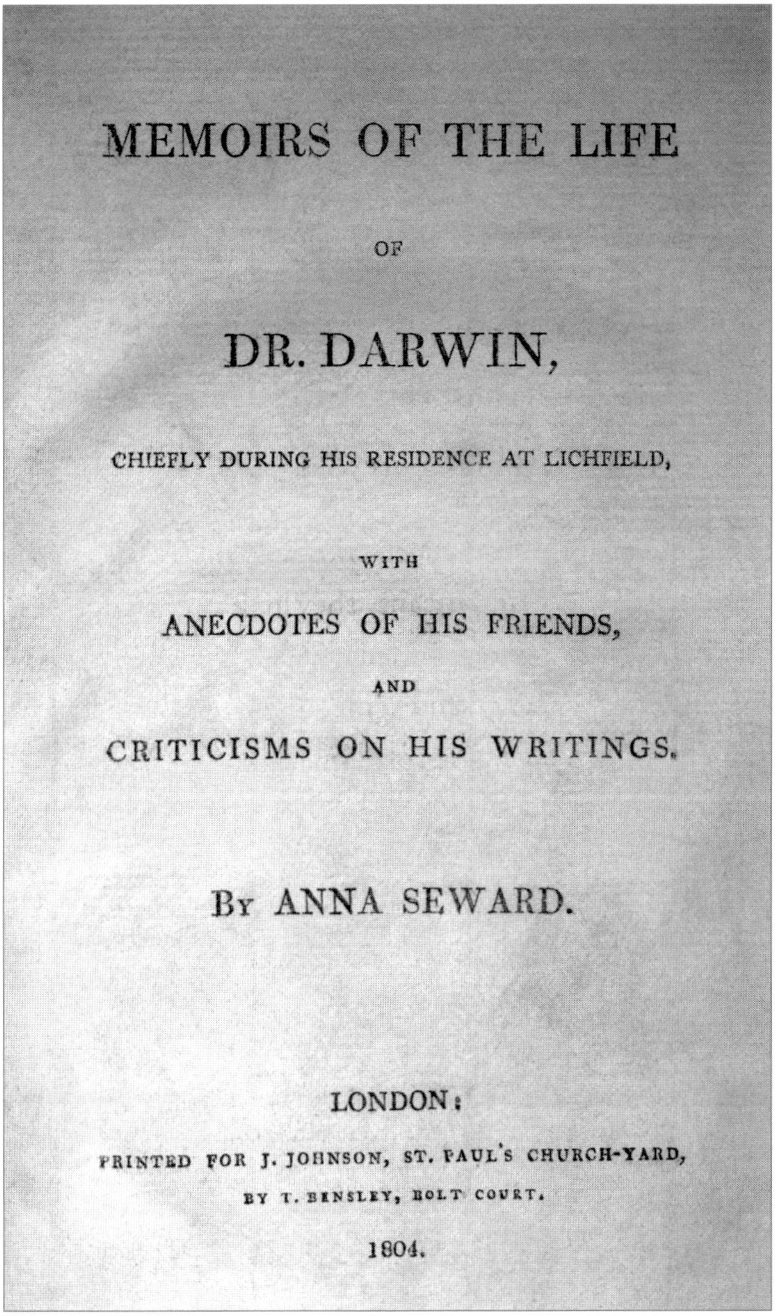

MEMOIRS OF THE LIFE

OF

DR. DARWIN,

CHIEFLY DURING HIS RESIDENCE AT LICHFIELD,

WITH

ANECDOTES OF HIS FRIENDS,

AND

CRITICISMS ON HIS WRITINGS.

By ANNA SEWARD.

LONDON:

PRINTED FOR J. JOHNSON, ST. PAUL'S CHURCH-YARD,

BY T. BENSLEY, BOLT COURT.

1804.

Figure 10: Title page of Seward's Life of Dr Darwin *(1804).*

Preface

In publishing these *Memoirs of the Life and Writings of Dr Darwin*, I am conscious of their defects; that they do not form a regular detail of biographical circumstances, even in that moiety of his professional existence formed by his residence at Lichfield; while of that which passed at Derby I am qualified to present no more than a merely general view.[4]

My work consists of the following particulars: the person, the mind, the temper of Dr Darwin; his powers as a Physician, Philosopher, and Poet; the peculiar traits of his manners; his excellencies and faults; the Petrarchan attachment of his middle life, more happy in its result than was that of the Bard of Vaucluse;[5] the beautiful poetic testimonies of its fervour, while yet it remained hopeless; an investigation of the constituent excellencies and defects of his magnificent poem, *The Botanic Garden*;[6] remarks upon his philosophic prose writings; the characters and talents of those who formed the circle of his friends while he resided in Lichfield; and the very singular and interesting history of one of them, well-known in the lettered world, whose domestic history, remarkable as it is, has been unaccountably omitted by the gentleman who wrote his life.

Dr Darwin's Letters make no part of these *Memoirs*.[7] Possessing few of them myself, and those perfectly inconsequential, no effort has here been made to obtain them from others. He lived not, like Pope and Swift, Gray and Johnson, in exclusive devotion to abstract literature.[8] During such hours of repose, compared to his busy and hurried life, he might have found leisure to pour his imagination and his knowledge on the epistolary page; but his epistles, though professionally numerous, were short from necessity, and by choice compressed. He has often said that he had not the talent of elegant letter-writing.

Like all other distinguished acquirements, it can only obtain excellence from frequent and diffuse practice, unrestrained by the interfering pressure of extrinsic considerations.

It was also his frequent remark, that literary fame invariably suffers by the publication of every thing which is below the level of that celebrity which it has already gained. Letters, through whose progress either wit scatters its scintillations, criticism its instruction, knowledge its treasures, or fancy its glow, are not beneath the dignity of the most eminent reputation; but since coercive circumstances in a great measure precluded those effusions to the letters of Darwin, there would be no kindness to his memory in obtruding them upon the public; none to the public in swelling out books with materials of no intrinsic value.[9] It is only zeal without judgment, and the enthusiasm of partiality, which can take pleasure in reading a great man's letters, which might have been those of any tolerably educated mind, on which genius had never shone.

Biography of recently departed Eminence is apt to want characteristic truth, since it is generally written either by a near relation,

Who writes to share the fame of the deceased,
So high in merit, and to him so dear!
Such dwell on praises which they think they share;[10]

or by an highly obliged friend, whom gratitude and affection render blindly partial, and who is influenced by a desire of gratifying, with a description of all-excelling endowment and angelic excellence, the surviving family of the author he commemorates; or by an editor who believes it highly conducive to his profits on the writings he publishes, or republishes, to claim for their author the unqualified admiration and reverence of mankind. All these classes of biographers do for the person whom they commemorate, what our generally wise Queen Elizabeth had the weakness to request her painters would do for her portrait on the canvass [sic]; they draw a picture without shades.[11]

But though people of credulous and effervescent zeal may be gratified by seeing a writer, whose works have charmed them, thus invested with unrivalled genius and super-human virtue, the judicious few, whose approbation is genuine honour, are aware of this truth, asserted by Mrs Barbauld in her beautiful, her inestimable *Essay against Inconsistency in our Expectations*: "Nature is much too frugal to heap together all manner of shining qualities in one glaring mass".[12] Every man has his errors, and the errors of public characters are too well known not to expose unfounded eulogium to the distaste of all who prefer truth to enthusiasm. They are conscious that the mind, as well as the person, of a celebrated character, ought to be drawn with dispassionate fidelity, or not attempted; that though just biographic record will touch the failings of the good and the eminent with tenderness, it ought not to spread over them the veil of suppression. A portrait painter might as well omit each appropriate distinction of feature, countenance, and form, because it may not be elegant, and, like the Limner in Gay's *Fables*, finish his pictures from casts of the Venus and Apollo, as the historian conceal the faults, foibles, and weaknesses of the individual whom he delineates.[13]

It is this fidelity of representation which makes Mrs Piozzi's *Memoirs of Dr Johnson*, and Mr Boswell's *Tour*, and his *Life* of that wonderful being, so valuable to those who wish not for an idol to worship, instead of a great man to contemplate, as nature, passion, and habit, compounded his character.[14]

If those biographers had invested their deceased friend with excellence, which no sombre irritability had ever overshadowed; ... with justice and candour,[15] which no literary jealousy, no party prejudice, no bigot zeal had ever warped; ... the public might have been led, through boundless veneration of *one*, into injustice towards *many*. The world might have been induced to believe that all whose merit he has depreciated, whose talents he has undervalued, through the course of his *Lives of the Poets*, had *deserved* the fate they met on those pages.[16] Then, to the injury of our national taste, and to the literary and moral character of the great English Classics, more universal confidence had been placed in the sophistries of those volumes, which seem to have put on the whole armour of truth by the force of their eloquence and the wit of their satire.

A paragraph which appeared in several of the late newspapers, and which contained a ridiculously false print, *political* for *poetical*, mentioned that these expected *Memoirs* were undertaken at the request of the late Dr Darwin's family.[17] A mistaken rumour; though they certainly had their rise in the expressed desire of Dr Robert Darwin of Shrewsbury, that I would supply him with such anecdotes of his father's earlier life, as my intimacy with him, during that period, had enabled me to obtain, and which might assist in forming a biographic sketch, to be prefixed to his writings at some future time.[18] In purposed obedience these records were begun, but they became too extended to form only materials for another person's composition; and too impartial to pass with propriety through the filial channel, though fervently just to the excellencies of the commemorated.

Of those years in which the talents and social virtues of this extraordinary man shed their lustre over the city which I inhabit, no historian remains, who, with vicinity of habitation, and domestic intercourse with Dr Darwin, took equal interest with myself in all that marked, by traits of him, that period of twenty-three years, and which engaged my attention from my very earliest youth. Some few of his contemporaries in this town yet remain; but not one who could be induced to publish what their observation may have traced, and their memory treasured.

His sometime pupil, and late years friend, the ingenious Mr Bilsborrow,[19] is writing, or has written, his *Life*; but since Dr Darwin constantly shrunk with reserved pride from all that candour would deem confidential conversation, and which the world is so apt to ridicule as vain egotism; since it is understood that he has not left biographic documents; since Mr Bilsborrow was scarcely in existence when his illustrious friend first changed his sphere of action; he must find himself as much a stranger to the particulars of his Lichfield residence, as I am of those which were most prominent in the equal number of years he passed at Derby. Between us, all will probably be known that can now with accuracy be traced of Dr Darwin.

To the best of my power I have presumed to be the recorder of vanished Genius, beneath the ever-present consciousness that biography and criticism have their sacred duties, alike to the deceased, and to the public; precluding, on one hand, unjust depreciation, on the other, over-valuing partiality.

Notes

1   Varied use of either "His Residence *at* Lichfield" and "His Residence *in* Lichfield" are found among different printings of the same edition of this work that Joseph Johnson (1738–1809) published in London in 1804. William Poyntell (1756–1811) of the Classic Press in Philadelphia, Pennsylvania published a pirated edition that same year. Slight variations of wording in the Philadelphia printing are noted throughout this annotated text.

2   Frederick Howard, the Fifth Earl of Carlisle (1748–1825).

3   Lord Carlisle prepared one of the first translations of Dante into English. This appeared, together with his own work, in *Poems, Consisting of the Following Pieces, I. Ode Written upon the Death of Mr Gray. II. For the Monument of a Favourite Spaniel. III. Another Inscription for the Same. IV. Translation from Dante, Canto XXXIII*, 2nd ed. (London: J. Ridley, 1773).

4   Dr Darwin resided in Lichfield from November 1756 to March 1781, at which time he moved to Radburn Hall, near Derby. In March 1802, he and his family moved to Breadsall Priory, four miles north of Derby, where he died on 18 April 1802.

5   Francesco Petrarca (1304–1374), the Italian poet and founding Renaissance humanist. Seward published a sonnet, "Petrarch to Vaucluse", in imitation of Petrarch, Number XXV in *Original Sonnets on Various Subjects; And Odes Paraphrased from Horace* (London: G. Sael, 1799), which also appeared in her *Poetical Works*, Vol.3, p.146.

6   For a bibliography of versions of *The Botanic Garden*, as well as a listing of Dr Darwin's other publications, see Appendix I.

7   Extant letters to and from Dr Darwin are found in repositories throughout the world. The most complete collection of known letters is Desmond King-Hele's edited *The Collected Letters of Erasmus Darwin* (Cambridge: Cambridge University Press, 2006).

8   Alexander Pope (1688–1744), Jonathan Swift (1667–1745), Thomas Gray (1716–1771), and Samuel Johnson (1709–1784).

9   Anne Katherine Elwood informed us that it was Seward's "habit to transcribe into a book every letter of her own which appeared to her worth the attention of the public, omitting those passages which were without interest but to the person to whom they were addressed. She left twelve volumes of letters, thus copied by herself; … from this it is evident [that] she always had in view the possibility of publication, [and thus] their studied and highly ornamented style is easily accounted for". *Memoirs of Literary Ladies of England, From the Commencement of the Last Century* (London: Henry Colburn, 1843), available online at http://198.82.142.160/spenser/BiographyRecord.php?action=GET&bioid=34457.

10   Edward Young, *The Complaint, or, Night-Thoughts on Life, Death, and Immortality* (London, R. Dodsley, and sold by M. Cooper, 1742–46), V.531–533. Seward altered the original lines: "Some weep to share the fame of the deceased,/So high in merit, and to them so dear./They dwell on praises which they think they share". In this long didactic poem on death, the English poet, dramatist, and literary critic, Edward Young (1683–1765) also extolled the open space within the natural world as well as the omnipotent power of God.

11   Nicholas Hilliard (1547–1619), portrait painter to Elizabeth I, composed *The Art of Limning* (*c*.1600), i.e., illustrating medieval manuscripts, in the course of which he records conversations with the Queen and, in particular, their agreement that portrait-painting should be done without shadows. Such painting is "best in plaine lines without shadowing, for the line without shadows showeth all to a good judgment, but the shadows without line showeth nothing". Resulting portraits of the Queen, by English artists, were more diagrammatic than lifelike, and they represented the Queen's body as a fixed symbol of stable monarchy. For further reference, see Peter and Linda Murray, *Dictionary of Artists*, 5th ed (Middlesex: Penguin, 1983), p.192, and David Starkey, *Elizabeth I* (London: Chatto and Windus for the National Maritime Museum, 2003), p.177.

12   John Aikin and Anna Letitia Barbauld (née Aikin), "Against Inconsistency in Our Expectations", in *Miscellaneous Pieces in Prose* (London: J. Johnson, 1773), p.35. Seward altered the original sentence: "But nature is much more frugal than to heap together all manner of shining qualities in one glaring mass". In her letters, Seward compared this essay favorably with Samuel Johnson's *Rambler* essays (Anna Seward to Mr [Henry] C[ary], 31 July 1795, *Letters*, Vol.4, p.85).

13   William Kent (1685–1748) and John Wootton (1682–1764) were the limners (i.e., illustrators) of the first edition of John Gay's (1685–1732) *Fables* (London: J Tonson, J Watts, 1727). Many later editions of these *Fables* were published, some of which included illustrations by Hubert François Bourguignon (1699–1773), (better known as Gravelot), Thomas Bewick (1753–1828), and William Blake (1757–1827). Venus was the Roman goddess of love and beauty; Apollo the Greek god of poetry, music, healing, prophecy, and the sun.

14   Authors of works in that "Life and Letters" genre had approached Seward for insightful anecdotes about other individuals. For instance, Hester Lynch Thrale Piozzi and James Boswell asked her for material to use in their respective life stories of Samuel Johnson, although neither ultimately used the anecdotes that Seward provided. See Woolley, "Johnson as Despot: Anna Seward's Rejected Contribution to Boswell's *Life*", pp.140–145, and Heiland, "Swan Songs: The Correspondence of Anna Seward and James Boswell", pp.381–391. Seward's anecdotes regarding Johnson are more conspicuous in *Johnsonian; or, Supplement to Boswell: Being Anecdotes and Sayings of Dr Johnson* (London: John Murray, 1836), pp.314–325.

15   Throughout the text, Seward used a variety of dashes and other forms of punctuation which we have standardized into ellipses.

16   Samuel Johnson, *The Lives of the Most Eminent English Poets; With Critical Observations on Their Works* (London: J. Nichols, 1781).

17   Including the *General Morning Post* and *Aris's Gazette*.

18   At the time, Robert Waring Darwin (1766–1848) was a "successful, prosperous and admired" physician practicing in Shrewsbury (Ashmum, *Singing Swan*, pp.234–235).

19   Dewhurst Bilsborrow (alternatively spelled Bilsboro, *b.*1776).

Memoirs of the Life and

Writings of Doctor Darwin

Chapter I

Doctor Erasmus Darwin was the son of a private gentleman, near Newark, in Nottinghamshire.[1] He came to Lichfield to practise physic in the autumn of the year 1756, at the age of twenty-four; bringing high recommendations from the University of Edinburgh, in which he had studied, and from that of Cambridge, to which he belonged.[2]

He was somewhat above the middle size, his form athletic, and inclined to corpulence; his limbs too heavy for exact proportion. The traces of a severe small-pox;[3] features, and countenance, which, when they were not animated by social pleasure, were rather saturnine than sprightly; a stoop in the shoulders, and the then professional appendage, a large full-bottomed wig, gave, at that early period of life, an appearance of nearly twice the years he bore. *(Figure 11)* Florid health, and the earnest of good humour, a sunny smile, on entering a room, and on first accosting his friends, rendered, in his youth, that exterior agreeable, to which beauty and symmetry had not been propitious.

He stammered extremely; but whatever he said, whether gravely or in jest, was always well worth waiting for, though the inevitable impression it made might not always be pleasant to individual self-love.[4] Conscious of great native elevation above the general standard of intellect, he became, early in life, sore upon opposition, whether in argument or conduct, and always revenged it by sarcasm of very keen edge. Nor was he less impatient of the sallies of egotism and vanity, even when they were in so slight a degree, that strict politeness would rather tolerate than ridicule them. Dr Darwin seldom failed to present their caricature in jocose but wounding irony. If these ingredients of colloquial despotism were discernible in unworn existence, they increased as it advanced, fed by an ever-growing reputation within and without the pale of medicine.

Figure 11: Sketch of Dr Erasmus Darwin based upon Joseph Wright's portrait (1792/93), used with permission of Dr Denis Gibbs.

Extreme was his scepticism to human truth. From that cause he often disregarded the accounts his patients gave of themselves, and rather chose to collect his information by indirect inquiry and by cross-examining them, than from their voluntary testimony. That distrust and that habit were probably favourable to his skill in discovering the origin of diseases, and thence to his preeminent success in effecting their cure; … but they impressed his mind and tinctured his conversation with an apparent want of confidence in mankind, which was apt to wound the ingenuous and confiding spirit, whether seeking his medical assistance, or his counsel as a friend. Perhaps this proneness to suspicion mingled too much of art in his wisdom.

From the time at which Dr Darwin, first came to Lichfield, he avowed a conviction of the pernicious effects of all vinous fluid on the youthful and healthy constitution; an absolute horror of spirits of all sorts, and however diluted.[5] His own example, with very few exceptions, supported his exhortations. From strong malt liquor he totally abstained, and if he drank a glass or two of English wine, he mixed it with water. Acid fruits, with sugar, and all sort of creams, and butter, were his luxuries; but he always ate plentifully of animal food. This liberal alimentary regimen he prescribed to people of every age, where unvitiated appetite rendered them capable of following it; even to infants. He despised the prejudice, which deems foreign wines more wholesome than the wines of the country. If you must drink wine, said he, let it be home-made. It is well known, that Dr Darwin's influence and example have sobered the county of Derby; that intemperance in fermented fluid of every species is almost unknown amongst its gentlemen.[6]

Professional generosity distinguished Dr Darwin's medical practice. While resident in Lichfield, to the priest and lay-vicars of its cathedral, and their families, he always cheerfully gave his advice, but never took fees from any of them. Diligently, also, did he attend to the health of the poor in that city, and afterwards at Derby, and supplied their necessities by food, and all sort of charitable assistance. In each of those towns, his was the cheerful board of almost open-housed hospitality, without extravagance or parade; deeming ever the first unjust, the latter unmanly. Generosity, wit, and science, were his household gods.

To those many rich presents, which Nature bestowed on the mind of Dr Darwin, she added the seducing, and often dangerous gift of a highly poetic imagination; but he remembered how fatal that gift professionally became to the young physicians, Akenside and Armstrong.[7] Concerning them, the public could not be persuaded, that so much excellence in an ornamental science was compatible with intense application to a severer study; with such application as it held necessary to a responsibility, towards which it might look for the source of disease, on which it might lean for the struggle with mortality. Thus, through the first twenty-three years of his practice as a physician, Dr Darwin, with the wisdom of Ulysses,[8] bound himself to the medical mast, that he might not follow those delusive syrens, the muses, or be considered as their avowed votary. Occasional little pieces, however, stole at seldom occurring periods from his pen; though he cautiously precluded their passing the press, before his latent genius for poetry became unveiled to the public eye in its copious and dazzling splendour. Most of these minute gems have stolen into newspapers and magazines,[9] since the impregnable rock, on which his medicinal and philosophical reputation were placed, induced him to contend for that species of fame, which should entwine the Parnassian laurel with the balm of Pharmacy.[10]

After this sketch of Dr Darwin's character and manners, let us return to the dawn of his professional establishment. A few weeks after his arrival at Lichfield, in the latter end of the year 1756,[11] the intuitive discernment, the skill, spirit, and decision which marked the long course of his successful practice, were first called into action, and brilliantly opened his career of fame. The late Mr Inge of Thorpe, in Staffordshire, a young gentleman of family, fortune, and consequence, lay sick of a dangerous fever.[12] The justly celebrated Dr Wilks [sic] of Willenhall, who had many years possessed, in wide extent, the business and confidence of the Lichfield neighbourhood, attended Mr Inge, and had unsuccessfully combated his disease.[13] At length he pronounced it hopeless; that speedy death must ensue, and took his leave. It was then that a fond mother, wild with terror for the life of an only son, as drowning wretches catch at twigs, sent to Lichfield for the young, and yet inexperienced physician, of recent arrival there. By a reverse and entirely novel course of treatment, Dr Darwin gave his dying patient back to existence, to health, prosperity, and all that high reputation, which Mr Inge afterwards possessed as a public magistrate.

The far-spreading report of this judiciously daring and fortunate exertion brought Dr Darwin into immediate and extensive employment, and soon eclipsed the hopes of an ingenious rival, who resigned the contest; nor, afterwards, did any other competitor bring his certainly ineffectual lamp into that sphere, in which so bright a luminary shone.

Equal success, as in the case of Mr Inge, continued to result from the powers of Dr Darwin's genius, his frequent and intense meditation, and the avidity with which he, through life, devoted his leisure to scientific acquirement, and the investigation of disease. Ignorance and timidity, superstition, prejudice, and envy, sedulously strove to attach to his practice the terms, *rash, experimental, theoretic*; not considering, that without experimental theory, the restoring science could have made no progress; that neither time, nor all its accumulation of premature death, could have enlarged the circle, in which the merely practical physician condemns himself to walk. Strength of mind, fortitude unappalled, and the perpetual success which attended this great man's deviations from the beaten track, enabled him to shake those mists from his reputation, as the lion shakes to air the dewdrops on his mane.

In 1757, he married Miss Howard, of the Close of Lichfield, a blooming and lovely young lady of eighteen.[14] A mind, which had native strength; an awakened taste for the works of imagination; ingenuous sweetness; delicacy animated by sprightliness, and sustained by fortitude, made her a capable, as well as fascinating companion, even to a man of talents so illustrious ....To her he could, with confidence, commit the important task of rendering his childrens' minds a soil fit to receive, and bring to fruit, the stamina of wisdom and science.

Mrs Darwin's own mind, by nature so well endowed, strengthened and expanded in the friendship, conversation, and confidence of so beloved, so revered a preceptor. But alas! upon her early youth, and a too delicate constitution, the frequency of her maternal situation, during the first five years of her marriage, had probably a baneful effect.[15] The potent skill, and assiduous cares of him, before whom disease daily vanished from the frame of others, could not expel it radically from that of her he loved. It was however kept at bay thirteen years.[16]

Upon the distinguished happiness of those years, she spoke with fervour to two intimate female friends in the last week of her existence, which closed at the latter end of the summer of 1770.[17] "Do not weep for my impending fate", said the dying angel, with a smile of unaffected cheerfulness. "In the short term of my life, a great deal of happiness has been comprised. The maladies of my frame were peculiar; the pains in my head and stomach, which no medicine could eradicate, were spasmodic and violent; and required stronger measures to render them supportable while they lasted, than my constitution could sustain without injury. The periods of exemption from those pains were frequently of several days duration, and in my intermissions I felt no indication of malady. Pain taught me the value of ease, and I enjoyed it with a glow of spirit, seldom, perhaps, felt by the habitually healthy. While Dr Darwin combated and assuaged my disease from time to time, his indulgence to all my wishes, his active desire to see me amused and happy, proved incessant. His house, as you know, has ever been the resort of people of science and merit.[18] If, from my husband's great and extensive practice, I had much less of his society than I wished, yet the conversation of his friends, and of my own, was ever ready to enliven the hours of his absence. As occasional malady made me doubly enjoy health, so did those frequent absences give a zest, even to delight, when I could be indulged with his company. My three boys have ever been docile, and affectionate [19] .... Children as they are, I could trust them with important secrets, so sacred do they hold every promise they make. They scorn deceit, and falsehood of every kind, and have less selfishness than generally belongs to childhood .... Married to another man, I do not suppose I could have lived a third part of those years, which I have passed with Dr Darwin; he has prolonged my days, and he has blessed them".[20]

Thus died this superior woman, in the bloom of life, sincerely regretted by all, who knew how to value her excellence, and passionately regretted by the selected few, whom she honoured with her personal and confidential friendship.[21] The year after his marriage, Dr Darwin purchased an old half timbered house in the cathedral vicarage, adding a handsome new front, with venetian windows, and commodious apartments.[22] *(Figure 12)* This front looked towards Beacon street, but had no street annoyance, being separated from it by a narrow, deep dingle, which, when the Doctor purchased the premises, was overgrown with tangled briars and knot-grass. In ancient days it was the receptacle of that water, which moated the Close in a semicircle, the other half being defended by the Minster pool. A fortunate opening, between the opposite houses and this which has been described, gives it a prospect, sufficiently extensive, of pleasant and umbrageous fields. Across the dell, between his house and the street, Dr Darwin flung a broad bridge of shallow steps with Chinese paling, descending from his hall-door to the pavement.[23] The tangled and hollow bottom he cleared away into lawny smoothness, and made a terrace on the bank, which stretched in a line, level with the floor of his apartments, planting the steep declivity with lilacs and rose-bushes; while he screened his terrace from the gaze of passengers, and the summer sun,

> "By all that higher grew,
> Of firm and fragrant leaf. Then swiftly rose
> Acanthus, and each odorous, bushy shrub,
> To fence the verdant wall".[24]

Figure 12: Erasmus Darwin House, Lichfield. Wood engraving of John Sanders, used with permission of Stephen Sanders.

The last gentleman who purchased this house and its gardens, has destroyed the verdure and plantations of that dell, for the purpose of making a circular coach-road from the street to the hall-door; a sacrifice of beauty to convenience, and one of many proofs, that alteration and improvement are not always synonimous [sic] terms.[25] To this *rus in urbe*, of Darwinian creation, resorted, from its early rising, a knot of philosophic friends, in frequent visitation. The Revd. Mr Michell, many years deceased.[26] He was skilled in astronomic science, modest and wise. The ingenious Mr Keir, of West Bromwich, then Captain Keir *(Figure 13)*.[27] Mr Boulton, known and respected wherever mechanic philosophy is understood.[28] Mr Watt, the celebrated improver of the steam engine.[29] And, above all others in Dr Darwin's personal regard, the accomplished Dr Small, of Birmingham, who bore the blushing honours of his talents and virtues to an untimely grave.[30] About the year 1765, came to Lichfield, from the neighbourhood of Reading, the young and gay philosopher, Mr Edgeworth, a man of fortune, and recently married to a Miss Ellars of Oxfordshire.[31] The fame of Dr Darwin's various talents allured Mr E[dgeworth] to the city they graced. Then scarcely two and twenty, and with an exterior yet more juvenile, he had mathematic science, mechanic ingenuity, and a competent portion of classical learning, with the possession of the modern languages. His address was gracefully spirited, and his conversation eloquent. He danced, he fenced, and winged his arrows with more than philosophic skill; yet did not the consciousness of these lighter endowments abate his ardour in the pursuit of knowledge.

After having established a friendship and correspondence with Dr Darwin, Mr Edgeworth did not return to Lichfield till the summer of the year 1770.[32] With him, at that period, came the late Mr Day, of Bear-hill, in Berkshire. These young men had been fellow-students in the university of Oxford.[33] Mr Day was also attracted by the same celebrated abilities, which, five years before, had drawn his friend into their sphere. He was then twenty-four, in possession of a clear estate, about twelve hundred pounds per annum.[34]

Mr Day *(Figure 14)* looked the philosopher. Powder and fine clothes were, at that time, the appendages of gentlemen. Mr Day wore not either. He was tall and stooped in the shoulders, full made, but not corpulent; and in his meditative and

Figure 13: James Keir (1735-1820). Courtesy of Archives and Heritage, Birmingham Central Library.

melancholy air a degree of awkwardness and dignity were blended. We found his features interesting and agreeable amidst the traces of a severe small-pox. There was a sort of weight upon the lids of his large hazel eyes; yet when he declaimed,

> "Of good and evil
> Passion and apathy, and glory, and shame".[35]

very expressive were the energies gleaming from them beneath the shade of sable hair, which, Adam-like, curled about his brows. Less graceful, less amusing, less brilliant than Mr E[dgeworth], but more highly imaginative, more classical, and a deeper reasoner; while strict integrity, energetic friendship, openhanded bounty, sedulous and diffusive charity, greatly overbalanced, on the side of virtue, the tincture of misanthropic gloom and proud contempt of common-life society, that marked the peculiar character, which shall unfold itself on these pages. In succeeding years, Mr Day published two noble poems, *The Dying Negro*, and *The Devoted Legions*; also *Sandford and Merton*, which by wise parents is put into every youthful hand.[36]

Mr Day dedicated the third edition of *The Dying Negro* to Rousseau.[37] That dedication has every force and every grace of eloquence. The sentiments are strongly characteristic of their writer except in the philippic against American resistance, only just commenced when the address to Rousseau was composed. Generous indignation of the slave trade, practised without remorse in the southern colonies of North America, induced Mr Day to refuse them all credit for the patriotic virtue of that their resistance to new and unconstitutional claims, which threatened their liberties.

In the course of the year 1770, Mr Day stood for a full-length picture to Mr Wright of Derby.[38] A strong likeness and a dignified portrait were the result. Drawn as in the open air, the surrounding sky is tempestuous, lurid, and dark. He stands leaning his left arm against a column inscribed to Hambden [sic].[39] Mr Day looks upward, as enthusiastically meditating on the contents of a book, held in his dropped right hand. The open leaf is the oration of that virtuous patriot in the senate, against the grant of ship-money, demanded by King Charles the first.[40] A flash of lightning plays in Mr Day's hair, and illuminates the contents of the volume. The poetic fancy, and what were then the politics of the original, appear in the choice of subject and attitude. Dr Darwin sat to Mr Wright about the same period.[41] The result was a simply contemplative portrait, of the most perfect resemblance.

Figure 14: Thomas Day (1748-1789). Courtesy of Archives and Heritage, Birmingham Central Library.

During the summer and autumn of that year, was found, in Dr Darwin's circle, as Mr Day's visitor, the late Mr William Seward of London; yet, though a young man whose talents were considerably above the common level, he was rather a satellite than a planet in that little sphere.[42] He afterwards became known to the literary world as one of Dr Johnson's habitual companions, and, in the year 1795, he published *Anecdotes of Distinguished Persons*; a compilation of more industry in the collection, than grace in the dress.[43] Mr W. Seward has not displayed in those volumes, the happy art of animating narration. Common occurrences, even in the lives of eminent people, weary attention, unless they are told with elegance and spirit. From the ardently sought society of men of genius, this gentleman acquired a striking degree of wit and ingenious allusion in conversation, though it was too uniformly, and too caustically, of the sarcastic species; but every sort of fire seems to have evaporated from the language of Mr W. Seward in passing through his pen.

Mr Day and Mr Edgeworth took the house now inhabited by Mr Moresby, in the little green valley of Stow, that slopes from the east end of the cathedral, and forms, with its old grey tower on the banks of its lake, so lovely a landscape.[44] That house was Mr Day's bachelor mansion through the year 1770; that of Mr Edgeworth, and his wife and family, in the ensuing year. All of this city and its vicinity, who comprehended and tasted those powers of mind which take the higher range of intellect, were delighted to mingle in such associations.

In February 1775, died Dr Small *(Figure 15)*, nor were so much talent and merit suffered to pass away,

"Without the meed [sic] of some melodious tears".[45]

They were given in a short elegy, by his most valued friend, Dr Darwin; which elegy is engraven on a vase in Mr Boulton's garden,[46] sacred to the memory of the ingenious deceased.

> Ye Gay, and Young, who, thoughtless of your doom,
>   Shun the disgustful mansions of the dead,
> Where Melancholy broods o'er many a tomb,
>   Mouldering beneath the yew's unwholesome shade,
>
> If chance ye enter these sequester'd groves,
>   And day's bright sunshine, for a while, forego,
> O leave to Folly's cheek, the laughs and loves,
>   And give one hour to philosophic woe!
>
> Here, while no titled dust, no sainted bone,
>   No lover, weeping over beauty's bier,
> No warrior, frowning in historic stone,
>   Extorts your praises, or requests your tear.
>
> Cold Contemplation leans her aching head,
>   And as on human woe her broad eye turns,
> Waves her meek hand, and sighs for science dead,
>   For science, virtue, and for Small she mourns![47]

Epitaph on Dr Small of Birmingham, by Mr Day

> Beyond the rage of Time, or Fortune's power,
> Remain, cold stone! … remain, and mark the hour
> When all the noblest gifts that Heaven e'er gave
> Were destined to a dark, untimely grave.
> O taught on reason's boldest wing to rise,
> And catch each glimmer of the opening skies!
> O gentle bosom! O unspotted mind!
> O friend to truth, to virtue, and mankind,
> Thy lov'd remains we trust to this pale shrine,
> Secure to meet no second loss like thine![48]

Figure 15: Dr William Small (1734-1775). Courtesy of Archives and Heritage, Birmingham Central Library.

In Mr Day's epitaph there is some pathos, and more poetry; but it is far from being faultless. Perhaps it may be its least error, that the name of the bewailed is omitted, which

Dr Johnson has well observed, ought always to be involved in the verses.[49] It must, however, be confessed, that, in this case, the noun personal was not calculated to appear with grace in verse; but that consideration, though it doubtless caused, will not justify, the omission. In Dr Darwin's *Elegy*, it is placed out of all possibility of ludicrous equivoque, and so accents the last line, as to produce no mean or inharmonious sound. The commendation, also, is, in the elegy, of much more dignified modesty. Praise may be allowed to glow even upon a tombstone, but should never be hyperbolic. The epitaph is too exclamatory; and to assert that no second loss, so deplorable, can be sustained, is infinitely too much for one, who, however endowed and adorned, left the world at large no written testimony of that imputed superiority. It is finely observed by the charming Prior,

> "That the distinguish'd part of men,
> By pencil, compass, sword, or pen,
> Should, in life's visit leave their name,
> In characters, which may proclaim
> That they, with ardour, strove to raise
> At once their art, and country's praise;
> And, in the working, took great care
> That all was full, and round, and fair".[50]

The circumstances of Mr Day's disposition, habits, and destiny were so peculiar, as to justify digression from the principal subject of these pages.[51]

Their author would deem it inexcusable to introduce any thing fabulous; to embellish truth by the slightest colouring of fiction, even by exaggerating singularity, or heightening what is extraordinary; … but when realities are of a nature to interest and to amuse in a collateral branch of the memoir, the reader will not be displeased to turn from its principal personage, distinguished rather by wonderful endowment than by uncommon occurrences, while the picture of his friend's more eventful story passes before their eyes.

Mr Day's father died during his infancy, and left him an estate of twelve hundred pounds per annum.[52] Soon after his mother married a gentleman of the name of Philips.[53] The author of this narrative has often heard Mr Day describe him as one of those common characters, who seek to supply their inherent want of consequence, by a busy teizing [sic] interference in circumstances, with which they have no real concern.

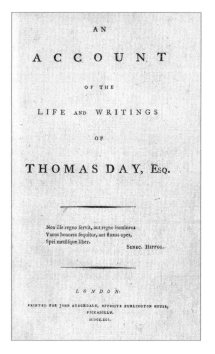

Figure 16: Title page of James Keir's Life of Thomas Day (1791).

Mrs Philips, jointured with three hundred pounds a year out of her son's estate, was left his sole guardian, or united with another person in the trust, whom she influenced. Herself, influenced by such a husband, often rendered uncomfortable the domestic situation of a high-spirited youth of genius. We may well suppose he impatiently brooked the preceptive impertinence, and troublesome authority of a man whom he despised, and who had no claim upon his obedience, though he considered it as a duty to pay some outward respect to the husband of his mother.

She frequently repined at the narrowness of her jointure, and still oftener expressed solicitude lest Mr Philips, who had no fortune of his own, should lose in the decline of life, by losing her, all comfortable subsistence. It was Mr Day's first act, on coming of age, and into possession of his estate, to augment his mother's jointure to four hundred, and to settle it upon Mr Philips during his life. This bounty, to a man who had needlessly mortified and embittered so many years of his own infancy and youth, evinced a very elevated mind. That mind had also been wounded by the caprice of a young lady, who "claimed the triumph of a lettered heart", without knowing how to value and retain her prize. Before her fickleness became indisputable, he wrote the following beautiful elegy,

> Yet once again, in yonder myrtle bowers,
> Whence rose-lipp'd zephyrs, hovering, shed perfume,
> I weave the painted radiance of the flowers,
> And press coy Nature in her days of bloom.
>
> Shall she, benignant, to the wondering eyes
> Of the lone hermit all her charms unfold?
> Or, gemm'd with dew, bid her gay florets rise
> To grace the rustic master of the fold?
>
> Shall these possess her bright, her fragrant store,
> These snatch the wreath, by plastic Nature wove,
> Nor wanton summer yield one garland more
> To grace the bosom of the nymph I love?
>
> For she shall come; with her each sister grace,
> With her the kindred powers of harmony,
> The deep recesses of the grove shall trace,
> And hang with flowers each consecrated tree.
>
> Blithe Fancy too shall spread her glittering plumes,
> She loves the white cliffs of Britannia's isle,
> She loves the spot where infant Genius blooms,
> She loves the spot, where Peace and Freedom smile.

Unless her aid the mimic queen bestow,
In vain fresh garlands the low vales adorn;
In vain with brighter tints the florets glow,
Or dewdrops sparkle on the brow of morn.

Opes not one blossom to the spicy gale,
Throws not one elm its moss-wreath'd branches wide,
Wanders no rill through the luxuriant vale,
Or, glist'ning, rushes down the mountain side,

But thither, with the morning's earliest ray,
Fancy has wing'd her ever-mazy flight,
To hymn wild carols to returning day,
And catch the fairest beams of orient light.

Proud of the theft she mounts her lucid car,
Her car the rainbow's painted arch supplies;
Her swift wing'd steeds unnumber'd loves prepare,
And countless zephyrs waft her through the skies.

There, while her bright wheels pause in cloudless air,
She waves the magic sceptre of command,
And all her flattering visions, wild as fair,
Start into life beneath the potent wand.

Here, proudly nodding o'er the vale below,
High rocks of pearl reflect the morning ray,
Whence gushing streams of azure nectar flow,
And tinge the trickling herbage on their way.

There, cull'd from every mountain, every plain,
Perennial flowers the ambient air perfume,
Far off stern Boreas [54] holds his drear domain,
Nor chains the streams, nor blights the sacred bloom.

Through all the year, in copse and tangled dale,
Lone Philomel [55] her song to Venus pours,
What time pale Evening spreads the dewy veil,
What time the red Morn blushes on the shores.

Illusive visions! O, not here, ... not here,
Does Spring eternal hold her placid reign,
Already Boreas chills the altering year,
And blasts the purple daughters of the plain.

So fade my promis'd joys! ... fair scenes of bliss,
Ideal scenes, too long believ'd in vain,
Plung'd down and swallow'd deep in Time's abyss!
So veering Chance, and ruthless fates ordain.

Thee, Laura,[56] thee, by fount, or mazy stream,
Or thicket rude, unpress'd by human feet,
I sigh, unheeded, to the moon's pale beam;
Thee, Laura, thee, the echoing hills repeat.

Oh! long of billows wild, and winds the sport,
Seize, seize the safe asylum that remains!
Here Truth, Love, Freedom, Innocence resort,
And offer long oblivion to thy pains.

When panting, gasping, breathless, on the strand
The shipwreck'd mariner reclines his breast,
Say, shall he scorn the hospitable hand,
That points to safety, liberty, and rest?

But thou, too soon forgetful of past woe,
Again would'st tempt the winds, and treacherous sea;
Ah! shall the raging blast forget to blow,
Shall every wintry storm be hush'd for thee?

Not so! I dread the elemental war,
Too soon, too soon the calm, deceitful, flies;
I hear the blast come whistling from afar,
I see the tempest gathering in the skies.

Yet let the tempest roar! ... love scorns all harms,
I plunge amid the storm, resolved to save;
This hour, at least, I clasp thee in my arms,
The next let ruin join us in the grave.[57]

The above verses imply some perfidy, or disappointment experienced by the lady to whom they are addressed. She probably accepted Mr Day's addresses in resentment, and afterwards found she had not a heart to give him. This is no uncommon case; and it is surely better to recede, even at the church-porch, than to plight at its altar the vow of unexisting love, which no effort of the will can implant in the bosom. It has been observed, that marriage is often the grave of love, but scarcely ever its cradle; and what hope of happiness, what hope of a blessing on nuptials, which commence with perjury!

Even at that period, "when youth, elate and gay, steps into life", Mr Day was a rigid moralist, who proudly imposed on himself cold abstinence, even from the most innocent pleasures; nor would he allow an action to be virtuous, which was performed upon any hope of reward, here, or hereafter. This severity of principle, more abstract and specious, than natural or useful, rendered Mr Day sceptical towards revealed religion, though by no means a confirmed deist. Most unlike Doctor Johnson in those doubts, he resembled him in want of sympathy with such miseries as spring from refinement and the softer affections; resembled him also, in true compassion for the sufferings of cold and hunger. To the power of relieving them he nobly sacrificed all the parade of life, and all the pleasures of luxury. For that mass of human character which constitutes polished society, he avowed a sovereign contempt; above all things he expressed aversion to the modern plans of female education, attributing to their influence the fickleness which had stung him. He thought it, however, his duty to marry; nursed systematic ideas of the force of philosophic tuition to produce future virtue, and loved to mould the infant and youthful mind.[58]

Ever despicable in Mr Day's estimation were the distinctions of birth, and the advantages of wealth; and he had learnt to look back with resentment to the allurements of the Graces.[59] He resolved, if possible, that his wife should have a taste for literature and science, for moral and patriotic philosophy. So might she be his companion in that retirement, to which he had destined himself; and assist him in forming the minds of his children to stubborn virtue and high exertion. He resolved also, that she should be simple as a mountain girl, in her dress, her diet, and her manners; fearless and intrepid as the Spartan wives and Roman heroines.... There was no finding such a creature ready made; philosophical romance could not hope it. He must mould some infant into the being his fancy had imaged.

With the late Mr Bicknell, then a barrister, in considerable practice, and of taintless reputation, and several years older than himself, Mr Day lived on terms of intimate friendship.[60] Credentials were procured of Mr Day's moral probity, and with them, on his coming of age, these two friends journied [sic] to Shrewsbury, to explore the hospital in that town for foundling girls.[61] From the little train, Mr Day, in the presence of Mr Bicknell, selected two of twelve years each; both beautiful; one fair, with flaxen locks, and light eyes; her he called Lucretia.[62] The other, a clear, auburn brunette, with darker eyes, more glowing bloom, and chestnut tresses, he named Sabrina.[63]

These girls were obtained on written conditions, for the performance of which Mr Bicknell was guarantee. They were to this effect; that Mr Day should, within the twelvemonth after taking them, resign one into the protection of some reputable tradeswoman, giving one hundred pounds to bind her apprentice; maintaining her, if she behaved well, till she married, or began business for herself. Upon either of these events, he promised to advance four hundred more. He avowed his intention of educating the girl he should retain, with a view to making her his future wife; solemnly engaged never to violate her innocence; and if he should renounce his plan, to maintain her decently in some creditable family till she married, when he promised five hundred pounds as her wedding portion.

Mr Day went instantly into France with these girls; not taking an English servant, that they might receive no ideas, except those which [he] himself might choose to impart.[64]

They teized [sic] and perplexed him; they quarrelled, and fought incessantly; they sickened of the small-pox; they chained him to their bed-side by crying, and screaming if they were ever left a moment with any person who could not speak to them in English. He was obliged to sit up with them many nights; to perform for them the lowest offices of assistance.

They lost no beauty by their disease. Soon after they had recovered, crossing the Rhone with his wards in a tempestuous day, the boat overset. Being an excellent swimmer he saved them both, though with difficulty and danger to himself.

Mr Day came back to England in eight months, heartily glad to separate the little squabblers. Sabrina was become the favourite. He placed the fair Lucretia with a chamber milliner.[65] She behaved well, and became the wife of a respectable linen-draper in London. On his return to his native country, he entrusted Sabrina to the care of Mr Bicknell's mother, with whom she resided some months in a country village, while he settled his affairs at his own mansion-house, from which he promised not to remove his mother.[66]

It has been said before, that the fame of Dr Darwin's talents allured Mr Day to Lichfield. Thither he led, in the spring of the year 1770, the beauteous Sabrina, then thirteen years old, and taking a twelve month's possession of the pleasant mansion in Stowe Valley, resumed his preparations for implanting in her young mind the characteristic virtues of Arria, Portia, and Cornelia.[67] His experiments had not the success he wished and expected. Her spirit could not be armed against the dread of pain, and the appearance of danger. When he dropped melted sealing-wax upon her arms she did not endure it heroically, nor when he fired pistols at her petticoats, which she believed to be charged with balls, could she help starting, or suppress her screams.

When he tried her fidelity in secret-keeping, by telling her of well-invented dangers to himself, in which greater danger would result from its being discovered that he was aware of them, he once or twice detected her having imparted them to the servants, and to her play-fellows.

She betrayed an averseness to the study of books, and of the rudiments of science, which gave little promise of ability, that should, one day, be responsible for the education of youths, who were to emulate the Gracchi.[68]

Mr Day persisted in these experiments, and sustained their continual disappointment during a year's residence in the vicinity of Lichfield.[69] The difficulty seemed to lie in giving her motive to exertion, self-denial, and heroism. It was against his plan to draw it from the usual sources, pecuniary reward, luxury, ambition, or vanity. His watchful cares had precluded all knowledge of the value of money, the reputation of beauty, and its concomitant desire of ornamented dress. The only inducement, therefore, which this lovely artless girl could have to combat and subdue the natural preference, in youth so blossoming, of ease to pain, of vacant sport to the labour of thinking, was the desire of pleasing her protector, though she knew not how, or why he became such. In that desire, fear had greatly the ascendant of affection, and fear is a cold and indolent feeling.

Thus, after a series of fruitless trials, Mr Day renounced all hope of moulding Sabrina into the being his imagination had formed; and ceasing to behold her as his future wife, he placed her at a boarding school in Sutton-Coldfield, Warwickshire. His trust in the power of education faltered; his aversion to modern elegance subsided. From the time he first lived in the Vale of Stowe, he had daily conversed with the beautiful Miss Honora Sneyd of Lichfield.[70] Without having received a Spartan education, she united a disinterested desire to please, fortitude of spirit, native strength of intellect, literary and scientific taste, to unswerving truth, and to all the graces. She was the very Honora Sneyd, for whom the gallant and unfortunate Major Andre's inextinguishable passion is on poetic, as his military fame and hapless destiny are on patriot, record.[71] Parental authority having dissolved the juvenile engagements of this distinguished youth and maid, Mr Day offered to Honora his philosophic hand.[72] She admired his talents; she revered his virtues; she tried to school her heart into softer sentiments in his favour. She did not succeed in that attempt, and ingenuously told him so. Her sister, Miss Elizabeth Sneyd, one year younger than herself, was very pretty, very sprightly, very artless, and very engaging, though countless degrees inferior to the endowed and adorned Honora.[73] To her the yet love-luckless sage transferred the heart, which Honora had with sighs resigned. Elizabeth told Mr Day she could have loved him, if he had acquired the manners of the world, instead of those austere singularities of air, habit, and address.

He began to impute to them the fickleness of his first love; the involuntary iciness of the charming Honora, as well as that for which her sister accounted. He told Elizabeth, that, for her sake, he would renounce his prejudices to external refinements, and try to acquire them. He would go to Paris for a year, and commit himself to dancing and fencing masters. He did so; stood daily an hour or two in frames, to screw back his shoulders, and point his feet; he practiced the military gait, the fashionable bow, minuets, and cotillions; but it was too late; habits, so long fixed, could no more than partially be overcome. The endeavour, made at intervals, and by visible effort, was more really ungraceful than the natural stoop, and unfashionable air. The studied bow on entrance, the suddenly recollected assumption of attitude, prompted the risible instead of the admiring sensation; neither was the showy dress, in which he came back to his fair one, a jot more becoming.

Poor Elizabeth reproached her reluctant but insuppressive ingratitude, upon which all this labour, these sacrifices had been wasted. She confessed, that Thomas Day, blackguard, as he used jestingly to style himself, less displeased her eye than Thomas Day, fine gentleman.

Thus again disappointed, he resumed his accustomed plainness of garb, and neglect of his person, and went again upon the continent for another year, with pursuits of higher aim, more congenial to his talents and former principles. Returning to England in the year 1773, he saw, that spring, Miss Honora Sneyd united to his friend Mr Edgeworth *(Figure 17)*, who was become a widower; and, in the year 1780, he learned that his second love of that name, Miss Elizabeth Sneyd, was also, after the death of Honora married to Mr Edgeworth.[74]

It was singular that Mr Day should thus, in the course of seven years, find himself doubly rivalled by his most intimate friend; but his own previously renounced pursuit of those beautiful young women, left him without either cause or sensations of resentment on their account.

From the year 1773 this hitherto love-renounced philosopher resided chiefly in London, and amid the small and select circle which he frequented there, often met the pretty and elegant Miss Esther Mills [sic] of Derbyshire, who, with modern acquirements, and amongst modish luxuries, suited to her large fortune, had cultivated her understanding by books, and her virtues by benevolence.[75] The again unpolished stoic had every charm in her eyes,

"She saw Othello's visage in his mind".[76]

But, from indignant recollection of hopes so repeatedly baffled, Mr Day looked with distrust on female attention of however flattering semblance; nor was it till after years of her modest, yet tender devotion to his talents and merit, that he deigned to ask Miss Mills [sic], if she could, for his sake, resign all that the world calls pleasures; all its luxuries, all its ostentation. If, with him, she could resolve to employ, after the ordinary comforts of life were supplied, the surplus of her affluent fortune in clothing the naked, and feeding the hungry; retire with him into the country, and shun, through remaining existence, the infectious taint of human society.

Figure 17: Richard Lovell Edgeworth (1744-1817).

Mr Day's constitutional fault, like poor Cowper's, seemed that of looking with severe and disgusted eyes upon those venial errors in his species, which are mutually tolerated by mankind.[77] This stain of misanthropy was extremely deepened by his commerce with the world, restrained as that commerce had ever been. Satiric, jealous, and discerning, it was not easy to deceive him; yet, in a few instances, he was deceived by the appearance of virtues congenial to his own:

"For neither man, nor angel can discern
Hypocrisy, the only evil that walks
Invisible, except to God alone".[78]

To proposals so formidable, so sure to be rejected by a heart less than infinitely attached, Miss Mills [sic] gladly assented; but something more remained. Mr Day insisted, that her whole fortune should be settled upon herself, totally out of his present or future control; that if she grew tired of a system of life so likely to weary a woman of the world, she might return to that world any hour she chose, fully empowered to resume its habits, and its pleasures.

They married, and retired into the country about the year 1780, according to the best recollection of the author of these memoirs.[79] No carriage; no appointed servant about Mrs Day's own person; no luxury of any sort. Music, in which she was a distinguished proficient, was deemed trivial. She banished her harpsichord and music-books. Frequent experiments upon her temper, and her attachment, were made by him, whom she lived but to obey and love. Over these she often wept, but never repined. No wife, bound in the strictest fetters, as to the incapacity of claiming separate maintenance, ever made more absolute sacrifices to the most imperious husband, than did this lady, whose independence had been secured, and of whom nothing was demanded as a duty.

Thus Mr Day found, at last, amid the very class he dreaded, that of fashionable women, a heart whose passion for him supplied all the requisites of his high-toned expectations.

Some eight or ten years after his marriage, the life of this singular being became, in its meridian, a victim to one of his uncommon systems. He thought highly of the gratitude, generosity, and sensibility of horses; and that whenever they were disobedient, unruly, or vicious, it was owing to previous ill usage from men. He had reared, fed, and tamed a favourite foal. When it was time it should become serviceable, disdaining to employ a horsebreaker, he would use it to the bit and the burden himself. He was not a good horseman. The animal disliking his new situation, heeded not the soothing voice to which he had been accustomed. He plunged, threw his master, and then, with his heels, struck him on the head an instantly fatal blow.[80] It was said that Mrs Day never afterwards saw the sun; that she lay in bed, into the curtains of which no light was admitted during the day, and only rose to stray alone through her garden, when night gave her sorrows congenial gloom. She survived this adored husband two years, and then died, broken-hearted, for his loss.

Ere the principal subject of this biographic tract is resumed, the reader will not be sorry to learn the future destiny of Sabrina. She remained at school three years; gained the esteem of her instructress; grew feminine, elegant, and amiable. This young woman proved one of many instances that those modes of education, which have been sanctioned by long experience, are seldom abandoned to advantage by ingenious system-mongers.

When Sabrina left school, Mr Day allowed her fifty pounds annually. She boarded some years near Birmingham, and afterwards at Newport, in Shropshire. Wherever she resided, wherever she paid visits, she secured to herself friends. Beautiful and admired, she passed the dangerous interval between sixteen and twenty-five, without one reflection upon her conduct, one stain upon her discretion. Often the guest of Dr Darwin, and other of her friends in Lichfield, esteem and affection formed the tribute to her virtues.

Mr Day corresponded with her parentally, but seldom saw her, and never without witnesses. Two years after his marriage, and in her twenty-sixth year, his friend, Mr Bicknell, proposed himself; that very Mr Bicknell, who went with Mr Day to the Foundling Hospital at Shrewsbury, and by whose suretyship for his upright intentions the governors of that charity permitted Mr Day to take from thence that beauteous girl, and the young Lucretia.

Mr Bicknell, high in practice as a barrister, was generally thought an advantageous match for Sabrina. More from prudential, than impassioned impulse, did she accept his addresses, yet became one of the most affectionate, as well as the best of wives.[81] When Mr Day's consent was asked by his *protégée*, he gave it in these ungracious words: "I do not refuse my consent to your marrying Mr Bicknell; but remember you have not asked my advice". He gave her the promised dower, five hundred pounds.

Mr Bicknell, without patrimonial fortune, and living up to his professional income, did not save money. His beloved wife brought him two boys.[82] When the eldest was about five years old, their father was seized with a paralytic stroke, which, in a few weeks, became fatal. His charming widow had no means of independent support for herself and infants. Mr Day said he would allow her thirty pounds annually, to assist the efforts which he expected she would make for the maintenance of herself and children. To have been more bounteous must surely have been in his heart, but it was not in his system. Through the benevolent exertions of Mr Harding [sic], Solicitor General to the Queen, the sum of eight hundred pounds was raised among the gentlemen of the bar for Mrs Bicknell and her sons; the interest to be the mother's during her life, and the principal, at her decease, to be divided between her children.[83]

That excellent woman has lived many years, and yet lives with the good Dr Burney of Greenwich, as his housekeeper, and assistant in the cares of his academy.[84] She is treated by him, and his friends, with every mark of esteem and respect due to a gentlewoman, and one whose virtues entitle her to universal approbation. Her name was not in Mr Day's will, but Mrs Day continued the allowance he had made her, and bequeathed its continuance from her own fortune during Mrs Bicknell's life. Mr and Mrs Day left no child. Mr Edgeworth, having also lost his third wife, Elizabeth, is now the husband of a fourth, a daughter of the reverend Dr Beaufort of Ireland.[85] He had four children by his first; a son, who of late years died in America;[86] Miss Edgeworth, the celebrated writer of *Stories for Children*, and *Moral Tales for Young People*, &c.;[87] Miss Anna, married to the ingenious Dr Beddoes of Bristol;[88] and Miss Emmeline, married to Mr King, surgeon of the same place.[89] Honora left him an infant girl [90] and boy,[91] when she died in the year 1780. The former inherited her mother's name, her beauty, and her malady, and died of consumption at sixteen. The amiable son yet lives, with fine talents, but infirm health. By his third wife, Elizabeth, he has several children;[92] and by the present, two or three.[93] From Mr Edgeworth's large family elaborate systems of infantile education have proceeded: of them, the author of these memoirs cannot speak, as she has never seen them. Other compositions, which are said to be humorous and brilliant, are from the same source.[94]

Figure 18: Maria Edgeworth (1767-1849). Courtesy of Archives and Heritage, Birmingham Central Library.

Notes

1   Erasmus Darwin was born on 12 December 1731, the son of the solicitor, Robert Darwin (1682–1754) and Elizabeth Hill (1702–1797), daughter of John Hill (1658–1717) of Sleaford, Lincolnshire. His parents lived at Elston Hall, near Newark, Nottinghamshire. Erasmus was their seventh, and last, child.

2   Darwin matriculated at St John's College, Cambridge, in 1750 where he resided through 1753, and from which he received an MB degree in 1755. He spent much of 1753–55, and part of 1756, in Edinburgh studying under a number of skilled, Leiden-trained physicians including John Rutherford (1695–1779) and Alexander Monro, primus

(1697–1767) on medicine, William Cullen (1710–1790) on chemistry and medicine, and Charles Alston (1683–1760) on botany. Darwin received his MB from Cambridge in 1756. For an overview of the importance of Edinburgh as a center of medical education during the period, see, among others, Christopher J. Lawrence, "Early Edinburgh Medicine: Theory and Practice", in R. G. W. Anderson and A. D. C. Simpson (eds) *The Early Years of the Edinburgh Medical School* (Edinburgh: Royal Scottish Museum, 1976), pp.81–94, and Guenter B. Risse, *Hospital Life in Enlightenment Scotland: Care and Teaching at the Royal Infirmary of Edinburgh* (Cambridge: Cambridge University Press, 1986).

3 King-Hele suggests that Darwin contracted this disease "presumably in his schooldays" (*Doctor of Revolution*, p.24).

4 Throughout his career, Dr Darwin devoted a considerable amount of time to the study of language production. Philip J.B. Jackson explored this interest in "Mama and Papa: The Ancestors of Modern-Day Speech Science", in Smith and Arnott (eds) *Genius of Erasmus Darwin*, pp.217–236.

5 In Lichfield – the city known for its "Preachers, Pubs, and Prostitutes" – Dr Darwin was, as Chris Upton (*History of Lichfield*, p.94), recently noted, "one customer the local publican might not have wanted to see". Dr Darwin, a non-conformist in his Christian beliefs, admonished the community of the Cathedral Close in which he lived for further exacerbating the problem of the vine. In *The Botanic Garden*, Darwin argued, the "chemical process of fermentation … converts food into poison! And it has thus become the curse of the Christian world, producing more than half of our chronical diseases; which Mohamet [sic] observed, and forbade the use of it to his disciples" (*The Loves of the Plants*, III, p.119, note). Darwin viewed intemperance (i.e., alcoholism) as the foundational hereditary disease. In the words of his grandson, Charles, "No man ever inculcated more persistently and strongly the evil effects of intemperance than did Dr Darwin; but chiefly on the grounds of ill-health, with its inherited consequences" (C. Darwin, "Preliminary Notice", p.56). Dr Darwin himself argued (*The Temple of Nature; or, The Origin of Society*, New York: T. and J. Sword, 1804, p.178) that all the "hereditary diseases of this country" originated as "the consequence of drinking much fermented or spiritous liquor". Consequently, overcoming the hereditary tendency to intemperance was "perhaps … the most practical line of attack" against all "ill-health" (C. Darwin, "Preliminary Notice", p.56). For further insight into Dr Darwin's thoughts about heredity, see Philip K. Wilson's writings including "Erasmus Darwin on Animal Generation: Placing Heredity within early 19th-Century Contexts", in Smith and Arnott (eds) *Genius of Erasmus Darwin*, pp.113–132; "Erasmus Darwin and the 'Noble' Disease (Gout): Conceptualizing Heredity and Disease in Enlightenment England", in S. Müller-Willie and H-J. Rheinberger (eds) *Heredity Produced: At the Crossroads of Biology, Politics and Culture 1500–1870* (Cambridge, MA: MIT Press, 2007), 133–154, and "Drinks, Dames & Diseases: Erasmus Darwin on Inheritance", *Vesalius: Official Journal of the International Society for the History of Medicine* 13 (2007): 60–67.

6 Maria Edgeworth's (1767–1849) letters corroborate Dr Darwin's crusade to stop the ruin created by hereditary tendencies towards alcoholism. According to her, Dr Darwin vehemently argued that "almost all destroyers of the higher classes of people arise from drinking, in some form or another, too much vinous spirit". We have long known of Darwin's claims in his own writings, but Edgeworth goes beyond this and helpfully informs us that Darwin supported them "still more in conversation, by all of those powers of wit, satire, and peculiar humour, which never appeared fully to the public in his works, but which gained him strong ascendancy in private society". Indeed, she claimed that during his life in Lichfield, Darwin "almost banished wine from the tables of the rich … and persuaded most of the gentry in his own and the neighbouring countries, to become water-drinking" *(Memoirs of Richard L. Edgeworth,* Vol.2, p.88).

7 King-Hele noted that Dr Darwin feared that his devotion to poetry might impair his medical reputation (*Erasmus Darwin: Life of Unequalled Achievement*, p.201, and *Collected Letters of Erasmus Darwin*, p.236, footnote 3). It was only after Darwin established his financial future by marrying Elizabeth that he allowed the second poetic half of *The Botanic Garden* to be published, and even then it appeared anonymously.

8   Among the challenges that Ulysses (Odysseus), the wise and crafty King of Ithaca, faced on his long voyage after the Trojan War back to Ithaca, was to escape the lure of the Sirens, those sea nymphs who used their entrancing song to tempt sailors from their duties, thereby causing their ships to crash on the nearby rocky islands. The goddess Circe assisted Ulysses by tying him to the ship's mast before he encountered the Sirens' alluring music.

9   See Erasmus Darwin's Writings, Appendix I.

10   The crown wreath from Parnassus that was awarded to select poets. Parnassus was the mountain of Greek mythology near Delphi that Apollo and the Muses viewed as sacred.

11   12 November 1756.

12   William Inge (1737–1785), a nephew of Dr Wilkes' second wife. Inge lived at Constantine Hall in Thorpe, just northeast of Tamworth. Inge later served as High Sheriff of Staffordshire in 1766.

13   Richard Wilkes (1691–1760) of Willenhall.

14   Mary Howard (1740–1770), married Darwin on 30 December 1757 in St Mary's Church, Lichfield. Mary, known locally as Polly, was the daughter of the Lichfield solicitor, Charles Howard (1707–1771) and Penelope Foley (1708–1748). Charles had been a Lichfield Free Grammar School classmate and friend of Samuel Johnson, and Penelope was descended via the Pagets from Mary, that "other Boleyn Girl" (*c.*1499–1543). For a recent historical, though fictitious, account of Mrs Darwin's relative, see Philippa Gregory, *The Other Boleyn Girl* (Touchstone: Old Tappan, New Jersey, 2002). Anna Seward's "Ode to Euphrosyne, An Epithalamium on the Marriage of Doctor D___ to Miss M___", appeared in her *Poetical Works*, Vol.1, pp.161–164. In a letter to his son Robert Waring Darwin, Erasmus discussed his uncle, also named Charles Howard (1742–1791). It was this uncle Charles Howard who was, so Darwin claimed, a drunkard both in public and private – and when he went to London he became connected with a woman and lived a deba[u]ched life in respect to drink, hence he always had the Gout of which he died" (Erasmus Darwin to Robert Waring Darwin, 5 January [1792], as reprinted in Nora Barlow, *The Autobiography of Charles Darwin, 1809–1882*, New York: W.W. Norton, 1958, p.224). These effects carried forth into Polly's life for early in their married life, she began to drink excessively – though attempting to conceal this from her husband – in order to overcome episodes of "temporary delirium, or … insanity" (Ralph Colp, Jr., *To Be An Invalid: The Illness of Charles Darwin*, Chicago: University of Chicago Press, 1977, p.119). Even Anna Seward, who lashed out viciously at many people in her letters, was kinder than she might have been about what we would call Polly Darwin's addiction, claiming that "stronger measures" [i.e., alcohol] were required "to render" Polly's pains "supportable while they lasted", yet they proved even stronger measures than her "constitution could sustain without injury" (Desmond King-Hele, "Erasmus Darwin's Life at Lichfield: Fresh Evidence", *Notes and Records of the Royal Society of London* 49 [1995]: 236). Donald H. Reiman substantiates this in his introductory essay to the reprint of *The Botanic Garden; a Poem, in Two Parts* (New York: Garland Press, 1978), Vol.1, p.vii.

15   Together, Polly and Erasmus had five children, Charles Darwin (*b.*1758), Erasmus Darwin, Jr., (*b.*1759), Elizabeth Darwin (*b.*1763), Robert Waring Darwin (*b.*1766), and William Alvey Darwin (*b.*1767); Elizabeth Darwin and William Darwin predeceased their mother.

16   Referring to their married life, 1757–1770.

17   One of these was likely Miss Mary Newton, one of two sisters who lived with their brother, Andrew Newton (*d.*1806, known locally as 'The Nabob'), in Lichfield. Their brother Thomas Newton (1704–1782), later served as Chaplain to George II and as Bishop of Bristol and Dean of St Paul's Cathedral.

18   Especially that group of predominantly liberal, Whig technocrats who comprised a "troop of philosophers" later known as the Lunar Society. Curiously, Seward never mentioned this Society in her *Life of Dr Darwin*. Some, including John Brewer, have speculated that this omission was due to Seward's being "excluded as a woman" from this all-male Society (*Pleasures of the Imagination*, p.600). Benedict Nicholson reminds us that Seward's Bishops Palace

was "the hub of intellectual life in the Midlands until Matthew Boulton collected a group of scientists around him in Birmingham" (*Joseph Wright of Derby: Painter of Light*, New Haven: Yale University Press, 1968, p.100). Thus, perhaps Seward intentionally neglected mentioning the Lunar Society as it had detracted from her central position of luminary gatherings in the Midlands.

19 Her three living children, Charles Darwin, Erasmus Darwin, Jr., and Robert Waring Darwin.

20 From an account of Polly's life as relayed to Anna Seward who sat with Polly several times during her last weeks. King-Hele, "Erasmus Darwin's Life at Lichfield", p.236. Dr Darwin, as well, composed an eight-page elegiac "Account" of Polly's last months and days (King-Hele, *Collected Letters of Erasmus Darwin*, p.105, note, 2).

21 Polly died on 30 June 1770, supposedly of gallstones and liver disease. She was buried in the Lady Choir of Lichfield Cathedral.

22 As Desmond King-Hele uncovered, it may have been a bit more than a year after his marriage before Dr Darwin actually purchased the property. It was not until 8 August 1760 that he "paid £210 to Lady [Gertrude] Gresley (*c.*1715–1790) for a forty-year lease" for a house on the western boundary of Lichfield's Cathedral Close (*Doctor of Revolution*, p.42). This house currently serves as the international memorial to Dr Darwin in its function as a museum and as the venue for a wide variety of educational and social events. For further information, you may contact Erasmus Darwin House, Beacon Street, Lichfield, Staffordshire, WS13 7AD, United Kingdom, or consult the House's website at www.erasmusdarwin.org.

23 The work of Sir William Chambers (1723–1796) became the standard source for realistic Chinese architecture of the era, expanding the earlier 18th-century fashion for Chinoiserie.

24 John Milton (1608–1674), *Paradise Lost* (London: S. Simons, 1668), Book IV, ll. 694–97. Seward slightly altered the original passage: "and what higher grew/ Of firm and fragrant leaf; on each side/ Acanthus and each odorous bushy shrub/ Fenc'd up the verdant wall".

25 Nigel Bower Gresley "followed Darwin into the premises and not long afterwards, Charles Howard moved in, perhaps intending from the outset to carry out alterations to the house". Based on Lichfield Record Office "Lease Book" D30/XXXVIII, f.3.v., as cited in *Darwin House Lichfield: An Archaeological Watching Brief 1998–1999*, Vol.1, Report No. 99/2 (Tamworth, Staffordshire: Bob Meeson Historic Buildings Consultant, February 1999).

26 John Michell (1724–1793).

27 Erasmus established a friendship with James Keir (1735–1820) while they were both students at Edinburgh University. West Bromwich is located in Staffordshire, south of Walsall.

28 Matthew Boulton (1728–1809), a leader among the entrepreneurs of the Industrial Revolution.

29 James Watt (1736–1819). According to Dr Darwin, a "few years ago Mr Watt of Glasgow much improved this machine, and with Mr Boulton of Birmingham has applied it to a variety of purposes, such as raising water from mines, blowing bellows to fuse the ore, supplying towns with water, grinding corn and many other purposes. There is reason to believe it may in time be applied to the rowing of barges, and the moving of carriages along the road. As the specific levity of air is too great for the support of great burthens by balloons, there seems no probable method of flying conveniently but by the power of steam, or some other explosive material; which another half century may probable discover" (*Economy of Vegetation*, I, p.26, note).

30 William Small (1734–1775).

31 Richard Lovell Edgeworth (1744–1817), father of novelist, Maria.

32 The meeting of Edgeworth and Dr Darwin was quite a memorable scene. On Edgeworth's arrival in Lichfield during the summer of 1766, Dr Darwin was away, but Polly welcomed him in the Darwin home until the Doctor's return later that evening. According to Edgeworth, "When supper was nearly finished, a loud rapping at the door announced the Doctor. There was a bustle in the hall, which made Mrs Darwin get up and go to the door. Upon her exclaiming

that they were bringing in a dead man, I went to the hall: I saw some persons, directed by one whom I guessed to be Doctor Darwin, carrying a man who appeared motionless. 'He is not dead', said Doctor Darwin. 'He is only dead drunk. I found him', continued the Doctor, 'nearly suffocated in a ditch; I had him lifted into my carriage, and brought hither, that we might take care of him to-night'. Candles came, and what was the surprise of the Doctor, and of Mrs Darwin, to find that the person whom he had saved was Mrs Darwin's brother! Who, for the first time in his life, as I was assured, had been intoxicated in this manner, and who would undoubtedly have perished, had it not been for Doctor Darwin's humanity", *Memoirs of Edgeworth*, Vol. 1, pp. 162–164. Dr Darwin applied the accolade upon his Lunar friend, the "very ingenious Mechanic Philosopher, Mr Edgeworth". (*Loves of the Plants*, III, line 131, note).

33 Thomas Day (1748–1789).

34 Thomas's father, also Thomas Day (*c*.1690–1749), died when his son was but a year old. As Deputy Collector Outwards of the Customs of the Port of London, Thomas, Sr, left his son significant financial backing upon his death. The younger Thomas inherited a considerable amount of stock in the Eddystone and Portland lighthouses as well as receiving his father's estate, Barehill, Berkshire, close to Edgeworth's Hare Hatch in Wargrave, Berkshire.

35 Slightly modified from Milton, *Paradise Lost*, Book II, lines 562–564.

36 John Laurens Bicknell (1746–1787) wrote the original poem, *The Dying Negro*, and Day expanded and revised this poem, borrowing much from Michel Adanson's (1727–1806) *A Voyage to Senegal, The Isle of Goree, and The River Gambia* (London: J. Nourse and W. Johnston, 1759), turning the Bicknell/Day work into what became an "immensely popular" version, *The Dying Negro, a Poetical Epistle, Supposed to be Written by a Black, (Who Lately Shot Himself on Board a Vessel in the River Thames) to His Intended Wife* (London: W. Flexney, 1773). For further comment, see P. Rowland, *Life of Thomas Day*, p.57. In *The Devoted Legions: A Poem Addressed to Lord George Germain and the Commanders of the Forces Against America* (London: J. Ridley and G. Kearsly, 1776), as well as in *The Desolation of America: A Poem* (London: Kearsly, Richardson, Urquhart, and Flexney, 1777), Day's sympathy for the oppression felt by the American colonists was clearly displayed. Day delivered similar arguments for reaching an early peace with the revolutionaries in his 1780 arguments in Parliament. *Sandford and Merton: A Work Intended for the Use of Children* (London: J. Stockdale, 1783–1789), a work prompted by *Practical Education: Or, The History of Harry and Lucy* (Lichfield: J. Jackson, 1780), which was begun by Richard and Honora Edgeworth, and to which Maria later contributed, has become Day's most enduring work. Under a heavy influence of Jean-Jacques Rousseau (1712–1778), this work depicts the wholesome education story of the rich and noble, though spoiled, Tommy Merton and his poor but virtuous friend, Harry Sandford. Through a series of events, the boys' tutor, together with Sandford, teach Merton the true value of labour as well as the evils of the idle rich.

37 It was actually the second revised edition that appeared in 1774 which Day dedicated to Rousseau.

38 August 1770.

39 Sir John Hampden (*c*.1595–1643), an English Parliamentarian from Buckinghamshire viewed by many as a central figure at the start of the English Civil War (1642), was always ready to use his persuasive tactics to defend Parliament's rights and privileges. Peter Rowland (*The Life of Thomas* Day, p.27) notes that "on this point we can see for ourselves that she was mistaken", as no such inscription appears on the known portrait. However, Wright produced two versions of this portrait, one of which, as well as preliminary sketches, may have included the inscription.

40 Coastal communities had long been called upon to provide ships to defend the realm. If they had no ships, Charles I (1600–1649) argued that "ship money" should be collected. In 1635, Charles I demanded "ship money" from all English counties. In the Midlands, many landowners viewed this request as an arbitrary, non-Parliamentary tax. Hampden refused to pay, and The King brought a case against him in 1637/8. Hampden offered a notable oration and, despite Charles's judicial victory, considerable opposition was raised in support of Hampden.

41 Wright painted Darwin in 1770 and again in 1792–93. Darwin's eight lines of admiration to Wright, which first appeared in *The Loves of the Plants*, II, lines 175–182, were reprinted in Robert Simpson, *A Collection of Fragments Illustrative of the History and Antiquities of Derby* (Derby: G. Wilkins and Sons, 1826), Vol.1, p.679. This tribute to Wright's volcanic, landscape, and moonlight painting is as follows:

> So Wright's bold pencil from Vesuvio's height
>
> Hurls his red lavas to the troubled night;
>
> From Calpè starts the intolerable flash,
>
> Skies burst in flames, and blazing oceans dash;
>
> Or bids in sweet repose his shades recede,
>
> Winds the still vale, and slopes the velvet mead;
>
> On the pale stream expiring Zephyrs sink,
>
> And Moonlight sleeps upon its hoary brink.

42 William Seward (1747–1799), unrelated to Anna, was educated at Oriel College, Oxford. He became a friend of Samuel Johnson and of Thomas Day, whom he met at Oxford. Seward was later a guest of Day's at Stowe House, Lichfield (P. Rowland, *Life of Day*, p.26).

43 *Anecdotes of Some Distinguished Persons, Chiefly of the Present and Two Preceding Centuries* (London: Cadell and Davies, 1795–96), and its one volume *Supplement* (London: Cadell and Davies, 1797). No members of the Lunar Society were included in this work nor was William Seward's style of life-story writing something that Anna desired to emulate.

44 Mr Fairfax Moresby occupied Stowe House from *c*.1793–1817. Day leased it from the previous owner, Mrs Elizabeth Aston (1708–1785), during his stay there in 1770/71.

45 Milton, "Lycidas: A Lament for a Friend Drowned in his Passage from Chester on the Irish Seas, 1637", 1.14. Dr Small died on 25 February, reputedly of ague (recurrent fever, perhaps malaria). His lead-lined coffin was placed in St Philip's Cathedral Churchyard, Birmingham, on 15 March by his friends who could not agree on a suitable monument for him. The coffin was buried under the floor in 1970 when the crypt was converted into meetings rooms. A memorial stone set in the cathedral floor marks the spot, beneath which, he is buried.

46 At his Soho House residence. This vase remained there through the 1940s, though its whereabouts are unknown since that time.

47 Darwin's epitaph for Small was also cited in Muirhead, *The Origin and Progress of the Mechanical Inventions of James Watt*, Vol.1, pp.clvi–clviii.

48 A slightly altered version appeared in *A New and General Biographical Dictionary: Containing an Historical and Critical Account of the Lives and Writings of the Most Eminent Persons in Every Nation; Particularly the British and Irish*, New Ed, Vol.4 (London: G.G. and J. Robinson, J. Johnson, J. Nichols, J. Sewell, H.L. Gardner [and 23 others], 1798), p.528. Here, line 4 reads, "Were centred in a dark and gloomy grave"; line 6, "glimmering" instead of "glimmer"; line 7, "unsullied" instead of "unspotted"; line 9, "dear" instead of "lov'd"; and "sad" instead of "pale"; line 10, "feel" instead of "meet".

49 Samuel Johnson, "An Essay on Epitaphs", *Gentleman's Magazine*, X (Nov. 1740): 593–6.

50 Matthew Prior, "Protogenes and Apelles" (1781), II. 95–102.

51 At the time, the only available biographical work on Day in English *(Figure 16)* was that of Fellow Lunar Society member, James Keir, *Life and Writings of Thomas Day* (1791).

52 Thomas Day, his father, died in 1749.

53 His mother, Jane Bonham Day (*c*.1728–1796), married Thomas Phillips (*d*.1781) in 1754. Phillips had been a friend of her husband, Thomas, and had served as a Trustee of his will (P. Rowland, *Life of Day*, p.9).

54 The Greek god of the North Wind.

55 The poetic personification of a nightingale. In his *Odyssey*, Homer makes reference to Philomela, an unfortunate woman whom Zeus transformed into a nightingale out of pity for her sad plight.

56 According to Marion Roberts, Laura may be Thomas Day's reference to Honora Sneyd, whom he loved but lost to Richard Lovell Edgeworth. Kate Iles adds that Day may have been referring to Margaret Edgeworth, Richard Lovell's sister, to whom this Elegy was reputedly written and who, for a short time, was the object of Day's affection (Personal communication).

57 "Elegy on a Young Lady", in *Select Miscellaneous Productions, of Mrs Day, and Thomas Day, Esq., in Verse and Prose: Also, Some Detached Pieces of Poetry By Esther Milnes Day, Esther Day, Thomas Day, Thomas Lowndes* (London: T. Jones, 1805), pp. 14–18. As Kate Iles suggests, "Seward would have known of the poem before its publication here, if this is indeed the first time it appeared in print" (Personal communication).

58 Day's ideas of female education stemmed from Rousseau. Specifically, it was the education of Sophie in Rousseau's *Emilius and Sophie; or, An Essay on Education* (London: J. Nourse and P. Vaillant, 1763) that he viewed as the model educational experience through which he hoped to nurture a girl into his own wife.

59 Aglaia, Thalia, and Euphrosyne were the Roman Graces, or goddesses, who served as attendants upon Venus and the nine Muses.

60 John Laurens Bicknell (1746–1787), the second son of Robert (d. 1781), barrister, author, and admirer of Rousseau. Together with Day, Bicknell worked to put Rousseau's doctrines on education into practice.

61 In 1758, the Shrewsbury Foundling Hospital was opened as a branch of the Foundling Hospital in London once the London facility could no longer accommodate the increasing number of foundling children. Later, these premises were leased to His Majesty's Commissioners for Taking Care of Sick and Wounded Seamen and for Exchange of Prisoners of War, then becoming the House of Industry. Since 1882, it has served as the central building of the famed Shrewsbury School, where Charles Darwin, the naturalist, studied, albeit in a different building.

62 The girl that Day named Sabrina (1757–1843) was taken on as a pseudo-apprentice to Day and an official ward of Edgeworth from the Shrewsbury Foundling Hospital. Lucretia (b. 1758), taken under similar arrangements from the Thomas Coram's (1668–1751) Foundling Hospital in London was given a name indicative of Day's love of classical heroines.

63 Day gave this young girl the name Sabrina Sidney; Sabrina, the poetical Latinate name for the River Severn that flows through Shrewsbury, and Sidney after his hero, Algernon Sidney (1622–1683).

64 Although initially intending to go as far as Africa, they remained in France where they spent considerable time in Avignon and Lyon. While in France, they visited Rousseau in 1771.

65 On Ludgate Hill, London.

66 Sarah Campbell Bicknell (1717–1806), of the Clan of the Breadalbane Scots.

67 Arria was a virtuous, heroic woman in Ancient Rome whose husband had been ordered by the Emperor to commit suicide. Initially unable to do so, Arria grabbed her husband's dagger, stabbed herself, and then handed it back to her husband claiming, "It does not hurt". Portia was the Stoic daughter of the Roman statesman Marcus Proclus Cato Uticensis (95–46 BC) and the wife of the Roman Senator Marcus Julius Brutus (85–42 BC) who, when she finally learned of Brutus's conspiracy against Julius Caesar, took her own life by swallowing burning coals in order to keep silent about what she knew of her husband's role in Caesar's death. Cornelia Scipionis Africana (c. 190–100 BC) was the daughter of Punic War hero, Publius Cornelius Scipio Africanus (236–183 BC) and the wife of Tiberius Sempronius Gracchus (217–164 BC). As an ideal model of Roman beauty and virtue, Cornelia, after her husband's death, declined the suitor King Ptolemy VIII Physcon in order to devote her attention toward educating her children whom she considered as her true jewels. Anna Seward wrote an "Epistle to Cornelia" which appeared in her *Poetical Works*.

68 The brothers, Tiberius Sempronius Gracchus (168–133 BC) and Gaius Gracchus (154–121 BC), were sons of Cornelia. Plutarch (46–120 AD) featured their reform efforts in his widely read *Parallel Lives*, a work translated by Dryden which was influential to Boswell's biographical thinking. Chief among these brothers' efforts were their attempts to modify agrarian laws such that lands illegally acquired should be redistributed to the poor and to limit the number of years and campaigns that a Roman soldier was obliged to serve. Their ideas, unpopular among the Senators, eventually led to their demise.

69 During 1770–1771, Day leased Stowe House.

70 Honora Sneyd (*c.*1751–1780).

71 The lasting memory of John André (1750–1780) rests primarily upon his military plights during much of the War of Independence (1775–1783).

72 Major Sneyd did not view André's background and future prospects as acceptable for his daughter. According to Sargent (*Life and Career of Major John Andre*, p.15), the "absence of present means to enable them to be provided with such a maintenance as they had each been brought up to anticipate" caused Honora's caretakers to look "coldly" upon the matter.

73 Elizabeth Sneyd (1753–1797).

74 The first Mrs Edgeworth, Anna Maria Elers Edgeworth, died in March 1773, following childbirth. While facing her own death, Honora Edgeworth urged her husband to marry her sister, Elizabeth, upon her demise. After a holiday with the Sneyds at Scarborough, Richard and Elizabeth became engaged. Although they faced considerable opposition from the Sneyds and the church, they were married on 25 December 1780. The marriage took place at St Andrew's Church, Holborn, London, for Lichfield clergy opposed this union between kindreds. Seward held a grudge against Edgeworth for the rest of her life, envisioning him, at least figuratively, as Honora's "murderer" in that he did not attend well to her illness. In a letter to The Revd. Thomas Whalley, Seward characterized Edgeworth as "the specious, the false, the cruel, the murderous Edgeworth, who cankered first and then crushed to Earth, the Finest of all human flowers". Seward to Whalley, 3 September 1791, as reprinted in *Journals and Correspondence of Thomas Sedgewick Whalley*, Vol.2, p.56. Anna Seward's "Honora, An Elegy" appeared in her *Poetical Works*, Vol.1, pp.65–67.

75 Esther Milnes (1753–1792).

76 Shakespeare, *Othello* (1604), I.iii.252.

77 William Cowper (1731–1800).

78 Milton, *Paradise Lost*, Book III, ll. 682–684.

79 Day and Milnes were married on 7 August 1778, and they moved first to Hampstead, then to a small estate at Stapleford Abbotts, near Abridge in Essex. In 1780, they moved to Anningsley in Surrey, three miles south of Chertsey, where Day bought a new estate. There, they expended considerable effort to improve the lot of the working class.

80 Day died on 28 September 1789 at Anningsley, as Uglow (*Lunar Men*, p.434) states, a "master of his own philosophy of kindness", gently taming a horse.

81 Bicknell married Sabrina in 1784.

82 John Laurens Bicknell (*c.*1785–1845), named after his father, became a solicitor, a Fellow of the Society of Antiquaries, a founder of the Westminster Bank, and a trustee of Sir John Soane's unique museum in Lincoln's Inn Fields. Henry Edgeworth Bicknell (*c.*1788–1879) became senior Registrar of the Court of Chancery.

83 George Hardinge (1743–1816), with whom Anna Seward corresponded, had been a Member of Parliament for the borough of Old Sarum and, after 1787, served as Senior Justice for the counties of Brecon, Glamorgan, and Radnor.

84 The Reverend Charles Burney (1757–1817), a classical scholar and clergyman. Kate Iles is currently pursuing work on a doctoral dissertation at the University of Birmingham under the provisional title, "Constructing the Eighteenth-Century Woman: The Life and Education of Sabrina Sidney". (Personal communication, 2008).

85 Elizabeth Edgeworth died of consumption in 1797. The fourth Mrs Edgeworth was Frances Anne Beaufort (1769–1865).

86 Richard Edgeworth (1764–1796).

87 Maria Edgeworth (1767–1849).

88 Anna Edgeworth (1772–1824) married the Clifton physician, Thomas Beddoes (1760–1808) in 1798. Beddoes treated Coleridge and many other influential Romantic thinkers. For more on Beddoes' career, see Roy Porter, *Doctor of Society: Thomas Beddoes and the Sick Trade in Late-Enlightenment England* (London: Routledge, 1992), and Trevor H. Levere, "Dr Thomas Beddoes (1760–1808) and the Lunar Society of Birmingham: Collaborations in Medicine and Science", *British Journal for Eighteenth-Century Studies* 30 (2007): 209–226.

89 Emmeline Edgeworth (1770–1847) married John King (1766–1840), the Swiss-born Johannes Koenig, in 1803.

90 Honora Edgeworth (1774–1790).

91 Lovell Edgeworth (1775–1842).

92 Elizabeth Edgeworth (1781–1805), Henry Edgeworth (1782–1813), Charlotte Edgeworth (1783–1807), Charles Sneyd Edgeworth (1786–1864), Honora Edgeworth (1792–1858), and William Edgeworth (1794–1829).

93 Francis Maria Edgeworth (1799–1848), Harriet Edgeworth (1801–1889), Sophia Edgeworth (1803–1836), Lucy Jane Edgeworth (1805–1897), and Francis Beaufort Edgeworth (1809–1846).

94 Maria Edgeworth's *(Figure 18)* prolific literary output, a few of which works were prepared in collaboration with her father, which have not been previously cited, include *Letters for Literary Ladies* (London: J. Johnson, 1795); *Practical Education* (London: J. Johnson, 1798); *A Rational Primer* (London: J. Johnson, 1799); *Castle Rackrent: An Hibernian Tale* (London: L. Hansard for J. Johnson, 1800); *Early Lessons* (London: J. Johnson, 1801); *Belinda* (London: J. Johnson, 1801); *An Essay on Irish Bulls* (London: J. Johnson, 1802); *Popular Tales* (London: J. Johnson, 1804); *The Modern Griselda: A Tale* (London: J. Johnson, 1804); *Leonora* (London: J. Johnson, 1806); *The Match Girl: A Novel* (London: J. Dennett for J. F. Hughes, 1808); *Tales of Fashionable Life* (London: J. Johnson, 1809); *Ennui; or, Memoirs of the Earl of Glenthorn* (London: J. Johnson, 1809); *The Absentee* (London: J. Johnson, 1812), *Vivian* (London: J. Johnson, 1812); *Patronage* (London: J. Johnson, 1813); *Continuation of Early Lessons* (London: J. Johnson, 1814); *Harrington: A Tale* (London: R. Hunter, 1817); *Ormond: A Tale* (London: R. Hunter, 1817); *Comic Dramas* (London: R. Hunter, 1817); *Rosamond: A Sequel to Early Lessons* (London: Hunter & Baldwin, Cradock & Joy, 1821); *Frank, A Sequel to Early Lessons* (London: R. Hunter, 1822); *Harry and Lucy Concluded: Being the Last Part of Early Lessons* (London: R. Hunter, 1825); *Little Plays for Children* (London: R. Hunter, 1827); *Garry Owen, or The Snow-Woman and Poor Bob the Chimney Sweeper* (London: J. Murray, 1832); and *Helen: A Tale* (London: Bentley, 1834). Among these writings, *Castle Rackrent* holds the enduring reputation of being the first novel written by an Irish author on an Irish theme. Many of these have been included in Marilyn Butler (ed) *The Works of Maria Edgeworth* (London: Pickering and Chatto, 2003). For an overview of the Edgeworth's devotion to education, see Alice Paterson, *The Edgeworths: A Study of Later Eighteenth Century Education* (London: WB Clive, 1914). See also Mitzi Myers' many excellent essays on Maria Edgeworth's literature, for example: "Shot from Canons; Or, Maria Edgeworth and the Cultural Production and Consumption of the Late Eighteenth-Century Woman Writer" in Ann Bermingham and John Brewer (eds) *The Consumption of Culture 1600-1800: Image, Object, Text* (London & New York: Routledge, 1995), pp.193-214; "'Like the Pictures in a Magic Lantern': Gender, History, and Edgeworth's Rebellion Narratives", *Nineteenth-Century Contexts* 19 (1996): 373-412; "Child's Play as Woman's Peace Work: Maria Edgeworth's 'The Cherry Orchard,' Historical Rebellion Narratives, and Contemporary

Cultural Studies" in Beverly Lyon Clark and Margaret R. Higonnet (eds) *Girls, Boys, Books, Toys: Gender in Children's Literature and Culture* (Baltimore: Johns Hopkins University Press, 1999), pp.25-39; "'Anecdotes from the Nursery' in Maria Edgeworth's *Practical Education* (1798): Learning from Children 'Abroad and At Home'", *Princeton University Library Chronicle* 60 (1999): 220-250; and "My Art Belongs to Daddy? Thomas Day, Maria Edgeworth, and the Pre-Texts of *Belinda*: Women Writers and Patriarchal Authority" in Paula R. Backscheider (ed) *Revising Women: Eighteenth-Century "Women's Fiction" and Social Engagement* (Baltimore: Johns Hopkins University Press, 2000), pp.104-146.

Chapter II

It is now perhaps more than time to resume the recollected circumstances of Dr Darwin's life.

After Dr Small and Mr Michell vanished from the earth, and Mr Day and Mr Edgeworth, in the year 1772, left the Darwinian sphere, the present Sir Brooke Boothby became an occasional inhabitant of Lichfield; sought, on every possibility, the conversation of Dr Darwin, and obtained his lasting friendship.[1] Sir Brooke had not less poetic fancy than Mr Day, and even more external elegance than Mr Edgeworth possessed when he won Honora's heart; elegance, which time, its general foe, has to this hour but little tarnished in the frame of Sir Brooke Boothby.

A votary to botanic science, a deep reasoner, and a clear-sighted politician, is Sir Brooke Boothby, as his convincing refutation of that splendid, dazzling, and misleading sophistry, Burke on the French Revolution, has proved.[2] Ever to be lamented is it, that national pride, and jealousy, made our efficient senate, and a large majority of people in these kingdoms, unable to discern the fallacy which Sir Brooke's answer unveiled. Fallacy, which has eventually overthrown the balance of power in Europe; built up, by the strong cement of opposition, the Republic's menacing and commanding tower, and wasted in combat with the phantom, Jacobinism, the nerves and sinews of defence against the time when real danger may assault Great Britain.

About the period at which Sir Brooke first sought Dr Darwin, sought him, also, Mr Munday [sic] of Marketon,[3] whose exertions, as a public magistrate, have through life been most benignly sedulous and wise; with whom

"The fair ey'd Virtues in retirement dwell".[4]

and whose *Needwood Forest* is one of the most beautiful local poems that has been written. Its landscapes vivid and appropriate; its episodes sweet and interesting; its machinery well fancied and original; its numbers spirited, correct, and harmonious; while an infusion of sweet and gentle morality pervades the whole, and renders it dear to the heart as to the eye and ear. Great is the loss to poetic literature, that, of this delightful composition, only a few copies were privately printed, for presents to the author's friends and acquaintance; that he cannot overcome his reluctance to expose it to the danger of illiberal criticism from some of the self-elected censors in every periodical publication. The public imagines, that, on each subject discussed in a review and magazine, it obtains the joint opinion of a set of learned men, employed to appreciate the value of publications.... That in every such work many writers are engaged is true; yet is it no less true that in each separate tract the opinion is merely individual on every various theme. One person is appointed to review the medical, another the chirurgical, another the clerical, another the historical, another the philosophical articles, another the ethics in prose, and another the poetry; and each criticises singly, and unassisted, in his appointed range.

The most distinguished of Dr Darwin's scientific friends, who visited him from a distance when he lived in Lichfield, have now been enumerated.

He once thought inoculation for the measles might, as in the small-pox, materially soften the disease;[5] and, after the patriotic example of lady Mary Wortley Montague [sic],[6] he made the trial in his own family, upon his youngest son, Robert, now Dr Darwin of Shrewsbury, and upon an infant daughter,[7] who died within her first year. Each had, in consequence, the disease so severely, as to repel, in their father's mind, all future desire of repeating the experiment.

In the year 1768, Dr Darwin met with an accident of irretrievable injury in the human frame. His propensity to mechanics had unfortunately led him to construct a very singular carriage. It was a platform, with a seat fixed upon a very high pair of wheels, and supported in the front, upon the back of the horse, by means of a kind of proboscis, which, forming an arch, reached over the hind quarters of the horse; and passed through a ring, placed on an upright piece of iron, which worked in a socket, fixed in the saddle. The horse could thus move from one side of the road to the other, quartering, as it is called, at the will of the driver, whose constant attention was necessarily employed to regulate a piece of machinery contrived, but not well contrived for that purpose.[8] From this whimsical carriage the Doctor was several times thrown, and the last time he used it, had the misfortune, from a similar accident, to break the patella of his right knee, which caused, as it always must cause, an incurable weakness in the fractured part, and a lameness, not very discernible indeed, when walking on even ground.[9]

It is remarkable, that this uncommon accident happened to three of the inhabitants of Lichfield in the course of one year; first, to the author of these memoirs in the prime of her youth; next, to Dr Darwin; and, lastly, to the late Mr Levett, a gentleman of wealth and consequence in the town.[10] No such misfortune was previously remembered in that city, nor has it once recurred through all the years which have since elapsed.

Dr Darwin was happy in the talents, docility, and obedience, of his three sons.[11] An high degree of stammering retarded and embarrassed his utterance. The eldest boy, Charles, had contracted the propensity. With that wisdom, which marked the Doctor's observations on the habits of life; with that decision of conduct, which always instantly followed the conviction of his mind, he sent Charles abroad;[12] at once to break the force of habit, formed on the contagion of daily example, and from a belief, that in the pronunciation of a foreign language, hesitation would be less likely to recur, than in speaking those words and sentences, in which he had been accustomed to hesitate. About his twelfth year he was committed to the care of the scientific, the learned, the modest, and worthy Mr Dickinson, now rector of Blimel [sic], in Shropshire.[13]

That the purpose of the experiment might not be frustrated, Dr Darwin impressed that good man's mind with the necessity of not permitting his pupil to converse in English; nor ever to hear it uttered after he could at all comprehend the French language. Charles Darwin returned to England, after a two year's residence on the continent, completely cured of stammering; with which he was not afterwards troubled; but his utterance was, from that time, somewhat thick and hurried.

Since these memoirs commenced, an odd anecdote of Dr Darwin's early residence at Lichfield was narrated to a friend of the author by a gentleman, who was of the party in which it happened. Mr Sneyd, then of Bishton,[14] and a few more gentlemen of Staffordshire, prevailed upon the Doctor to join them in an expedition by water, from Burton to Nottingham, and on to Newark. They had cold provision on board, and plenty of wine. It was midsummer; the day ardent and sultry. The noontide meal had been made, and the glass gone gayly round. It was one of those few instances, in which the medical votary of the Naiads transgressed his general and strict sobriety.[15] If not absolutely intoxicated, his spirits were in a high state of vinous exhilaration. On the boat approaching Nottingham, within the distance of a few fields, he surprised his companions by stepping, without any previous notice, from the boat into the middle of the river, and swimming to shore. They saw him get upon the bank, and walk coolly over the meadows toward the town: they called to him in vain, he did not once turn his head.

Anxious lest he should take a dangerous cold by remaining in his wet clothes, and uncertain whether or not he intended to desert the party, they rowed instantly to the town, at which they had not designed to have touched, and went in search of their river-god.

In passing through the market-place they saw him standing upon a tub, encircled by a crowd of people, and resisting the entreaties of an apothecary of the place, one of his old acquaintance,[16] who was importuning him to go to his house, and accept of other raiments till his own could be dried.

The party, on pressing through the crowd, were surprised to hear him speaking without any degree of his usual stammer.

"Have I not told you, my friend, that I had drank a considerable quantity of wine before I committed myself to the river. You know my general sobriety; and, as a professional man, you ought to know, that the unusual existence of internal stimulus, would, in its effects upon the system, counteract the external cold and moisture".[17]

Then, perceiving his companions near him, he nodded, smiled, and waved his hand, as enjoining them silence, thus, without hesitation, addressing the populace:

"Ye men of Nottingham, listen to me. You are ingenious and industrious mechanics.[18] By your industry life's comforts are procured for yourselves and families. If you lose your health, the power of being industrious will forsake you. That you know; but you may not know, that to breathe fresh and changed air constantly, is not less necessary to preserve health, than sobriety itself. Air becomes unwholesome in a few hours if the windows are shut. Open those of your sleeping-rooms whenever you quit them to go to your workshops. Keep the windows of your workshops open whenever the weather is not insupportably cold. I have no interest in giving you this advice. Remember what I, your countryman, and a physician, tell you. If you would not bring infection and disease upon yourselves, and to your wives and little ones, change the air you breathe, change it many times in a day, by opening your windows".[19]

So saying, he stept down from the tub, and returning with his party to their boat, they pursued their voyage.

Dr Johnson was several times at Lichfield, on visits to Mrs Lucy Porter his daughter-in-law, while Dr Darwin was one of its inhabitants.[20] They had one or two interviews, but never afterwards sought each other.[21] Mutual and strong dislike subsisted between them. It is curious that in Dr Johnson's various letters to Mrs Thrale, now Mrs Piozzi,[22] published by that lady after his death, many of them, at different periods, dated from Lichfield, the name of Darwin cannot be found; nor indeed, that of any of the ingenious and lettered people who lived there; while of its mere common-life characters there is frequent mention, with many hints of Lichfield's intellectual barrenness, while it could boast a Darwin, and other men of classical learning, poetic talents, and liberal information. Of that number was the Revd. Thomas Seward Canon-Residentiary of its Cathedral; known to the lettered world as critical editor of *Beaumont and Fletcher's Plays*, in concert with Mr Simpson.[23] Their edition came out in the year 1750.[24] By people of literary taste and judgment, it is allowed to be the best commentary on those dramatic poets which has appeared; and that from the lucid ability of Mr Seward's readings and notes. Strange, that dramas, so entirely of the Shakespearian school, in the business and interest of their plots; in the strength and variety of their characters; and which, in their sentiments and language, possess so much of Shakespeare's fire, should be coldly and stupidly neglected in the present day, which has not yet forgotten to proclaim the Bard of Avon to be, what he surely is, the first poet the world has produced. Shakespeare has had few more spirited eulogists than Mr Seward, in the following lines, written about the year 1740, and published, together with other little poems of his, in Dodsley's *Miscellany*.[25]

> Great Homer's birth seven rival cities claim,
> Too mighty such monopoly of fame!
> Yet not to birth alone did Homer owe
> His wond'rous worth, what Egypt could bestow,
> With all the schools of Greece, and Asia join'd,
> Enlarg'd th' immense expansion of his mind.
> Nor yet unrivall'd the Meonian [26] strain,
> The British Eagle and the Mantuan Swan
> Tower equal heights; but happier, Stratford, thou
> With uncontested laurels deck thy brow!
> Thy Bard was thine unschool'd, and from thee brought
> More than all Egypt, Greece, or Asia taught;
> Not Homer's self such peerless honours won,
> The Greek has rivals, but thy Shakespeare none!

In the later editions of Dodsley's *Miscellany*, the word *Swan*, in the fourth couplet, is most absurdly changed to *Swain*, because it chimed more completely to the foregoing rhyme, *Strain*, at the expense of everything like sense and accuracy in the apposite terms; at the expense of making a bird and a man fly equal heights ere balloons were dreamed of. Mr Seward was often heard to laugh at this instance of editorial presumption and stupidity.[27]

Another of the Lichfield literati, overlooked by the arrogant Johnson, was the Reverend Arch-Deacon Vyse, the amiable the excellent father of the present ingenious Dr Vyse of Lambeth, and his gallant brother General Vyse.[28] Mr Vyse was not only a man of learning, but of Prioric talents in the metrical impromptu.[29] Gentle reader, behold an instance! and if thou hatest not rhyme, as does many an ungentle reader, "worse than toad or asp", thou wilt not think it intrusive.

Mrs Vyse,[30] herself a beautiful woman, had a fair friend whose name was Charlotte Lynes.[31] At a convivial meeting of Lichfield gentlemen, most of whom could make agreeable verses, it was proposed that every person in company should give a ballad or epigram on the lady whose health he drank. Mr Vyse toasted Miss Lynes, and, taking out his pencil, wrote the following stanzas extempore.

> Shall Pope sing his flames
> With quality dames,
> And duchesses toast when he dines;
> Shall Swift verses compose
> On the Girl at the Rose,
> While unsung is my fair Charlotte Lynes?

> O! were Phoebus [32] my friend,
> Or would Bacchus [33] but lend
> The spirit that flows from his vines,
> The lass of the mill,
> Molly Mogg, and Lepell,[34]
> Should be dowdies to fair Charlotte Lynes.

> Any porter may serve,
> For a copy, to carve
> An Alcides,[35] with muscular chines [sic];
> But a Venus to draw,
> Bright as sun ever saw,
> Let him copy my fair Charlotte Lynes.

> In the midst of gay sights,
> And foreign delights,
> For his country the banish'd man pines;
> Thus, from her when away,
> Though my glances may stray,
> Yet my heart is with fair Charlotte Lynes.

> It is Atropus' sport,[36]
> With her sheers to cut short
> The thread, which dame Lachesis [37] twines;
> But forbear, you curst jade,
> Or cut mine, not the thread
> That was spun for my fair Charlotte Lynes!

For quadrille when the fair
Cards and counters prepare
They cast out the tens, eights, and nines,
And in love 'tis my fear
The like fate I shall share,
Discarded by fair Charlotte Lynes.

With hearts full of rapture
Our good dean and chapter
Count over, and finger their fines;
But I'd give their estate,
Were it ten times as great,
For one kiss of my fair Charlotte Lynes.

The young pair, for a crown,
On the book laid him down,
The sacrist obsequiously joins,
Were I bishop I swear
I'd resign him my chair,
To unite me with fair Charlotte Lynes.

For my first night I'd go
To those regions of snow,
Where the sun, for six months, never shines,
And O! there should complain
He too soon came again
To disturb me with fair Charlotte Lynes![38]

These verses were much read, admired, and copied. Mr Vyse thought his fair Charlotte growing too vain in consequence, and once, when she was complimented on the subject in a large company, he said smilingly,

"Charlotte the power of song can tell,
For 'twas the ballad made the belle".

The late Reverend William Robinson[39] was also a choice spirit amongst those Lichfieldians, whose talents illuminated the little city at that period. Too indolent for authorism, he was, by wit and learning, fully empowered to have shone in that sphere. More of him hereafter.

These were the men whose intellectual existence passed unnoticed by Dr Johnson in his depreciating estimate of Lichfield talents. But Johnson liked only worshippers. Arch-deacon Vyse, Mr Seward, and Mr Robinson,[40] paid all the respect and attention to Dr Johnson, on these his visits to their town, due to his great abilities, his high reputation, and to whatever was estimable in his mixed character; but they were not in the herd that "paged his heels", and sunk, in servile silence, under the force of his dogmas, when their hearts and their judgments bore contrary testimony.

Certainly, however, it was an arduous hazard to the feelings of the company to oppose, in the slightest degree, Dr Johnson's opinions. His stentor lungs; that combination of wit, humour, and eloquence, which "could make the worse appear the better reason"; that sarcastic contempt of his antagonist, never suppressed or even softened by the due restraints of good-breeding, were sufficient to close the lips, in his presence, of men, who could have met him in fair argument, on any ground, literary or political, moral or characteristic.

Where Dr Johnson was, Dr Darwin had no chance of being heard, though at least his equal in genius, his superior in science; nor indeed, from his impeded utterance, in the company of any overbearing declaimer; and he was too intellectually great to be an humble listener to Johnson, therefore he shunned him, on having experienced what manner of man he was. The surly dictator felt the mortification, and revenged it, by affecting to avow his disdain of powers too distinguished to be an object of genuine scorn.

Dr Darwin, in his turn, was not much more just to Dr Johnson's genius. He uniformly spoke of him in terms, which, had they been deserved, would have justified Churchill's [41] "immane Pomposo", as an appellation of scorn; since, if his person was huge, and his manners pompous and violent, so were his talents vast and powerful, in a degree from which only prejudice and resentment could withhold respect.

Though Dr Darwin's hesitation in speaking precluded his flow of colloquial eloquence, it did not impede, or at all lessen, the force of that concise quality, wit. Of satiric wit he possessed a very peculiar species. It was neither the dead-doing broadside of Dr Johnson's satire, nor the aurora borealis of Gray,[42] whose arch, yet coy and quiet fastidiousness of taste and feeling, as recorded by Mason,[43] glanced bright and cold through his conversation, while it seemed difficult to define its nature; and while its effects were rather perceived than felt, exciting surprise more than mirth, and never awakening the pained sense of being the object of its ridicule. That unique and humorous verse, the *Long Story*, is a complete and beautiful specimen of Gray's singular vein.

Darwinian wit is not more easy to be defined; instances will best convey an idea of its character to those who never conversed with its possessor. To give such as are recollected at this moment, it will be necessary to recall Mr Robinson, already mentioned as a choice spirit of Lichfield. His perpetual stream of frolic raillery was of a species so singular, as to have exclusively obtained, wherever he was known, the title of rector, "The Rector", as if there were no other. The odd excursions of his fancy were enriched by an exhaustless store of classic, historic, and theological learning, grotesquely applied to the passing subjects of conversation, and that with unrivalled ease and happiness. It is to be regretted that no records remain of talents so uncommon, except in the fading traces of contemporary recollection, which time and mortality obliterate so soon. ... Frequently, during his youth and middle life, in the fashionable circles of Bath, London, and the summer public places, the whimsical sallies of the Rector's sportive imagination, which were never coarse or low, common place or ill-natured, had considerable publicity and éclat. They were like the lambent lightning of a calm summer evening, brilliant, but not dangerous. The sweetness of his temper was the security of every man's self-love; and, while his humorous gayety "set the table in a roar", the company laughed at their ease.

But then good-nature was the only curb his wit could endure. Without the slightest taint of infidelity, Robinson could not resist the temptation of lancing it even at the most serious objects and themes.

One evening, when he and Dr Darwin were in company together, the Rector had, as usual, thrown the bridle upon the neck of his fancy, and it was scampering over the church-yard, and into the chancel, when the Doctor exclaimed ... "Excellent! Mr Robinson is not only a clever fellow, but a d...d clever fellow".[44]

Soon after the subject of common swearing was introduced, Mr R. made a mock eulogium upon its power to animate dullness, and to season wit .... Dr Darwin observed, "Christ says, Swear not at all. St Paul tells us we may swear occasionally. Mr Robinson advises us to swear incessantly. Let us compromise between these counsellors, and swear by non-en-ti-ties. I will swear by my im-pu-dence, and Mr Robinson by his mo-dest-y".

That gentleman, whose wit, where it met no equal resistance, kept an untired and sparkling course, could seldom recover its track when the jest and the laugh were with his adversary. So often was it thus when Dr Darwin and he met, that Mr R. rather shunned than sought the rencounter. It was curious, that he, who met indulgence from his clerical and pious brethren for those frolic emanations, wont to play upon the themes his heart revered, should so often find himself reproved, with cutting raillery, for the practice, by one not famous for holding religious subjects in veneration.

Dr Darwin was conversing with a brother Botanist, concerning the plant *Kalmia*, then just an imported stranger in our green-houses and gardens.[45] A lady, who was present, concluding he had seen it, which in fact he had not, asked the Doctor what were the colours of the plant. He replied, "Madam, the *Kalmia* has precisely the colours of a seraph's wing". So fancifully did he express his want of consciousness respecting the appearance of a flower whose name and rareness were all he knew of the matter.

Dr Darwin had a large company at tea. His servant announced a stranger lady and gentleman. The female was a conspicuous figure, ruddy, corpulent, and tall. She held by the arm a little, meek-looking, pale, effeminate man, who, from his close adherence to the side of the lady, seemed to consider himself as under her protection.

"Dr Darwin, I seek you not as a physician, but as a *Belle Esprit*. I make this husband of mine", and she looked down with a sideglance upon the animal, "treat me every summer with a tour through one of the British counties, to explore whatever it contains worth the attention of ingenious people. On arriving at the several inns in our route, I always search out the man of the vicinity most distinguished for his genius and taste, and introduce myself, that he may direct, as the objects of our examination, whatever is curious in nature, art, or science. Lichfield will be our headquarters during several days. Come, Doctor, whither must we go, what must we investigate to-morrow, and the next day, and the next? here are my tablets and pencil".[46]

"You arrive, madam, at a fortunate juncture. To-morrow you will have an opportunity of surveying an annual exhibition perfectly worth your attention. To-morrow, madam, you will go to Tutbury bull-running".

The satiric laugh with which he stammered out the last word, more keenly pointed this sly, yet broad rebuke to the vanity and arrogance of her speech. She had been up amongst the boughs, and little expected they would break under her so suddenly, and with so little mercy. Her large features swelled, and her eyes flashed with anger .... I "was recommended to a man of genius, and I find him insolent and ill-bred".... Then, gathering up her meek and alarmed husband, whom she had loosed when she first spoke, under the shadow of her broad arm and shoulder, she strutted out of the room.

After the departure of this curious couple, his guests told their host he had been very unmerciful. I chose, replied he, to avenge the cause of the little man, whose nothingness was so ostentatiously displayed by his lady-wife. Her vanity has had a smart emetic. If it abates the symptoms, she will have reason to thank her physician who administered without hope of a fee.

Notes

1   Sir Brooke Boothby (1744–1824), 6th Baronet of Broadlow, lived at Ashbourne Hall, Derbyshire.

2   Boothby responded to Edmund Burke's (1729-1797) pro-aristocracy *Reflections on the Revolution in France* (1790) with his *A Letter to the Right Honourable Edmund Burke* (London: J. Debrett, 1790), thereby joining many other radical writers in "the pamphlet war".

3   Francis Noel Clarke Mundy (1739–1815).

4   Possibly drawn from Nahum Tate (1652–1715), "A Pastoral Dialogue" (1691), l. 10: "The chast [sic] delights that in retirement dwell".

5   Dr Darwin advocated for smallpox vaccination in *Zoonomia* and in the *Temple of Nature*. He also wrote to Edward Jenner on 24 February 1802, claiming that Jenner's "discovery of preventing this dreadful havoc made among mankind by smallpox ... may in time eradicate the smallpox from all civilized countries", as cited by King-Hele in *Doctor of Revolution*, p, 284.

6   Lady Mary Wortley Montagu (1689–1762).

7   Elizabeth Darwin (1763–1764).

8   Desmond King-Hele discussed Dr Darwin's carriages in "Erasmus Darwin's Improved Design for Steering Carriages – and Cars", *Notes and Records of the Royal Society of London* 56 (2002): 41–62, and in "Designing Better Steering for Carriages (and Cars); with a Glance at Other Inventions", in Smith and Arnott (eds) *Genius of Erasmus Darwin*, pp.197–216.

9   Curiously, it was during this same year that Anna Seward also broke her patella. These injuries, accidents that Seward claims later in her *Life of Dr Darwin*, were "irretrievable to the human frame", troubled them physically for the rest of their respective lives. At the time however, they may also have been mentally troubled about the maintenance of these injuries, for this was the year that Lunar Man, Josiah Wedgwood (1730–1795) had his leg amputated. Dr Darwin attended this operation which the Newcastle surgeon, Mr James Bent (1739–1812) performed. For further discussion of Wedgwood's health, see E. Posner, "Josiah Wedgwood's Doctors", *Pharmaceutical Historian* 3, no. 1 (1973):6–8, and 3, no. 2 (1973): 2–5. Accidents were common during this period, as Roy Porter discussed in "Accidents in the Eighteenth Century", in Roger Cooter and Bill Luckin (eds) *Accidents in History: Injuries, Fatalities and Social Relations* (Amsterdam and Atlanta, GA: Rodopi, 1997), pp.90–106.

10   John Levett (1721–1799).

11   Charles, Erasmus, Jr., and Robert.

12   Charles left Lichfield in October 1766, returning the next autumn.

13   While in France, Charles was accompanied by a tutor, The Reverend Samuel Dickenson (1733–1823), whom Erasmus had known at St John's College, Cambridge. Dickenson later served as Rector of Blymhill in southern Staffordshire, on the Shropshire border, for forty-six years, beginning in 1777. Dickenson's obituary in *Gentleman's Magazine* 1 (1823): 650, notes his invaluable assistance to Reverend Stebbing Shaw's (1762–1802) completion of *The History and Antiquities of Staffordshire* (London: J. Nichols and Son, 1798, 1801), not only for his antiquarian knowledge of the area, but also for his "catalogue of plants found in the county". Shaw's work also included an article by Lunar Man James Keir on "Mineralogy". For an overview of Shaw's contributions, see M.W. Greenslade and G.C. Baugh, "Stebbing Shaw and the History of Staffordshire", in M.W. Greenslade (ed) *Essays in Staffordshire History, Presented to S.A.H. Burne*. Collections for a History of Staffordshire, 4th ser., vol.6 (Stafford: Staffordshire Record Society, 1970), pp.224–254.

14   Ralph Sneyd (1723–1793), of Bishton, in Staffordshire, near Stone on the Lichfield Road.

15   Naiads were the nymphs of classical mythology that lived in, and thus gave life to, bodies of water.

16   Dr Darwin had initially set up a short-lived medical practice in Nottingham in 1756, prior to moving to Lichfield that same year.

17   DAR.227.7:44 (Archives: Cambridge University Library). This scene was quite unbecoming of Dr Darwin who, as a matter of habit, regularly abstained from alcoholic drink.

18   Nottingham was a major industrial centre known particularly for the production of cotton hosiery.

19   According to Desmond King-Hele, Seward likely "heard about this speech from an elderly Lichfield man who was on the boat". (Personal communication, 19 August 2008).

20   As background to the family connections, Elizabeth Hunter (*d.*1768), Mrs Elizabeth Seward's stepmother, was the wife of the Reverend John Hunter (*c.*1674–1741), Headmaster of Lichfield's Free Grammar School. Mrs Hunter was the sister of Harry Porter (*d.*1734). After Henry died, his widow, Elizabeth "Tetty" Jervis Porter (1689–1752), married Samuel Johnson, who received her daughter, Lucy Porter (1715–1786), as his step-daughter. Anna Seward's sister, Sarah, (1744–1764), called Sally, was betrothed to Lucy's brother, Joseph Porter (*c.*1724–1783), at the time of her death. For more information of these relations, see Sir R. White-Thomson, "Anna Seward's Relationship to Johnson", *Johnson Society Transactions* 1 (1910):3–30. Seward's "Visions, An Elegy [for her sister, Sarah]" appeared in her *Poetical Works*, Vol.1, 1–9.

21   According to King-Hele (*Doctor of Revolution*, p.73), their first meeting most likely took place in Lichfield when Johnson spent time in the city of his birth from July to October 1767.

22   Hester Lynch Thrale [Piozzi] (1740–1821), *Letters To and From the Late Samuel Johnson* (London: 1788).

23   Thomas Seward (1708–1790).

24   Lewis Theobald (1688–1744), Thomas Seward and J. Sympson (of Gainsborough), *The Works of Mr Francis Beaumont [1584–1616] and Mr John Fletcher [1579–1625], In Ten Volumes. Collated with all the Former Editions and Corrected.* (London: J. and R. Tonson and S. Draper, 1750).

25   Robert Dodsley (1703–1764), bookseller and author.

26   Likely drawn from Samuel Johnson's *The Rambler*, No. 158 (21 September 1751), though possibly borrowed from Virgil's *Aneid* (LXVI), "An aged seer thus warns them to refrain, Expounding Fate: Choice youths, the flower and show Of ancient warriors of Meonian strain, Whom just resentment arms against the foe, Whose souls with hatred of Mezentius glow, No man of Italy is fit to lead So vast a multitude, the Fates say 'No'".

27   Seward's own footnote, "This gentleman was father of the writer of these memoirs".

28   Seward had a great interest in the Vyse family, having been pursued by Richard Vyse (1746–1824), later General, in the mid 1760s.

29   In the manner of the poet Matthew Prior. Seward noted that The Reverend William Vyse was known for "Epigrams, and gay ballads, of exquisite spirit, [which] flowed extempore from his lips", but that he "declined

publishing them" (Seward, *Poetical Works*, Vol.2, p.337, note 1.) It seems that clergy seldom published their lighter writings and verse thinking, as Mary Alden Hopkins maintains, that doing so would "detract from their dignity" (*Dr Johnson's Lichfield*, p.50).

30   Catherine Smallbrooke Vyse (*c.*1715–1790).

31   Although Lynes's identity remains somewhat puzzling, Mary Alden Hopkins described Charlotte Lynes as a "very beautiful woman who was visiting" Mrs William Vyse (*Dr Johnson's Lichfield*, p.49).

32   Phoebus is Apollo, the Greek and Roman god of poetry and music, and of the Sun.

33   The Greek god of Wine.

34   Mary Lepell, Lady Hervey (1706–1768), the wife of John Hervey, 2nd Baron Hervey of Ickworth (1696–1743), a court beauty, whom Alexander Pope satirized by placing her in the lyrics of a bar song as "Molly Mogg".

35   Alcides, the original name of the son of Zeus and Alcmene, better known as Hercules.

36   In Greek mythology, Atropos was one of the three Fates, the one responsible for cutting the thread of life that Clotho had spun.

37   Lachesis, the third Fate, measured the thread of life.

38   Patrick Delany, "A Song", included in *A Collection of the Most Esteemed Pieces of Poetry, That Have Appeared for Several Years* (London: Richardson and Urquhart, 1767). Delany (*c.*1686–1768), matriculated at Trinity College Dublin, served as Dean of Downpatrick, and became an intimate of Jonathan Swift (1667–1745). The version in this collection includes seven additional stanzas, but not stanzas 6 and 7. The date of this collection suggests that the poem included might have been written first by Richard Vyse, and then perhaps was "read, admired, and copied" by Delany.

39   "The Rector" referred to here is most likely William Robinson (*c.*1718–1797), a son of James Robinson of Lichfield and an Oxford alumnus who served as Rector of Swinnerton and Stoke. A later Revd. William Robinson (1777–1812), who also served as Rector of Stoke and of Swinnerton and as a Prebend of Lichfield Cathedral, was still living when Seward's *Life of Dr Darwin* was published.

40   Seward here refers to Revd. Richard George Robinson (1736–1825), Vicar of Harborne and of Barrow-upon-Trent, later served as Chancellor's Vicar of Lichfield Cathedral.

41   Charles Churchill (1731–1764).

42   Thomas Gray (1716–1771).

43   William Mason (1725–1797).

44   Untraceable.

45   *Kalmia*, a genus of 7 species of evergreen shrubs native to eastern North America, named after the Finnish botanist and student of Linnaeus, Pehr Kalm (1716–1779). Kalm's reputation grew considerably after the publication of his *Travels into North America. Containing its Natural History, and a Circumstantial Account of its Plantations and Agriculture in General … [and] the Civil, Ecclesiastical and Commercial State of the Country*, Translated by John Reinhold Forster (1729–1798) (Warrington: William Eyres, 1770–1771). Forster, who replaced Joseph Banks when he refused to sail on Cook's Second Voyage, had been a Warrington Academy tutor alongside Priestley.

46   Although the identity of this woman is unknown, those familiar with BBC television might envision a tinge of Hyacinth Bucket from Roy Clarke's sitcom, "Keeping Up Appearances" which ran between 1990–1995. Tutbury (also known as Stutebury) is a Staffordshire village on the bank of the River Dove just before it joins the River Trent, three miles from Burton, on the border of Derbyshire. In Tutbury, locals practiced an ancient barbaric tradition of "bull-running" each August at the close of the Feast of the Assumption. The Prior released a bull whose horns, ears and tail had been cut off, and which was lathered with soap and had ground pepper blown up its nose. Minstrels tried to catch the bull before it escaped across the bridge into Derbyshire. William Cavendish, 5th Duke of Devonshire (1748–1811) banned this tradition in 1788.

Chapter III

About the year 1771, commenced that great work, the *Zoonomia*, first published in 1794; the gathered wisdom of three-and-twenty years.[1] Ingenious, beyond all precedent, in its conjectures, and embracing, with giant-grasp, almost every branch of philosophic science; discovering their bearings upon each other, and those subtle, and, till then, concealed links by which they are united; and with their separate, conjunctive and collective influence upon human organization; their sometimes probable, and at others demonstrative, power, under judicious application, of restoring that regularity to the mechanism of animal life, which is comprehended under the term health.

It cannot be denied that in the pursuit of a new and favourite system, Dr Darwin has, in some instances, imperiously rejected the adverse facts which opposed his theory. His chapter on Instinct, highly ingenious as it is, affords proof of his hypothetical devotion. He there denies, at least by strong implication, the existence of that faculty so termed, and which God has given to his inferior family, in lieu of the rational. But this wonderfully ingenious philosopher seeks in vain to melt down in his system of imitation amongst brutes, the eternal boundaries which separate instinct and reason.

God, who has exempted the orders of brutal life from responsibility for their actions in this terrestrial sphere, gave them instinct, incapable of error, but also, beyond a certain very limited degree, incapable of improvement; incapable of all that are termed the artificial passions.

God, who made man accountable, and earthly life his state of trial, gave him the nobler faculty of reason, liable to err, but, in countless degrees, more connected with volition; and, according to its different degrees of native strength, almost interminably capable of improvement.

Instinct cannot be that lower degree of reason which empowers the animal to observe, and, by will and choice, to imitate the actions, and acquire the arts of his species; since, were it so, imitation would not be confined to his own particular genus, but extend to the actions, the customs, and the arts of other animals; as men observe, and emulate, the actions, customs, and arts of the natives of other countries. Thus, improvement would have advanced amongst brutes, in proportion as it has advanced in mankind. That it has not advanced in brutal life, through countless generations, we have the testimony of all records to ascertain. Therefore is it, that the instinctive faculty must be a totally different power to the rational; in as much as it has a perfection unknown to reason, and as it has an incapacity of progression which counteracts that limited perfection, and renders it a thousand fold inferior to the expanding, aspiring, and strengthening power of human intelligence. Between the separate nature of those faculties, insurmountable and everlasting are the barriers. Philosophy cannot throw them down; but in the attempt, as in many another,

"Vaulting AMBITION doth o'erleap itself,
And falls where it would mount".[2]

If the Creator had indeed given to brutal life that degree of reason, which Dr Darwin allots to it, when he asserts, that its various orders act from imitation, which must be voluntary, rather than from impulse, which is resistless, the resulting mischief of disorder and confusion amongst those classes had outweighed the aggregate good of improvement. It is reasonless, will-less instinct, limited but undeviating, which alone could have preserved, as they were in the beginning, are now, and ever shall be, the numberless divisions and subdivisions of all merely animal life. As attraction is the planetary curb of the solar system, confining all orbs to their proper spheres, so is instinct the restraint, by which brutes are withheld from incroaching upon the allotted ranges and privileges of their fellow-brutes; from losing their distinct natures in imitation, blending and endless. If imitation were the source of brutal acquirements, whence the undeviating sameness of those acquirements? whence their never extended limit? Wherefore, since the ear of the feathered warbler is open to the immense variety of strains, poured from the throat of birds of other plume, whence its invariable choice of the family song? And, when the female sees such numbers of different nests building around her for the reception of the callow brood, whence her inflexible attachment to the family nest?

Dr Darwin read his chapter on Instinct to a lady, who was in the habit of breeding canary-birds.[3] She observed that the pair, which he then saw building their nest in her cage, were a male and female, who had been hatched, and reared in that very cage, and were not in existence when the mossy cradle was fabricated, in which they first saw light. She asked him how, upon his principle of imitation, he could account for the nest he then saw building, being constructed, even to the precise disposal of every hair and shred of wool, upon the model of that, in which the pair were born, and on which every other canary-bird's nest is constructed, where the proper materials are furnished. That of the pyefinch, added she, is of much compacter form, warmer, and more comfortable. Pull one of them to pieces for its materials; place another before these canary-birds, as a pattern, and see if they will make the slightest effort to imitate their model! No, the result of their labors will, upon instinctive, hereditary impulse, be exactly the slovenly little mansion of their race; the same with that which their parents built before themselves were hatched. The Doctor could not do away the force of that single fact, with which his system was incompatible; yet he maintained that system with philosophic sturdiness, though experience brought confutation from a thousand sources.

Mr Fellowes,[4] the eminent champion in our day, of true and perfect Christianity, against the gloomy misrepresentations of the Calvinists, has not less truly than ingeniously observed, that "Dr Darwin's understanding had some of the properties of the microscope; that he looked with singularly curious and prying eyes, into the economy of plants and the habits of animals, and laid open the labyrinth of nature in some of her most elaborate processes and most subtle combinations; that he was acquainted with more links in the chain of second causes than had probably been known to any individual, who went before him; but that he dwelt so much, and so exclusively on second causes, that he too generally seems to have forgotten that there is a first".[5]

Certainly Dr Darwin's distinguished power of disclosing the arcana of nature, enabled him to explore, and detect, the fallacy of many received and long-established opinions; but the proud consciousness that his scientific wand so often possessed the power attributed by Milton to Ithuriel's spear, betrayed him at times, into systematic error.[6] Convinced, by deep thought and philosophic experience, that mankind received so many prejudices for truths, he looked too jealously at all its most revered and sacred axioms. Beneath the force of that jealousy he denied the power of instinct, and solved it into imitation. To have admitted, on the testimony of all impartial observation, all fair experiment, the unblending natures of instinct and reason, must have involved that responsibility of man to his Creator for his actions in this his state of trial, which Dr Darwin considered as a gloomy unfounded superstition. Unquestionably, if reason, like instinct, were incapable of warp from the power of volition, man could have no vice which might justly render him amenable to punishment in a future state; neither could he have any virtue for whose cultivation he might hope eternal reward. But, since his rational faculty is choice, not impulse, capable, at will, of refinement or degradation; whether it shall be his pole-star to virtue and piety, or his ignis fatuus to vice and irreligion, it inevitably follows that man is accountable to God for his conduct; that there is a future and retributory state.

If this brilliant and dazzling philosopher had not closed the lynx's eye of his understanding on that clear emanation from the source of intellectual as well as of planetary light, he had indeed been great and illuminated above the sons of men. Then had he disdained to have mingled that art in his wisdom, which was sometimes found in his common-life actions, and of which he not unfrequently boasted.

That noble simplicity which disdains the varnish of disingenuous design in principal and in conduct, in conversation and in writing, was the desideratum of Dr Darwin's strong and comprehensive mind. Its absence rendered his systems, which were so often luminous, at times impenetrably dark by paradox. Its absence rendered his poetic taste somewhat meretricious from his rage for ornament; chilled his heart against the ardour of devotion, and chained his mighty powers within the limits of second causes, though formed to soar to INFINITE.

If, however, the doctrines of the *Zoonomia* are not always infallible, it is a work which must spread the fame of its author over lands and seas, to whatever clime the sun of science has irradiated and warmed. The *Zoonomia* is an exhaustless repository of interesting facts, of curious experiments in natural productions, and in medical effects; a vast and complicated scheme of disquisition, incalculably important to the health and comforts of mankind, so far as they relate to objects merely terrestrial; throwing novel, useful, and beautiful light on the secrets of physiology, botanical, chemical, and aerological.

The world may consider the publication of the *Zoonomia* as a new era of pathologic science; the source of important advance in the power of disclosing, abating, and expelling disease.[7] Every young professor of medicine, if God has given him comprehension, assiduity, and energy, should devote his nights and days to studying this great work. It will teach him more than the pages of Galen and Hippocrates; than schools and universities know to impart.[8] Those instructions which, through the channel of its pages, flow to the world, enabled Dr Robert Darwin of Shrewsbury to attain instant eminence as a physician in that county, at his first outsetting, and in the bloom of scarcely ripened youth; to continue a course of practice, which has been the blessing of Shropshire; its sphere expanding with his growing fame. That son, who joins to a large portion of his father's science and skill, all the ingenuous kindness of his mother's heart. That son, whose rising abilities and their early éclat, recompensed to Dr Darwin a severe deprivation in the death of his eldest and darling son, Charles, of whom this memoir has already spoken. He was snatched from the world in the prime of his youth, and with the highest character at the university of Edinburgh, by a putrid fever, supposed to have been caught from dissecting, with a slightly wounded finger, a corpse in a state of dangerously advanced putrefaction.[9] When society became deprived of his luxuriantly blossoming talents, Mr Charles Darwin had recently received an honorary medal from the Society of Arts and Sciences, for having discovered a criterion by which pus may be distinguished from mucus.[10]

A few years before Dr Darwin left Lichfield as a residence he commenced a botanical society in that city.[11] It consisted of himself, Sir Brooke Boothby, then Mr Boothby, and a Proctor in the Cathedral jurisdiction, whose name was Jackson.[12] Sprung from the lowest possible origin, and wholly uneducated, that man had, by the force of literary ambition and unwearied industry, obtained admittance into the courts of the spiritual law, a profitable share of their emoluments, and had made a tolerable proficiency in the Latin and French languages. His life, which closed at sixty, was probably shortened by late acquired habits of ebriety. He passed through its course a would-be philosopher, a turgid and solemn coxcomb, whose morals were not the best, and who was vain of lancing his pointless sneers at Revealed Religion.

Jackson admired Sir Brooke Boothby, and worshipped and aped Dr Darwin. He became a useful drudge to each in their joint work, the translation of the Linnaean system of vegetation into English from the Latin.[13] His illustrious coadjutors exacted of him fidelity to the sense of their author, and they corrected Jackson's inelegant English, weeding it of its pompous coarseness.

The Doctor was probably disappointed that no recruits flocked to his botanical standard at Lichfield. The young men of the genteel classes in that city devoted themselves to professions with which natural history had no inseparable connexion [sic]. However useful, entertaining, and creditable

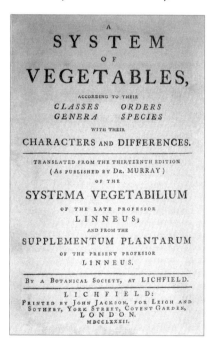

Figure 19: The Lichfield Botanical Society (consisting of Erasmus Darwin, Sir Brooke Boothby, and William Jackson) prepared this English translation of Linnaeus's Systema Vegetabilium.

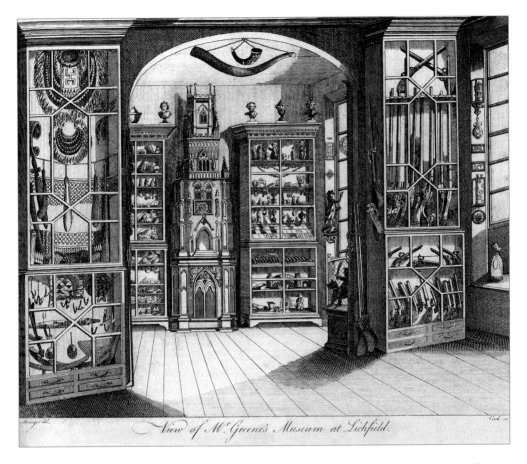

Figure 20: Richard Greene's Museum, Lichfield. Courtesy of Archives and Heritage, Birmingham Central Library.

might be its studies, they felt little desire to deck the board of session, the pulpit, or the ensigns of war, with the Linnaean wreaths and the chemical crystalines. Thus the original triumvirate received no augmentation, yet the title was maintained. Various observations, signed Lichfield Botanical Society, were sent to the periodical publications, and it was amusing to hear scientific travellers, on their transit over Lichfield, inquiring after the state of the botanical society there.

About the year 1779, at the house of his friend, Mr Sneyd of Belmont,[14] whose seat in the wild and hilly part of Staffordshire Moorlands is eminent for its boldly romantic features, Dr Darwin wrote an address to its owner, from the Naiad of that scene. Her rivulet originally took its course along the deep bottom of cradling woods, luxuriantly clothing the steeply-sloping mountains, which a rough glen, and this its brook, divided.

Mr Sneyd caused the rough and tangled glen to be cleared and hollowed into one entire basin, which the brook immediately filled with the purest and most transparent water. Only a very narrow, marginal path is left on each side, between the water and those high woody mountains which shut the liquid scene from every other earthly object. This lake covers more than five acres, yet is not more than seventy yards across at the broadest part. The length is, therefore, considerable. It gradually narrows on its flow, till suddenly, and with loud noise, it is precipitated down a craggy, darkling, and nearly perpendicular fall of forty feet. The stream then takes its natural channel, losing itself in the sombre and pathless woods which stretch far onward.

While we walk on the brink of this liquid concave; while we listen to the roar, with which the tumbling torrent passes away; while we look up, on each side, to the umbrageous eminences, which leave us only themselves, the water, and the sky, we are impressed with a sense of solemn seclusion, and might fancy ourselves in the solitudes of Tinian [15] or Juan-Fernandes.[16] The trees and shrubs which, from such great elevation, impend over the flood, give it their own green tint without lessening its transparency. Glassy smooth, this lake has not a wave till within a few yards of its precipitance. But it is time to introduce Dr Darwin's verses, already mentioned. They were written before the existence of the Lake, and while the brook, which formed it, had the silence imputed to it by the poet.

Address of a Water Nymph, at Belmont, to the Owner of that place.

O! Friend to peace and Virtue, ever flows
For thee my silent and unsullied stream,
Pure and untainted as thy blameless life!
Let no gay converse lead thy steps astray
To mix my chaste wave with immodest wine,
Nor with the poisonous cup, which Chemia's hand
Deals, fell enchantress, to the sons of folly!
So shall young Health thy daily walks attend,
Weave for thy hoary brow the vernal flower
Of cheerfulness, and with his nervous arm
Arrest th' inexorable scythe of Time.[17]

The exhortation was not disobeyed; the benediction was not fruitless. Mr Sneyd still lives to exhilarate the spirits of his friends, and to be the blessing of his neighbourhood. The duties of a public magistrate, exerted with energy, and tempered with kindness; the hospitality of his social mansion; his pursuit of natural history, and taste for the arts, are unlessened by time, and no corporal infirmity allays their enjoyment. After a lapse of seventy years he passes several hours every day, in all seasons when the weather is dry, in the open air, forming for his scenes new plans of cultivation and ornament. Look at Mr Sneyd, ye young men of fortune, and reflect upon the robust and happy consequence of youthful sobriety, of religion, morality, and a cultivated mind!

"The age of such is as a lusty winter,
Frosty, but kindly".[18]

In the spring of the year 1778 the children of Colonel and Mrs Pole of Radburn,[19] in Derbyshire, had been injured by a dangerous quantity of the cicuta,[20] injudiciously administered to them in the hooping-cough, by a physician of the neighbourhood. Mrs Pole brought them to the house of Dr Darwin, in Lichfield, remaining with them there a few weeks, till, by his art, the poison was expelled from their constitutions, and their health restored.

Mrs Pole was then in the full bloom of her youth and beauty. Agreeable features; the glow of health; a fascinating smile; a fine form, tall and graceful; playful sprightliness of manners; a benevolent heart, and maternal affection, in all its unwearied cares and touching tenderness, contributed to inspire Dr Darwin's admiration, and to secure his esteem. Soon after she left Lichfield, with her renovated little ones, their restorer sent to his friend, Mr Bolton of Birmingham,[21] the following directions for making a tea-vase, designed as a present from the Doctor to Mrs Pole.

Friend Bolton, take these ingots fine
From rich Potosi's sparkling mine;[22]
With your nice art a tea-vase mould,
Your art, more valu'd than the gold.

With orient pearl, in letters white,
Around it, "To the Fairest", write;
And, where proud Radburn's turrets rise,
To bright Eliza [23] send the prize.

I'll have no bending serpents kiss
The foaming wave, and seem to hiss;
No sprawling dragons gape with ire,
And snort out steam, and vomit fire;
No Naiads weep; no sphinxes stare;
No tail-hung dolphins swim in air.

Let leaves of myrtle round the rim,
With rose-buds twisting, shade the brim;
Each side let woodbine stalks descend,
And form the branches as they bend;
While on the foot a Cupid stands
And twines the wreath with both his hands.
Perch'd on the rising lid above,
O place a lovelorn, turtle dove,
With hanging wing, and ruffled plume,
With gasping [24] beak, and eye of gloom.

Last, let the swelling bosses shine
With silver, white, and burnish'd fine,
Bright as the fount, whose banks beside
Narcissus [25] gaz'd, and lov'd, and died.

Vase, when Eliza deigns to pour,
With snowy hand, thy boiling shower;
And sweetly talks, and smiles, and sips
The fragrant steam,[26] with ruby lips,
More charms thy polish'd orb shall shew
Than Titian's glowing pencil drew;
More than his chisel soft unfurl'd,
Whose heav'n-wrought statue charms the world.[27]

Soon after the composition of these gallant verses to Mrs Pole, circumstances arose which gave rise to the following ode, not less beautiful, though much less gay.

Fly, gentle steeds![28] O'er yon unfriendly towers
Malignant stars, with baleful influence reign;
Cold Beauty's frown infects [29] the cheerless hours,
And Avarice dwells in Love's polluted fane!

Dim, distant towers! whose ample roof protects
All that my beating bosom holds so dear,
Far shining lake! whose silver wave reflects
Of Nature's fairest forms, the form most fair;

Groves, where at noon the sleeping Beauty lies;
Lawns, where at eve her graceful footsteps rove;
For ye full oft have heard my secret sighs,
And caught unseen, the tear of hopeless love;

Farewell! a long farewell! Your shades among
No more these eyes shall drink Eliza's charms:
No more these ears the music of her tongue!
O! doom'd for ever to another's arms!

Fly, gentle steeds! My bleeding heart convey
Where brighter scenes [30] and milder planets shine;
Where Joy's white pinion glitters in the ray,[31]
And Love sits smiling on his crystal [32] shrine![33]

About the summer 1778 the Countess of Northesk rested at one of the inns in Lichfield, on her way to Scotland by the shortest possible stages.[34] She had been a year in England, for the benefit of her health, wasting rapidly by hemorrhage. Ineffectually had the most eminent physicians of London and Bath endeavoured to check the progress of her disease. Her youngest daughter, Lady Marianne Carnegie,[35] then an amiable girl of thirteen, now, alas no more, and their friend, Mrs Scott,[36] were the companions of Lady Northesk's journey. Her ladyship told the mistress of the inn that she was going home to die, the physicians having confessed that art could do no more in her case. The person replied, "I wish, Madam, that you would send for our Doctor, he is so Famous". Lady Northesk consented.

When Dr Darwin came, he observed that he could do little on transient observation, where the disease was so obstinate, and of such long continuance; pressed her to remove with her daughter and friend to his house, and to remain his guests during a fortnight. The invitation was accepted. He requested the author of these memoirs frequently to visit his new patient, contribute to amuse her, and abate the inevitable injury of perpetual self-attention.

Miss Seward [37] felt herself extremely interested in this lady, and anxious to see those sufferings relieved which were so patiently sustained. Lady Northesk lay on a couch, through the day, in Dr Darwin's parlour, drawing with difficulty that breath, which seemed often on the point of final evaporation. She was thin, even to transparency; her cheeks suffused at times with a flush, beautiful, though hectic. Her eyes remarkably lucid and full of intelligence. If the languor of disease frequently overshadowed them, they were always relumined by every observation to which she listened, on lettered excellence, on the powers of science, or the ingenuity of art. Her language, in the high Scotch accent, had every happiness of perspicuity, and always expressed rectitude of heart and susceptibility of taste.

Whenever her great and friendly physician perceived his patient's attention engaged by the conversation of the rest of the circle, he sat considering her in meditative silence, with looks that expressed, …. "You shall not die thus prematurely, if my efforts can prevent it".[38]

One evening, after a long and intense reverie, he said, "Lady Northesk, an art was practised in former years, which the medical world has very long disused; that of injecting blood into the veins by a syringe, and thus repairing the waste of diseases like yours. Human blood, and that of calves and sheep, were used promiscuously. Superstition attached impiety to the practice. It was put a stop to in England by a bull of excommunication from some of our Popish Princes, against the practitioners of sanguinary injection …. That it had been practised with success, we may, from this interdiction, fairly conclude; else restraint upon its continuance must have been superfluous.[39] We have a very ingenious watch-maker here, whom I think I could instruct to form a proper instrument for the purpose, if you chose to submit to the experiment". She replied cheerfully, "that she had not the least objection, if he thought it eligible".

Miss Seward then said – "If the trial should be determined upon, perhaps Lady Northesk would prefer a supply from an healthy human subject, rather than from an animal. My health is perfect, neither am I conscious of any lurking disease, hereditary or accidental. I have no dread of the lancet, and will gladly spare, from time to time, such a portion from my veins to Lady Northesk, as Dr Darwin shall think proper to inject".

He seemed much pleased with the proposal, and his amiable patient expressed gratitude far above the just claim of the circumstance. Dr Darwin said he would consult his pillow upon it.

The next day, when Miss S.[40] called upon Lady N. the Doctor took her previously into his study, telling her, that he had resigned all thoughts of trying the experiment upon Lady Northesk; that it had occurred to him as a last resource, to save an excellent woman, whose disorder, he feared, was beyond the reach of medicine; "but", added he, "the construction of a proper machine is so nice an affair, the least failure in its power of acting so hazardous, the chance at last from the experiment, so precarious, that I do not choose to stake my reputation upon the risque. If she die, the world will say I killed Lady Northesk, though the London and Bath physicians have pronounced her case hopeless, and sent her home to expire. They have given her a great deal too much medicine, I shall give her very little. Their system of nutritious food, their gravy jellies, and strong wines, I have already changed for milk, vegetables, and fruit. No wines ever; no meat, no strong broth, at present. If this alteration of diet prove unavailing, her family and friends must lose her".

It was not unavailing; she gathered strength under the change from day to day. The disease abated, and in three weeks time she pursued her journey to Scotland, a convalescent, full of hope for herself, of grateful veneration towards her physician, whose rescuing skill had saved her from the grave; and full, also, of overrating thankfulness to Miss S.[41] for the offer she had made. With her, Lady Northesk regularly corresponded from that time till her sudden and deplorable death. All Lady N.'s letters spoke of completely recovered health and strength. She sent Miss Seward a present of some beautiful Scotch pebbles for a necklace, picked up by her own hands in her Lord's park, and polished at Edinburgh.

Lady Northesk might have lived to old age, the blessing of her family and friends. Alas! the time had passed by in which Miss Seward was accustomed to expect a letter from her friend!

Inquiry taught her that Lady Northesk had perished by the dreadfully-frequent accident of having set fire to her clothes. Lady Marianne Carnegie wrote to Miss S. the year after, and continued to honour her with several letters while her Ladyship lived with her father at Ethic [sic] House,[42] on the ocean's edge. It was there that she dedicated many of her youthful years to the pious endeavour of mitigating Lord Northesk's deep anguish for the loss of his Lady, which had induced him inflexibly to renounce all society, except with his own family. That might be said of Ethic [sic] House which Dr Johnson said of the Isle of Raasay,[43] in the Hebrides. "Without were the dark rocks, the roaring winds, and tumultuous deep"; but, alas for Lady Marianne! it could not also be said, as of Raasay, that "within were the social comforts, the voice of gaiety, the dance, and the song". Yet did she support, with uncomplaining patience, in the flower of her youth, this deep solitude; this monotony of natural objects, in which little variety could be found, beyond the change of smiling and frowning seas, the hushed and the bellowing waters.

In the autumn of this year Mrs Pole of Radburn was taken ill; her disorder a violent fever.[44] Dr Darwin was called in, and perhaps never, since the death of Mrs Darwin, prescribed with such deep anxiety. Not being requested to continue in the house through the ensuing night, which he apprehended might prove critical, he passed the remaining hours till day-dawn beneath a tree opposite her apartment, watching the passing and repassing lights in the chamber. During the period in which a life he so passionately valued was in danger, he paraphrased Petrarch's celebrated sonnet, narrating a dream, whose prophecy was accomplished by the death of Laura.[45] It took place the night on which the vision arose amid his slumber. Dr Darwin extended the thoughts of that sonnet into the following elegy.

Dread Dream, that, hovering in the midnight air,
Clasp'd, with thy dusky wing, my aching head,
While, to Imagination's startled ear,
Toll'd the slow bell, for bright Eliza dead.

Stretch 'd on her [46] sable bier, the grave beside,
A snow-white shroud her breathless bosom bound,
O'er her wan brow the mimic lace was tied,[47]
And Loves, and Virtues, hung their garlands round.

From those cold lips did softest accents flow?
Round that pale mouth did sweetest dimples play?
On this dull cheek the rose of beauty blow,
And those dim eyes diffuse [48] celestial day?

Did this cold hand unasking want relieve,
Or wake the lyre to every rapturous sound?
How sad, for other's woe, this breast would heave!
How light this heart, for other's transport, bound!

Beats not the bell again? … Heav'ns! do I wake?
Why heave my sighs, why gush my tears anew?
Unreal forms my trembling doubts mistake,
And frantic Sorrow fears the vision true.

Dream! to Eliza bend thy airy flight,
Go, tell my charmer all my tender fears,
How Love's fond woes alarm [49] the silent night,
And steep [50] my pillow in unpitied tears.

The second verse of this charming elegy affords an instance of Dr Darwin's too exclusive devotion to distinct picture in poetry; that it sometimes betrayed him into bringing objects so precisely to the eye, as to lose in such precision their power of striking forcibly upon the heart. The pathos in that second verse is injured by the words, "mimic lace", which allude to the perforated borders of the shroud. The expression is too minute for the solemnity of the subject. Certainly it cannot be natural for a shocked and agitated mind to observe, or to describe with such petty accuracy. Besides the allusion is not sufficiently obvious. The reader pauses to consider what the poet means by "mimic lace". Such pauses deaden sensation, and break the course of attention. A friend of the Doctor's pleaded strongly that the line might run thus,

"On her wan brow the *shadowy crape* was tied";[51]

but the alteration was rejected. Inattention to the rules of grammar in the first verse, was also pointed out to him at the same time. The dream is addressed,

"Dread dream, that clasped my aching head",[52]

but nothing is said to it; and therefore the sense is left unfinished, while the elegy proceeds to give a picture of the lifeless beauty. The same friend suggested a change, which would have remedied the defect, thus,

"Dread *was the dream*, that, in the midnight air,
Clasp'd, with its dusky wing, my aching head,
While to, &c".[53]

Hence, not only the grammatic error would have been done away, but the grating sound, produced by the near alliteration of the harsh *dr*, in "*dread dream*", removed, by placing those words at a greater distance from each other.

This alteration was, for the same reason, rejected. The Doctor would not spare the word *hovering*, which he said strengthened the picture; but surely the image ought not to be elaborately precise, by which a dream is transformed into an animal, with black wings.

Soon after Mrs Pole's recovery from her dangerous illness, Dr Darwin wrote the following little poem.

Ode To The River Derwent[54]
Written, in a romantic Valley near its source.

Derwent, what scenes thy wandering waves behold,
As bursting from thine hundred springs they stray,
And down these vales, in sounding torrents roll'd,
Seek to the shining East their mazy way!

Here dusky alders, leaning from the cliff,
Dip their long arms, and wave their branches wide;
There, as the loose rocks thwart my bounding skiff,
White moonbeams tremble on the foaming tide.

Pass on, ye waves, where, dress'd in lavish pride,
Mid roseate bowers, the gorgeous Chatsworth [55] beams,
Spreads her smooth lawns along your willowy side,
And eyes her gilded turrets in your streams.

Pass on, ye waves, where Nature's rudest child,
Frowning incumbent o'er the darken'd floods,
Rock rear'd on rock, mountain on mountain pil'd,
Old Matlock sits,[56] and shakes his crest of woods.

But when fair Derby's stately towers you view;
Where his bright meads your sparkling currents drink,
O! should Eliza press the morning dew,
And bend her graceful footsteps to your brink,

Uncurl your eddies, all your gales confine,
And, as your scaly nations gaze around,
Bid your gay nymphs pourtray, with pencil fine,
Her radiant form upon your silver ground.

With playful malice, from her kindling cheek
Steal the warm blush, and tinge your passing stream;
Mock the sweet transient dimples, as she speaks,
And, as she turns her eye, reflect the beam!

And tell her, Derwent, as you murmur by,
How in these wilds with hopeless love I burn,
Teach your lone vales and echoing caves to sigh,
And mix my briny sorrows with your urn?

This elegiac ode is rich in poetic beauty. The epithet willowy, in the third stanza, appeared questionable, till it was recollected that it is the weeping willow that was meant, with which art has adorned the Derwent in his course through the lawns of Chatsworth. The common species of that tree has no spontaneous growth on the edge of rivers which alternately rush and flow through their rocky channel in mountainous countries. Common willows border the heavy, sluggish streams of flat and swampy situations. Dwarf-alders, nut-trees, and other bushes of more stinted height, and darker verdure, fringe the banks of the Derwent, the Wie[sic],[57] and the Larkin,[58] on their passage through the Peak scenery, and form a more rich and beautiful curtain than the taller, the straggling, and pale-hued willow.

Matlock is not justly called Nature's rudest child. If his rocks were without clothing, he might properly be so called. Rude gives an idea of barrenness, and Matlock is luxuriantly umbraged; much more luxuriantly than Dove-Dale;[59] while every traveler through Derbyshire must recollect, how rich and smiling the Matlock-scenery, compared to the savage magnificence of Eyam-Dale,[60] commonly, though not properly, called Middleton-Dale.[61]

There, indeed, we see rocks piled on rocks, unfoliaged and frowning. They form a wall, of vast height, on either side the white limestone bottom of that deep and narrow valley, with the little sparkling rill which speeds through it.

In several reaches of the curves, made by this Salvatorial Dale,[62] it is from the temperature of the air alone that the seasons can be ascertained; since there are no trees, to mark by their foliage the reign of sylvan beauty; no grass, to denote it by its lively hue. Nothing but the grey, the barren, and lonely rocks, with, perhaps, a few straggling Scotch firs waving on the tops of the cliffs above; and their dusky sprays neither winter strips nor spring enlivens.

This dale is, indeed, "Peak's rudest child". Of late years, injury has been done to the towery and fantastic forms of many of the rocks, from their having been broken in pieces by gunpowder explosion, for the sake of mending the turnpike roads. The mills, for smelting the lead-ore in this dale, blot the summer noon, and increase its sultriness by those volumes of black smoke which pour out from their chimnies [sic]; but in the night they have a grand effect, from the flare of the pointed flames which stream amid the smoke, and appear like so many small volcanos.

Mr Longston,[63] of Eyam, has adorned a part of this scene by a hanging garden and imitative fort. The steep, winding paths of the garden are planted with wild shrubs, natives of the steril [sic] soil, and which root their fibres in the fissures of the rocks. The effect, in descending those paths from the cliffs above, is very striking. They command the stupendous depths of the vale below and a considerable portion of its curve.

About the year 1777, Dr Darwin purchased a little, wild, umbrageous valley, a mile from Lichfield, amongst the only rocks which neighbour that city so nearly. *(Figure 21)* It was irriguous from various springs, and swampy from their plenitude. A mossy fountain, of the purest and coldest water imaginable, had, near a century back, induced the inhabitants of Lichfield to build a cold bath in the bosom of the vale.[64] That, till the Doctor took it into his possession, was the only mark of human industry which could be found in the tangled and sequestered scene.

Figure 21: Area of Darwin's Botanic Garden, Abnalls, near Lichfield.

One of its native features had long excited the attention of the curious; a rock, which, in the central depth of the glen, drops perpetually, about three times in a minute. Aquatic plants border its top and branch from its fissures. No length of summer drought abates, no rains increase its humidity, no frost congeals its droppings. The Doctor cultivated this spot,

"And Paradise was open'd in the wild".[65]

In some parts he widened the brook into small lakes, that mirrored the valley; in others, he taught it to wind between shrubby margins. Not only with trees of various growth did he adorn the borders of the fountain, the brook, and the lakes, but with various classes of plants, uniting the Linnaean science with the charm of landscape.

For the Naiad of the fountain, he wrote the following inscription.

Speech of a Water Nymph

If the meek flower of bashful dye,
Attract not thy incurious eye;
If the soft, murmuring rill to rest
Encharm not thy tumultuous breast,
Go, where Ambition lures the vain,
Or Avarice barters peace for gain![66]

Dr Darwin restrained his friend Miss Seward's *(Figure 22)* steps to this her always favourite scene till it had assumed its new beauties from cultivation. He purposed accompanying her on her first visit to his botanic garden, but a medical summons into the country deprived her of that pleasure. She took her tablets and pencil, and, seated on a flower-bank, in the midst of that luxuriant retreat, wrote the following lines, while the sun was gilding the glen, and while birds, of every plume, poured their song from the boughs.

Figure 22: Anna Seward (1742-1809). Courtesy of Archives and Heritage, Birmingham Central Library.

O, come not here, ye Proud, whose breasts infold
Th' insatiate wish of glory, or of gold;
O come not ye, whose branded foreheads wear
Th' eternal frown of envy, or of care;
For you no Dryad [67] decks her fragrant bowers,
For you her sparkling urn no Naiad pours;
Unmark'd by you light Graces skim the green,

And hovering Cupids aim their shafts unseen.
But, thou! whose mind the well attemper'd ray
Of Taste, and Virtue, lights with purer day;
Whose finer sense each soft vibration owns,
Mute and unfeeling to discorded tones;
Like the fair flower that spreads its lucid form
To meet the sun, but shuts it to the storm;
For thee my borders nurse the glowing wreath,
My fountains murmur, and my zephyrs breathe;
My painted birds their vivid plumes unfold,
And insect armies wave their wings of gold.

And if with thee some hapless maid should stray,
Disastrous love companion of her way,
O lead her timid step to yonder glade,
Whose weeping rock incumbent alders shade!
There, as meek Evening wakes the temperate breeze,
And moonbeams glimmer through the trembling trees,
The rills, that gurgle round, shall sooth her ear,
The weeping rock shall number tear for tear;
And as sad Philomel,[68] alike forlorn,
Sings to the night, reclining on her thorn,
While, at sweet intervals, each falling note
Sighs in the gale, and whispers round the grot,
The sister-woe shall calm her aching breast,
And softest slumbers steal her cares to rest.

Thus spoke the Genius [69] as he stept along,
And bade these lawns to Peace and Truth belong;
Down the steep slopes he led, with modest skill,
The grassy pathway and the vagrant rill;
Stretch'd o'er the marshy vale the willowy mound,
Where shines the lake amid the cultur'd ground;
Rais'd the young woodland, smoo'th'd the wavy green,
And gave to Beauty all the quiet scene.

O! may no ruder step these bowers prophane,
No midnight wassailers deface the plain;
And when the tempests of the wintry day
Blow golden Autumn's varied leaves away,
Winds of the North, restrain your icy gales,
Nor chill the bosom of these HALLOWED VALES![70]

When Miss Seward gave this little poem to Dr Darwin, he seemed pleased with it, and said, "I shall send it to the periodical publications; but it ought to form the exordium of a great work. The Linnaean System is unexplored poetic ground, and an happy subject for the muse. It affords fine scope for poetic landscape; it suggests metamorphoses of the Ovidian kind, though reversed. Ovid [71] made men and women into flowers, plants, and trees. You should make flowers, plants, and trees, into men and women. I", continued he, "will write the notes, which must be scientific; and you shall write the verse".

Miss S. observed, that, besides her want of botanic knowledge, the plan was not strictly proper for a female pen; that she felt how eminently it was adapted to the efflorescence of his own fancy.

He objected the professional danger of coming forward an acknowledged poet. It was pleaded, that on his first commencing medical professor, there might have been no[72] danger; but that, beneath the unbounded confidence his experienced skill in medicine had obtained from the public, all risque of injury by reputation flowing in upon him from a new source was precluded; especially since the subject of the poetry, and still more the notes, would be connected with pathology.

Dr Darwin took his friend's advice, and very soon began his great poetic work; but previously, a few weeks after they were composed, sent the verses Miss S. wrote in his *Botanic Garden*, to the *Gentleman's Magazine*, and in her name. From thence they were copied in the *Annual Register*; but, without consulting her, he had substituted for the last six lines, eight of his own.[73] He afterwards, and again without the knowledge of their author, made them the exordium to the first part of his poem, published, for certain reasons, some years after the second part had appeared. No acknowledgment was made that those verses were the work of another pen. Such acknowledgment ought to have been made, especially since they passed the press in the name of their real author. They are somewhat altered in the exordium to Dr Darwin's Poem, and eighteen lines of his own are interwoven with them.

In September 1780, a playful correspondence passed between Dr Darwin and Miss Seward, in the name of their respective cats.[74] The subject was ludicrous as it was singular, but the mock-heroic result pleased very generally, as the permission of taking copies had been solicited and obtained by several of their acquaintance[s]. Some literary friends of the writer of these pages, remembering the bagatelles with pleasure, persuaded her to insert them. She is apprehensive that they may be considered as below the dignity which a biographic sketch of deceased Eminence ought perhaps to preserve; yet, as in this whimsically gay effusion, Dr Darwin appears in a new light of comic wit and sportive ingenuity, she ventures to comply with their request.

From the Persian Snow, at Dr Darwin's, to Miss
　　Po Felina, at the Palace, Lichfield.

Lichfield Vicarage, Sept. 7, 1780.

Dear Miss Pussey,

As I sat, the other day, basking myself in the Dean's Walk,[75] I saw you, in your stately palace, washing your beautiful round face, and elegantly brinded ears, with your velvet paws, and whisking about, with graceful sinuosity, your meandering tail. That treacherous hedgehog, Cupid, concealed himself behind your tabby beauties, and darting one of his too well aimed quills, pierced, O cruel imp! my fluttering heart.

Ever since that fatal hour have I watched, day and night, in my balcony, hoping that the stillness of the starlight evenings might induce you to take the air on the leads of the palace. Many serenades have I sung under your windows; and, when you failed to appear, with the sound of my voice made the vicarage re-echo through all its winding lanes and dirty alleys. All heard me but my cruel Fair-one; she, wrapped in fur, sat purring with contented insensibility, or slept with untroubled dreams.

Though I cannot boast those delicate varieties of melody with which you sometimes ravish the ear of night, and stay the listening stars; though you sleep hourly on the lap of the favourite of the muses, and are patted by those fingers which hold the pen of science; and every day, with her permission, dip your white whiskers in delicious cream; yet am I not destitute of all advantages of birth, education, and beauty. Derived from Persian kings, my snowy fur yet retains the whiteness and splendor of their ermine.

This morning, as I sat upon the Doctor's tea-table, and saw my reflected features in the slop-basin, my long white whiskers, ivory teeth, and topaz eyes, I felt an agreeable presentiment of my suit; and certainly the slop-basin did not flatter me, which shews the azure flowers upon its borders less beauteous than they are.

You know not, dear Miss Pussey Po, the value of the address you neglect. New milk have I, in flowing abundance, and mice pent up in twenty garrets, for your food and amusement.

Permit me, this afternoon, to lay at your divine feet the head of an enormous Norway Rat, which has even now stained my paws with its gore. If you will do me the honour to sing the following song, which I have taken the liberty to write, as expressing the sentiments I wish you to entertain, I will bring a band of catgut and catcall, to accompany you in chorus.

Air: ... spirituuosi.

Cats I scorn, who, sleek and fat,
Shiver at a Norway rat;
Rough and hardy, bold and free,
Be the cat that's made for me!
He, whose nervous paw can take
My lady's lapdog by the neck;
With furious hiss attack the hen,
And snatch a chicken from the pen.
If the treacherous swain should prove
Rebellious to my tender love,
My scorn the vengeful paw shall dart,
Shall tear his fur, and pierce his heart.

Chorus.

Qu-ow wow, quall, wawl, moon.

Deign, most adorable charmer, to pur your assent to this my request, and believe me to be with the profoundest respect, your true admirer.

Snow.[76]

Answer.

Palace, Lichfield, Sept. 8, 1780.

I am but too sensible of the charms of Mr Snow; but while I admire the spotless whiteness of his ermine, and the tyger-strength of his commanding form, I sigh in secret, that he, who sucked the milk of benevolence and philosophy, should yet retain the extreme of that fierceness, too justly imputed to the Grimalkin [77] race. Our hereditary violence is perhaps commendable when we exert it against the foes of our protectors, but deserves much blame when it annoys their friends.

The happiness of a refined education was mine; yet, dear Mr Snow, my advantages in that respect were not equal to what yours might have been: but, while you give unbounded indulgence to your [78] carnivorous desires, I have so far subdued mine, that the lark pours his mattin song, the canary-bird warbles wild and loud, and the robin pipes his farewell song to the setting sun, unmolested in my presence; nay, the plump and tempting dove has reposed securely upon my soft back, and bent her glossy neck in graceful curves as she walked around me.

But let me hasten to tell thee how my sensibilities in thy favour were, last month, unfortunately repressed. Once, in the noon of one of its most beautiful nights, I was invited abroad by the serenity of the amorous hour, secretly stimulated by the hope of meeting my admired Persian. With silent steps I paced around the dimly-gleaming leads of the palace. I had acquired a taste for scenic beauty and poetic imagery, by listening to ingenious observations upon their nature from the lips of thy own lord, as I lay purring at the feet of my mistress.

I admired the lovely scene, and breathed my sighs for thee to the listening moon. She threw the long shadows of the majestic cathedral upon the silvered lawn. I beheld the pearly meadows of Stow Valley, and the lake in its bosom, which, reflecting the lunar rays, seemed a sheet of diamonds. The trees of the Dean's Walk, which, the hand of Dulness [sic] had been restrained from torturing into trim and detestable regularity, met each other in a thousand various and beautiful forms. Their liberated boughs danced on the midnight gale, and the edges of their leaves were whitened by the moonbeams. I descended to the lawn, that I might throw the beauties of the valley into perspective through the graceful arches, formed by their meeting branches. Suddenly my ear was startled, not by the voice of my lover, but by the loud and dissonant noise of the war-song, which six black grimalkins were raising in honour of the numerous victories obtained by the Persian Snow; compared with which, they acknowledged those of English cats had little brilliance, eclipsed, like the unimportant victories of the Howes,[79] by the puissant Clinton [80] and Arbuthnot,[81] and the still more puissant Cornwallis.[82] It sung that thou [83] didst owe thy matchless might to thy lineal descent from the invincible Alexander,[84] as he derived his more than mortal valour from his mother Olympia's [85] illicit commerce with Jupiter.[86] They sung that, amid the renowned siege of Persepolis,[87] while Roxana [88] and Statira [89] were contending for the honour of his attentions, the conqueror of the world deigned to bestow them upon a large white female cat, thy grandmother, warlike Mr Snow, in the ten thousandth and ninety-ninth ascent.

Thus far their triumphant din was music to my ear; and even when it sung that lakes of milk ran curdling into whey, within the ebon concave of their pancheons, with terror at thine approach; that mice squealed from all the neighbouring garrets; and that whole armies of Norway rats, crying out amain, "the devil take the hindmost", ran violently into the minster-pool, at the first gleam of thy white mail through the shrubs of Mr Howard's [90] garden.

But O! when they sung, or rather yelled, of larks warbling on sunbeams, fascinated suddenly by the glare of thine eyes, and falling into thy remorseless talons; of robins, warbling soft and solitary upon the leafless branch, till the pale cheek of winter dimpled into joy; of hundreds of those bright breasted songsters, torn from their barren sprays by thy pitiless fangs! … Alas! my heart died within me at the idea of so preposterous a union!

Marry you, Mr Snow, I am afraid I cannot; since, though the laws of our community might not oppose our connection, yet those of principle, of delicacy, of duty to my mistress, do very powerfully oppose it.

As to presiding at your concert, if you extremely wish it, I may perhaps grant your request; but then you must allow me to sing a song of my own composition, applicable to our present situation, and set to music by my sister Sophy at Mr Brown's [91] the organist's, thus,

Air: … affettuoso.

He, whom Pussy Po detains
A captive in her silken chains,
Must curb the furious thirst of prey,
Nor rend the warbler from his spray!
Nor let his wild, ungenerous rage
An unprotected foe engage.

O, should cat of Darwin prove
Foe to pity, foe to love!
Cat, that listens day by day,
To mercy's mild and honied lay,
Too surely would the dire disgrace
More deeply brand our future race,
The stigma fix, where'er they range,
That cats can ne'er their nature change.

Should I consent with thee to wed,
These sanguine crimes upon thy head,
And ere the wish'd reform I see,
Adieu to lapping Seward's tea!
Adieu to purring gentle praise,
Charm'd as she quotes thy master's lays! ...
Could I, alas! our kittens bring
Where sweet her plumy favourites sing,
Would not the watchful nymph espy
Their father's fierceness in their eye,
And drive us far and wide away,
In cold and lonely barn to stray?
Where the dark owl, with hideous scream,
Shall mock our yells for forfeit cream,
As on starv'd mice we swearing dine,
And grumble that our lives are nine.

Chorus: ... *largo.*

Waal, woee, trone, moan, mall, oll, moule.

The still too much admired Mr Snow will have the goodness to pardon the freedom of these expostulations, and excuse their imperfections. The morning, O Snow! had been devoted to this my correspondence with thee, but I was interrupted in that employment by the visit of two females of our species, who fed my ill-starred passion by praising thy wit and endowments, exemplified by thy elegant letter, to which the delicacy of my sentiments obliges me to send so inauspicious a reply.

    I am, dear Mr Snow,

        Your ever obliged,

            Po Felina

Notes

1   *Zoonomia; or, The Laws of Organic Life*. Part I (London: J. Johnson, 1794), Parts II and III (London: J. Johnson, 1796, with 2nd ed. of Part I, corrected). Dr Darwin began writing this project in Lichfield in 1770–1771, soon after Polly Darwin's death.

2   Shakespeare, *Macbeth* (1606), I, vii, 27–28. The original lines are: "Vaulting ambition, which o'erleaps itself, / And falls on th' other −".

3   As Anna Seward kept "yellow-breasted songsters", it may well have been herself to whom she was referring to as this "lady".

4   At the time of Darwin's biography, Robert Fellowes (1770/71–1847) was editor of the *Critical Review, or, Annals of Literature* and had become quite well known for his many religious writings.

5   *Critical Review* 68 (1789): 375–379.

6   With the touch of his spear, the angel Ithuriel exposed deceit. John Milton (1608–1674), employed this allegorical imagery in *Paradise Lost. A Poem Written in Ten Books* (London: P. Parker, 1667), IV, 810–813, showing how Ithuriel exposed Satan. The angel Gabriel sent the angels Ithuriel and Zephon to search the Garden of Eden for "some infernal spirit … who escaped the barrs of Hell on errand bad". They find Satan disguised "like a toad, close at the ear of Eve". Ithuriel touches the toad with his spear, and Satan returns to his original form, for "no falsehood can endure the touch of" Ithuriel's spear. Dustin Griffin focused upon the importance of Milton in Dr Darwin's era in *Regaining Paradise: Milton and the Eighteenth Century* (Cambridge: Cambridge University Press, 1986).

7   Anna Seward called Dr Darwin the "great system monger" (Anna Seward to H. Cary, 9 March 1793, *Letters*, Vol.III, p.211). As Lester L. King noted in *The Medical World of the Eighteenth Century* (Chicago: University of Chicago Press, 1958, esp. pp.220–223), *Zoonomia* is distinct from other contemporary medical-oriented nosologies in that Darwin based his distinguishing characteristics on the causes, not the signs, of disease. Dr Darwin's nosology was consistent with his view of society in that he viewed diseases in dynamic, evolving terms. See, for example, P. Bowler, "Evolutionism and the Enlightenment", *History of Science* 12 (1974): 159–183, and M. McNeil, *Under the Banner of Science*, pp.86–124. To establish the nosological context, see James L. Larson's two works, *Reason and Experience: The Representation of Natural Order in the Work of Carl von Linné* (Berkeley: University of California Press, 1971), and *Interpreting Nature: The Science of Living Form from Linnaeus to Kant* (Baltimore: The Johns Hopkins University Press, 1994).

8   Hippocrates (460–*c*.377 BC), of Cos, has been looked upon as the founding figure of Western medicine for centuries. For recent overviews of the use of Hippocratic wisdom in his own era as well as in Darwin's era, see, respectively, Owsei Temkin, *Hippocrates in a World of Pagans and Christians* (Baltimore: The Johns Hopkins University Press, 1991) and David Cantor (ed) *Reinventing Hippocrates* (Aldershot: Ashgate, 2002). Galen was born in 129 AD in Pergamum and combined the study of medicine with the study of philosophy. For an important contextualization of Galen among the Ancients, see Vivian Nutton, *Ancient Medicine* (London: Routledge, 2004). In addition to the writings of Hippocrates and Galen available to Darwin, two important medical history works were also widely read during the eighteenth century, namely Daniel Le Clerc (1652–1728) *Histoire de la Médecine* (Amsterdam: G. Gallet, 1702), and John Friend (1675–1728), *History of Physick from the Time of Galen to the Beginning of the Sixteenth Century* (London: J. Walthoe, 1725).

9   Upon learning of this accident, Darwin hurried to Edinburgh to attend to his son, but to no avail. Charles died on 15 May 1778. Dr Darwin composed the inscription for his son's tomb in the family vault of Dr Andrew Duncan (1744–1828), one of Charles' cherished professors, in St Cuthbert Chapel churchyard, Edinburgh. Dr Darwin also wrote a tributary elegy which was published anonymously as, *An Elegy on the Much-Lamented Death of a Most Ingenious Young Gentleman* (London: G. Robinson, sold by M. Morgan, Lichfield, 1778).

10   Dr Darwin published Charles' thesis, *Experiments Establishing a Criterion between Mucaginous and Purulent Matter. And an Account of the Retrograde Motions of the Absorbent Vessels of Animal Bodies in Some Diseases* (Lichfield: J. Jackson; London: T. Cadell, and Edinburgh: W. Creech, 1780). In this work, Dr Darwin added a few cases of his own, five of which involved the use of digitalis, prepared from the plant commonly known as Foxglove. Although this work established Dr Darwin's priority of publication, it is his fellow Lunar Society colleague, the Birmingham physician William Withering (1741–1799), who typically gets credit for the first use of digitalis. See G.C. Cook, "Erasmus Darwin FRS (1731–1802) and the Foxglove Controversy", *Journal of Medical Biography* 7 (1999): 86–92. For a more complete account of Withering, see T.W. Peck and K.D. Wilkinson, *William Withering of Birmingham* (Bristol: John Wright & Sons, 1950) and Peter Sheldon, *The Life and Times of William Withering: His Work, His Legacy* (Studley: Brewin Books, 2004).

11   The Lichfield Botanical Society *(Figure 19)* existed essentially of Darwin, Boothby, and William Jackson (1735–1798). As Mary Alden Hopkins related in *Dr Johnson's Lichfield* (London: Peter Owen, 1956), p.194, "John

Saville was invited to join, but he refused because he knew he would have to do all the paperwork". "Learned men interested in botany" when "passing through Lichfield sometimes paused to consult with" this group, and were "astonished to discover that the erudite society was only a threesome". *(Figure 20)* Boothby and Darwin also prepared an encouraging forward for a work published by Boothby's Derbyshire cousin, Maria Elizabeth Jackson (also Jacson, 1755–1829). This work, anonymously published, was *Botanical Dialogues, between Hortensia and her Four Children, Charles, Harriet, Juliette and Henry. Designed for Use of Schools* (London: J. Johnson, 1797). Dr Darwin noted "Maria Jackson of Tarporly, in Cheshire" as "a Lady who adds much botanical knowledge to many other elegant acquirements" (*Loves of the Plants*, Additional Notes, p.181). For a thorough placement of Jacson in the arena of female botanical writing, see Ann B. Shteir "Botanical Dialogues: Maria Jacson and Women's Popular Science Writing in England", *Eighteenth-Century Studies* 23 (1990): 301–317. See also Ann B. Shteir, *Cultivating Women, Cultivating Science: Flora's Daughters and Botany in England, 1760–1860* (Baltimore: The Johns Hopkins University Press, 1996) and Samantha George, *Botany, Sexuality and Women's Writing, 1760–1830: From Modest Shoot to Forward Plant* (Manchester: Manchester University Press, 2008).

12   William Jackson (1735–1798). For more biographical information, see King-Hele, *Letters of Erasmus Darwin* (1981), pp.110–111.

13   *A System of Vegetables according to their Classes Orders Genera Species with their Characters and Differences.* Translated from the Thirteenth Edition of the *Systema Vegetabilium* of the late Professor Linneus (as published by Dr [Johann Andreas] Murray [1740-1791]) by a Botanical Society at Lichfield, 2 vols. (Lichfield: J. Jackson, for Leigh and Sotheby, London, 1783). See also *The Families of Plants, Translated from [Johann Jacob] Reichard's (1743-1782) Edition of the 'Genera Plantarum' and the Mantissae Plantarum of the Elder Linnaeus; and the Supplementum Plantarum of the Younger Linnaeus* by a Botanical Society at Lichfield. 2 vols. (Lichfield: J. Jackson for J Johnson, London: T. Byrne, Dublin: and Edinburgh: J. Balfour, 1787). Both this work and Darwin's *Botanical Garden* have recently been reprinted in Judith Hawley (ed) *Literature and Science: 1660-1834*, Volume 4: *Flora* (London: Pickering & Chatto, 2003). John Dean addressed some of the difficulties surrounding botanical classification of this era in "Controversy over Classification: A Case Study from the History of Botany", in Barry Barnes and Steven Shapin (eds) *Natural Order: Historical Studies of Scientific Culture* (Beverly Hills, CA: Sage, 1979), pp.211-228. See also Charlie Jarvis, *Order out of Chaos: Linnaean Plant Names and Their Types* (London: The Linnean Society of London in association with the Natural History Museum, 2007), and Peter Bernhardt, *Gods and Goddesses in the Garden: Greco-Roman Mythology and the Scientific Names of Plants* (New Brunswick: Rutgers University Press, 2008). Dr Darwin is hailed as "one of the great promoters of the Linnaean ideas" in Frans A. Stefleu, *Linnaeus and the Linnaeans: The Spreading of the Ideas in Systematic Botany, 1735-1789* (Utrecht: A. Oosthoek, 1971), p.216. More generally on botanical classification up to the period of England's John Ray (1627-1705), see Anna Pavord, *The Naming of Names: The Search for Order in the World of Plants* (London: Bloomsbury, 2005).

14   John Sneyd (1734–1809) of Bishton and later Belmont Hall, near Hazles, Staffordshire, who was an uncle to Honora, served as Sheriff of Staffordshire in 1763. He was a descendant of the Sneyd's of Keele Hall, Staffordshire, now part of Keele University.

15   Pacific island, part of the Northern Marianas group just south of Saipan.

16   Pacific islands west of Chile.

17   Written by Darwin in 1779 before the lake was formed.

18   Shakespeare, *As You Like It* (1599), II.iii.52–53. The original lines are, "Therefore my age is as a lusty winter,/Frosty, but kindly".

19   Colonel Edward Sacheveral Pole (1707–1780) and Elizabeth Pole (1747–1832) had three children: Sacheveral (1769–1813), Elizabeth (1770–1821), and Millicent (1774–1857). Dr Darwin mentions having treated Millicent in

1777. Radburn Hall (today, known as Radbourne Hall) was built around 1750 by the Jacobite, German (pronounced Jarman) Pole (*c.*1690–1765), uncle to Colonel Edward Pole. It is situated four miles west of Derby on property that has been the location of the Chandos-Pole family estate since the 15th century and of the Chandos family since the reign of Henry IV. Colonel Pole, graduate of Repton, Harrow, and Cambridge, inherited Radburn Hall from his uncle in 1765.

20 Most likely *Cicuta virosa*, commonly known as Cowbane or Northern Water Hemlock, a species native to northern and central Europe. This poisonous plant's clusters of white tuberous roots have frequently been mistaken for parsnips, often leading to death.

21 Darwin's Lunar Society colleague, Matthew Boulton.

22 Silver mines in Potosi, Bolivia.

23 Elizabeth Pole.

24 "Gaping" used in Desmond King-Hele's reprinting as Erasmus Darwin's collection of poems, *To Elizabeth, With Love* (Sheffield: Stuart Harris, 2008), p.23.

25 The youth in Greek mythology who, upon seeing his own reflection, pined for the love of what he saw and was turned into a flower bearing the same name.

26 "Stream" used in *To Elizabeth, With Love*, p.24.

27 For the manuscript versions of this poem, see Archives, Cambridge University Library, DAR 267.38, and Dr Erasmus Darwin's 'Early Poems' Letter ii, p.13. Univ. College, London. Pearson Papers.577. It has recently appeared in print, with slight variation, as "Directions for Making a Vase" in King-Hele's *The Collected Letters of Erasmus Darwin*, pp.146–147.

28 "Steed" in the singular in King-Hele's reprinting in a poem entitled "Jealousy: An Ode", in *To Elizabeth, With Love*, p.42.

29 "The frown of Beauty chills" is the opening of this line in *To Elizabeth, With Love*, p.24.

30 "Suns" used in *To Elizabeth, With Love*, p.42.

31 This line appears as "Where Beauty's eyes give luster to the day" in *To Elizabeth, With Love*, p.42.

32 "Golden" used in *To Elizabeth, With Love*, p.42.

33 Dr Erasmus Darwin's 'Early Poems': "Jealousy: An Ode", p.76. Univ. College, London. Pearson Papers.577.

34 Anne Melville Carnegie, Countess Northesk (*c.*1730–1779), wife of Admiral George Carnegie, 6th Earl of Northesk (1716–1792).

35 Lady Mary Anne Carnegie (*d.*1798).

36 We have been unable to identify this individual.

37 Anna Seward, the author.

38 This appears to be Seward's interpretation of Darwin's thoughts from the look on his face.

39 Following ethical controversies over whether the process of transfusing blood was playing God, the Pope outlawed the procedure in 1675 and England's Parliament banned it three years later. For a stirring account of this controversy, see Pete Moore *Blood & Justice – the Seventeenth Century Parisian Doctor Who Made Blood Transfusion History* (Hoboken, NJ: John Wiley and Sons, 2002).

40 Anna Seward.

41 Anna Seward.

42 Ethie Castle is on Scotland's East coast, north of Dundee, Carnoustie, and Arbroath. The Carnegie family, which later became the family lineage of the Earl of Northesk, purchased this estate in 1665. It remained with that family until 1928.

43 Situated between the Isle of Skye and the Scottish mainland, separated by the Sound of Raasay. Johnson and Boswell visited Raasay House on that Isle during their tour of 1773.

44 A "violent fever" typically expressed itself as a persistent burning heat felt throughout the body that can last for a few days.

45 Francesco Petrarca (1304–1374), the poet and humanist scholar who idealized his love to "Laura", the individual to whom he addressed his lyric poems, *Rime in Vita di Laura* and *Rime in Morte di Laura*, collectively known as his *Canzoniere*. In Seward's poems and letters, she frequently referred to the "Mistress of Batheaston", Lady Anne Miller (1741–1781), as "Laura". See R.A. Hesselgrave *Lady Miller and the Batheaston Literary Circle* (New Haven: Yale University Press, 1927), p.37.

46 "The" in King-Hele's reprinting in a poem entitled "Elegy for Elizabeth, After a Dream", in *To Elizabeth, With Love*, p.35.

47 This line concludes as the variation "the gather'd folds were tied" in *To Elizabeth, With Love*, p.35.

48 "Effuse" in *To Elizabeth, With Love*, p.35.

49 "Woe alarms" in *To Elizabeth, With Love*, p.35.

50 "Steeps" in the plural in *To Elizabeth, With Love*, p.35.

51 Likely Seward's own suggestion.

52 Seward's concise version of Darwin's first two lines.

53 According to Seward scholar, Marion Roberts, the "friend" who supplied this "was probably Seward herself" as suggested by the alliteration which she so liked. (Personal communication, 8 July 2008).

54 A manuscript version of this poem is available at the Bodleian Library Oxford (MS Eng. Poet. D.10 fol.82), and it first appeared in print as "Ode Written on the River Derwent" in *Gentleman's Magazine* 55 (1785): 641. King-Hele provides a recent printing of this work in *To Elizabeth, With Love*, pp.25–26. The local historian, James Pilkington noted in 1789 that the Derwent "flows in some parts with a noisy and rapid current, and in others with such a deep and gentle stream, that its unruffled surface ... clearly reflects the rocks and wood near its margin. Thus do rocks, trees, shrubs, and water conspire at once to fill the mind of the spectator with admiration and delight". *A View of the Present State of Derbyshire* (Derby: J. Drewry for J. Johnson and J. Deighton, London, 1789). Dr Darwin's friend, F.N.C. Mundy, composed the following in honor of his Darby residence on the Derwent.

"Address to the River Derwent, on whose Banks the Author of the Botanic Garden Resides".

DERWENT, like thee thy Poet's splendid song
With sweet vicissitudes of ease and force
Now with enchanting smoothness glides along,
Now pours impetuous its resounding course;

While Science marches down thy wond'ring dells,
And all the Muses round her banners crowd,
Pleas'd to assemble in thy sparry cells,
And chant her lessons to thy echoes proud;

While here Philosophy and Truth display
The shining robes those heaven-born sisters wove,
While Fays and Graces beck'ning smooth their way,
And hand in hand with Flora follows Love.

Well may such radiant state increase thy pride,

Delighted stream! tho' rich in native charms,

Tho' inborn worth and honour still reside,

Where thy chill banks the glow of Chatsworth warm.

Tho' here her new-found art, as that of yore,

The spinster Goddess to thy rule assigns;

Tho', where her temples crowd thy peopled shore,

Wealth gilds thy urn, and Fame thy chaplet twines.

Ah, while thy nymphs in Derby's towered vale

Lead their sad Quires around MILCENA'S bier,

What soothing sweetness breathes along the gale,

Comes o'er the consort's heart, and balms a brother's tear!

55   Chatsworth is the ancestral home of the Duke of Devonshire. Redesigned by James Paine (*c*.1716–89), Lancelot (Capability) Brown (1716–83), and John Carr of York (1723–1807) in the 18th century, the property gained new renown for its fashionable natural and romantic appearance. At the time of Darwin's writing, Chatsworth was the home of William Cavendish, the 5th Duke of Devonshire (1748–1811), who had married the charming and beautiful Lady Georgiana Spencer (1757–1806), who was the great-great-great-great aunt of Diana, Princess of Wales (1961–1997). For more on this influential woman of the late English Enlightenment period whose political views and personal lifestyle were both intriguing and reviling to her contemporaries, see Amanda Foreman, *Georgiana: Duchess of Devonshire* (London: Harper Collins, 1999).

56   High Tor, a lofty limestone crag between Matlock and Matlock Bath, towers above the River Derwent. Joseph Wright, among others, captured the beauty of natural composition in his "Matlock High Tor-Moonlight" (*c*.1777–1779). For a splendid account of the exploration of this area during Seward's time, see Trevor Brighton, *The Discovery of the Peak District* (Shopwyke Manor Barn, Chichester: Phillimore, 2004).

57   The beautiful River Wye rises above Buxton and flows south easterly through Buxton and Bakewell to join the River Derwent at Rowsley. According to Anna Seward, the River Wye "runs through Mensaldale, the loveliest of the Peak Vallies, and through the rich meads below Bakewell, where it winds and curves with capricious wantonness. The waters of the Derwent have a tint of amber, which seems to suit the dark and luxuriant foliage on their banks, and is well contrasted by the white foam almost perpetually formed by its rocky channel. The clearness of the Wie [sic] is still more beautiful. Hence, it becomes the mirror of the exquisite scenery on its borders", in "Ode to William Boothby, Esq", in Seward's *Poetical Works*, Vol.1, pp.115–118.

58   A small Derbyshire river, the Lathkill ravine runs from the ancient lead mining village of Monyash, snaking along until it meets up with the River Wye near Rowsley.

59   Dale surrounding the River Dove, running for 3 miles from Milldale in the north through a wooded ravine near Thorpe Cloud and Bunster Hill in the south. As William Bray noted of Dove Dale in 1783, the "rocks, on both sides of the water, are of grey limestone, of every wild and grotesque variety of height and shape. Sometimes they stand single, like the fragments of a wall, or the tower of an old castle; sometimes they rise from a broad base in a kind of pyramid, at others, slender like a pinnacle", in *Sketch of a Tour into Derbyshire and Yorkshire*, 2nd Ed., (London: B. White, 1783). Wright painted several memorable landscapes of Dove Dale.

60   Eyam was the village home of Anna Seward, where her father was Rector before moving his family to Lichfield. For a general history, see William Wood, *The History and Antiquities of Eyam, with a Minute Account of the Great Plague*

Which Desolated That Village in 1666 (Little Longstone: Country Books, 2006, reprint of 1842 edition). Seward's tribute "Eyam" appeared in her *Poetical Works*, Vol.3, pp.1–4.

61 Middleton Dale is known for a vertical narrow cave (an old mine) along the cliffs called Fingal's Cave, around the entrance of which one finds sparkly lead ore, fluorspar and barytes.

62 Figurative reference, in the manner of Salvator Rosa (1615–1673), the Neapolitan painter and artist best known for his wild, savage landscapes and whose work inspired the eighteenth-century "rage for the picturesque" in British landscape art.

63 Mr Longston of Little Longstone, Derbyshire.

64 Best known as Dr Floyer's Cold Bath, after the Lichfield physician, Sir John Floyer, MD (1649–1734). According to Dr Darwin, this "scenery" of his botanical writing is taken from this garden, where there is "a grotto surrounded by projecting rocks, from the edges of which trickles a perpetual shower of water; and it is here represented as adapted to love-scenes, as being thence a proper residence for the modern goddess of Botany" (*Economy of Vegetation*, note, p.3).

65 Alexander Pope (1688–1744), *Eloisa to Abelard* (1717), l.134.

66 A manuscript version exists in Darwin's "Early Poems" as "Speech to a Water Nymph, Inscribed on a Weeping Rock in a Botanic garden near Lichfield", p.19. University College London. Pearson Papers. 577. In many ways it parallels Darwin's "Speech of a Wood Nymph" written to Mrs Pole (*c.*1775), cited in King-Hele's *Collected Letters of Erasmus Darwin*, pp.138–139, and included in the recently collected poems published as *To Elizabeth, With Love*, p.21.

67 A wood nymph.

68 A nightingale.

69 Seward's own footnote, "By the Genius of the place is meant its first cultivator, Dr Darwin".

70 Seward's own footnote, "These verses, in their original state, as inscribed here, will be found in Mr [Stebbing] Shaw's *History of Staffordshire*, published in 1798, near four years before the death of Dr Darwin; see Article "Lichfield", Vol.1, page 347. Their author chose to assert her claim to them in the Doctor's lifetime, since they had appeared in the periodical publications many years before *The Botanic Garden* passed the press, and had borne her signature".

71 Ovid (43 BC–17 AD), a noted Roman poet remembered for his *Metamorphosis*, an epic poem of myth and legend involving a transformation in terms of an ordering of chaos over time from the creation of the universe through the Augustan organization of peace following the Civil Wars. The mythical characters in Ovid's poem are rewarded (or punished) for their obedience (or lack thereof) by a metamorphosis into some lasting form of an animal, vegetable, or astronomical figure. Dr Darwin described his playful use of Ovid thusly, that "great Necromancer in the famous Court of Augustus Caesar, did by art poetic transmute Men, Women, and even Gods and Goddesses, into Trees and Flowers; I have undertaken by similar art to restore some of them to their original animality, after having remained prisoners so long in their respective vegetable mansions; and have here exhibited them before thee. Which thou may'st contemplate as diverse little pictures suspended over the chimney of a Lady's dressing-room, connected only by a slight festoon of ribbons. And which, though thou may'st not be acquainted with the originals, may amuse thee by the beauty of their persons, their graceful attitudes, or the brilliancy of their dress" (*Loves of the Plants*, Proem). In short, Darwin performed the reversal of Ovid's transformations. Linnaeus also incorporated Greek mythological references into his nomenclature. See John L. Heller, "Classical Mythology in the *Systema Naturae* of Linnaeus", *Transactions of the American Philological Association* 76 (1945): 333–357.

72 The word "no" does not appear in the 1804 version of Seward's *Life* published in Philadelphia.

73 The specific lines in question were these which Seward composed as "Verses Written in Dr Darwin's Botanic Garden", Near Lichfield, July, 1778.

O come not here, ye proud, who breasts enfold
Th' insatiate wish of glory, or of gold!
O come not here, whose branded foreheads wear
The eternal frown of envy or of care!
For you no Dryad decks her fragrant bowers,
For you her sparkling urn no Naiad pours;
Unmask'd by you, light Graces skim the green,
And hovering Cupids aim their shafts unseen.

But THOU, whose mind the well-attemper'd ray
Of taste and virtue lights with purer day;
Whose finer sense each soft vibration owns,
Mute and unfeeling to discordant tones;
Like the fair flower, that spreads it lucid form
To meet the sun, but shuts it to the storm;
For thee my borders name the glowing wreath,
My fountains murmur and my zephyrs breathe;
To charm thine eye, amid the crystal tide,
With sinuous track, my silvery nations glide;

Darwin modified and published the following in the opening lines of his *Botanic Garden* as his own verse:

Stay your rude steps! whose throbbing breasts infold
The legion-fiends of Glory, or of Gold!
Stay! whose false lips seductive simpers part,
While Cunning nestles in the harlot-heart! –
For you no Dryads dress the roseate bower,
For you no Nymphs their sparkling vases pour;
Unmark'd by you, light Graces swim the green,
And hovering Cupids aim their, shafts, unseen.

But THOU! whose mind the well-attemper'd ray
Of Taste and Virtue lights with purer day;
Whose finer sense each soft vibration owns
With sweet responsive sympathy of tones;
So the fair flower expands its lucid form
To meet the sun, and shuts it to the storm; –
For thee my borders nurse the fragrant wreath,
My fountains murmur, and my zephyrs breathe;
Slow slides the painted snail, the gilded fly
Smoothes his fine down, to charm thy curious eye;
On twinkling fins my pearly nations play,
Or win with sinuous train their trackless way;

74   This flirtation, in the form of a whimsical *billet doux* cast between two cats, Mr Snow and Miss Po Felina, is perhaps most readily accessible in "Love Letters of Clerical Cats: Erasmus Darwin and Anna Seward" in Mark Bryant (ed) *The Church Cat: Clerical Cats in Stories and Verse* (London: Hodder and Stoughton, 1997), pp.141–148.

75   The Dean's Walk in front of the Bishop's Palace, on the north side of the Cathedral, is a shaded avenue dating back to 1703. The Dean's Walk was a favorite area for many of Lichfield's literary circle.

76   Seward's own footnote, "The cat, to whom the above letter was addressed, had been broken of her propensity to kill birds, and lived several years without molesting a dove, a tame lark, and a redbreast, all which used to fly about the room where the cat was daily admitted. The dove frequently sat on pussey's back, and the little birds would peck fearlessly from the plate in which she was eating".

77   Grimalkin, an evil-looking and acting female cat, derived from being "gray" in her colour plus "malkin" (or daemon-like) in her actions.

78   The word "you" appears here instead of "your" in the 1804 version of Seward's *Life of Dr Darwin* published in Philadelphia.

79   William Howe, 5th Viscount Howe (1729–1814).

80   Sir Henry Clinton (1730–1795).

81   Marriot Arbuthnot (1711–1794).

82   Charles Cornwallis, 1st Marquis and 2nd Earl, Viscount Brome, Baron Cornwallis (1738–1805).

83   The work "thou" appeared as "though" in the 1804 version of Seward's *Life of Dr Darwin* published in Philadelphia.

84   Alexander the Great, also known as Alexander III of Macedonia (356–323 BC) was a student of Aristotle (384–322 BC) and later King of Macedonia, succeeding his father, Philip II of Macedon (382–336 BC). As a ruler, Alexander conquered the Persian Empire.

85   Olympias (376–316 BC), a princess, daughter of Neoptolemus (*d. c.*360 BC), King of Epirus was the mother of Alexander.

86   In mythology, Jupiter was King of the gods.

87   Persepolis was a capital of the ancient Achaemenid Empire, in Northern Iran of today. It was founded by Darius (550–486 BC) and destroyed by Alexander in 330 BC.

88   Roxana (d.310 BC), daughter of Oxyartes, a nobleman of Bactria or Sogdia, who became Alexander's first wife. After Alexander the Great's death (323 BC), she had Stateira killed so that her son, Alexander IV Aegus (323–309 BC) would rule Macedonia jointly with Phillip III Arrhidaues (359–317 BC), Alexander's half brother.

89   Stateira, also called Barsine, was the daughter of Darius III Codomannus, who reigned from 336 to 330 BC as the last Persian king of the Achaemenid Empire. She was captured by Alexander at the battle of Issus (333 BC) and was married to him in an attempt to merge the Macedonian and Persian lineages.

90   Charles Howard (1707–1771), Proctor in the Ecclesiastical Court and father of Mrs Mary (Polly) Darwin. Charles married Penelope Foley, a descendant via the Pagets of Mary Boleyn (*c.*1499–1543).

91   William Brown served as Organist of Lichfield Cathedral from 1776–1807.

Chapter IV

During the course of the year 1780, died Colonel Pole. Dr Darwin, more fortunate than Petrarch, whose destiny his own had resembled in poetic endowment and hopeless love, then saw his adored Laura free, and himself at liberty to court her favor, whose coldness his muse had recorded; to "drink softer effusion from those eyes", which duty and discretion had rendered repulsive. He soon, however, saw her surrounded by rivals, whose time of life had nearer parity with her own, yet in its summer bloom, while his age nearly approached its half century; whose fortunes were affluent and patrimonial; while his were professional; who were jocund bachelors, while he had children for whom he must provide.

Colonel Pole had numbered twice the years of his fair wife.[1] His temper was said to have been peevish and suspicious, yet not beneath those circumstances had her kind and cheerful attentions to him grown cold or remiss. He left her a jointure of six hundred pounds per annum; a son to inherit his estate,[2] and two female children amply portioned.[3]

Mrs Pole, it has already been remarked, had much vivacity and sportive humor, with very engaging frankness of temper and manners. Early in her widowhood she was rallied, in a large company upon Dr Darwin's passion for her, and was asked what she would do with her captive philosopher. "He is not very fond of churches, I believe, and if he would go there for my sake, I shall scarcely follow him. He is too old for me"…. Nay madam, what are fifteen years on the right side?" She replied, with an arch smile, "I have had so much of that right side!"[4]

The confession was thought inauspicious to the Doctor's hopes; but it did not prove so; the triumph of intellect was complete. Without that native perception and awakened taste for literary excellence, which the first charming Mrs Darwin possessed, this lady became tenderly sensible of the flattering difference between the attachment of a man of genius, and wide celebrity, and that of young fox-hunting esquires; dashing militaries, and pedantic gownsmen; for she was said to have specimens of all these classes in her train. They could speak their own passion, but could not immortalize her charms. However benevolent, friendly, and sweet-tempered, she was not perhaps exactly the woman to have exclaimed with Akenside,

> "Mind, mind alone, bear witness earth and heaven!
> The living fountain in itself contains
> Of beauteous and sublime!"[5]

Yet did her choice support his axiom when she took Dr Darwin for her husband. Darwin, never handsome, or personally graceful, with extremely impeded utterance; with hard features on a rough surface; older much in appearance than in reality; lame and clumsy! …

and this, when half the wealthy youth of Derbyshire were said to have disputed the prize with him.

But it was not without some stipulations, apparently hazardous to his pecuniary interest, that Mrs Pole was persuaded to descend from her Laura-eminence to wifehood, and probably to silence for ever, in the repose of possession, those tender strains, which romantic love and despair, and afterwards the stimulating restlessness of doubtful hope, had occasionally awakened.

During that visit to Dr Darwin, in which Mrs Pole had brought her sick children to be healed by his skill, she had taken a dislike to Lichfield, and decidedly said, nothing could induce her to live there. His addresses did not subdue that resolve.

After so long and prosperous a residence, to quit that city, central in the Mercian district,[6] from whence his fame had diffused itself through the circling counties, seemed a great sacrifice; but the philosopher was too much in love to hesitate one moment. He married Mrs Pole in 1781, and removed directly to Derby.[7] His reputation and the unlimited confidence of the public followed him thither, and would have followed him to the metropolis, or to any provincial town, to which he might have chosen to remove.[8]

Why he constantly, from time to time, withstood solicitations from countless families of rank and opulence, to remove to London, was never exactly understood by the writer of these memoirs. She knows that the most brilliant prospects of success in the capital were opened to him, from various quarters, early on his residence at Lichfield, and that his attention to them was perpetually requested by eminent people. Undoubtedly those prospects acquired added strength and lustre each year beneath the ever-widening spread of his fame. Conscious of his full habit of body, he probably thought that the established custom of imbibing changed and pure air by almost daily journies into the country, essential to his health; perhaps to the duration of his life. In allusion to that perpetual travelling, a gentleman once humorously directed a letter "Dr Darwin upon the road". When himself wrote to Dr Franklin, complimenting him on having united philosophy to modern science, he directed his letter merely thus, "Dr Franklin, America"; and said, he felt inclined to make a still more flattering superscription[,] "Dr Franklin, the World".[9] His letter reached the sage, who first disarmed the lightning of its fatal power, for the answer to it arrived, and was shown in the Darwinian circles; in which had been questioned the likelihood of Dr Franklin ever receiving a letter of such general superscription as the whole western empire. Its safe arrival was amongst the triumphs of genius combined with exertion, "they make the world their country".

From the time of Dr Darwin's marriage [10] and removal to Derby, his limited biographer can only trace the outline of his remaining existence; remark the dawn and expansion of his poetic fame, and comment upon the claims which secure its immortality. The less does she regret this limitation, as Mr Dewhurst Bilsbury,[11] his pupil in infancy, his confidential friend, and frequent companion through ripened youth, is now writing at large, the life of Dr Darwin, who once more became an happy husband, with a second family of children, springing fast around him.[12] To those children the Miss Poles, as themselves grew up to womanhood, were very meritoriously attentive and attached. The eldest Miss Pole married Mr Bromley,[13] and is said to be happy in her choice of a worthy and amiable man. The second Miss Pole gave her lovely self to Mr John Gisborne,[14] younger brother to the celebrated moralist and poet of that name.[15]

Mr John Gisborne's philosophic energies, poetic genius, extensive benevolence, ingenuous modesty, and true piety, render him a pattern for all young men of fortune, and an honour to human nature. In the year 1797, he published a spirited and elegant local poem, entitled, *The Vales of Weaver*.[16] It is evidently of the Darwinian school, though in a shorter measure, and has genius to support the peculiar manner of poetic writing which it emulates and has caught. In this poem we meet appropriate and vivid landscape. Some of the epithets are perhaps exceptionable, and too free use is made of the word *glory* in several instances, particularly in its application to moon-light. Pope's faulty, though admired simile, in the last passage of the eighth book of the Iliad, has misled succeeding poets; inducing them to lavish upon the lunar effusions those terms of superlative splendour which they should reserve for the sun in his strength.[17] The Bard of Twickenham,[18] so generally discriminating, is indiscriminate when he styles the moon "refulgent lamp of night", and its white and modest beams "a flood of glory". Scholars say, he found no example in the original passage for this sun-defrauding magnificence. We do not find it for the moon in Cowper's more literal translation of the Homeric landscape, two sins against truth pardoned, and the scene, as penciled by Cowper, is beautiful; thus:

> As when around the clear, bright moon, the stars
> Shine in full splendour, and the winds are hush'd,
> The groves, the mountain tops, the headland heights,
> Stand all apparent; not a vapor streaks
> The boundless blue, but aether, open'd wide,
> All glitters, and the shepherd's heart is cheer'd.[19]

Surely the original does not sanction an image which nature never presents, since, when the moon is clear and bright, the stars do not spangle the firmament plenteously, or splendidly. A few stars, and never more than a few, sometimes glimmer through her flood of snowy and absorbing light. At any rate, splendour is a false term. When the night is cloudless, and the moon absent, the stellar host glows and sparkles very brightly; but its resulting mass of light by no means amounts to splendour.

Nature hallows, and poetry consecrates all the moon-light scenery in Milton. It is never more charming than in the following instance.

> Now glow'd the firmament
> With living saphirs [sic]. Hesperus, that led
> The starry host, rode brightest, till the moon,
> Rising in clouded majesty, o'er all
> Apparent queen, unveil'd her peerless light,
> And o'er the dark her silver mantle threw.[20]

Since Pope and Cowper, as translators of Homer, have been brought into a degree of comparison on these pages, the writer of them cannot resist the avowal of her opinion, that, on the whole, and considered merely as poems, great superiority is with Pope, as to perspicuity, elegance, and interest; the grace of picture, and the harmony of numbers. In a few striking passages Cowper may be the nobler, but his muse is for ever visibly and awkwardly struggling for literality, where he should have remembered the painter's adage, "It is better to sin against truth than beauty", so long as the sense is not perverted, and nature is not outraged by inappropriate epithets, which must always injure the distinctness of imagery and landscape.

If, in the preceding instance, Cowper's moon-light is chaster than Pope's, see how much more grandly the rhyme translation gives the remaining lines of that closing passage.

> So numerous seem'd those fires, the bank between
> Of Zanthus,[21] blazing, and the fleet of Greece,
> In prospect all of Troy; a thousand fires
> Each watch'd by fifty warriors, seated near.
> The steeds beside the chariot stood, their corn
> Chewing, and waiting till the golden-thron'd
> Aurora should restore the light of day.
>
> Cowper's Homer, First Edition[22]

Nothing can be more confused and unhappy than the language of this passage. It is left doubtful whether it is the fires that are blazing, or the river that by reflection blazes; and, "the bank between", is strange language for "between the banks". Chewing seems below the dignity of heroic verse, and the compound epithet golden-thron'd, fine in itself, is ruined as to effect, by closing the line when its substantive begins the next. Observe how exempt from all these faults is Pope's translation of the same paragraph.

> So many flames before proud Ilion [23] blaze,
> And lighten glimmering Zanthus with their rays.
> The long reflection of the distant fires
> Gleam on the walls, and tremble on the spires.
> A thousand piles the dusky horrors gild,
> And shoot a shady lustre o'er the field.
> Full fifty guards each flaming pile attend,
> Whole umber'd arms, by fits, thick flashes send.
> Loud neigh the coursers o'er their heaps of corn,
> And ardent warriors wait the rising morn.[24]

Poetry has no picture more exquisite than we meet in the second, third, and fourth lines; but an infinite number, equally vivid and beautiful, rise to the reader's eye, as it explores the pages of Doctor Darwin's *Botanic Garden*.

While the powers of metrical landscape-painting are the theme, not unwelcome to those who feel its inchantment [sic], will be instances which must prove that they are possessed by Mr John Gisborne in a degree which would disgrace the national taste if they should be suffered to pass away without their fame. *The Vales of Weaver* is this young man's first publication. Beneath thankless neglect the efflorescence of a rich imagination will probably sink blighted, like the opening flowers of the spring before an eastern mildew, no more to rise in future compositions to the view of that public which had estimated so coldly the value of the first.

We have read various descriptions of a winter's night, and its ensuing morning; but the following sketch is not borrowed from any of them. We feel that it was drawn beneath a lively remembrance of real impression made on the author's mind by the circumstances themselves; therefore, it will not fail to touch the vibrating chords of recollected sensation in every reader of sensibility. Book-made descriptions are trite and vapid; but nature is inexhaustible in her varieties, and will always present to the eye of genius either new images, or such combination of images as must render them new; and they will rise on his page in the morning freshness of originality. These sacred arcana she reserves for the poet, and leaves the mere versifier to his dull thefts.

Vales of Weaver

O Wootton![25] oft I love to hear
Thy wintry whirlwinds, loud and clear;
With dreadful pleasure bid them fill
My listening ear, my bosom chill.
As the sonorous North assails
Weaver's bleak wilds, and leafless vales,
With awful majesty of might
He bursts the billowy clouds of night;
Booms [26] the resounding glens among,
And roaring rolls his snows along.
In clouds against my groaning sash
Broad, feathery flakes incessant dash,
Or wheel below, and mingling form
The frolic pageants of the storm.
Hark! with what aggravated roar
Echo repeats her midnight lore;
Rends her dark solitudes and caves,
And bellowing shakes the mighty graves.[27]

Couch'd on her seat the timid hare
Listens each boisterous sweep of air;
Or peeps, yon blasted furze between,
And eyes the snow-bewildered scene;
Instant retracts her shuddering head,
And nestles closer in her bed.
All sad and ruffled, in the grove
The fieldfare wakes from dreams of love;

Hears the loud north and sleety snow,
And views the drifted brakes below;
Swift to her wing returns her beak,
And shivers as the tempests break.

Up starts the village-dog aloof,
And howls beneath his rifted roof;
Looks from his den, and blinking hears
The driving tumult at his ears!
Instant withdraws his fearful breast,
Shrinks from the storm, and steals to rest.
So [28] shrinks the pining fold, and sleeps
Beneath the valley's vaulted deeps;
Or crops the fescue's dewy blade,
And treads unseen the milky glade;
Forms by its breath fair opening bowers,
Transparent domes, and pearly showers.

Thus night rolls on till orient dawn
Unbars the purple gates of morn,
Unfolds each vale and snow-clad grove,
Mute founts and glossy banks above.
Thin streaky clouds, convex'd by storms,
Slowly expand their tissued forms;
Long bars of grey and crimson bright
Divert the golden threads of light;
Till glory's nascent curve displays
One splendid orb, a world of rays!
Then lightens heaven's etherial bound,
And all the spangled country glows around.[29]

Now that we have observed what power this author possesses to bring back to our recollection a stormy night in winter, succeeded by a ruddy dawn, blazing upon its frosted landscape, let us turn to his misty morning, in the same season, gradually clearing up into a mild and sunny day.

When winter's icy hand
Whitens Britannia's shivering land,
Then slow the billowy vapors glide,
And roll their lazy oceans wide.
Oft have I mark'd from Mathfield's [sic] [30] brow,
Her mist-embosom'd realms below,
While, here and there, a soaring tree

Waded amid the vapory sea,
And Ashbourn's [31] spire to distant sight
Tower'd, like a mast, in dubious light.
If, through the paly gloom, the sun
With struggling beams his journey won,
Soon as he rais'd his crimson eye
With transport flash'd th' illumin'd sky;
The vane, rekindling at his blaze,
Shot, like a meteor, through the haze;
The trees in liquid lustre flow'd,
And all the dim transparence glow'd,

...

The rustic, on his fields below,
Shoves from his lot the melting snow;
Salutes the welcome change, and seems
To taste of life's diviner streams;
Breathes with delight the temperate air
And views, with half-clos'd eyes, the boundless glare.[32]

What a pretty summer scene rises in the following verses from the same poem!

... Wide spread
An elm uprears his reverend head;
His front the whispering breeze receives,
The blue sky trembles through its leaves;
A cottage group beneath his shade,
Their locks with flowers and rushes braid;
And, gurgling round dark beds of sedge,
A brook just shows its silver edge.[33]

But now, turning from *The Vales of Weaver*, let us seek the *Botanic Garden*. The commencement of that poem in 1779 has been previously mentioned, with the circumstance which gave it birth. It consists of two parts; the first contains the *Economy of Vegetation*, the second the *Loves of the Plants*. Each is enriched by a number of philosophical notes. They state a great variety of theories and experiments in botany, chemistry, electricity, mechanics, and in the various species of air, salubrious, noxious, and deadly. The discoveries of the modern professors in all those sciences, are frequently mentioned with praise highly gratifying to them. In these notes explanations are found of every personified plant,[34] its generic history, its local situation, and the nature of the soil and climate to which it is indigenous; its botanic and its common name.

The verse corrected, polished, and modulated with the most sedulous attention; the notes involving such great diversity of matter relating to natural history; and the composition going forward in the short recesses of professional attendance, but chiefly in his chaise, as he travelled [35] from one place to another, the *Botanic Garden* could not be the work of one, two, or three years; it was ten from its primal lines to its first publication.[36] The immense price which the bookseller gave for this work,[37] was doubtless owing to considerations which inspired his trust in its popularity. Botany was, at that time, and still continues a very fashionable study. Not only philosophers, but fine ladies and gentlemen, sought to explore its arcana.[38] This poem, therefore, involved two classes of readers by whom it would probably be purchased. Every skilful Botanist, every mere Tyro in the science, would wish to possess it for the sake of the notes, though insensible, perhaps, as the veriest rustic, to the charms of poetry; while every reader, awakened to them, must be ambitious to see such a constellation of poetic stars in his library; all that gave immortality to Ovid's fame, without the slightest imitation of his manner, the least debt to his ideas; since, though Dr Darwin often retells that poet's stories, it is always with new imagery and heightened interest.

Certainly it was by an inversion of all custom that Dr Darwin published the second part of his poem first. The reason given for so extraordinary a manoeuvre in that advertisement which led the younger sister before the elder on the field of public exhibition, is this, that the appearance of the first part had been deferred till another year, for the purpose of repeating some experiments in vegetation.[39]

The Doctor was accustomed to remark, that whenever a strange step had been taken, if any way obnoxious to censure, the alleged reason was scarcely ever the real motive. His own singular management in this instance, and the way in which he accounted for it, proved a case in point. He was conscious that the second part of his work would be more level than the first to the comprehension, more congenial to the taste of the superficial reader, from its being much less abstract and metaphysic, while it possessed more than sufficient poetic matter to entertain and charm the enlightened and judicious few. They, however, he well knew, when his first part should appear, would feel its superiority to the earlier publication, its grander conceptions, its more splendid imagery, though less calculated to amuse and to be understood by common readers. Those of that last number who had purchased the first part would not like to possess the poem incomplete, and therefore would purchase the second. The observations of this paragraph refer to the poetry of the work, and to the two classes of readers who would value it chiefly on that account. The notes to each part must render them equally valuable to the votaries of botany, and other modern sciences.

It is with just and delicate criticism that Mr Fellowes [40] again observes of Dr Darwin's poetry: "In perspicuity, which is one of the first excellences in poetic as well as prose composition, this author has perhaps few equals. He is clear, even when describing the most intricate operations of nature, or the most complex works of art; and there is a lucid transparency in his style through which we see objects in their exact figure and proportion; but Dr Darwin's poetry wants sensation; that sort of excellence which, while it enables us to see distinctly the objects described, makes us feel them acting on our nerves".[41]

A little reflection is, perhaps, necessary precisely to understand this criticism, distinguishing between vivid poetry which does *not* excite sensation, and vivid poetry which *does* excite it. Instances will best elucidate the distinction. See the two following descriptions of a wintery evening, late in autumn.

Botanic Garden

Then o'er [42] the cultur'd lawns and dreary waste,
Retiring Autumn flings her howling blast,
Bends in tumultuous waves the struggling woods,
And showers her leafy honours on the floods,
In withering heaps collects the flowery spoil,
And each chill insect sleeps [43] beneath the soil.[44]

Quoted from a sonnet of Mr C. Lloyd's [45] published with Mr Colridge's[sic] [46] poems.

Dismal November! me it sooths to view,
At parting day, the scanty foliage fall
From the wet fruit-tree, or the grey stone wall,
Whose cold films glisten with unwholesome dew;
To watch the sweepy mists from the dank earth
Enfold the neighbouring copse, while, as they pass,
The silent rain-drop bends the long, rank grass,
Which wraps some blossom's immatured birth;
And, through my cot's lone lattice, glimmering grey,
Thy damp chill evenings have a charm for me,
Dismal November![47]

The picture is equally just and striking in both the above quotations; but the first, though more dignified, does *not* thrill our nerves, and the second *does*. We admire in the former the power and grace of the poet; in the latter we forget the poet and his art, and only yearn to see images reflected in his mirror, which we have annually, and many times shuddered to survey in real life.

When Dr Darwin describes the glow-worm,[48] supposing its light to be phosphoric, he thus exhorts his allegoric personages, the nymphs of fire, meaning the electrical powers.

Warm, on her mossy couch, the radiant worm,
Guard from cold dews her love-illum'd form,
From leaf to leaf conduct the virgin light,
Star of the earth, and diamond of the night![49]

Nothing can be more poetic, more brilliant than this picture; yet, when Shakespear [sic] says,

"The glow-worm shows the morning to be near,
And 'gins to pale his ineffectual fire",[50]

132

we feel sensation which the more resplendent picture of this insect had failed to inspire, notwithstanding the pleasure it had given us, the admiration it had excited.

Probably the reason why Dr Darwin's poetry, while it delights the imagination, leaves the nerves at rest, may be, that he seldom mixes with the picturesque the (as it is termed in criticism) *moral epithet*, meaning that quality of the thing mentioned, which pertains more to the mind, or heart, than to the eye, and which, instead of picture, excites sensation. Shakespear [sic] gives no distinct picture of the glow-worm, since the only epithet he uses for it is not descriptive of its appropriate lustre, which has a tint specified in the ensuing quotation.

"… From the bloom that spreads
Resplendent in the lucid morn of May,
To the green light the little glow-worm sheds
On mossy banks, when midnight glooms prevail,
And Silence broods o'er all the shelter'd dale".[51]

If Dr Darwin also omits to mention the particular hue of this insect, when it is luminous, he conveys that hue to the imagination when he says, "Star of the earth", since the largest and brightest stars have the same master-tint. Ossian [52] says, "Night is dull and dark, no star with its green, trembling beams!"

But Shakespear's [sic] moral epithet, ineffectual, does better than paint its object. It excites a sort of tender pity for the little insect, shining without either warmth or useful light, in the dark and lonely hours.

Botanic Garden

And now the rising moon, with lustre pale,
O'er heaven's dark arch unfurls her milky veil.[53]

This picture is charming: yet when Milton paints the same object thus,

"… Now reigns,
Full orb'd, the moon, and with more pleasant light,
Shadowy, sets off the face of things",[54]

the charm is on the nerves, as well as on the eye. The moral epithet *pleasant*, excites sensation, while the picturesque epithet, *shadowy*, has all the truth, the grace, and power of the pencil. It is that charm on the nerves to which Mr Fellowes so well applies the word, *sensation*.[55] It seems a new term in criticism, and is useful to express what pathos would express too strongly, and therefore with less accuracy. Pathos is the power of affecting the heart; by sensation is meant that of acting upon the nerves.

Beneath their torpor, the heart, or the passions, cannot be affected; but the nerves may be awakened to lively, or pensive pleasure, by composition which, not exciting any positive passion, may not act upon the heart in a degree to justify the application of the word, *pathetic*; and for this gentler, subtler, and more evanescent influence, which almost imperceptibly touches the passions without agitating them, Mr F.'s [56] term is happy.

Dr Darwin's excellence consists in delighting the eye, the taste, and the fancy, by the strength, distinctness, elegance, and perfect originality of his pictures; and in delighting the ear by the rich cadence of his numbers; but the passions are generally asleep, and seldom are the nerves thrilled by his imagery, impressive and beauteous as it is, or by his landscapes, with all their vividness.

It may, however, be justly pleaded for his great work, that its ingenious and novel plan did not involve any claim upon the affections. We are presented with an highly imaginative and splendidly descriptive poem, whose successive pictures alternately possess the sublimity of Michael Angelo,[57] the correctness and elegance of Raphael,[58] with the glow of Titian;[59] whose landscapes have, at times, the strength of Salvator,[60] and at others the softness of Claude;[61] whose numbers are of stately grace, and artful harmony; while its allusions to ancient and modern history and fable, and its interspersion of recent and extraordinary anecdotes, render it extremely entertaining. Adapting the past and recent discoveries in natural and scientific philosophy to the purposes of heroic verse, the *Botanic Garden* forms a new class in poetry, and by so doing, gives to the British Parnassus a wider extent than it possessed in Greece, or in ancient, or modern Rome.

Nor is it only that this composition takes unbeaten ground, and forms an additional order in the fanes of the Muses, it forms that new order so brilliantly, that though it may have many imitators, it will probably never have an equal in its particular class; neither would its style apply happily to subjects less intrinsically picturesque. The species of praise here given to this work is all that its author desired to excite. We have no right to complain of any writer, or to censure him for not possessing those powers at which he did not aim, and which are not necessarily connected with his plan.

To the subject Dr Darwin chose, his talents were eminently calculated. Neither Pope nor Gray would have executed it so well; nor would Darwin have written so fine an *Essay on Man*,[62] so interesting a Churchyard,[63] or so lovely an Ode [64] on the prospect of the school at which he was educated, had that school been Eton. He would not have succeeded so transcendently on themes, which demanded either pathos, or that sort of tender and delicate feeling in the poet, which excites in the reader sympathetic sensation; or yet in the sacred morality of ethic poetry, which however it may admit, or require that fancy adorn it with some rare, and lovely flowers, "allows to ornament but a second place, and always renders it subordinate to intrinsic worth and just design".[65] To whomsoever he might have been practically inferior on themes he has left unattempted, he is surely not inferior to Ovid; and if poetic taste is not much degenerated, or shall not hereafter degenerate, the *Botanic Garden* will live as long as the *Metamorphoses*.[66]

That in his poetic style Dr Darwin is a mannerist cannot be denied; but so was Milton, in the *Paradise Lost*;[67] so was Young, in the *Night Thoughts*;[68] so was Akenside, in the *Pleasures of Imagination*.[69] The Darwinian peculiarity is in part formed by the very frequent use of the imperative mood, generally beginning the couplet either with that, or with the verb active, or the noun personal. Hence, the accent lies oftener on the first syllable of each couplet in his verse than in that of any other rhymist [sic]; and it is, in consequence, peculiarly spirited and energetic. Dr Darwin's style is also distinguished by the liberal use of the spondee, viz. two monosyllables, equally accented, following each other instantly in some part of the line.[70]

Spondees, judiciously used, vary and increase the general harmony in every species of verse, whether blank or rhyme. They preserve the numbers from too luscious sweetness, from cloying sameness, from feeble elegance, and *that*, by contrasting the smoothness of the dactyls,[71] and the rich melodies of the iambic [72] accents. So discords resolving into concords, inspirit the strains of musical composition. But it is possible to make too frequent use of the spondee in poetry, as of the discord in music. Dr Darwin's ear preserved him from that exuberance; but Mr Bowles,[73] one of the finest poets of this day, often renders his versification, which is, at times, most exquisitely sweet, harsh, by the too frequently-recurring spondee.

From that gentleman's verse a couple of instances may be selected, to show, in one, that harmony may be improved by a sparing use of that accent, and injured in the other by using it too freely.

Mr Bowles' *Hope*

But lusty Enterprise, with looks of glee,
Approach'd the drooping youth, as he would say,
Come to the *wild woods* and the hills with me,
And throw thy sullen myrtle wreath away![74]

Bowles' *Elegiac Stanzas*

Hast thou [75] not visited that pleasant place,
Where in this *hard world* I have happiest been,
And shall I tremble at thy lifted mace,
That hath *pierc'd* all on which *life seem'd* to lean?[76]

The recurrence of two equally accented words three times in the stanza, and twice in the last line, incumbers [sic] the versification, while the single use of the spondee in the preceding four lines, from Hope, gives it grace and beauty. Dr Darwin, in the following passage, has used it frequently, without producing any such dead weight upon the verse. The quotation is from the charge of the Botanic Queen to the Nymphs of Fire, a poetic allegory for the influence of the fluid matter of heat in forwarding the germination and growth of plants.

Pervade, pellucid forms, their cold retreat!
Ray, from *bright orbs*, your viewless floods of heats!
From earth's *deep wastes* electric torrents pour,
Or shed from heav'n the scintillating shower!
Pierce the *dull root*, relax its fibre trains,
Thaw the *thick blood* that lingers in its veins!

Melt with *warm breath*, the fragrant gums that bind
Th' expanding foliage in its scaly rind!
And as in air the laughing leaflets play,
And turn their shining bosoms to the ray,
Nymphs, with *sweet smile*, each opening flower invite,
And on its damask eyelids pour the light![77]

On reflection, it should seem that it is the situation of these twin accents in the line, which prevents their frequent recurrence from producing harshness. It will be observed in the last quotation, that all the many spondees are preceded by two syllables; and that it is only when they are preceded by an odd syllable, either one or three, that they increase the harmony by their sparing, and injure it by their frequent appearance. One syllable only goes before the spondee in this line from the *Botanic Garden*.

The *wan stars* glimmering through the silver train.[78]

Three syllables in this verse from the same poem.

Where now the *South-sea* heaves its waste of frost.[79]

Again,

Loud shrieks the *lone thrush* from his leafless thorn.[80]

And, in that last instance, the spondee recurring twice in one line, harshness is the result. Once used only, and the harshness had been avoided; thus,

And shrieks the *lone thrush* from the leafless thorn.[81]

The following is a couplet where the spondee succeeding to three monosyllables has an exquisite effect of sound echoing sense.

Botanic Garden

With paler lustre where Aquarius [82] burns,
And showers the *still snow* from his hoary urns.[83]

We find another striking peculiarity in Dr Darwin's, style, that of invariably presenting a class by an impersonified individual; thus,

Where, nurs'd in night, incumbent Tempest shrouds
The seeds of thunder in circumfluent clouds.[84]

Again,

> Where, with chill frown, enormous Alps alarms
> A thousand realms horizon'd in his arms.[85]

Again,

> Sailing in air, when dark Monsoon enshrouds
> His trophic mountains in a night of clouds.[86]

Similar instances crowd the pages of the *Botanic Garden*. There is extreme sublimity in the whole of that passage; which converts the monsoon winds into an individual monster,

> That showers on Afric all his thousand urns.[87]

Dr Johnson, Mr Burke, and Dr Parr,[88] have the same habit in their prose; "Criticism pronounces", instead of "Critics pronounce". "Malignance will not allow", instead of "Malignant people will not allow". "Good-nature refuses to listen", instead of "a good natured man refuses to listen", and so on.

This manner of writing, whether in verse or prose, sweeps from the polished marble of poetry and eloquence, a number of the sticks and straws of our language; its articles, conjunctives, and prepositions. Addison's serious *Essays* are so littered with them and with idioms, as to render it strange that they should still be considered as patterns of didactic oratory.[89] No man of genius, however, adopts their diffuse and feeble style, now that the strength, the grace, and harmony of prose-writing, on the dignified examples of our *later* essayists, senators, and pleaders, give us better examples. These observations relate solely to the grave compositions of celebrated Atticus.[90] The quiet, easy, elegant gaiety of his comic papers in the Spectator, remains unrivalled.

It has been already observed in the course of this tract, that Dr Darwin's muse ranges through nature and art, through history, fable, and recent anecdote, to vary, inspirit, and adorn this her luxuriant work. If she impersonizes too lavishly; if devoted to picture, she covers every inch of the walls of her mansion with landscapes, allegoric groups, and with single figures; if no intersticial [sic] space is left to increase the effect of these splendid forms of the imagination; yet be it remembered, that it is always in the reader's power to draw each picture from the mass, and to insulate it by his attention. It will recompense by its grandeur, its beauty, or its terrific grace, the pains he may take to view it in every light, ere he proceeds to examine other objects in the work, which he will find of equal force and skill in their formation.

Dr Darwin gives us, in this poem, classic fables from Homer, Virgil, and Ovid, and *so* gives them, places the persons of each little drama in such new and interesting situations and attitudes, that he must indeed be a dull prose-man who shall exclaim undelighted, "This is an old story".

Notes

1   Colonel Pole was born in 1707, whereas Elizabeth Pole was born in 1747.

2   Sacheveral Pole (1769–1813). Another son, German Pole, died in his third month, in November 1774.

3   Elizabeth (1770–1821) and Millicent (1774–1857).

4   Attributed to Anna Seward.

5   Mark Akenside (1721–1770), *Pleasures of the Imagination* (1744), Book I, l.480. The original version places parentheses around "bear witness earth and heaven!" and has "fountains" in the plural.

6   Mercia, a kingdom of Anglo-Saxon England consisting of what today is England's Midlands, was settled by Angles *c.*500 along the Trent valley. The Venerable Bede (*c.*672–735) records in his *Historia Ecclesiastica Gentis Anglorum* that St Chad (*d.*672), who became Bishop of the Mercians, established the Episcopal See of the Mercians in Lichfield in 699. Thereafter, Lichfield's cathedral became the burial site for the Kings of Mercia.

7   Colonel Pole died 27 November 1780, and Mrs Pole and Dr Darwin were married 6 March 1781.

8   Following upon his experience with the Lunar Society, Dr Darwin organized the formation of the Derby Philosophical Society at his home in February 1783, formally bringing together a "group of men whose interest in the subject was already firmly established", as noted by R.P. Sturges, "The Membership of the Derby Philosophical Society, 1783–1802", *Midland History* 48 (1978):215. The original members were, in addition to Dr Darwin, Richard French (*c.*1738/39–1801), John Sneyd (1734–1809), Dr John Beridge (1745–1788), Dr John Hollis Pigot (1756/57–1794), Mr Erasmus Darwin, Jr. (1759–1799), John Leaper (1754–1819), Thomas Gisborne (1758–1846), William Strutt (1756–1830), and Mr Fox (either the hosier, Samuel, 1765–1851, or the surgeon, Francis). For further insight into the activity of this Society, see Eric Robinson, "The Derby Philosophical Society", *Annals of Science* 9 (1953): 359–367, Paul Elliott, "The Birth of Public Science in the English Provinces: Natural Philosophy in Derby, *c.*1690–1760", *Annals of Science* 57 (2000):61–100, and Paul Elliott, "The Derbyshire General Infirmary and the Derby Philosophers: The Application of Industrial Architecture and Technology to Medical Institutions in Early-Nineteenth-Century England", *Medical History* 46 (2000): 65–92.

9   Dr Darwin exchanged many letters with Benjamin Franklin (1707–1790) on topics ranging from pond gases, Darwin's 'Speaking Machine', the colours seen in the closed eye after having gazed some time upon luminous objects, the opportunity of reprinting the Lichfield Botanic Society's translation of Linnaeus, Sir Frederick William Herschel's (1738–1822) telescopic discovery of three volcanoes on the moon, and, of course, electricity. Darwin likely first met Franklin in Birmingham in 1758 while he was visiting Matthew Boulton and his scientific friends. Franklin was officially in England as a representative of the Pennsylvania Assembly to petition the Crown for more equity in taxation, but he wanted to further explore the Midlands, the regional homeland of some of his ancestors. In 1765, Franklin provided Dr Small letters of introduction to Boulton and Darwin upon Small's return from teaching in the American Colonies. Franklin also met up with Dr Darwin in Lichfield in Spring 1771.

10   Married 6 March 1781 during which month they left Lichfield for Radburn Hall, near Derby.

11   Bilsborrow.

12   Edward Darwin (1782–1829), Frances Anne Violetta Darwin (1783–1874), Emma Georgina Elizabeth Darwin (1784–1818), Francis Sacheveral Darwin (1786–1859), John Darwin (1787–1818), Henry Darwin (1789–1790), and Harriot Darwin (1790–1825).

13   Elizabeth Anne Pole (1770–1821), when 21 years old, married Colonel Henry Bromley (*b. c.*1767), a natural son of Thomas Bromley, 2nd Lord Montfort (1732–1799). Elizabeth and Henry lived at Abberley, Worcestershire where they raised their seven daughters.

14   Millicent Pole married John Gisborne (1770–1851) in 1792, and they had eleven children. The Gisbornes lived at Holly Bush, at Newborough, Staffordshire, in the heart of the ancient Needwood Forest, just a mile from the

Gisborne family estate, Yoxall Lodge. They became close friends of Jane Austen's (1775–1817) cousin, their neighbour Edward Cooper (1770–1835) and his wife, Carolina Isabella Powys (1775–1838). The men shared an evangelical passion as well as a strong interest in botany. For a contemporary account of Gisborne, see the work of his daughter, Emma Nixon, *A Brief Memoir of the Life of John Gisborne, Esq., To which are Added, Extracts from his Diary* (Derby, 1852).

15   The Revd. Thomas Gisborne (1758–1846), divine, poet, writer, and drawing and musical companion of Joseph Wright of Derby. Seward acknowledged Gisborne's *An Enquiry into the Duties of the Female Sex* (London: T. Cadell and W. Davies, 1797), together with his earlier *An Enquiry Into the Duties of Men in the Higher and Middle Classes of Society in Great Britain* (London: J. Davis for B. and J. White, 1794), to be "books of high reputation, and certainly [to] contain many excellent things", but, "Admirable receipt books [as they are] … to make human angels", she found "both [to be] … too strict", and thought that they "might have been more generally useful upon a less rigid plan of admonition, especially the volume dedicated to females …. could the volatile and joyous spirit of my youth have borne curbs so continual and such Argus-eyed watchfulness?" she wrote. "Remembering those trusted pleasures, which Mr Gisborne's system would restrain as dangerous, he cannot convince me to consider such restraints necessary where the young heart is pure, or capable of improving it where it is otherwise" (Seward, *Letters,* IV, pp.350–51).

16   *The Vales of Weaver: A Loco-Descriptive Poem Inscribed to the Reverend John Granville of Calwich, Staffordshire* (London: John Stockdale, 1797).

17   Alexander Pope's (1688–1744) translation of Homer's *Iliad* was published in six volumes from 1715 to 1720; a translation of the *Odyssey* followed in 1725–26. Among the cameo reliefs that Wedgwood used on his pottery was that of the "Apotheosis of Homer".

18   In 1717, Pope moved to Twickenham, west of London on the River Thames, where he was visited by many celebrities and where he lived for the rest of his life. Seward composed a sonnet "On Reading a Description of Pope's Garden at Twickenham", Number XX in *Original Sonnets on Various Subjects; And Odes Paraphrased from Horace* (London: G. Sael, 1799).

19   William Cowper (1731–1800), trans. of *The Iliad and Odyssey of Homer* (1791), *Iliad*, Book 8, ll.643–48.

20   Milton, *Paradise Lost*, Book IV, ll.604–609. Seward used "o'er all" instead of Milton's "at length".

21   The ancient capital city of Lycia which stood on the River Zanthus, or Xanthus. In the *Iliad*, the River Zanthus took on human form and tried to stop Achilles' slaughter of the Trojans.

22   Cowper, trans. of *The Iliad and Odyssey of Homer* (1791), *Iliad*, Book 8, ll.649–55.

23   Ilion ('Ιλιον) or *Ilium* in Latin, the ancient name for the city of Troy, as used in the title of Homer's *Iliad*.

24   Pope, *The Iliad* (1715–20), Book 8, ll.698–708.

25   This poem describes the wide river valley of Weaver, Derbyshire. In 1776, Rousseau lived in Richard Davenport's country home, Wootton Hall, near Wootton Lodge, at the foot of the lofty Weaver Hills. On walks around Wootton, to and from his beloved Dovedale, Rousseau studied local flora. The River Wootton flows across west Cheshire, linking with the Trent and Mersey Canal.

26   Seward's own footnote, "A word admirably expressing the noise of winds, and applied to here for the first time in poetry".

27   Seward's own footnote, "The numerous tumuli on Weaver and the adjacent hills".

28   Seward's own footnote, "*So shrinks the pining fold*. It often happens that sheep in this and in the Peak country, are immersed many feet deep in snow for several days before they are discovered. The perpetual steam from their nostrils keeps the snow, immediately over their heads, in a dissolving state, and hence a tunnel is constantly forming through the heaps above. This tunnel greatly facilitates their discovery, and supplies them with abundance of fresh

air. The warmth of these animals soon dissolves the surrounding snow, and at length the drift is so completely vaulted, that they are able to stretch their limbs, and search for subsistence. It is asserted that sheep have been frequently found alive after having been entombed in the snow during a fortnight".

29   John Gisborne (1770–1851), *The Vales of Weaver: a Loco-Descriptive Poem* (1797), ll.371–88, 391–426. Seward omits ll. 389–90: "Appals [sic] with horror Fancy's mind,/While ghosts disturb'd shrill-shriek upon the wind". Gisborne used "ears" in the plural, line 374, "closer nestles to" instead of "nestles closer in" in line 396, "beating" instead of "sleety" in line 399, "Regards" for "And views" in line 400, "fear froze" instead of "fearful" in line 407, "towers" instead of "showers" in line 414, and "twinkles round" instead of "glows around" in line 426.

30   Mayfield, on the River Dove, near Ashbourne, Derbyshire.

31   In Derbyshire, on the Staffordshire border, along the east side of the River Dove, ten miles from Derby. This was the location where Dr Darwin established a boarding school for girls, where the teachers were his natural daughters Mary Parker (1774–1859) and Susanna Parker (1772–1856), both daughters of Dr Darwin's Lichfield housemaid, Mary Parker, born after the death of Mrs Polly Darwin.

32   Seward's own footnote, "A Lapland scene, which succeeds to the last line, is omitted, not from its want of poetic beauty, but merely to shorten the quotation". Gisborne, *The Vales of Weaver*, ll.121–38, 151–56. Gisborne used "lucid" instead of "paly" in line 131, "lawns" for "fields" in line 151, "cot" for "lot" in line 152, "wondrous" for "welcome" in line 153, and "half-shut" for "half-clos'd" in line 156.

33   Gisborne, *The Vales of Weaver*, ll.29–36. Gisborne used "his" instead of "its" in line 32.

34   On personification in Darwin's poetry in particular, see James Venable Logan, "The Poetry and Aesthetics of Erasmus Darwin", *Princeton Studies in English* 15 (1936): 46–92; King-Hele, *Erasmus Darwin and the Romantic Poets*; Maureen McNeil, "The Scientific Muse: The Poetry of Erasmus Darwin" in L. J. Jordanova (ed) *Languages of Nature: Critical Essays on Science and Literature* (London: Free Association Books, 1986), pp.159–203; Janet Browne, "Botany for Gentlemen: Erasmus Darwin and the Loves of the Plants", *Isis* 80 (1989): 593–620; and Catherine Packham, "The Science and Poetry of Animation: Personification, Analogy, and Erasmus Darwin's *Loves of the Plants*", *Romanticism* 10 (2004): 191–208. For a popular work of recent years that takes on somewhat of a personification of plants, see Michael Pollen's bestselling, *The Botany of Desire: A Plant's-Eye View of the World* (New York: Random House, 2001).

35   According to King-Hele, *Erasmus Darwin: A Life of Unequalled Achievement*, p.82, Dr Darwin travelled up to 10,000 miles per year in his carriage.

36   Its origin, dating from Seward's lines composed in July 1778, until it appeared in the *The Loves of the Plants*, the earliest published section of *The Botanic Garden*, published in 1789.

37   Darwin received £300 for the copyright of *The Loves of the Plants* and £400 for *The Economy of Vegetation*. See King-Hele, *Collected Letters of Erasmus Darwin*, letter 90–2, p.360, and note 1.

38   For more thorough investigations into the women who investigated and wrote about botany during this era, see Londa Schiebinger, *Nature's Body: Gender in the Making of Modern Science* (Boston: Beacon Press, 1993); Ann B. Shteir, *Cultivating Women, Cultivating Science* (1996); Henrietta Nickels Shirk, "Contributions to Botany, the Female Science, by Two Eighteenth-Century Women Technical Communicators", *Technical Communication Quarterly* 6 (1997): 293–312; and Samantha George, *Botany, Sexuality and Women's Writing* (2007).

39   It remains unclear as to what experiments were being pursued. Although dated 1791, King-Hele (*Doctor of Revolution*, p.213) has noted that this second part was probably not published until June 1792.

40   The Revd. Robert Fellowes (1771–1847).

41   *Critical Review* 68 (1789): 375–379.

42   Darwin's actual opening of this *Loves of the Plants* passage was "When in" rather than "Then o'er".

43   Darwin used "sinks" rather than "sleeps".

44   *Loves of the Plants*, I, lines 198–204.

45   The poet, Charles Lloyd (1775–1839), part of the prominent Birmingham Quaker banking family.

46   Samuel Taylor Coleridge (1772–1834).

47   Charles Lloyd, "To November", in *Poems by S. T. Coleridge, Second Edition, To Which are Now Added Poems by Charles Lamb, and Charles Lloyd* (London: N. Biggs, 1797), ll.1–11.

48   The wingless female firefly (family *Lampyridae*) that emits lights from its abdomen.

49   Darwin, *Economy of Vegetation*, I, lines 193–196.

50   Shakespeare, *Hamlet* (1600–1601), I, v, 89–90.

51   Anna Seward, "Sonnet VII", *Original Sonnets on Various Subjects; And Odes Paraphrased from Horace*, 2nd ed (London: G. Sael, 1799). ll.10–14.

52   Ossian, reputed to be a 3rd century Irish war poet who conveyed heroic tales about Finn and his warriors, the Fianna Eirean. The Scottish poet James Macpherson (1736–1796) brought these tales to wide attention in his publications *Fingal, An Ancient Epic Poem, in Six Books* (London: T. Becket and P. A. DeHoudt, 1762) and *Temora, An Ancient Epic Poem in Eight Books, Together with Several Other Poems, Composed by Ossian, the Son of Fingal* (London: T. Becket and P. A. DeHoudt 1763). As many others eventually came to believe, Sir Walter Scott tried to persuade Seward that these supposed Gaelic ballads were actually Macpherson's own creations. See Samuel H. Monk, "Anna Seward and the Romantic Poets: A Study in Taste", in Earl Leslie Griggs (ed) *Wordsworth and Coleridge: Studies in honor of George McLean Harper* (New York: Russell and Russell, 1962). Seward wrote two poems based on Ossian, "Crugal's Ghost" and "The Ghost of Cuchullin" which appeared in her *Poetical Works*, vol.3, pp.15–20 and p.21, respectively.

53   Darwin, *Loves of the Plants*, II, lines 13–14. In Darwin's version, these lines read:
"Soft, when the pedant moon with lustres pale
O'er heaven's blue arch unfurls her milky veil".

54   Milton, *Paradise Lost*, V.41–3. Where Seward has "pleasant", Milton has "pleasing". The lines are from Satan's voice in Eve's dream, urging her to eat the fruit from the tree of knowledge.

55   Sensation or sensibility included actions like the opening and closing of sphincters, salivating upon the sight of food, and creating facial expressions. All of these motions were, according to Darwin, inherited traits. For more on the application of these ideas to human psychology, see Edward S. Reed*, From Soul to Mind: The Emergence of Psychology from Erasmus Darwin to William James* (New Haven: Yale University Press, 1997), and Noel Jackson, *Science and Sensation in Romantic Poetry* (Cambridge: Cambridge University Press, 2008).

56   Robert Fellowes.

57   Michelangelo di Lodovico Buonarroti Simoni (1475–1564), an artist who held a supreme influence over the development of Western art.

58   Raffaello Sanzio (1483–1520) was known for the clarity of his form.

59   Tiziano Vecellio (*c.*1488–1576), the Venetian school's paramount Renaissance painter.

60   Francesco de Rossi, known as Salviati (1510–1563), a master mannerist fresco painter.

61   Claude Gellée, called Claude Lorrain (1600–1682), a French master landscape artist.

62   Alexander Pope's *An Essay On Man, in Epistles to a Friend* (London: for J. Wilford, 1733–34).

63   Thomas Gray's *Elegy Written in a Country Churchyard* (London: Dodsley, 1751).

64   Gray, who matriculated at Eton in 1725, later composed *An Ode on a Distant Prospect of Eton College* (London: R. Dodsley, 1747).

65   James Beattie (1735–1803), *The Minstrel; or, the Progress of Genius* (1771), lviii. ll.5–7. The original lines, which Seward seems to paraphrase, are "but Nature now/To his experienced eye a modest grace/Presents, where Ornament the second place/Holds, to intrinsic worth and just design/Subservient still".

66 Joseph Addison, in particular, adapted Ovid's *Metamorphoses* for the Augustan age of English literature.

67 John Milton, *Paradise Lost* (1667).

68 Edward Young, *The Complaint; or, Night-thoughts* (1743).

69 Mark Akenside, *The Pleasures of Imagination* (1744).

70 Seward's own footnote, "This explanation is for the ladies".

71 Metrical pattern of one long (stressed) syllable and two short (unstressed) syllables.

72 Metrical pattern of one short (unstressed) syllable followed by one long (stressed) syllable.

73 William Lisle Bowles (1762–1850), divine and poet, whose sonnets significantly influenced Coleridge.

74 *Hope, An Allegorical Sketch on Recovering Slowly from Sickness* (1796) I. 141.

75 Seward's own footnote, "Death".

76 *Elegiac Stanzas, Written During a Sickness at Bath* (1796), II, 35–38.

77 Darwin, *Economy of Vegetation*, I, lines 461–472.

78 Darwin, *Economy of Vegetation*, I, line 134, though Darwin used "its" instead of the second "the".

79 Darwin, *Economy of Vegetation*, I, line 78, though Darwin used "tide" instead of "frost".

80 Darwin, *Loves of the Plants*, I, line 475.

81 Seward's own refinement of Darwin's lines.

82 Aquarius, the "Water-Bearer" constellation in the zodiac.

83 Darwin, *Economy of Vegetation*, II, line 27.

84 Darwin, *Economy of Vegetation*, II, lines 357–358.

85 Darwin, *Economy of Vegetation*, III, lines 103–104.

86 Darwin, *Economy of Vegetation*, III, line 130, though Darwin used "tropic" instead of "trophic".

87 Darwin, *Economy of Vegetation*, III, line 132.

88 Samuel Parr (1747–1825), educated at Harrow and Emmanuel College, Cambridge, a schoolmaster, divine, Whig pamphleteer, and admirer of Samuel Johnson.

89 Joseph Addison (1672–1719).

90 Atticus was Pope's satirical name for Addison.

Chapter V

Analysis of the first part of the *Botanic Garden*.[1]

The Economy of Vegetation[2]

After that landscape of the scene which forms the exordium, the Goddess of Botany[3] descends in gorgeous gaiety.

She comes! – the Goddess! – thro' the whispering air,
Bright as the morn, descends her blushing car;
Each circling wheel a wreath of flowers entwines;
And gemm'd with flowers the silken harness shines;
The golden bits with flowery studs are deck'd,
And knots of flowers the crimson reins connect.
And now on earth the silver axle rings,
And the shell sinks upon its slender springs;
Light from her airy seat the Goddess bounds,
And steps celestial press the pansied grounds.[4]

Spring welcomes her with fragrance and with song, and, to receive her commissions, the four Elements attend *(Figure 23)*. They are allegorised as Gnomes, Water-Nymphs, Sylphs, and Nymphs of Fire.[5] Her address to each class, and the business she allots to them, form the four Cantos of this first part of the poem.

The Ladies of Ignition [6] receive her primal attention. The picture with which her address commences, is of consummate brilliance and grace; behold it, reader, and judge if this praise be too glowing!

Nymphs of primeval fire, your vestal train
Hung with gold tresses o'er the vast inane;
Pierc'd with your silver shafts the throne of night,
And charm'd young Nature's opening eyes with light,
When Love Divine, with brooding wings unfurl'd,
Call'd from the rude abyss the living world.[7]

Figure 23: "Flora Attended by the Elements", engraved by Anker Smith based upon Henry Fuseli's design. Darwin used this engraving as the frontispiece of The Economy of Vegetation *(1792).*

The Darwinian creation, which ensues, charms us infinitely, even while we recollect its simpler greatness on the page of Moses,[8] and on its sublime paraphrase in the *Paradise Lost*.[9] The creation in this poem is astronomic, and involves the universe; and as such is of excellence yet unequalled in its kind, and never to be excelled in the grandeur of its conceptions.

> Let there be light, proclaim'd th' Almighty Lord,
> Astonish'd Chaos heard the potent word;
> Through all his realms the kindling ether runs,
> And the mass starts into a million suns.
> Earths round each sun, with quick explosion, burst,
> And second planets issue from the first;
> Bend, as they journey, with projectile force,
> In bright ellipsis, their reluctant course;
> Orbs wheel in orbs, round centres centres roll,
> And form, self-balanc'd, one revolving whole;
> Onward they move, amid their bright abode,
> Space without bound, the bosom of their God.[10]

The word of the Creator, by an allusion to the effects of a spark upon gunpowder, setting into instant and universal blaze the ignited particles in Chaos, till they burst into countless suns, is an idea sublime in the first degree.

The subsequent comments of the Goddess on the powers of the Nymphs of Fire,[11] introduce lovely pictures of the lightning and the rainbow; the exterior sky, the twilight, the meteor, and the aurora borealis; of the planets, the comet, and all the etherial blazes of the universe.

She next exhibits them as superintending the subterranean and external volcanos.

> You, from deep cauldrons and unmeasur'd caves,
> Blow flaming airs, or pour vitrescent waves;
> O'er shining oceans ray volcanic light,
> Or hurl innocuous embers through the night.[12]

She compares them to Venus[13] and her Nymphs,[14] after they had descended to the cave of Vulcan.[15] The classic fable forms a varied and lively little drama. The Goddess proceeds to remind her hand-maids of their employments; says, they lead their glittering bands around the sinking day, and when the sun retreats, confine, with folds of air, his lingering fires to the cold bosom of earth.

> O'er eve's pale forms diffuse phosphoric light,
> And deck with lambent flames the shrine of night.[16]

Surely there cannot be a more beautiful description of a vernal twilight. The phosphorescent quality of the Bolognian stone,[17] Beccari's prismatic shells,[18] and the harp of Memnon,[19] which is recorded to have breathed spontaneous chords when shone upon by the rising sun, are all compared to the twilight glimmerings of the horizon; so also the luminous insects, the glow-worm, the fire-flies of the tropics, the fabulous *ignis fatuus*,[20] and the *gymnotus electricus*,[21] brought to England from Surinam in South America, about the year 1783; a fish, whose electric power is, on provocation, mortal to his enemy. He is compared to the Olympic eagle, that bears the lightning in its talons.

Dr Darwin considers the discovery of the uses of fire, as the earliest and most important of the artificial comforts. Hence, the Goddess praises her nymphs of that element, as the primal instructers [sic] of savage man. Its dangerous excellence is illustrated by the severe beauty of the serpent-haired Medusa,[22] as it blazes on the shield of Minerva.[23]

They are next addressed as the patronesses of chemistry; teaching the uses of gunpowder, and inspiring Captain Savery [24] with the invention of the steam-engine. The unpoetical name renders this introduction of a real person amidst allegoric beings, unhappy; especially since no dramatic circumstance in his destiny recompenses the infelicity. A description of that eminently useful machine is given with the accuracy of a mechanic philosopher, and the dignity of a great poet. A prophecy follows, that its powers will, in future times, be applied to the purposes of facilitating land and water carriage, and in navigating balloons.

The wonderful effects of this vast machine are supposed to resemble the exploits of Hercules,[25] and several of those exploits are very finely pictured.

All the operations of electricity next pass in review; a lovely female receiving the shock on a waxen elevation; also a circle of young men and women electrified.[26] Their resulting sensations are described with perfect truth and elegance, and the effects of this discovery in paralytic cases are thus exquisitely mentioned.

Palsy's cold hands the fierce concussion own,
And Life clings trembling on her tottering throne.[27]

Such powers in this artful lightning are compared to those of the natural; its deleterious excess, to the fire of heaven that scathes the oak; its milder degree, to the fairy rings, which the poet believes to have been imprinted by the flashes of the thunder storm darting on the grass and circularly blighting it.

The disastrous fate of professor Richman,[28] at Petersburgh, pursuing electric experiment with fatal temerity, rises to the eye, and makes the reader a shuddering spectator of its progress and result.

Dr Franklin, with his preserving rods, is compared to the celebrated Florentine Gem,[29] Cupid snatching the lightnings from Jupiter, which the poet considers as a noble allegory, representing Divine Justice disarmed by Divine Love. The poetic scene, from the Gem, is one of the sweetest little dramas of this poem; so sweet, there is no resisting the temptation of here exhibiting it to those to whom the work itself may not instantly be accessible.

Thus when, on wanton wing, intrepid Love
Snatch'd the rais'd lightning from the arm of Jove,
Quick o'er his knee the triple bolt he bent,
The cluster'd darts and forky arrows rent;
Snapp'd, with illumin'd hands, each flaming shaft,
His tingling fingers shook, and stamp'd, and laugh'd.
Bright o'er the floor the scatter'd fragments blaz'd,
And Gods, retreating, trembled as they gaz'd.
Th' immortal Sire, indulgent to his child,
Bow'd his ambrosial locks, and Heav'n relenting, smil'd.[30]

Of the great superiority of poetic to actual picture, this passage is one of the countless proofs, perceived by every reader who has power to meet the ideas of the Bard.[31] Suppose the subject of this little fable to be engraven, or painted with the utmost excellence, yet the exquisitely natural action of the infant god shaking his fingers, and laughing and stamping, from that degree of pain experienced on slightly touching an ignited substance; the scattering over the floor the broken darts and arrows of the lightning; the alarmed deities retreating, and the indulgent nod and increasing smile of Jupiter, are all progressive circumstances which genius may paint on the imagination, but not on the canvass.

The Goddess next adverts to the influence of her nymphs on animal circulation, from the theory of the phosphoric acid [32] colouring and warming the blood, and hence becoming an indispensable ingredient in vital formation

From the crown'd forehead to the prostrate weed.[33]

This theory is illustrated by the noble fable of Eros,[34] or Divine Love, issuing from the great egg of night, floating in chaos; but surely the image of this celestial love is too gay for the sublimity of its birth; "gaudy wings", "soft smiles", "golden curls", and "silver darts",[35] might suit the cyprian [36] but not the hieroglyphic [37] Cupid.

… Higher far of *him*
And with mysterious reverence we deem.

Milton.[38]

Her Nymphs thus eulogized,

The Goddess paus'd, admir'd, with conscious pride,
Th' effulgent legions marshall'd by her side,
Forms spher'd in fire, with trembling light array'd,
Ens [39] without weight, and substance without shade.[40]

It may be observed of the two last lines that the imagination, which could with such appropriate and novel beauty invest its ideal personages, cannot be too highly appreciated, and we might as well disdain the sun for often dazzling us with excess of splendor, as to suffer the occasional redundance of ornament in this extraordinary work, to make us cold and insensible to its original, bold, and, in their class, peerless excellencies.

The use of words entirely Latin has been objected to this poem, as *ens* for *life*, in the last verse of the above quotation. Niceness of ear probably induced its substitution, and that from the proximity of the word *light* in the preceding line, which would have been of too similar sound to *life*, had life been used instead of its Latin synonism, *ens*.

The Botanic Queen now proceeds to appoint the nymphs of fire their tasks. She bids them awaken the west wind, chafe his wan cheeks, and wring the rain-drops from his hair; bids them blaze around the frosted rills, and stagnant waters, and charm the Naiad from her silent cave, where she sits enshrined in ice, clasping her empty urns. She is compared to Niobe.[41]

Our poet seems to have forgotten himself in thus throwing the year back into the skirts of winter; since, in opening this Canto, he had described the spring in all her glory, when the Botanic Queen descended, and the impersonized elements received her.

The nymphs are also commanded to assail the fiend of frost; to break his white towers and crystal mail; to drive him to Zembla, and chain him to the northern bear. A simile ensues, in which the grampus,[42] and the scene of the whale fishery, in all the strength of poetic colouring, meets the attention of the reader.

Supposed influence of the principle of internal heat in vegetation induces a command to these its agents to pour electric torrents from the deep wastes of earth, which may pierce the root, relax the fibres, and thaw the sap of plants, flowers, and trees. The asserted consequence of their obedience to this command produces a noble sketch of the umbrageous wilds of Canada. Their operations are oddly compared to the effects of the sympathetic inks, and of a picture drawn in them; and a receipt to make them is given in a note.

The nymphs are now exhorted to quit the summer regions when the dog-star [43] shall preside in them. Its often blighting influence on the fruits of the earth is illustrated by an allusion to the fate of Semele.[44] Then rises an iceland scene, and an astronomical personification. Look at it, courteous reader, and if with eyes of indifference, arraign the power of prejudice in thy mind, or suspect thy want of taste for the higher orders of poetry.

> There, in her azure coif, and starry stole,
> Grey Twilight sits, and rules the slumbering Pole;
> Bends the pale moon-beam round the sparkling coast,
> And strews with livid hands eternal frost.[45]

An agency of the ignited particles in creation, that of separating the ice-islands, fancifully induces a command from the Goddess, that her nymphs should float their broken masses of ice to the torrid climates. It is adorned with the scripture incident, Elijah, on mount Carmel, invoking fire from heaven,[46] and the incident is given with all the Darwinian power.

This Canto terminates with the obedience of the nymphs, and a simile for their departure. They start from the soil, and wing their duteous flight.

While vaulted skies, with streams of transient rays,
Shine as they pass, and earth and ocean blaze.[47]

A comparative description of the fire-works exhibited in great cities for the return of peace and liberty, after the cruel oppressions of war, is of the most accurate precision; but it is faulty as a simile, from its extreme inferiority to the imaginary objects which it is meant to illustrate. The nymphs of fire, flying on their appointed errands, in every direction, illuminating, with evanescent flashes, the whole horizon, the sea, and the land, is so grand an idea, that the wheels, the dragons, the serpents, the mock stars, and suns, of that ever childish exhibition, become ludicrous, as succeeding to a picture of such gay sublimity; for sublimity is not always confined to sombre objects. Proofs that it is not, are found in the *Paradise Lost*. When Adam observes to Eve, on the approach of the angel Michael,[48] that the glorious shape seems another morning risen on mid-noon, the idea is no less sublime than it is gay.

This apprehended injudiciousness of the fire-work simile suggests the remark, that a few such erratic luxuriances of a picturesque fancy, together with the peculiar construction of the Darwinian verse, and its lavish personification, enabled an highly ingenious satirist to burlesque the *Loves of the Plants*, by the *Loves of the Triangles*.[49] Eminently fortunate for its purpose was the thought of transforming cubes, and cones, and cylinders, and other technical terms of mathematic and mechanic science, into nymphs and swains, enamoured of each other. The verse of this ironical poem is not only Darwinian, but it is beautifully Darwinian. The very slightly allusive power of several of the similies in the *Botanic Garden*, is ridiculed with infinite subtleness and wit; while the little stories in this burlesque, so comic in their scantiness of resemblance, are very elegantly told. That brilliant satire amply refutes Lord Shaftesbury's [sic] system,[50] that ridicule is the test of truth, and that it is impossible to ridicule with effect what is intrinsically excellent. The warmest admirers of Dr Darwin's splendid poem, and of the ingenious theories and stated experiments of the notes, must yet be amused with such grotesque imitation of each; just as they are diverted with the burlesque, in the *Critic*, of the death of Hotspur,[51] and of Eve's beautiful protest to Adam,

Sweet is the breath of morn, &c.[52]

On the subject of this satire, Dr Darwin wanted presence of mind. Instead of pretending, as he did, never to have seen or heard of the *Loves of the Triangles*, when questioned on the subject, he should voluntarily have mentioned that satire every where, and praised its wit and ingenuity. He ought to have triumphed in a just consciousness, that his poem could lose none of its charms with the few, whose praise is fame, by the artful resemblance of this false Florimel;[53] secure that its mock graces, brilliant as they are, would soon melt away, like the Nymph of Snow in the *Fairie Queen*,[54] while the genuine charms of his muse must endure so long as the English language shall exist; nay, should that perish, Translation would preserve the *Botanic Garden* as one of its gems; if not in original brightness, would at least retain all that host of beauties which do not depend upon the perhaps intransfusible felicities of verbal expression. The lavish magnificence of the imagery in this work, Genius alone, bold, original, creative, and fertile in the extreme, could have produced. Its profusion may cloy the fastidious, its splendor may dazzle the poetically weak of sight; but still it is the result of that power, which Shakespear [sic] characterises when he says,

The Poet's eye, in a fine phrenzy rolling,
Doth glance from heaven to earth, from earth to heaven,
And as Imagination bodies forth
The form of things unknown, the Poet's pen
Turns them to shape, and gives to airy nothing
A local habitation, and a name.[55]

The Second Canto

Opens with the charge of the Botanic Queen to her Gnomes, who are here restored to that benevolent character allotted to them by Rosicrusius,[56] and which, to suit his purpose, Pope rendered malignant, in the *Rape of the Lock*.[57] She addresses them as ministrant spirits to subterranean vegetation, and spectators of all the astronomic and terraqueous wonders of creation; of the Sun exploding our planet, the earth, from his crater.

Except to introduce an extremely fine description of the sun's signs in the zodiac, it would be difficult to guess why the Gnomes [58] should be supposed to have pursued the flying sphere, and encircled the year's starry girdle. Those should seem employments better suited to the allotted nature of the Nymphs of Ignition, of at least of the Sylphs,[59] than of these their subterranean sisters. The epithet *ardent*, "your ardent troops", is a seldom-found instance of inaccuracy in this poem, corrected and polished with such elaborate care; eager, active, any thing rather than an adjective metaphorically taken from fire, the assigned element of the nymphs recently dismissed.

Next rises the golden age, and Earth is invested with Edenic privileges and exemptions. We are told, in a note, that there is an ancient gem, representing Venus rising out of the sea, supported by two Tritons;[60] that the allegory was originally an hieroglyphic picture, before letters were invented, descriptive of the formation of the earth from the ocean. The poet takes this opportunity of presenting to his readers the most beautiful portrait of Venus, first emerging from her parent deep, that has been given by any Bard, ancient or modern; and its features are unborrowed as they are peerless. She has about her the traces of the humid element, from which she rises, and they increase her general loveliness and grace; wringing, with rosy fingers, her golden tresses, as they hang uncurled around her fair brows, while bright drops of water roll from her lifted arms, wander round her neck, stand in pearls upon her polished shoulders and back, and star with glittering brine her whole lucid form. Thus the Darwinian Venus,

O'er the smooth surge, on silver sandals stood,
And look'd enchantment on the dazzled flood.[61]

The first terrestrial volcano is next described; an earthquake of incalculable magnitude, producing continents and islands on the before united and level earth, with separating oceans rolling between them. The birth of the Moon is now represented as thrown from the Earth near the south-pole, in consequence of this primal convulsion, by the explosion of water, or other vapors of greater power. The lunar birth is thus beautifully presented to the eye,

> When rose the continents, and sunk the main,
> And Earth's huge sphere, exploding, burst in twain;
> Gnomes, how you gaz'd, when from her wounded side,
> Where now the South-sea rolls its waste of tide,
> Rose, on swift wheels, the Moon's refulgent car,
> Circling the solar orb, a sister star;
> Dimpled with vales, with shining hills emboss'd,
> And roll'd round Earth her airless realms of frost.[62]

The difficulty of introducing these charming images any other way than by reminding the Gnomes of what they are supposed to have seen, gives us, in this address, the noun personal in apostrophe, with a frequency which, far from being graceful, becomes almost ludicrous; as, "Gnomes, how you gaz'd! &c ... ". Gnomes, how you shriek'd!"... "Gnomes, how you trembled!"[63] ... but infinite is the poetic fancy with which the hypothesis is maintained, of the earth being struck from the crater of the sun, and the moon from the first terrestrial volcano.

The Goddess now reminds her subterranean hand-maids of their assistance in having formed into marble and other petrific substances, the dissolving shells which covered the prominent parts of the earth, thrown up from her ocean in that first convulsion, by submarine fires. Sculpture is here introduced, and poetic casts of the famous ancient statues, the Hercules, Antinous,[64] Apollo,[65] and Venus, rise from the page. Roubilliac,[66] unquestionably the first statuary of the modern world, is praised with enthusiasm; and Mrs Damer,[67] the ingenious mistress of the chisel, with delight.

To the Gnomes is next imputed the power of extracting the saline particles from different kinds of earths; from prostrate woods, and from morasses; and this introduces the description of a town in the immense salt-mines of Poland.[68] With his peculiar ingenuity, this Bard of Fancy shows us the saline city; and that, and the statue supposed to be Lot's wife,[69] the river and temple, gleam and sparkle on the imagination of every reader who has imagination. To those who have it not, the magnificent pageantries of this poem will pass unreflected, unimpressive,

> And, like the baseless fabric of a vision,
> Leave not a wreck behind.[70]

Personification is surely carried too far when, in the next passage, azotic [71] gas is made the lover of the virgin air, and fire transformed into a jealous rival, indignant of the treacherous courtship. The trio are compared to Mars, Venus, and Vulcan, and the Homeric tale, of the enmeshed pair, is told again. The mechanism of the net; the struggles of the guilty goddess to escape; her impatient exhortations to her nymphs, to disunite the links of the iron net-work; her efforts to conceal her beauties from the surrounding deities, have all that truth to nature with which criticism has justly observed, Shakespeare draws the manners of his imaginary beings. With much more of that appropriate verity has Darwin told this story than Homer, and not more voluptuously. This is the only passage in the *Botanic Garden* which can justly be taxed with voluptuousness, and with Homer its author shares the censure. Homer, whose morality has been so loudly, but so partially applauded, since his deities are all either libertine or unjust; and of his heroes, only one is in himself a virtuous man, and he defends the cause of his guilty brother, and does not once urge the restoration of the stolen wife to her injured husband, an atonement not only in itself due, but which must have raised the siege, saved the city, and spared immense effusion of human blood. The story, if really founded on historic circumstances, might not have authorised the restoration of Helen,[72] but it was in the poet's power to have made Hector[73] urge it.

If the Homeric fable of Mars and Venus, in Vulcan's net, repeated by Darwin with new circumstances, more picturesque, not more indelicate, forms *one* somewhat licentious passage in the *Botanic Garden*, the *Iliad* contains several which are equally voluptuous, even after Pope has chastened them.[74] As to the amours of the Plants and Flowers, it is a burlesque upon morality to make them responsible at its tribunal. The floral harems do not form an imaginary but a real system, which philosophy has discovered, and with which poetry sports. The impurity is in the imagination of the reader, not on the pages of the poet, when the *Botanic Garden* is considered on the whole, as an immodest composition.

From the net of Vulcan, and the lovers it entangles, the Poet leads us to his forge, after the mention of iron, as produced by the decomposition of vegetable bodies. To perceive the strength and truth of the Forge-picture, no power of imagination, on the part of the reader, is necessary; memory is sufficient. Who has not seen a blacksmith's shop, and heard its din? Here it blazes and resounds on the page. The formation of magnetic bars ensues.[75] Though the power of the magnet has been known and applied to use from very early times, yet the Poet imputes these artificial magnets to their last improver, the personal friend of his youth, Mr Michell,[76] mentioned early in these memoirs. Of Mr Michell's process in this improvement Dr Darwin has formed another poetic description, so distinct that the operation may be performed from perusing it attentively.

And now we meet an animated apostrophe to Steel, praising its use in navigation, agriculture, and war. This applausive address is one of the grandest in the poem, where so *many* are grand. What has poetry more noble than these first six lines of that eulogium?

> Hail adamantine Steel! magnetic Lord,
> King of the prow, the ploughshare, and the sword!
> True to the pole, by thee the pilot guides
> His steady course amid the struggling tides!
> Braves, with broad sail, th'immeasurable sea,
> Cleaves the dark air, and asks no star but thee![77]

A description of Gems succeeds to that apostrophe, as a work of the Gnomes, by whom, from marine acids[78] mixed with the shells of marine animals, and of calcareous,[79] arid argillaceous[80] earths, they are here supposed to be, from time to time, produced. These natural transformations are comparatively illustrated by those of Ovidian fable; and Proteusgallantries [81] are retold even more beautifully than Ovid has told them, particularly the story of Europa.[82] It is here, beyond all possible transcendence, exquisite, and it closes with a spirited compliment to the natives of Europe.

Returning to the subject, the Goddess reminds her Gnomes of having seen the subterranean volcanos forming the various species of clay; from the porcelain of China, and of ancient Etruria,[83] to those used in the beautiful productions of its modern namesake, brought to so much perfection by the late Mr Wedgwood. The mechanism of the porcelain of China, with its ungraceful forms and gaudy ornaments, rises on the page. The superiority, in the two last circumstances, of our English Etruria, is asserted, as producing "uncopied beauty and ideal grace";[84] and its mechanism is also given, but in terms so technical as to spoil the harmony of the verse in that passage. Satire has caught hold of the seldom harshness, triumphantly displaying it in the *Loves of the Triangles*.

Mr Wedgwood is addressed as at once the friend of Art and Virtue. His medallion of the Negro-slave in chains *(See Figure 24)*, imploring mercy, is mentioned as reproaching our great national sin against justice and mercy, so long resisting the admonitions of Benevolence and Piety, in the senate; also another medallion of Hope, attended by Peace, and Art, and Labour. *(See Figure 25)* "It was made of clay from Botany Bay [85] and many of them were sent thither, to show the inhabitants what their materials would do, and to encourage their industry". The emblematic figures on the Portland Vase *(Figure 26)*,[86] so finely imitated in our new Etruria, next appear in all the charms of poetry, while the truth of their ingenious construction is supported in the notes with wonderful learning and precision, so as to leave

(Left) Figure 24: Josiah Wedgwood's image used on his popular Abolition of Slavery cameo medallion first produced in 1787. Erasmus Darwin used this engraving in The Economy of Vegetation *(1792). (Right) Figure 25: Josiah Wedgwood's image used on his Sydney Cove, Australia cameo medallion produced in 1789. Joseph Banks gave to Wedgwood the clay from this Cove with which these medallions were made. Hope is allegorically featured arriving on the shores of Sydney Cove, being met by three figures representing Peace, Art and Labour. Darwin used this engraving in* The Economy of Vegetation *(1792).*

no doubt on the unprejudiced mind, that the Bard of Linnaeus has explained their real design. This address to Mr Wedgwood closes with the asserted immortality of his productions.

Coal, Jet,[87] and Amber, are next impersonized [sic], an individual for the species. The latter is placed on his "electric throne", as a material, the natural properties of which were the source of the discoveries in electricity, and from which the name of that branch of modern science is derived, *electron* being the Greek word for *amber*. Led by its phosphoric light, Dr Franklin comes forward in the act of disarming the lightning of its dire effects, by his electrical rods. His influence in procuring the freedom of America is applauded with much poetic imagery.[88] The short-lived freedom of Ireland, in her acquirement of self-legislation, is allegorized by "the warrior Liberty, helming his course to her shores".[89]

Another bold figure of Liberty succeeds, presented as a giant form, slumbering within the iron cage and marble walls of the French Bastile [sic],[90] unconscious of his chains till, touched by the patriot flame, he rends his flimsy bonds, lifts his colossal form, and rears his hundred arms over his foes; calls to the good and brave of every country, with voice that echoes like the thunder of heaven, to the polar extremities;

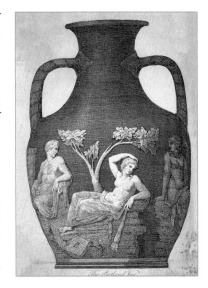

Figure 26: "Portland Vase". Engraving by William Blake. Darwin used this engraving in The Economy of Vegetation *(1792).*

> Gives to the winds his banner broad unfurl'd,
> And gathers in its shade the living world![91]

This sublime sally of a too-confiding imagination has made the poet and his work countless foes. They triumph over him on a result so contrary; on the mortal wounds given by French crimes to real liberty. They forget, or choose to forget, that this part of the poem (though published after the other) appeared in 1791, antecedent to the dire regicide, and to all those unprecedented scenes of sanguinary cruelty inflicted on France by three of her republican tyrants, compared to whom the most remorseless of her monarchs was mild and merciful.

The Botanic Queen now reminds her Gnomes of the means they had used to produce metallic substances; and, from the mention of silver and gold, she starts into a spirited and noble exclamation over the cruelties committed by catholic superstition, in the East and West Indies;[92] and from them she turns, with equal indignation, to the Slave Trade, that plague-spot on the reputation of our national humanity! that crying sin in the practice of our national religion! Greatly is it to the honour of our English poets, within the last twenty years, that, with very few exceptions, the best and most highly-gifted of them have fought their way to fame beneath the banners of Freedom and Mercy, whose eternal nature no national or individual abuse, no hypocritical assumption, can change.

These instances of unchristian barbarity lead to the story of the cruel and impious Cambyses [93] on his march to subdue Ethiopia, after having destroyed the temples and devasted [sic] the country of Thebes, and massacred its inhabitants. The fate of that army is described which he sent to plunder the temple of Jupiter, and which perished in the desert overwhelmed by sand. The Gnomes are considered as ministers of that just vengeance, and of the famine by which it was preceded; and this, by withholding the dews, and blasting vegetation, and by summoning the whirlwinds which cause the fatal rise of the sand-tornados. The successive horrors that overtook this army are depicted with the highest interest and grandeur. They rise in climax till the final overwhelming is thus brought to the shuddering imagination of the reader,

> ... awhile the living hill
> Heav'd with convulsive throes, ... and all was still![94]

language has nothing of more genuine sublimity.

Turning from this dread tragedy, the Botanic Queen assumes a livelier strain, and compares her little ministers to the planets in an orrery. That beautiful machine is described with its fairy-mimicry of the stellar evolutions. She exhorts her nymphs to the practice of several benevolent operations, guarding against the mischiefs of elementary excess. Hannibal's renowned march over the Alps, against tyrannic Rome, and the supposed means by which he facilitated his progress, are held up to their imitation.[95] To this succeeds an exhortation to feed the embryons, and forward the parturition of trees, plants, and flowers. For those offices a medical simile occurs, and afterwards a scripture story is told, Peter released from prison by an angel,[96] and to that angel the illustriously benevolent Howard is compared.[97]

Imputed assistance, on the part of these subterranean nymphs, in the chemical decomposition of animal and vegetable substances, introduces the ancient fable of the slaughtered, buried, and assurgent Adonis.[98] His story is told with not less added poetic excellence than, with accession of personal beauty, he is said to have arisen from the dark mansions of Proserpine,[99] and to have returned to Venus. Dr Darwin's reasons, given in the note to this passage, for rejecting former interpretations of that allegory, are convincing; and his substituted solution is not only highly ingenious, but deeply philosophic; and good sense sanctions the conjecture.

This fable closes the address of the Goddess to her Gnomes. Their elfin flight on their appointed errands, is described with playful elegance, and compared to the successive shadows that pass over a sunny vale beneath the light clouds. With that comparison the second Canto terminates. If the Gnomes make their exit with less poetic splendour than their predecessors, it must be considered that the Nymphs of Fire are personages of more intrinsic dignity.

The Third Canto

Opens with a charge to the Water Nymphs, and we are told that the Goddess gives it in tones so sweet and sonorous as to shake the wrinkling fountains, curl the deep wells, rimple the lakes, and thrill the rivers.

The three first words selected to express the different kind of actual vibration on the fountains, wells, and lakes, are instances of that nice discrimination which imparts so much vitality to verse, and gives back to the reader his faded recollection of the objects of nature in their comparative distinctions. Though he may have viewed them often with unexamining eyes, yet no sooner do they arise before him on the poetic page than he recognises their truth with the thrill of delight; for who that looks into the records of the Muses, however insensible to the creations of Fancy, can view without pleasure the faithfully reflected image of nature in the subtle variety of her lineaments.

> Thick as the dews which deck the morning flowers,
> Or rain-drops twinkling in the sun-bright showers,
> Fair nymphs, emerging in pellucid bands,
> Rise, as she turns, and whiten all the lands.[100]

Their mistress tells them also, how much she is conscious of their power and use, in the formation, substance, and protection of the vegetable world. In the exordium of this charge we meet a couplet rivalling [sic] in picturesque beauty the lines in Collins' charming, though rhymeless Ode to Evening,[101] when he tells the grey-stoled personage, that, from his hut on the mountain side, he loves to contemplate, in a showery twilight,

> The hamlets brown, and dim-discover'd spires,
> And hear their simple bells, and mark o'er all
> > Her dewy fingers draw
> > The gradual, dusky veil.[102]

The Botanic Queen says to her aqueous ministry in these rival lines,

> Your lucid hands condense, with fingers chill,
> The blue mist hovering round the gelid hill.[103]

This charge has one harsh line; thus,

> And as below she braids her hyaline hair.[104]

The employment gentle, the attitude graceful, that harshness of measure which is often skilful when used to express violent exertion, is here censurable.

These new vicegerents are praised as feeding the harvest, filling the wide-ribbed arch with hurrying torrents, to assist the operation of the mill and the progress of the barge, and leading the refluent water to its parent main. These operations on the water induce a simile for the progressive and returning course of the blood. The purpureal tint it gives to the fair complexion of youthful beauty; the warm glow to her hair, the laugh of health to her lip, and its lightning to her eyes, form a lovely picture in this simile; and it closes with a medical observation in a fine poetic figure.

Just discernment will not cease to admire the facile success and artful grace with which this Poet subdues the difficulty of rendering all sorts of science subservient to the purposes of high heroic verse; or to observe how seldom even the most technical terms diminish the harmony of his measure, or the elegance of his imagery.

Mighty sway is attributed to the aqueous ladies over those realms of scale and shell, which are covered by the sea; and they are considered as architects of the pearly palaces of the fish. The modern experiment of smoothing rough waves with oil, is considered as their suggestion; also various sub-marine and benevolent influences. To them the birth of rivers, from the Alpine snows. The Danube, the Rhine, and the Tiber, are mentioned; the last as flowing through his degenerate realms with diminished waters. The features of that degeneracy are marked; the race of patriots, heros [sic], and legislators, long since become singers, dancers, and monks; and the passage concludes with this sublime picture of the present state of that long-renowned river:

> Parts with chill stream, the dim religious bower,
> Time-moulder'd bastion, and dismantled tower;
> By alter'd fanes, and nameless villas glides,
> And classic domes, that tremble on his sides;
> Sighs o'er each broken urn and yawning tomb,
> And mourns the fall of Liberty and Rome.[105]

Rivers being the subject, the Nile and its annual overflow, gives rise to grand allegoric imagery, and to nobly-imagined scenes. That overflow is ascribed to the monsoon winds, which deluge Nubia and Abyssinia with rain.

> Sailing in air, when dark Monsoon enshrouds
> His tropic mountains in a night of clouds;
> Or, drawn by whirlwinds, from the Line returns,
> And showers on Afric all his thousand urns;
> High o'er his head the beams of Sirius [106] glow,
> And, dog of Nile, Anubis,[107] barks below.
> Nymphs, you from cliff to cliff attendant guide,
> In headlong cataracts, the impetuous tide;
> Or lead o'er wastes of Abyssinian sands
> The bright expanse to Egypt's showerless lands.[108]

Her towns, her temples, and sultry plains are contrasted with a sublime description of Hecla [109] and its burning mountain. Its column of boiling water is transformed into a malignant Sorceress, whose baleful spells had been broken by the power of these benevolent Naiads.

The hypothesis, that warm salubrious springs are produced by steam arising from water falling on subterranean fires, and that this steam is condensed between the strata of incumbent mountains, and collected into springs, occasions a sportive address to Buxton.[110]

It is succeeded by an elegant compliment to the Duchess of Devonshire,[111] leading a train of Graces from Chatsworth [112] to that tepid fountain. From the epithet *fairy* given to legions, we should suppose these Graces a part of the machinery of the Poet; but, as the passage proceeds, it describes beautiful young women bathing with such exquisite precision, that the scene of action considered, it becomes impossible to contemplate them as ideal personages, especially as the last couplet is utterly at war with aerial substance; thus,

> Round each fair Nymph her dropping mantle clings,
> And Loves emerging shake their showery wings.[113]

The Loves, which are indisputably machinery, confuse the picture, if the nymphs also are of that species. The expression, *fairy legions*, is to be regretted; it renders the lively and lovely description amenable to Dr Johnson's censure of a passage in one of our poets, "that it is metaphoric in one point of view, and literal in another".

The Duke of Devonshire's public spirit and architectural taste, next become the theme, and they involve a charming picture of the Crescent, that gem of Grecian art in Britain;[114] and of the new plantations which surround it. Derbyshire stone has an amber tint, and hence the Buxton Crescent rises a golden palace in the desert.

The Goddess next congratulates her Water Nymphs on having celebrated the odd nuptials of pure Air and inflammable Gas. We had heard of their courtship earlier in the poem. That courtship, and this their marriage, forms one of the wildest extravagances of the work; but the Homeric fable, which illustrates the airy bride and groom, is charming in the first degree. Juno, attired by Venus, to captivate Jove.[115] With the most luxuriant fancy, and with new circumstances, this little drama rises again on the Darwinian page. It will not lose, but gain in a just estimation of poetic merit, by comparison with the translations, by Cowper and Pope, of this celebrated part of the Greek poet's machinery. Let them be compared, and first Cowper's literal translation, first edition.

> … First, she lav'd all o'er
> Her beauteous body with ambrosial lymph;
> Then polish'd it with richest oil divine,
> Of boundless fragrance. Oil, that in the courts
> Eternal only shaken through the skies
> Breath'd odours, and through all the distant earth.[116]
> Her whole fair body with these sweets bedew'd,
> She pass'd the comb through her ambrosial hair,
> And braided her light locks streaming profuse
> From her immortal brows; with golden studs
> She made her gorgeous mantle fast before;
> Etherial texture, labour of the hands
> Of Pallas, beautified with various arts,
> And brac'd it with a zone, fring'd all around
> An hundred fold; her pendants, triple gemm'd,

Luminous, graceful in her ears she hung.[117]
And covering all her glories with a veil
Sun-bright, new woven, bound to her fair feet
Her sandals elegant. Thus full attir'd
In all her ornaments, she issued forth,
And beck'ning Venus from the other powers
Of Heav'n apart, the Goddess thus bespake.[118]

Pope's translation of the same passage.

Here first she bathes, and round her body pours
Soft oils of fragrance, and ambrosial showers.
The winds perfum'd, the balmy gale convey
Through heav'n, through earth, and all th' aerial way.
Spirit divine! whose exhalation greets
The sense of Gods with more than mortal sweets.
Thus, while she breath'd of heav'n, with decent pride
Her artful hands the radiant tresses tied;
Part o'er her head in shining ringlets roll'd,
Part o'er her shoulders wav'd like melted gold;
Around her neck a heavenly mantle flow'd
That rich with Pallas'[119] labour'd colours glow'd;
Large clasps of gold the foldings gather'd round;
A golden zone her swelling bosom hound;
Far-beaming pendants tremble in her ear,
Each gem illumin'd with a triple star;
Then o'er her head she casts a veil more white
Than new-fall'n snow, and dazzling as the light;
Last, her fair feet celestial sandals grace.
Thus issuing radiant, with majestic pace,
Forth from the dome th' imperial Goddess moves,
And calls the mother of the Smiles and Loves.[120]

Pope has shown better taste in female dress than his master. A zone with an hundred folds of fringe upon it, must be a very heavy and inelegant ornament. The zone of plain gold, substituted by the rhyme translator, is grander and more graceful as well as more simple.

Darwin, who gives this fable after his own manner, tells us, that Venus not only lent the cestus, but attired the Goddess herself; and passing over the classic ceremony of the bath, and the operation of the oils, which perhaps he thought too Hottentotish,[121] he describes more concisely, yet not less brilliantly, this magnificent labour of the toilette; thus,

So, rob'd by Beauty's Queen, with softer charms,
Saturnia [122] woo'd the Thunderer to her arms;
O'er her fair limbs a veil of light she spread,
And bound a starry diadem on her head;
Long braids of pearls her golden tresses grac'd,
And the charm'd cestus [123] sparkled round her waist.[124]

The cestus is here a visible and brilliant ornament, instead of being, as Homer afterwards tells us, *hid* in Juno's bosom. Pope, in a note to this passage, observes, that, by this disposal, the poet meant to convey an idea of the matron-like modesty of Juno, who *conceals* what is to render her engaging; while Venus, wearing the cestus in open sight, ostentatiously displays the means by which she captivates; but this sort of lesser morality belonged not to the times in which Homer lived; neither is peculiar delicacy at all characteristic of the Juno he has drawn. His more probable reason for making her hide this ornamental spell, was the danger that Jupiter, if he saw the borrowed zone, so often seen on the person of his daughter, would know it, and, conscious of its power to excite passion, would have been aware of the design of his wife, and either not allowed of the interview, or disarmed the girdle of its magic. Supreme wisdom must have foiled *discovered* art. Neither of these suppositions occurred to Dr Darwin, or perhaps his Juno also had hidden her gay talisman.

Homer expressly says, Juno did not take her chariot on this conjugal visit; but Darwin allots her that mode of conveyance, and the change enabled him to assign to the Empress of Heaven her due pomp and stately retinue. Upon this imperial and celestial equipage the modern poet has lavished all the splendours of his imagination. Cupid is the charioteer, and Zephyr [125] flies before, showering roses from his wings; Naiads and Dryads, Fawns and Wood-Boys [126] are in the train. The reader is empowered, by distinctness of poetic description, to pursue the chariot with his eye, as it ascends the steeps of Ida,[127] now lost in its thick woods, now in full blaze, winding around its rocks.

But surely there is an error of judgment in making Cupid wing an arrow to the breast of Jove, as the retinue approaches, since that mode of awakening the passions of Jupiter for his queen, renders the charmed cestus a superfluous gift. And again, this gay car is represented as drawn by doves; from which it should seem that Venus had lent her equipage, as well as her girdle, on that occasion.

The address of the God to his Goddess is incomparably more elegant in the verse of Darwin than in the translation of Cowper, or even of Pope. Thus says Cowper, with all that cramp literality which hobbles through his version.

Soon he accosted her, and thus inquir'd:
"Juno, what region seeking, hast thou left
Th'Olympian [128] summit, and hast here arriv'd
With neither steeds nor chariot in thy train?"[129]

159

Pope

Fix'd on her eyes he fed his eager look,
Then press'd her hand, and thus transported spoke:
"Why comes my Goddess from th' etherial sky,
And not her steeds, and flaming chariot nigh?"[130]

Darwin

Pierc'd on his throne, the starting Thund'rer turns,
Melts with soft sighs, with kindling rapture burns;
Clasps her fair hand, and eyes, in fond amaze,
The bright Intruder with enamour'd gaze:
"And leaves my Goddess, like a blooming bride,
The fanes of Argos, for the rocks of Ide;
Her gorgeous palaces, and amaranth bowers,
For cliff-top'd mountains, and aerial towers"?[131]

But to resume the Botanic Goddess and her enumeration of the interesting employments of her third class of Nymphs; their disposal of all those bright waters which make Britain irriguous, verdant, and fertile. We find this beautiful couplet in the course of the passage:

You, with nice ear, in tiptoe trains pervade
Dim walks of morn,[132] or evening's silent shade.[133]

She then places them on the shore, listening to its pausing murmurs, and to the song of the Nereid, as on her playful sea-horse she glides over the twilight-main. Another exquisite picture arises, professedly from an antique gem. Great skill is shown in varying the attitude, appearance, and employments of this beautiful Sea-Nymph, on *her* voyage, from those of Europa, crossing the sea on her bull, in the preceding Canto. Her's [sic] is a day, and this is a night voyage. Europa draws up her feet beneath her robe, fearful of touching the water; the *secure* Nereid drops them carelessly down. Europa clings timidly round the neck of her Taurus,[134] and rests her cheek upon the curls of his forehead, while her mantle floats unheeded on the breeze. The Nereid has no apprehension; she and her steed are both in their element. She gives him the rein, lifts her eyes to the evening star, and sings the birth of Venus. She restrains her arching veil, with her hands, from floating on the gales of night, while the mantle of Europa was abandoned to the day-breeze. The Nereid is without fear, and therefore attends to the preservation of her dress; Europa is somewhat frightened, and therefore pays no attention to hers. These differences, however apparently, are not really trivial. The mere versifier knows not *how* to create them. The Poet knows their importance; how much they will inspire his portraits, and distinguish them from each other. In the progress of this episode the Nereid [135] looses her veil (we may conclude the wind had fallen) and we meet the following description of a very graceful operation, that of a lovely female combing her lavish tresses:

O'er her fair brow her pearly comb unfurls
Her beryl locks, and parts the waving curls;
Each tangled braid, with glist'ning teeth unbinds,
And with the floating treasure musks the winds.[136]

This is not a repetition of the employment of the dew-born Venus, in the second Canto. She had recently emerged, and therefore *her* hair must necessarily hang uncurled, and she is in the attitude of wringing the water from her golden tresses; than which no position can be more favourable to female symmetry.

Doctor Darwin's poem paints every attitude and employment which, in either sex, can be rendered elegant. No author ever had a mind more keenly awakened to grace in all its varieties, or could more exquisitely paint it.

That perception, and that talent, the, in his class of composition, peerless Richardson [137] possessed in an equal degree. No prose-writer ever was, or perhaps ever will be, so great a painter; and to that power what a constellation of other endowments contributed to immortalize the pages of Clarissa [138] and Grandison![139] Novels no longer, but English Classics, translated into every European language, and in all foreign countries considered as some of the noblest efforts of British Genius.

But the Darwinian Nereid has been left a little before her time; other circumstances attend her, too poetic to remain unnoticed. Her song "thrills the waves"; and the shadowy Forms of Night gleam on the margin of the shore, "with pointed ears", to denote the act of listening. Perhaps that characteristic had been better omitted, since it belongs to brute, not to human animals, and is at war with the imaginary grace of these twilight forms. The Moon pauses, and the Stars shoot from their spheres to listen. That last circumstance is evidently from Shakespeare's allegory in *The Midsummer Night's Dream*, alluding to the conspiracies formed in favour of the imprisoned Queen of Scotland, by the Duke of Norfolk, and other noblemen of the court of Elizabeth. This is the allegory:

I saw a Mermaid on a Dolphin's back
Uttering such dulcet and harmonious sounds,
That the rude sea grew civil at her song,
And certain stars shot madly from their spheres,
To hear the Sea-Maid's music.[140]

That he might guard against the displeasure of Elizabeth for this sally, it is immediately followed by as high an allegoric compliment paid to herself.

On the Poet's dismissal of the Nereid, the death of Mrs French of Derby,[141] is introduced as a subject of sorrow to the Water-Nymphs of its river. This picture of Milcena [sic] is very lovely, straying with her infants on the banks of the Derwent, and pondering, with scientific eye, the insects and plants on the shores of that stream. There is a tender strain of morality in this passage; but the annexed epitaph on Mrs French, however beautiful as poetry, is by no means fit for its originally purposed situation, a tombstone in the great church at Derby. The author of these memoirs is ignorant whether, or not, it is there inscribed. "Clouds of silver, and Beauty pleading for her husband's errors at the throne of God", may form a very poetical, but it is a very heathenish resurrection.

The mention of Brindley,[142] the Father of commercial Canals, has propriety as well as happiness. Similitude for their course, to the sinuous track of a serpent, produces a fine picture of a gliding animal of that species, and it is succeeded by these supremely happy lines:

> So, with strong arm, immortal Brindley leads
> His long canals, and parts the velvet meads;
> Winding in lucid lines, the watery mass
> Mines the firm rock, or loads the deep morass;
> With rising locks a thousand hills alarms,
> Flings o'er a thousand streams its silver arms;
> Feeds the long vale, the nodding woodland laves,
> And Plenty, Arts, and Commerce, freight the waves.
>
> Nymphs, who erewhile on Brindley's early bier,
> On snow-white bosoms shower'd th'incessant tear,
> Adorn his tomb! … Oh, raise the marble bust,
> Proclaim his honours, and protect his dust!
> With urns inverted, round the sacred shrine
> Their ozier wreaths let weeping Naiads twine,
> While on the top mechanic Genius stands,
> Counts the fleet waves, and balances the sands![143]

There is a note to this passage, which urges the duty of erecting a monument to Brindley in Lichfield Cathedral.[144] Certainly it would be to the credit of those who should subscribe to raise it, since the county of Stafford has been so materially benefited by his successful plans; but in the above eulogium, Dr Darwin has given him a more enduring memorial than stone or marble could bestow.

The mechanism of the pump is next described with curious ingenuity. Common as is the machine, it is not unworthy of a place in this splendid composition, as being, after the sinking of wells, the earliest of those inventions, which, in situations of exterior aridness, gave ready accession to water. This familiar object is illustrated by a picture of Maternal Beauty administering sustenance to her infant. To that succeeds an energetic reproof, and pathetic admonition to mothers in affluent life, whom indolence, or dissipation, seduces to the unnatural neglect of that delightful duty. For an infant slumbering on the maternal bosom which has nourished him, there is the following allegoric simile, of no common elegance:

Thus, charm'd to sweet repose, when twilight hours
Shed their soft influence on celestial bowers,
The cherub, Innocence, with smile divine,
Shuts his white wings, and sleeps on Beauty's shrine.[145]

The "Ode to Morning", in *Elfrida*,[146] contains a nearly resembling image; thus,

Away, ye Elves, away,
Shrink at ambrosial morning's living ray!
That living ray, whose power benign
Unfolds this scene of glory to our eye,
Where, thron'd in artless majesty,
The cherub Beauty sits on Nature's rustic shrine.[147]

Probably to the involuntary plagiarism of forgotten impression, we owe this sister-picture on the page of Dr Darwin.

The use of water by the fire-engine next occurs. Poetry has nothing more sublime than this, the preceding picture of a Town on Fire:

From dome to dome when flames infuriate climb,
Sweep the long street, invest the tower sublime;
Gild the tall vanes amid th' astonish'd night,
And reddening heaven returns the sanguine light;
While, with vast strides and bristling hair, aloof
Pale Danger glides along the falling roof;
And giant Terror, howling in amaze,
Moves his dark limbs across the lurid blaze;
Nymphs, you first taught the gelid waves to rise,
Hurl'd in resplendent arches to the skies;
In iron cells condens'd the airy spring,
And imp'd the torrent with unfailing wing;
On the fierce flame the shower impetuous falls,
And sudden darkness shrouds the shatter'd walls;
Steam, smoke, and dust, in blended volumes roll,
And Night and Silence repossess the pole.[148]

Dryden, in his *Annus Mirabilis*,[149] has described the great fire in London. Some very fine lines occur in that description, but it is prolix and feeble in comparison with the above.

The melancholy circumstances of the Woodmason family,[150] and that of Lady Molesworth,[151] each of whom suffered dreadfully by fire, are next pourtrayed [sic] with much pathetic solemnity, and the Water-Nymphs are reproached for not having prevented those evils.

After this mournful little drama, the Botanic Queen allots new tasks to these her hand-maids in the care of vegetation, and they are beautifully specified. To them succeeds an highly interesting picture of Sympathy in a female form, bending over a rock to assist the ship-wrecked mariners; she is shown afterwards as supporting feeble Age on her arm, pouring balm into the wounds of Sorrow; snatching the dagger from Despair; lulling Envy to sleep, and while she reposes, stealing her envenomed arrows from her quiver. An animated eulogium on a benevolent young lady of Ireland, diversifies these commissions; also three of Hercules' labours. A flooded country is presented in the deluged Etolia;[152] and the Water Fiend, that [153] caused the inundation, and whom Hercules subdues a second time, when assuming the form of a snake, it attempts to escape from the hero. It is thus admirably pictured:

> Then to a snake the finny Demon turn'd,
> His lengthen'd form, with scales of silver burn'd;
> Lash'd, with resistless sweep, his dragon tail,
> And shot meandering o'er th' affrighted plain.[154]

Perhaps the description of the Fiend's next transformation into a Bull, is not eminently judicious; the terms "silver hoofs", and "flowery meadows", which might well have suited the gentle bull of Europa, are too nice and gay to harmonize well with the enraged monster, one of whose horns was torn off by Hercules. Of the habits and manners of that formidable Brute, when incensed, a very inferior Poet, lately deceased, has given a more impressive picture. We sometimes find one or two good passages in the writings of ordinary versifiers. Sternhold's [155] and Hopkins'[156] nonsensical and vulgar translation of the Psalms, contain eight lines which Pope professed to envy. Though Hurdis [157] was chosen Professor of Poetry in Oxford contrary to Pope's precept,

> Let such teach others who themselves excel.[158]

yet he has given a description of the only very terrific English animal, which, when weeded of a long interrupting digression in the middle of it, about a thunder-storm, forms the most natural portrait of a malicious Bull that can perhaps be found in any of our poets; thus,

> ... 'Tis pleasure to approach,
> And, by the strong fence shielded, view secure
> Thy terrors, Nature, in the savage Bull.
> Soon as he marks me,[159] be the tyrant fierce,
> To earth descends his head; hard breathe his lungs
> Upon the dusty sod....A sulky leer
> Gives double horror to the frowning curls
> That wrap his forehead; and ere long is heard,
> From the deep cavern of his lordly throat,
> The growl insufferable.[160]....Tramples then
> The surly Brute, impatient of disdain,

And spurns the soil with irritated hoof;
Himself inhaler of the dusty sod;
Himself insulted by the pebbly shower,
Which his vain fury raises. Nothing fear'd,
Let him, incens'd, from agitated lungs
Blow his shrill trump acute till echo ring,
And, with a leer of malice, steal away,
Assault and vengeance swearing ere be long![161]

The last command of the Botanic Goddess to her Water-Nymphs, enforces their duties to plants and flowers; to render the vales irriguous, and to feed with their rills the floral and herbaceous roots. To the course of this moist nutriment through the vegetable fibres, is compared that of the chyle through the human frame; and to that, another simile succeeds. As the first is scientific, so is the second picturesque; it is a Turkish pilgrimage to Mecca; consisting of various caravans on their road over the sultry and sandy desert, and meeting with a pure rill, which, descending from distant rocks, had taken its course through the waste plain. The parched Travellers alight, kneel on the brink in grateful joy, and, bending over it, assuage their thirst. This rill somewhat suddenly becomes a lake, and reflects the eager and delighted multitude. With this little scene the commissions to the Water-Nymphs conclude, and their obedient flight is scarcely less poetically featured than that of the Nymphs of Fire. The similies, which illustrate the flight of the aqueous ministers, are the evolutions of the water-spider, and the exercise of skaiting [sic] amongst the natives of northern climates. The last is thus admirably described:

So where [162] the North congeals his watery mass,
Piles high his snows, and floors his seas with glass,
While many a month, unknown to warmer rays,
Marks its slow chronicle by lunar days;
Stout youths and ruddy maids, a[163] sportive train,
Leave the white soil and rush upon the main.
From isle to isle the moon bright squadrons stray,
And win, in graceful curves, their easy way;[164]
On step alternate borne, with balance nice
Hang o'er the gliding steel, and hiss along the ice.[165]

Fourth and Last Canto of *The Economy of Vegetation,*

Consists of a charge to the Sylphs, as benevolent spirits, to protect the vegetable substances, after they had emerged to light and air; to defend them from all the malignant operations of nature, and to cherish and assist the influence they may receive from all her vital and benign powers.

The deadly and salubrious winds; the volcanic and pestilential airs; the Tornado, dreadful to mariners, &c.; every thing here has animal life and consciousness. It was the author's plan, and he could not, at least in his own idea, depart from it with propriety. Hence, the Sylphs also are reminded of having presided at the nuptials of the purest of the Airs with Light. The passage which ushers in this whimsical marriage, is very beautiful, the expression, "simpering lips", excepted; but it was difficult to find variety of terms equally happy where the effect of pleasurable sensations on the countenance must so often be described. From these aerial nuptials vital spirit is supposed to proceed, which pervades and animates all nature. The loves and marriage of Cupid and Psyche are presented, poetically pictured from the well-known gems.[166] This life-infusing air is contrasted with the Syroc[sic][167] of Italy, and the Simoon [168] of the African desert. The last is presented as a Demon. Universal personification was the order of the Muse in this work, not to be infringed; else, when circumstances are in themselves sublime (and most things terrible in nature become sublime in poetry), they are more likely to be of diminished than increased force, by the addition of *fabled* endowment. A comparison between the Simoon described literally by Southey,[169] in his *Joan of Arc*,[170] and figuratively by Darwin, will perhaps evince the truth of this observation.

The Botanic Queen says to her Sylphs,

Arrest Simoon amid his waste [171] of sand,
The poison'd javlin balanc'd in his hand!
Fierce on blue streams he rides the tainted air,
Points his keen eye, and waves his whistling hair;
While as he turns, the undulating soil
Rolls its red waves, and billowy deserts boil.[172]

This is a fine picture of the Demon of Pestilence. The speed of his approach is marked by the strong current of air in which he passed, and by the term *whistling* annexed to his hair. The winds have hitherto, almost exclusively, possessed that term. Here transferred to the lifted hair of the Demon, it increases the terrific power of his approach. But let the Simoon be viewed where its terrible graces are *native*, and no attempt made to heighten them by allegory.

Joan of Arc, Tenth Book

… Ominous fear
Seizes the traveller o'er the trackless sands,
Who marks the dread Simoon across the waste
Sweep its swift pestilence. To earth he falls,
Nor dares give utterance to the inward prayer,
Deeming the Genius of the desert breathes
The purple blast of Death.[173]

We are informed by travellers, that to inhale the least portion of this mephitic [174] blast is fatal. They therefore fall on their faces, and hold their breath till it has passed over them.

But the Darwinian personification of the Tornado sublimely heightens the horror of that watery pest. It succeeds that of the Simoon; and the Fog, invested with animality, forms an immediate and striking contrast to the preceding monsters. It is drawn with such singular felicity of imagination that there is no resisting the desire of quoting the passage here:

> Sylphs, with light shafts, you pierce the drowsy Fog,
> That lingering slumbers on the sedge-wove bog,
> And [175] with webb'd feet o'er midnight meadows creeps,
> Or flings his hairy limbs o'er [176] stagnant deeps. [177]

The benevolent little spirits are then exhorted to combat Contagion,[178] stealing from charnel-vaults to bring death to the people. The plague, which in 1636 raged in Holland, is here introduced, with a beautiful story of faithful Love prevailing over the desire of self-preservation.[179] A young [180] maid is first seized in a, till then, un-infected family. This admirable line denotes the dread of its other individuals to approach, assist, or comfort her,

> And starting Friendship shunn'd her as she pass'd.[181]

Perceiving herself deserted, and fearing to spread the infection amongst those she loved, she seeks the garden, determined to die there. Her betrothed lover hears of her situation, and pursues her thither; raises a tent; procures her food, covering, and medicines; binds her fevered brows, and strews aromatic herbs and flowers upon her pillow. He escapes the contagion himself, and restores his beloved mistress to health. The poet has very sweetly told this interesting tale; a single epithet is perhaps the only word it contains which could be altered to advantage. It is in the following line,

> And clasp'd the *bright* infection in his arms.[182]

The adjective *bright* is too gay for its situation; *fair*, or *lov'd*, would be more subdued, and in better keeping with the mournful tenderness of the narration.

Less bold, says the Poet, was Leander,[183] eying, as he swam, the love-lighted tower. Less bold also, Tobias,[184] instructed by an angel to drive away the demon from the fatal bride.

The Sylphs are now applauded by their Queen for having instructed Torricelli [185] and Boyle,[186] concerning the properties of air, its pressure and elasticity. The operations of the weather-glass and air-pump are described with philosophic accuracy and poetic elegance. Young Rossiere's [187] dire fate, precipitated from his flaming montgolfier,[188] comes forward here, and is pictured with great poetic strength; nor is the illustration of that lamentable event, by the fable of Icarus,[189] less happy in its novel and mournful graces; his faithless and scattered plumage dancing upon [190] the wave; the Mermaids decking his watry tomb, strewing over his corse [sic] the pearly sea-flowers, and striking, in the coral towers, the pausing bell, which echos [sic] through the caves of Ocean! Surely it is not possible to admire too fondly the beautiful and exhaustless varieties of this darling Bard of Fancy.

Critics have asserted, that the poetic mind has little efflorescence after middle life; that, however the judgment may strengthen, the vivid luxuriance of the imagination abates. Milton's *Paradise Lost*, Darwin's *Botanic Garden*, and Cowper's *Task*,[191] each begun[192] after life had many years declined from its meridian, confute the dogma. Dr Johnson has combated its fallacy; and with more truth observed, that so long as the understanding retains its strength, the fancy, from time to time, acquires added vigor and new stores of imagery. Nor does the extreme poetic inferiority of the *Paradise Regained* to the *Paradise Lost*, at all disprove the converse proposition. We are to look for that inferiority in the so much more restraining nature of the *subject*, for poetry, above all others, improper. Poetry! to whose very existence, if it is to deserve its name, an infinitely larger portion of inventive and figurative ornament is necessary than the hallowed sobriety of the New Testament and its mysteries, can admit without the most revolting impropriety. Its choice, as the theme of an Epic Poem, was a radical error, which necessarily involved those long trains of comparative prosaicism, over which we yawn, however sometimes awakened by noble passages to recognise strength, which, though seldom put forth, we feel to be undiminished; to discern some rays of light which, amidst their infrequency, we yet perceive to be unfaded.

Figure 27: Joseph Priestley (1733-1804). Courtesy of Archives and Heritage, Birmingham Central Library.

Fresh commendation is next given to the Sylphs for their inspirations in the mind of Dr Priestley (Figure 27), concerning his analysis of the atmosphere.[193] The passage is most poetic, although purely chemical. Air calcining[194] the phlogistic[195] ores is termed the marriage of Ether with the Mine. These nuptials are illustrated by the retold story of Pluto and Proserpine. There is much propriety in this illustration, since Lord Bacon[196] has explained that fable as an hieroglyphic allusion, to signify "the combination, or marriage of etherial spirit with earthly materials".

A whimsical possibility is next supposed; that Dr Priestley's discoveries will hereafter enable adventurers to travel beneath the ocean in large inverted ships and diving balloons. A note to this passage asserts, that the experiment was successfully made by a Frenchman[197] in the reign of James the First, and it states the particulars. A splendid sub-marine voyage next occurs. It is to the warm tropic seas and shadowy ice-isles of the polar regions, and to be performed by Britannia. Her tears are to flow as she passes over the sad and visible remains of ship-wrecked lovers, mercantile and scientific adventurers, particularly those of Day[198] and Spalding,[199] who each perished in their diving-bells. Here the deplored fate of Captain Pierce,[200] his family and fellow-voyagers, thus forms a tragic drama:

Oft o'er thy lovely daughters, hapless Pierce!
Her sighs shall breathe, her sorrows dew their hearse.
With brow upturn'd to heav'n, "We will not part",

He cried, and clasp'd them to his aching heart,
Dash'd in dread conflict on the rocky grounds,
Crash the shock'd masts, the staggering wreck rebounds;
Through gaping seams the rushing deluge swims;
Chills their pale bosoms, bathes their shuddering limbs;
Climbs their white shoulders, buoys their streaming hair,
And the last sea-shriek bellows in the air.
Each, with loud sobs, their tender sire caress'd,
And gasping, strain'd him closer to her breast.
Stretch'd on one bier they sleep beneath the brine,
And their white bones with ivory arms entwine.[201]

The third, fourth, and fifth, couplets of the above quotation, are extremely fine pictures, and "sound never echoed sense" with more solemn horror than "and the last sea-shriek bellowed in the air". The description ought to have closed with that line, and the next couplet should have immediately followed the paternal exclamation. Beyond the utmost power of the pencil do the six grand verses of this passage image death by ship-wreck; but the "white bones" and "ivory arms" of the concluding line, are every way exceptionable. They disturb the awful impression made on the mind by the last sea-shriek. Aiming to be pathetic they are in reality ludicrous, the ivory *arms* of *bones*! The bones of ivory arms we might understand, though it would be affected expression, but the converse terms seem nonsense. One of the first of our existing poets, Mr Crowe,[202] public orator at Oxford, whose compositions, by their genuine excellence, atone for their too limited quantity, has told this sad story with solemn and simple beauty in his *Lewesdon Hill*,[203] one of the noblest local poems in our language. In his *narration* we find nothing which can strictly be termed picturesque, though the four *introductory* lines are highly so; but we find a great deal of Milton's manner in the progress of the tale, written in view of the rocks on which the *Halsewell* struck.

Lewesdon Hill [204]

See how the sun, here clouded, afar off
Pours down the golden radiance of his light
Upon th' enridged sea, where the black ship
Sails on the phospher-seaming waves ... So fair,
But falsely flattering, was yon surface calm,
When forth for India sail'd, in evil hour,
That vessel, whose disastrous fate, when told,
Fill'd every breast with horror, and each eye
With piteous tears, so cruel was the loss!
Methhinks I see her, by the wintry storm
Shatter'd and driven along past yonder isle!
She strove, her latest hope by strength or art,

To gain the port within it; or at worst,
To shun that harbourless and hollow coast,
From Portland [205] eastward to the Promontory,[206]
Where still St Albans high-built chapel [207] stands.
But art nor strength avail her, on she drives,
In storm and darkness, to that fatal coast!
And there, mid rocks and high o'er-hanging cliffs,
Dash'd piteously, with all her precious freight
Was lost, by Neptune's wild and foamy jaws
Swallow'd up quick! The richest laden ship
Of spicy Ternate,[208] or that, annual sent
To the Philippines o'er the southern main
From Acapulco, carrying massy gold,
Were poor to this; freighted with hopeful youth
And beauty, and high courage undismay'd
By mortal terrors; and paternal love,
Strong and unconquerable, even in death.
Alas! they perish'd all, ... all in ONE HOUR?[209]

Resuming the principal subject of these strictures, we find the harmonic discoveries attributed to the aerial hand-maids. Their mistress supposes them to have breathed their grand and exquisite inspirations into the ear of Handel;[210] to wake the tones on the shell of Echo; to melt in sweet chords upon the Eolian [211] harp; and on the lips of Cecilia [212] to breathe the song. Another lovely picture arises here, from an ancient gem, Cupid on a Lion's back, playing on a lute.

The Goddess proceeds to consider her Nymphs of Air as Ministers of Divine Vengeance on the Guilty, through the medium of tempests, and the pestilential winds of the East, as Samiel, Harmattan,[213] &c. and the scripture story of the fate of Senacherib [214] is told. The ravage of death, produced by those pestilential gales, forms a sublime personification; thus,

Hark! o'er the camp the venom'd tempest sings!
Man falls on man; on buckler buckler rings;
Groan answers groan; to anguish anguish yields,
And death's dread [215] accents shake the tented fields.
High rears the Fiend his grinning jaws, and wide
Spans the pale nations with colossal stride;
Waves his broad falchion with uplifted hand,
And his vast shadow darkens all the land![216]

Whether by coincidence or plagiarism on the part of Dr Darwin, is uncertain, but in Mr Sergeant's noble prophetic *Ode on the Woes of the House of Stuart*,[217] commencing with fair unfortunate Mary's calamities, we find the last sublime image, thus,

From Orkney's stormy steep
The spirit of the isles infuriate came;
Round him flash'd the arctic flame,
His dark cloud shadow'd the contentious deep![218]

This *Ode* was published in 1788. The *Economy of Vegetation* in 1791.

That poem proceeds with another exhortation to the etherial Cohorts to protect the vernal children; impart the talisman which guides the veering winds, and, by its influence, enchain Boreas [219] and Eurus,[220] so often fatal to early luxuriance, vegetable and animal. Thus shall they, she beautifully says,

Rock th' uncurtain'd cradle of the year.[221]

The destruction and reproduction of the atmosphere, is allegorised by a monster of magnitude more immense than that of Satan, when, on the page of Milton, he strides from hill to hill. This is a Camelion [222] beneath the northern constellation. We find much grandeur of fancy in this aerial giant. His groan is the thunder, his sigh the tempest, as he steers his course to the south, and spreads his shadowy limbs over the line, with frost and famine in his track. The Sylphs are adjured to direct his course to benevolent purposes; to cool Arabian vales with his antarctic breathing; and, in the following harmonious line,

To scatter roses o'er Zelandic [223] snows.[224]

This allegory concludes unhappily, with a personal compliment to Mr Kirwan,[225] "who has published a valuable Treatise on the temperature of Climates".[226] Those compliments to ingenious professors would often find their more proper place in the notes, except where they form a simile; but, as in this instance, a living man placed between the dragon wings of an imaginary and immeasurable monster, is a ridiculous idea. Often, through the course of this work, does such intermixture of actual and ideal beings disturb and interrupt, rather than agreeably diversify, the course of the allegory. The soon-ensuing mention of the celebrated Herschel,[227] and his stellar discoveries, is made in the form of a simile, and is therefore unexceptionable; and it passes on to the following charming apostrophe to the Stars:

Roll on, ye Stars! exult in youthful prime,
Mark, with bright curves, the printless steps of Time!
Near, and more near, your beamy cars approach,
And lessening orbs on lessening orbs incroach.
Flowers of the sky! ye too to age must yield,
Frail as your silken sisters of the field;
Star after star from heavn's high arch shall rush,
Suns sink on suns, on systems systems rush;
Headlong, extinct, to one dark centre fall,
And Death, and Night, and Chaos cover all;

Till o'er the wreck, emerging from the storm,
Immortal nature lifts her changeful form;
Mounts from the funeral pyre on wings of flame,
And soars, and shines, another and the same.[228]

Returning to the vegetable embryons, of which this Goddess, between her mention of
Kirwan and Herschel had spoken, she thus beautifully says:

Lo! on each seed, within its tender rind,
Life's golden threads, in endless circles wind;
Maze within maze the lucid webs are roll'd,
And, as they burst, the living flames unfold.[229]

The whole passage is equally fine, and closes thus:

Life buds, or breathes, from Indus [230] to the Poles,
And the vast surface kindles as it rolls.[231]

We find the same image applied to Light in the first Canto, as it is here to Vitality. Speaking
of Chaos the Poet says:

Through all his realms the kindling Ether runs.[232]

Yet, far from censuring the very infrequent repetitions, which we may find through this
great work, wonder and praise will rise in the mind of every true lover of the poetic art,
contemplating that exhaustless variety of ideas, imagery and expression, which light up the
subject with a thousand torches, kindled at the orb of Genius.

Skilful blendings of philosophic knowledge with poetic fancy, now occur in the birth
and growth of plants and flowers. They are compared to the kindling and expansion of
animal life in the Crocodile, bursting from its egg on the shores of the Nile. It is a grand
picture, though of somewhat forced introduction. The charge on its progress contains
instruction to gardeners, though it is addressed to the Sylphs, and adorned by the parable of
Aaron's rod.[233] The banishment of noxious insects by their cares, is enforced by the example
of the *Cyprepedia*,[234] a flower curiously resembling the large American Spider. Linnaeus
asserts, that it catches small birds as well as insects, and has the venomous bite of a serpent;
and a French naturalist narrates, that it catches the humming-bird in its strong nets. The
circumstance is thus elegantly pictured in the Botanic Queen's horticultural adjurations,

So where the humming-bird, in Chili's bowers,
On murmuring pinions robs the pendent flowers;
Seeks where fine pores their dulcet balms distill,
And sucks the treasure with proboscis bill,
Fell Cyprepedia, &c.[235]

The diseases of plants are next pointed out, and they are illustrated by a curious fact in glass-making. The pictures of various flowers next rise on the page, in botanic discrimination, and in all the hues of poetry. The exotic wealth of the Royal Garden at Kew [236] is celebrated; and the conscious pride of its river, on the occasion, is thus sweetly fancied;

Delighted Thames through tropic umbrage glides,
The [237] flowers antarctic bending o'er his sides;[238]
Drinks the new tints, the scents [239] unknown inhales,
And calls the Sons of Science to the vales.[240]

Poetic homage is then paid to our King and Queen, to their virtues, their taste for Botanic Science, and to the fair human Scions which themselves have raised.

The Goddess compliments her aerial Legions on attending the chariot of the Morning round the earth, on leading the gay Hours along the horizon; on showering the light on every dun meridian, and on pursuing, from zone to zone, the perennial journey of the Spring. She commissions them, on this their radiant tour, to bring her rich balms from the hallowed glades of Mecca, Arabian flowers, Italian fruits, and the tea-plants of China; also,

Each spicy rind which sultry India boasts,
Scenting the night-air round her breezy coasts;
Roots, whose bold stems in bleak Siberia blow,
And gem with many a tint th' eternal snow;
Barks, whose broad umbrage high in ether waves
O'er Ande's steeps, and hides his golden caves.[241]

Thus, with happy art, the Poet diversifies and animates floral enumeration with gleams of every-regioned landscape.

The Sylphs are then commanded to raise an altar to Hygeia;[242] to call to its rites the dispersed Sisterhood, the Water Nymphs, from their floating clouds, their waves and fountains; to stamp with charmed foot, and convoke the Gnomes from their subterranean palaces; and to beckon from their spheres the vestal forms of fire; that thus, in full congregation, they may win the Goddess of Health with unwearied vows. The picturesque attitudes of supplication, which she dictates, are eminently beautiful; and, with a patriotic apostrophe to Hygeia, the British Queen of Botany concludes her embassy.

O wave, Hygeia, o'er Britannia's throne
Thy serpent wand, and mark it for thy own!
Lead round her breezy coasts thy guardian trains,
Her nodding forests, and her waving plains!
Shed o'er her peopled realms thy beamy smile,
And with thy airy temple crown her isle![243]

The Goddess of Botany now ascends with as much elegance as she had descended, and with more magnificence. If the reader is susceptible of poetic beauty; if he can feel that what never can be seen in reality, may yet be painted naturally; a strict survey of this poetical ascension will enable him to perceive, what indeed countless other instances in this Poem evince, that its author most eminently possessed that rare talent.

> The Goddess ceas'd, and calling from afar
> The wandering Zephyrs, joins them to her car;
> Mounts with light bound, and graceful as she bends,
> Whirls the long lash, the flexile rein extends;
> On whispering wheels the silver axle slides,
> Climbs into air, and cleaves the crystal tides;
> Burst from its pearly chains, her amber hair
> Streams o'er her ivory shoulders, buoy'd in air;
> Swells her white veil, with ruby clasp confin'd
> Round her fair brow, and undulates behind;
> The lessening coursers rise in spiral rings,
> Fierce the slow-sailing clouds, and stretch their shadowy wings.[244]

If we could see a light vehicle mount the horizon, its wheels would whisper, its axle slide; so would it climb into air, so divide the etherial currents, as a boat divides the waves of the river or the sea; the coursers would rise in spiral rings and pervade the clouds; their wings would appear shadowy till they melted into air. Thus concludes the *Economy of Vegetation*.

Notes

1   Many scholars have investigated the natural philosophical and literary aspects of this work of Darwin. Among the notable works not cited elsewhere in this book, see Ralph B. Crum, *Scientific Thought in Poetry* (New York: Columbia University Press, 1931), esp. pp.110–130; Clark Emery, "Scientific Theory in Erasmus Darwin's *The Botanic Garden* (1789–91)", *Isis* 33 (1941): 315–325; Eric Robinson, "Erasmus Darwin's *Botanic Garden* and Contemporary Opinion", *Annals of Science* 10 (1954): 314–320; Robert L. Chamberlain, "George Crabbe and Darwin's Amorous Plants", *Journal of English and Germanic Philology* 61 (1962): 833–852; Ivanka Kovacevich, "The Mechanical Muse: The Impact of Technical Inventions of Eighteenth-Century Neoclassical Poetry", *Huntington Library Quarterly* 28 (1965): 263–281; Robert N. Ross, "'To Charm Thy Curious Eye': Erasmus Darwin's Poetry at the Vestibule of Knowledge", *Journal of the History of Ideas* 32 (1971): 379–394; Pierre Danchin, "Erasmus Darwin's Scientific and Poetic Purpose in *The Botanic Garden*", in Sergio Rossi (ed) *Science and Imagination in XVIIIth-Century British Culture* (Milan: Unicopli, 1987), pp.133–150; Alan Bewell, "'Jacobin Plants': Botany as Social Theory in the 1790s", *Wordsworth Circle* 20 (1989): 132–139; Londa Shiebinger, "The Private Life of Plants: Sexual Politics in Carl Linnaeus and Erasmus Darwin", in Marina Benjamin (ed) *Science and Sensibility: Gender and Scientific Enquiry, 1780–1945* (Oxford: Basil Blackwell, 1994), pp.121–143; Marina Benjamin, "Elbow Room: Women Writers on Science, 1790–1840", in Marina Benjamin (ed) *Science and Sensibility: Gender and Scientific Enquiry, 1780–1945* (Oxford: Basil Blackwell, 1994), pp.27–59; Fredrika J. Teute, "*The Loves of the Plants*; or, The Cross-Fertilization and Desire at the End of the Eighteenth Century", *Huntington Library Quarterly* 63 (2000):

319–345; Donna Coffey, "Protecting the Botanic Garden: Seward, Darwin, and Coalbrookdale", *Women's Studies* 31 (2002): 141–164; Patricia Fara, *Sex, Botany & Empire: The Story of Carl Linnaeus and Joseph Banks* (Duxford, Cambridge: Icon, 2003); Patricia Fara, *Pandora's Breeches: Women, Science & Power in the Enlightenment* (London: Pimlico, 2004); Sam George, "Linnaeus in Letters and the Cultivation of the Female Mind: 'Botany in an English Dress', *British Journal of Eighteenth-Century Studies* 28 (2005): 1–18; Gavin Budge, "Erasmus Darwin and the Poetics of William Wordsworth: 'Excitement Without the Application of Gross and Violent Stimulants'", *British Journal for Eighteenth-Century Studies* 30 (2007): 279–308; M.M. Mahood, "Erasmus Darwin's Felling for the Organism" chapter in Mahood's *The Poet as Botanist* (Cambridge: Cambridge University Press, 2008), pp.49–81; Noel Jackson, *Sciences and Sensation in Romantic Poetry* (Cambridge: Cambridge University Press, 2008), and Peter Ayres, *The Aliveness of Plants: The Darwins at the Dawn of Plant Science* (London: Pickering & Chatto, 2008). For a broad context of naturalists and their work in Britain, see David E. Allen, *The Naturalist in Britain: A Social History* (Harmondsworth, Middlesex: Penguin Books, 1978). Desmond King-Hele provided an exemplary resource towards helping to identify particular passages from *The Botanic Garden* in his *A Concordance to Erasmus Darwin's Poem, "The Botanic Garden"*, Wellcome Institute for the History of Medicine Occasional Publication, No. 1 (London: Wellcome Institute, 1994).

2   Footnote citations are drawn from the 2nd edition of this book, published in 1791 by J. Johnson in London. This edition was also reprinted as part of Priestman's edited *Collected Writings of Erasmus Darwin* (Bristol: Thoemmes Continuum, 2004), Vol.1.

3   Flora.

4   Darwin, *Economy of Vegetation*, I, lines 59–68.

5   According to Dr Darwin, the "Rosicrucian doctrine of Gnomes, Sylphs, Nymphs, and Salamanders, was thought to afford a proper machinery for a Botanic poem; as it is probable, that they were originally the names of hieroglyphic figures representing elements" (*Economy of Vegetation*, Apology, p.vii). C.S. Lewis provided an historical literary context for these four wide-spread representations of the elements in *The Discarded Image: An Introduction tot Medieval and Renaissance Literature* (Cambridge: Cambridge University Press, 1964), esp. pp.122–138.

6   Nymphs of Primeval Fire (Darwin, *Economy of Vegetation*, I, line 97).

7   Darwin, *Economy of Vegetation*, I, lines 97–102.

8   The Biblical account of creation. *Genesis* I:1–31.

9   Raphael recounts the creation of the world to Adam in Milton, *Paradise Lost*, VII.221–640.

10   Darwin, *The Botanic Garden*, Part I "The Economy of Vegetation", Canto I.i.103–114. Seward has "explosion" for Darwin's "explosions" and "ellipsis" for Darwin's "ellipses".

11   Seward appears to be using this phrase as a shortened version of Darwin's "Nymphs of Primeval Fire" or heat. In other contexts, Nymphs of Fire referred to Salamanders. As we learn from Marco Polo's *Travels* to Cathay, what had once been commonly described as a beast that lived within the veins of mountains which could withstand fire, was not really an animal, but rather asbestos.

12   Darwin, *Economy of Vegetation*, I, lines 149–152, though Darwin used "to" instead of "through" in the last line.

13   In mythology, the Roman goddess of Love.

14   Female entities of Greek mythology which attended Venus.

15   Mythological husband of Venus and god of the forge and fire.

16   Darwin, *Economy of Vegetation*, I, lines 177–178.

17   In 1602, the alchemist Vincenzo Casciarolo discovered a natural stone (what Dr Darwin identifies as selenite or gypsum) on Monte Paderno, outside of Bologna (thus the name "Bolognian Stone"), that was studied for its luminescence.

18	According to Dr Darwin, Giacomo Bartolomeo Beccari (1682–1766) "made many curious experiments on the phosphoric light, as it is called, which becomes visible on bodies brought into a dark room, after having been previously exposed to the sunshine. It appears from these experiments, that almost all inflammable bodies possess this quality in a greater or less degree; white paper or linen thus examined after having been exposed to the sunshine, is luminous to an extraordinary degree; and if a person shut up in a dark room, puts one of his hands out into the sun's light for a short time and then retracts it, he will be able to see that hand distinctly and not the other" (*Economy of Vegetation*, I, p.17, note).

19	Greek mythological King of Ethiopia whose statue at his temple at Thebes held a lyre. Dr Darwin, drawing upon Claude Étienne Savary's *Letters on Egypt, Containing, A Parallel Between the Manners of its Ancient and Modern Inhabitants, its Commerce, Agriculture, Government and Religion* (London: G.G.J. and J. Robinson, 1787), claimed that it "sounded when the rising sun shone upon it. Some philosophers have supposed that the sun's light possesses a mechanical impulse", thus creating the sounds. Even after it was cut in two to uncover its internal structure during the reign of Cambyses II of Persia (*d*.522 BC), the "truncated statue is said for many centuries to have saluted the rising sun with chearful [sic] tones, and the setting sun with melancholy ones" (*Economy of Vegetation*, Additional note VIII).

20	In Dr Darwin's words, the ignis fatuus or "Jack a lantern" is "supposed to originate from the inflammable air, or Hydrogene, given up from morasses; which being of a heavier kind from its impurity than that obtained from iron and water, hovers near the surface of the earth, and uniting with common air gives out light by its slow ignition". Darwin questioned the existence of this phenomenon, claiming to "have travelled much in the night, in all seasons of the year, and over all kinds of soil, but never saw one of these Will o'wisps" (*Economy of Vegetation*, I, p.18, note).

21	Electric eel.

22	In mythology, one of the Gorgons, the monsters who turned their victims to stone.

23	In Roman mythology, the goddess of artisans, poets, teachers, and physicians.

24	Thomas Savery (*c*.1650–1715) patented the first steam engine (then called "fire engines") in 1698, designed to pump water out of coal mines. He later worked to refine this engine together with Thomas Newcomen (bap.1664–1729). These engines soon replaced the mills that had depended on a regular availability of water.

25	Whose remarkable strength allowed him to perform twelve great labours.

26	Like many of his era, Dr Darwin marveled at the potential of harnessing the wondrous power of electricity for practical applications to natural philosophy and medicine. See, for example, Paul Elliott, "'More Subtle that the Electric Aura': Georgian Medical Electricity, the Spirit of Animation and the Development of Erasmus Darwin's Psychophysiology", *Medical History* 52 (2008): 195–220.

27	Darwin, *Economy of Vegetation*, I, lines 367–368.

28	George William Richman (*d. c*.1755), Professor of Experimental Philosophy, a Member of the Imperial Academy of Sciences at Petersburg. According to Dr Darwin, Richman "elevated an insulated metallic rod to collect the aerial electricity, as Dr Franklin had previously done at Philadelphia; and as he was observing the repulsion of the balls of his electrometer [he] approached too near the conductor, and receiving the lightening in his head with a loud explosion, was struck dead…" (*Economy of Vegetation*, I, p.37, note).

29	This allegory is represented on an agate in the gem and mineral collection started by Lorenzo di Piero de' Medici, the Duke of Urbino (1492–1591) in Florence.

30	Darwin, *Economy of Vegetation*, I, lines 389–398.

31	"The Bard" here refers to poets in general, a part of Seward's argument that poetic representation is superior to painting. It should be noted that Seward also frequently referred to Dr Darwin as "The Bard".

32	In Dr Darwin's terms, phosphoric acid is "like all other acids united with vital air, and requires to be treated with charcoal or phlogiston to deprive it of this air, it then becomes a kind of animal sulphur, but of so inflammable a nature, that on the access of air it takes fire spontaneously, and as it burns becomes again united with vital air, and re-assumes its form of phosphoric acid" (*Economy of Vegetation*, Additional note X, "Phosphorous", p.19).

33 Darwin, *Economy of Vegetation*, I, line 404.

34 In mythology, the Greek god of love who, as Hesiod relates, is associated with Dawn at the beginning of the cosmos.

35 Darwin, *Economy of Vegetation*, I, drawn from lines 415–417.

36 Prostitute, based upon Cyprus as the birthplace of Aphrodite.

37 Any ancient pictorial representations that was, at the time, thought to have existed before the use of letters.

38 Milton, *Paradise Lost*, VIII.598–99. Adam refers to Eve in this passage, thus Seward italicizes the change to the masculine pronoun in her paraphrase. The original lines read, "In procreation common to all kindes/(Though higher of the genial bed by far,/And with mysterious reverence I deem)".

39 Ens, "Ens Entium" or "Being of Beings", phrasing used philosophically in order to avoid any religious reference to God. According to Dr Darwin, "That there exists a superior Ens Entium, which formed these wonderful creatures [i.e., human beings] is mathematical demonstration. That HE influences things by a particular providence, is not so evident. The probability, according to my notion, is against it, since general laws seem sufficient for that end....The light of Nature afford us not a single argument for a future state; this is the only one – that it is possible with God; since he who made us out of nothing can surely re-create us" (Erasmus Darwin to Thomas Oakes, November 1754, as reprinted in King-Hele (ed) *The Collected Letters of Erasmus Darwin*, p.22). For further discussion of Ens, see Darwin's *Economy of Vegetation*, II, p.107, note in reference to line 574.

40 Darwin, *Economy of Vegetation*, I, lines 421–424.

41 A tragic figure of Greek mythology, the daughter of Tantalus and wife of Amphion, King of Thebes, who wept for her slain children and was turned into a stone from which her continual tears formed a stream, the Achelous. Among the cameo reliefs that Wedgwood used on his pottery was that of "Niobe's Children".

42 A dolphin (L. *Grampus griseus*).

43 Sirius, the brightest star in the sky, part of the constellation Canis Major.

44 Dionysius, mother of Hera, Zeus's wife, tricked Semele into having Zeus visit her as he would his goddess wife, but the thunderbolts which he released killed the mortal Semele.

45 Darwin, *Economy of Vegetation*, I, lines 523–526.

46 I *Kings* 18:34.

47 Darwin, *Economy of Vegetation*, I, lines 587–588, though Darwin begins this passage with "The" instead of "While".

48 In Milton's *Paradise Lost*, it is the lead archangel, Michael, who describes a history of the future to Adam.

49 A silly parody in imitation of Darwin's poetic use of heroic couplet in which a parabola, a hyperbola, and an ellipse vie for the love of a rectangle. At the core, it was designed to destroy Dr Darwin's ideas which, the authors deemed, undermined the established Anti-Jacobin government and the Anglican religion. Namely, as King-Hele described (*Erasmus Darwin: A Life of Unequalled Achievement*, p.316), they opposed the idea of humans having evolved from lower forms of life, the practical implications of electricity, and the argument that the earth's mountains are more than 6000 years old. Moreover, they opposed the notion of free love in which Darwin's sexualized plants participated. The work originally appeared in three numbers of *The Anti-Jacobin* (16 and 23 April and 7 May 1798). George Canning (1770–1827), at the time, Under-Secretary for Foreign Affairs in William Pitt's Government, initiated the work, together with the assistance of John Hookham Frere (1769–1846) and George Ellis (1753–1815). Their critique dramatically diminished Darwin's reputation as a poet. Moreover, in volatile times with revolution in the air, Pitt's government viewed the atheism and sexual immorality in *The Botanic Garden* as indicative of the causes underlying the revolution in France. On another level, readers on the Continent like Johann Wolfgang von Goethe (1749–1832), as expressed in a 26 January 1798 letter to Johann Christoph Friedrich von Schiller (1759–1805), mocked *The Botanic Garden*, claiming that "among

all these oddities" of this book, "the oddest, I think, is that in this botanic work you can find everything, except plants". This letter is translated in Lisbet Koerner's *Isis* article, "Goethe's Botany: Lessons of a Feminine Science", reprinted in Sally Gregory Kohlstedt (ed) *History of Women in the Sciences: Readings from Isis* (Chicago: University of Chicago, 1999), p.145.

50   Oft repeated phrases which appear in the politician and neoplatonic philosopher, Anthony Ashley Cooper, 3rd Earl of Shaftesbury's (1671–1713) *The Moralists, a Philosophical Rhapsody* (London: J. Wyat, 1709) and *Characteristics of Men, Manners, Opinions, Times* (London: J. Darby, 1711), including his "Miscellaneous Reflections on the Said Treatises, and Other Critical Subjects".

51   Sir Henry Percy (1364–1403), known as Hotspur, led a rebellious uprising against Henry IV in July 1403, during which battle he was killed. Hotspur's enduring reputation owes much to his prominent appearance in Shakespeare's *Henry IV*.

52   Milton, *Paradise Lost*, IV.641.

53   Literally, the honey flower; figuratively, a woman of great beauty. Florimel is a lady in love with the knight Marinell in Edmund Spenser's *The Faerie Queene*. In the poem, a witch creates a "false Florimel" out of wax.

54   Edmund Spenser (*c*.1552–1599).

55   Shakespeare, *A Midsummer Night's Dream* (1595–96), V.i.12–17. Seward has "form" where Shakespeare has "forms".

56   Christian Rosenkreuz, the reputed 15th-century founder of a movement, although likely founded by the alchemist Paracelsus (1493–1541). The underlying Rosicrucian beliefs, which embodied occult wisdom and spiritual enlightenment of the ancients, regained popularity during the 18th century. For further information, see Frank Wittemans, *A New and Authentic History of the Rosicrucians* (Chicago: Aries Press, 1938), and Frances Amelia Yates, *The Rosicrucian Enlightenment* (New York: Routledge, 1999).

57   Alexander Pope's mock epic morality poem, *Rape of the Lock* (London: B. Lintott, 1712).

58   An elemental substance which, in Paracelsian alchemy, was thought to inhabit the earth.

59   An elemental substance which, in Paracelsian alchemy, was thought to inhabit the air.

60   Human-bodied, fish-tailed sea gods.

61   Darwin, *Economy of Vegetation*, II, lines 57–58.

62   Darwin, *Economy of Vegetation*, II, lines 75–82, though Darwin used "heaves" instead of "rolls" in line 78.

63   Darwin, *Economy of Vegetation*, II, drawn from lines 73, 77 and 83.

64   The suitor of Penelope, Odysseus's wife.

65   God of Arts and the Sun.

66   Louis-François Roubiliac (*c*.1695–1762), prominent late Baroque sculptor who worked in England.

67   Anne Seymour Damer, née Conway, (1748–1828), English sculptor supported by a number of Whig patrons, whose sculptured busts she created, as well as a number of classical scenes.

68   As Dr Darwin described, "There is a town in the immense salt-mines of Cracow in Poland, with a market-place, a river, a church, and a famous statue, (here supposed to be of Lot's wife) by the moist or dry appearance of which the subterranean inhabitants are said to know when the weather is fair above ground. The galleries in these mines are so numerous and so intricate, that workmen have frequently lost their way, their lights having been burnt out, and have perished before they could be found" (*Economy of Vegetation*, II, p.71, note).

69   See *Genesis* 19:26. An angel warned Lot's family of the impending destruction of Sodom, the city they inhabited. They were commanded to "Flee for your lives! Don't look back, and don't stop anywhere on the plain!" Alas, Lot's wife was not obedient to God's command, and, for this action, she was turned into a pillar of salt.

70   Shakespeare, *The Tempest* (1611), IV.i.151, 156. Seward elides several of Prospero's lines: "And like the baseless fabric of this vision,/The cloud-capp'd tow'rs, the gorgeous palaces,/The solemn temples, the great globe itself,/Yea, all which it inherit, shall dissolve,/And like this insubstantial pageant faded/Leave not a rack behind".

71   An inflammable, phlogisticated gas containing azote (nitrogen).

72   Homer's heroine who, when abducted by Paris, the son of Troy's King Priam, initiated the Trojan War.

73   Trojan King Priam's son, husband of Andromache, who was slain by Achilles. Among the cameo reliefs that Wedgwood used on his pottery were "Priam Begging the Body of Hector" and the "Birth of Achilles".

74   Alexander Pope's translation of *The Iliad of Homer* (London: B. Lintot, 1715–20).

75   As Dr Darwin relates, the "method of rendering bars of hardened steel magnetical consists in holding vertically two or more magnetic bars nearly parallel to each other with their opposite poles very near each other (but nevertheless separated to a small distance), these are to be slided over a line of bars laid horizontally a few times backward and forward" (*Economy of Vegetation*, II, p.78, note). For a superb analysis of the contemporary philosophy surrounding the use of magnets, see Patricia Fara, *Sympathetic Attractions: Magnetic Practices, Beliefs, and Symbolism in Eighteenth-Century England* (Princeton: Princeton University Press, 1996).

76   John Michell (1724–1793). In Dr Darwin's words, "What Mr Michell proposed by this method was to include a very small portion of the horizontal bars, intended to be made magnetical, between the joint forces of two or more bars already magnetical, and by sliding them from end to end every part of the line of bars became successively included, and thus bars possessed of a very small degree of magnetism to begin with, would in a few times sliding backwards and forwards make the other ones much more magnetical than themselves, which are then to be taken up and used to touch the former, which are in succession to be laid down horizontally in a line" (*Economy of Vegetation*, II, p.78, note).

77   Darwin, *Economy of Vegetation*, II, lines 201–206, though Darwin used "helm" instead of "course" in line 204.

78   Hydrogen chloride.

79   Calcium oxide (lime).

80   Clay.

81   Proteus was the Greek mythological sea god noted for his abilities of metamorphosis and of prophecy.

82   When Zeus became enamored of Europa, a member of the reigning Phoenician family, he transformed himself into a tame white bull and intermixed with her family's herds. Europa was attracted to this bull, eventually mounting its back, at which time the bull (Zeus) ran to the sea and swam to the island of Crete. There, after Zeus revealed his true identity, Europa became the first Queen of Crete.

83   The ancient country inhabited by the Etruscans after which the master potter, Josiah Wedgwood (1730–1795), named his factory town. According to Dr Darwin, the "peculiar character of their [Etrurian] earthen vases consists in the admirable beauty, simplicity, and diversity of forms, which continue the best models of taste to the artists of the present times; and in a species of non-vitreous encaustic painting, which was reckoned, even in the time of Pliny, among the lost arts of antiquity, but which has lately been recovered by the ingenuity and industry of Mr Wedgwood. It is supposed that the principal manufactories were about Nola, at the foot of Vesuvius; for it is in that neighbourhood that the greatest quantities of antique vases have been found; and it is said that the general taste of the inhabitants is apparently influenced by them; insomuch that strangers coming to Naples, are commonly struck with the diversity and elegance even of the most ordinary vases for common uses" (*Economy of Vegetation*, II, p.86, note). For an accessible modern biography of Wedgwood, see Brian Dolan, *Wedgwood: The First Tycoon* (New York: Viking, 2004). For an illustrative overview of Wedgwood's works, see Hilary Young (ed) *The Genius of Wedgwood* (London: The Victoria and Albert Museum, 1995).

84   Darwin, *Economy of Vegetation*, II, line 296.

85   Sir Joseph Banks offered Wedgwood some clay that he had retrieved from New South Wales in 1789 which, after analysis, the potter found to be of excellent quality. Using that clay, he created some medallions "with a view to encourage the arts and to inspire hope, amidst many difficulties, in the breasts of those distant colonies". The figure

of Hope appeared on a rock, holding an anchor, with a cornucopia at her feet, addressing Peace, Labour, and Plenty (Meteyard, *Life of Wedgwood*, 1866, Vol.2, pp.567–568). For further discussion of this medallion, see L. Richard Smith, *The Sydney Cove Medallion* (Sydney: The Wedgwood Press, 1987) and John Pearn, "The Antipodes and Erasmus Darwin: The Place of Erasmus Darwin in the Heritage of Australian Literature and Biology", in Smith and Arnott (eds) *The Genius of Erasmus Darwin*, pp.103–111.

86 An ancient vase purchased by Sir William Hamilton (1730–1803), British envoy to the Kingdom of Naples, upon its excavation from Pompeii, and eventually sold to Margaret Cavendish Bentinck, Duchess of Portland (1715–1785) from whose estate, William Henry Cavendish-Bentinck, 3rd Duke of Portland (1738–1809) purchased the vase.

87 A compact form of coal abundant in England's north east coastal region of Whitby, Yorkshire, which, when polished, was frequently used in jewellery.

88 For an accessible overview of the study of electricity in Darwin's era, see Patricia Fara, *An Entertainment for Angels: Electricity in the Enlightenment* (Duxford, Cambridge: Icon, 2002).

89 Of all of Dr Darwin's acquaintances, Richard Lovell Edgeworth knew the Irish situation the best. Edgeworth oversaw his vast estate in an exemplary fashion. He was, as recently noted, the "best example" of a landowner, one who was not an absentee landlord, but rather one who "showed a commendable involvement in the welfare of their tenantry", claims Gearóid Ó Tuathaight, *Ireland Before the Famine 1798–1848* (Dublin: Gill and Macmillan, 2007), p.130. Edgeworth held a seat in the Irish Parliament and, although he claimed that the Irish people would benefit greatly if Ireland would join together under the rule of England, he voted, in the minority, against the Act of Union in 1800. For more on Edgeworth's life and politics in Ireland, see Clarke, *The Ingenious Mr Edgeworth*, esp. pp.152–175. As the Parliamentarians removed their wealth, their culture, and themselves from Dublin following the Act of Union, the city experienced the end of a century's worth of unprecedented cosmopolitanism.

90 The prison in Paris stormed by "the people" on 14 July 1789, symbolically beginning the French Revolution. One of Richard Lovell Edgeworth's cousins, Henry Essex Edgeworth (1745–1807), later The Abbé Edgeworth de Firmont, born in Edgeworthstown, was brought up by Jesuits in Toulouse and Paris. As a priest, he gained respect among those on both sides of the Revolution. As a confessor to Louis XVI (1754–1793), he attended him on the scaffold. For further details, see Violette M. Montagu, *The Abbe Edgeworth and His Friends* (London: Herbert Jenkins, 1913).

91 Darwin, *Economy of Vegetation*, II, lines 393–394.

92 For further discussion of superstition and science in this era, see Philip Shorr, *Science and Superstition in the Eighteenth Century* (New York: Columbia University Press, 1932), and Keith Thomas, *Man and the Natural World: A History of the Modern Sensibility* (New York: Pantheon, 1983).

93 Cambyses II (*d*.522 BC), the Achaemenid King of Persia who conquered Egypt in 523 BC and whose atrocities there were recorded (and perhaps amplified) in *The Histories* of Herodotus of Halicarnassus (*c*.484–425 BC).

94 Darwin, *Economy of Vegetation*, II, lines 497–498.

95 Hannibal (247–*c*.181 BC), the Carthaginian general and commander of forces against the Roman Army in the Second Punic War (218–201 BC). After a fifteen-day arduous climb and descent over the Alps, with considerable loss of forces and supplies, Hannibal arrived, with his famous elephants, at the Roman held territory of Taurini (modern day Turin). For a recent overview of this journey, see John Prevas, *Hannibal Crosses the Alps: The Invasion of Italy and the Second Punic War* (New York: Da Capo Press, 2001).

96 *Acts* 12: 1–8. The apostle, St Simon, also called Peter (*d. c*.64), escaped from prison in Rome, was later martyred as a Christian, and is considered, by tradition, to be the first Pope of the Roman Catholic Church.

97 John Howard (1726–1790), as High Sheriff of Bedfordshire in 1773, began reform measures to legally release discharged prisoners rather than, as had frequently been practiced, keeping them in prison merely to pay the gaolers salaries.

98   In Greek mythology, the god of vegetation who was loved by Venus.

99   In Roman mythology, Proserpine was kidnapped by Pluto and taken to his kingdom in the Underworld, where she became his wife. With the intervention of her mother, Ceres, Proserpine was able to return to the world of the living for half a year, but must spend the other half in the Underworld.

100 Darwin, *Economy of Vegetation*, III, lines 7–10.

101 William Collins (1721–1759), an English lyric poet known for his *Odes* which, though Neoclassical in their style, were Romantic in their themes. See, for example, his *Odes on Several Descriptive and Allegorical Subjects* (London: A. Millar, 1747), which contains his "Ode to Evening".

102 William Collins, "Ode to Evening" (1747), ll.37–40. Seward has "The Hamlets" where Collins has "And Hamlets", "hear" for "hears", "bells" for "bell", "mark" for "marks", and "Her dewy" for "Thy dewy".

103 Darwin, *Economy of Vegetation*, III, lines 19–20, though Darwin used "bands" instead of "hands".

104 Darwin, *Economy of Vegetation*, III, line 31.

105 Darwin, *Economy of Vegetation*, III, lines 123–128.

106 Also known as the Dog-Star.

107 In Egyptian mythology, the jackal-headed god responsible for leading the dead to their judgment.

108 Darwin, *Economy of Vegetation*, III, lines 124–138, though Darwin used "o'er" instead of "on" in line 127.

109 Mount Hekla, the most active volcano in Iceland, is situated in the south, some seventy miles east of Reykjavik.

110 Spa town in the High Peaks of Derbyshire noted for its hot sulphur water. Anna Seward frequented these spa waters, as did many of her associates including the Wedgwoods. It was at Buxton, in 1769, that Anna Seward and Honora Sneyd met John André. Many years later, in 1793, Seward took herself to Buxton in attempt to soothe her woes over the death of her inamorato, John Saville, the very spot where their futures had become "harmonized" on a holiday in 1768, as noted P. Rowland in his *Life of Thomas Day*, p.44. Dr Darwin described the content of spa waters thusly, "The water of many springs contains much azotic gas, or phlogistic air [also known as inflammable air or hydrogen], besides carbonic gas, or fixed air, as that of Buxton and Bath; this being set at liberty may more readily contribute to the production of nitre by means of the putrescent matters which it is exposed to by being spread upon the surface of the land; in the same manner as frequently turning over heaps of manure facilitates the nitrous process by imprisoning atmospheric air in the interstices of the putrescent materials. Water arising by land-floods brings along with it much of the most soluble parts of the manure from the higher lands to the lower ones. River-water in its clear state and those springs which are called soft are less beneficial for the purpose of watering lands, as they contain less earthy or saline matter; and water from dissolving snow from its slow solution brings but little earth along with it, as may be seen by the comparative clearness of the water of snow-floods" (*Economy of Vegetation*, III, p.154, note). Dr Darwin articulated his belief in the salubrity of spa waters in "Of the Medicinal Waters of Buxton and Matlock", in James Pilkington's *A View of the Present State of Derbyshire* (Derby: J. Drewry for J. Johnson and J. Deighton, London, 1789), pp.256–75. For further discussion of the importance of the spa towns during this era, both in terms of medical therapy and social gathering spots, see Phyllis Hembry, *The English Spa 1560–1815: A Social History* (London: Athlone, 1990), and Roy Porter (ed) *The Medical History of Waters and Spas, Medical History*, Supplement 10 (1990).

111 Georgiana Cavendish, Duchess of Devonshire (1757–1806).

112 Home of the Duke and Duchess of Devonshire.

113 Darwin, *Economy of Vegetation*, III, lines 191–192.

114 William Cavendish, 5th Duke of Devonshire (1748–1811) used profits from his investments into copper mines to erect a crescent-shaped edifice at Buxton with rooms and shops above, in imitation of The Crescent at Bath. He

also provided funds for the Devonshire Royal Hospital. Soon after Dr Darwin arrived in Derby, he began advising the Duke on diet, drinking, and gout (Uglow, *The Lunar Men*, p.378).

115 As wife of Jove (Jupiter), Juno was considered the patron goddess of Rome and its Empire.

116 Seward's own footnote, "Obscure and very awkward expression".

117 Seward's own footnote, "Most unpoetic".

118 Cowper, *The Iliad and Odyssey of Homer*, *Iliad*, XVI.202–23. Where Seward has "various arts", Cowper has "various art".

119 In Greek mythology, Pallas Athena was the goddess of wisdom, arts and crafts, spinning and weaving, war and the guardian of Athens, the city named for her.

120 Pope, *The Iliad*, XIV.197–218. Where Seward has "Part o'er her head", Pope has "Part on her head".

121 The Khoikhoin people of South Africa were encountered by the first European explorers of this area around 1500 and were also visited by Cook and his voyagers in Cape Town in 1771. The term "Hottentot", meaning "stutterer" or "stammerer", was used to describe the clicking sounds of the *Khoisan languages*. Saartjie "Sarah" Baartman (1789-1815), the woman shown in sideshow fashion in London as the "Hottentot Venus", gained exotic and erotic notoriety for her large buttocks and her large, apron-like, external genitalia. However, as she did not appear in London until 1810, this was not a specific reference to her. For further reading on the notoriety surrounding the act of displaying Sarah Baartman, see Sadiah Qureshi, "'Displaying Sara Baartman, the 'Hottentot Venus'", *History of Science* 42 (2004): 233-257, Rachel Holmes, *African Queen: The Real Life of the Hottentot Venus* (New York: Random House, 2007), and Clifton Crasis and Pamela Scully, *Sara Baartman and the Hottentot Venus: A Ghost Story and a Biography* (Princeton: Princeton University Press, 2008). According to physiognomists of Darwin's era, Hottentots occupied a "liminal classificatory status between humans and brutes", as Moi Rickman noted in "'Tied to the Species by the Strongest of All Relations': Mary Wollstonecraft and the Rewriting of Race as Sensibility", in Jennie Batchelor and Cora Kaplan (eds) *British Women's Writing in the Long Eighteenth Century* (Basingstoke, Hampshire: Palgrave Macmillan, 2005), p.150. For more detail on thinking about the Hottentots' placement within classification categories during this period, see L. Schiebinger, *Nature's Body*, esp. pp.160-172, and Peter J. Kitson, *Romantic Literature, Race, and Colonial Literature* (New York: Palgrave Macmillan, 2007).

122 Equivalent to Juno, wife of Jupiter, daughter of Saturn.

123 A belt worn by women in Ancient Greece.

124 Darwin, *Economy of Vegetation*, III, lines 211–216.

125 Literally, the West Wind.

126 Most likely male dryads, or perhaps elves.

127 Turkish mountain near ancient Troy, (modern day Kaz Dagi).

128 The mountain sanctuary of Zeus in the western Peloponnese.

129 Cowper, *The Iliad and Odyssey of Homer*, *Iliad*, XVI.354–57. Seward has "steeds" where Cowper has "steed".

130 Pope, *The Iliad*, XVI.337–40.

131 Darwin, *Economy of Vegetation*, III, lines 245–252.

132 Seward's own footnote, "What an exquisite picture!"

133 Darwin, *Economy of Vegetation*, III, lines 277–278.

134 Bull.

135 In Greek mythology, the sea nymphs, often accompanying Poseidon, were helpful to sailors who encountered storms.

136 Darwin, *Economy of Vegetation*, III, lines 287–290.

137 Samuel Richardson (bap.1689–1761).

138 Richardson's *Clarissa; or, The Story of a Young Lady* (London: S. Richardson, sold by A. Millar, J. and J. Rivington, J. Osborn; and Bath: J. Leake, Bath. 1747–48).

139 Richardson's *The History of Sir Charles Grandison, In a Series of Letters* (London: S. Richardson, sold by C. Hitch and L. Hawes, J. and J. Rivington, A. Millar, R. and J. Dodsley; and Bath: J. Leake, 1753–54).

140 Shakespeare, *A Midsummer Night's Dream*, II, i, 150–154. Seward has "I saw a Mermaid" for Shakespeare's "And heard a mermaid", and "harmonious sounds" for "harmonious breath".

141 Millicent Mundy French (1746–1789) who, according to Dr Darwin, was "a lady who to many other elegant accomplishments [is] added a proficiency in botany and natural history" (*Economy of Vegetation*, p.139, note). Millicent married Richard French (*c*.1738/39–1801), a Captain of the Royal House Guards, (The Blues) and an original member of the Derby Philosophical Society.

142 James Brindley (1716–1772), a Staffordshire millwright who became one of England's most prominent "Inland Navigation" (i.e., canal) surveyors and engineers.

143 Darwin, *Economy of Vegetation*, III, lines 329–344, though Darwin ends this passage with the word "Lands" instead of "sands".

144 No such monument exists. Brindley died at Turnhurst, Staffordshire, from complications associated with diabetes, for which he was being treated by Dr Darwin. Brindley's life is celebrated in Brindley Mill and James Brindley Museum, Mill Street, Leek, England, as described online at www.brindleymill.net/index.html. (15 September 2008).

145 Darwin, *Economy of Vegetation*, III, lines 373–376.

146 The Reverend William Mason (1725–1797), *Elfrida: A Dramatic Poem. Written on the Model of the Antient Greek Tragedy* (London: J. and P. Knapton, 1752).

147 William Mason, *Elfrida* (1752), ll.83–88.

148 Darwin, *Economy of Vegetation*, III, lines 377–392.

149 John Dryden (1631–1700), poet, dramatist, and literary critic who studied at Trinity College, Cambridge, composed *Annus Mirabilis. The Year of Wonders, M.DC.LXVI. An Heroic Poem Containing the Progress and Various Successes of our Naval War with Holland, under the Conduct of His Highness Prince Rupert, and His Grace the Duke of Albemarl: and Describing the Fire of London* (London: Henry Herringman, 1667).

150 The seven children of the stationer James Mason of Leadenhall Street, London, were killed in a great fire on 18 January 1782.

151 Mary Usher Molesworth, wife of Richard Molesworth, 3rd Viscount Molesworth of Swords (*d*.1758), died in a London fire on 6 May 1763, together with her daughters, Melosina and Mary, and six servants. Two other daughters were badly injured after jumping from upper windows, one requiring a leg amputation, and a third daughter was severely burned.

152 According to Dr Darwin, the River Achelous "deluged Etolia, by one of its branches or arms, which in the ancient languages are called horns, and produced famine throughout a great tract of country, this was represented in hieroglyphic emblems by the winding course of a serpent and the roaring of a bull with large horns. Hercules, or the emblem of strength, strangled the serpent, and tore off one horn from the bull; that is, he stopped and turned the course of one arm of the river, and restored plenty to the country. Whence the ancient emblem of the horn of plenty" (*Economy of Vegetation*, III, p.151, note).

153 The word "that" appears as "who" in the 1804 version of Seward's *Life* published in Philadelphia.

154 Darwin, *Economy of Vegetation*, III, lines 485–488, though Darwin ends line 487 with "dragon-train" rather than "dragon tail".

155 Thomas Sternhold (*c.*1500–1549), poet and Groom of the Robes to Henry VIII and to Edward VI. He set fifty one of David's *Psalms* to music in hopes that they would replace the amorous and bawdy sonnets that were commonly sung at Court.

156 John Hopkins (*d.*1570), Suffolk clergyman and schoolmaster who turned eighty five additional *Psalms* to music which, together with Sternhold's, were included in the 1562 *Psalter*. During Darwin's and Seward's era, these works were reprinted as *The Whole Book of Psalms, Collected into English Metre, by Thomas Sternhold, John Hopkins, And Others; Conferred with the Hebrew* (London: A. Wilde, 1760).

157 James Hurdis (1763–1801), divine and poet, known for his *The Village Curate, a Poem* (London: J. Johnson, 1788). A protégé of William Cowper, he was appointed Professor of Poetry at Oxford in 1793.

158 Pope, *Essay on Criticism* (1709), l. 15.

159 An additional word, "be" appears here in the 1804 version of Seward's *Life* published in Philadelphia.

160 Seward's own footnote, "Here comes in the impertinent thunder storm".

161 James Hurdis, *The Favorite Village: A Poem* (Bishopstone, Sussex: At the Author's Press, 1800), ll. 331–40, 345–54.

162 Darwin used "when" instead of "where".

163 No "a" appears in Darwin's version.

164 Darwin's line reads "And win, in easy curves, their graceful way".

165 Darwin, *Economy of Vegetation*, III, lines 561–570.

166 Among the cameo reliefs that Wedgwood used on his pottery was that of the "Marriage of Cupid and Psyche".

167 Sirocco or siroc Mediterranean winds of hurricane strength originating from the Sahara that can reach Southern Europe.

168 A "poisonous" wind of red dust and sand that blows across the Sahara and other deserts.

169 Robert Southey (1774–1843), an English poet and prose writer.

170 While a student at Oxford, Southey expressed his sympathy for the French Revolution in *Joan of Arc, An Epic Poem* (Bristol: J. Cottle, 1796). Like his friends and fellow poets, Coleridge and Wordsworth, he eventually tempered his radicalism towards conservatism. See Adam Sisman, *The Friendship: Wordsworth and Coleridge* (New York: Viking, 2007).

171 Darwin used "realms" instead of "waste".

172 Darwin, *Economy of Vegetation*, IV, lines 65–71.

173 Robert Southey (1774–1843), *Joan of Arc* (1796), 10.372–78.

174 A noxious, foul-smelling stench.

175 The word "and" does not appear in Darwin's version.

176 Darwin used "on" instead of "o'er".

177 Darwin, *Economy of Vegetation*, IV, lines 79–82.

178 Many of the physician and poet Hieronymus Fracastorius's (1478–1553) ideas presented in *De Contagione et Contagiosis Morbis* (Venice: Lucaeantonij Iuntae Florentini, 1546) were still current in Dr Darwin's day. Namely, diseases were thought to be contagious in their ability to spread either by direct contact with infected people, by coming into contact with an item previously touched or worn by an infected individual, or by spreading through the air, even over considerable distances.

179 According to Dr Darwin, when the plague "raged in Holland in 1636, a young girl was seized with it, had three carbuncles, and was removed to a garden, where her lover, who was betrothed to her, attended her as a nurse, and slept with her as his wife. He remained uninfected, and she recovered, and was married to him" (*Economy of Vegetation*, IV, p.169, note).

180 The word "beautiful" rather than "young" appears in the 1804 version of Seward's *Life* published in Philadelphia.

181 Darwin, *Economy of Vegetation*, IV, line 94.

182 Darwin, *Economy of Vegetation*, IV, line 106, though Darwin used "clasps" instead of "clasp'd".

183 The youth of Greek mythology who swam the Hellespont nightly to visit Hero, but drowned one night. Among Joseph Wright's many paintings were two "Hero and Leander" works which he produced for Wedgwood, one depicting a Storm, the other a Moonlight scene.

184 The Apocryphal Book of Tobit relates how the Jewish hero, Tobias, married the widow Sarah, whose previous husbands had each been killed by the demon Asmodeus on their respective wedding nights. With the intervention of the angel Raphael, Tobias was not killed by the demon when he married Sarah.

185 Evangelista Torricelli (1608–1647) used his invention, the barometer, to demonstrate the pressure of the atmosphere, having, in Dr Darwin's words, "previously found that the air had weight" (*Economy of Vegetation*, IV, p.171, note).

186 Robert Boyle (1627–1691), prominent Irish experimental natural philosopher known for devising an improved air pump in 1659.

187 As Dr Darwin relates, Jean-François Pilâtre de Rozier (1754–1785), historian to Louis XVI, together with Pierre-Jules Romain (*d.*1785) "rose in a balloon from Boulogne in June 1785, and after having been about a mile high for about half an hour the balloon took fire, and the two adventurers were dashed to pieces on their fall to the ground" (*Economy of Vegetation*, IV, p.173, note).

188 De Rozier had witnessed the first flight by the famed pioneers of ballooning, Joseph-Michel Montgolfier (1740-1810) and Jacques-Étienne Montgolfier (1745-1799) in their hot air balloon, which soon became colloquially known as the Montgolfière. Richard Gillespie describes more of this early ballooning era in "Ballooning in France and Britain, 1783-1786", *Isis* 75 (1984): 249-268. See also, Paul Keen, "The 'Balloonomania': Science and Spectacle in 1780s England", *Eighteenth-Century Studies* 39 (2006): 507-535, and L.T.C. Rolt, *The Balloonists: The History of the First Aeronauts* (Stroud, Gloucestershire: Sutton Publishing, 2006). Seward composed a sonnet "when the balloon enthusiasm was at its height", Number XLV in *Original Sonnets on Various Subjects; And Odes Paraphrased from Horace* (London: G. Sael, 1799).

189 In Greek mythology, despite the warnings of his father, Daedalus, Icarus flew with his waxen artificial wings too close to the sun, fell into the sea, and drowned.

190 "On" rather than "upon" in the 1804 version of Seward's *Life* published in Philadelphia.

191 William Cowper's *The Task, A Poem, In Six Books* (London, J. Johnson, 1785) was a long, discursive poem crafted to show his sympathy with the beauty of rural life and leisure.

192 "Began" rather than "begun" in the 1804 version of Seward's *Life* published in Philadelphia.

193 "The experiments here alluded to", according to Dr Darwin, are "1. Concerning the production of nitrous gas from dissolving iron and many other metals in nitrous acid, which … was fully investigated, and applied to the important purpose of distinguishing the purity of atmospheric air by Dr Priestley. When about two measures of common air and one of nitrous gas are mixed together a red effervescence takes place, and the two airs occupy about one fourth less space than was previously occupied by the common air alone. 2. Concerning the green substance which grows at the bottom of reservoirs of water, which Dr Priestley discovered to yield much pure air when the sun shone on it. His method of collecting this air is by placing over the green substance, which he believes to be a vegetable of the genus conserva, an inverted bell-glass previously filled with water, which subsides as the air arises; it has since been found that all vegetables give up pure air from their leaves, when the sun shines upon them, but not in the night, which may be owing to the sleep of the plant. 3. The third refers to the great quantity of pure air contained in the calces of metals. The calces were long known to weigh much more than the metallic bodies before calcination, insomuch that 100 pounds of lead will produce 112 pounds of minium; the ore of manganese, which is always found near the surface of the earth, is replete with pure air, which is now used for the purpose of

bleaching. Other metals when exposed to the atmosphere attract the pure air from it, and become calces by its combination, as zinc, lead, iron; and increase in weight in proportion to the air, which they imbibe" (*Economy of Vegetation*, IV, p.175, note).

194 Heating in order to remove impurities.

195 Pertaining to the fire-laden substances within the earth.

196 Sir Francis Bacon, Viscount St Albans, Baron Verulam (1561–1626), matriculated at Trinity College, Cambridge, a philosopher, essayist, and progenitor of the Scientific Method who later served as Lord Chancellor of England. Dr Darwin drew this quote from the *Works of Francis Bacon* (London: J. Rivington, 1778), Vol.5, p.470, and noted that this "allusion is still more curiously exact, from the late discovery of pure air being given up from vegetables, and that then in its unmixed state it more readily combines with metallic or inflammable bodies. From these fables which were probably taken from antient hieroglyphics there is frequently reason to believe that the Egyptians possessed much chemical knowledge, which for want of alphabetical writing perished with their philosophers" (*Economy of Vegetation*, IV, pp.176–177, note).

197 The Dutchman, Cornelius Drebbel (1572–1633). Citing Boyle, Dr Darwin relates that "Cornelius Drebelle contrived not only a vessel to be rowed under water, but also a liquor to be carried in that vessel, which would supply the want of fresh air. The vessel was made by order of James I and carried twelve rowers besides passengers" (*Economy of Vegetation*, IV, p.178, note).

198 Mr J. Day "perished in a diving bell, or diving boat, of his own construction at Plymouth [Sound] in June 1774, in which he was to have continued for a wager twelve hours one hundred feet deep in water, and probably perished from his not possessing all the hydrostatic knowledge that was necessary" (*Economy of Vegetation*, IV, p.179, note). See also "An authentic account of the rise and consequence of a new experiment to live under water, as lately tried at Plymouth", *Gentleman's Magazine* xliv (1774): 304–305, for additional details about Day's experiment and the circumstances of his death.

199 Mr Charles Spalding was, according to Dr Darwin, "professionally ingenious in the art of constructing and managing the diving bell, and had practised the business many years with success. He went down accompanied by one of his young men twice to view the wreck of the Imperial East-Indiaman at the Kish bank in Ireland. On descending the third time in June, 1783, they remained about an hour under water, and had two barrels of air sent down to them, but on the signals from below not being again repeated, after a certain time, they were drawn up by their assistants and both found dead in the bell" (*Economy of Vegetation*, IV, pp.179–180, note). For an extended obituary and description of the accident, see *Gentleman's Magazine* 53 (1783):541–42. Nearly a century earlier, the Secretary of the Royal Society, Sir Edmund Halley (1656–1742) better known today for his works in the astronomical region, developed the diving bell that served as a forerunner for all that came afterwards. For further discussion, see Lisa Jardine, *Ingenious Pursuits: Building the Scientific Revolution* (London: Little, Brown, and Co, 1999), esp. pp.216–220. The pioneering civil engineer, John Smeaton (1724–1792), made Halley's type of bell more practical with the addition of an air pump.

200 As Dr Darwin relates, the "*Haslewell East-Indiaman*, outward bound, was wrecked off Seacomb in the isle of Purbec [off England's south Dorsetshire coast] on the 6th of January, 1786; when Capt. [Richard] Pierce, the commander, with two young ladies, his daughters, and the greatest part of the crew and passengers perished in the sea. Some of the officers and about seventy seamen escaped with great difficulty on the rocks, but Capt. Pierce finding it was impossible to save the lives of the young ladies refused to quit the ship, and perished with them" (*Economy of Vegetation*, IV, p.180, note). An anonymously composed *Monody on the Death of Captain Pierce* appeared a few months after this disaster at sea.

201 Darwin, *Economy of Vegetation*, IV, lines 219–232.

202   William Crowe (1745–1829), divine and poet, served as rector of Stoke Abbot, Fellow of New College, Oxford, and Public Orator at Oxford University.

203   The hill itself is the largest in Dorset.

204   Seward provided her own bibliographical detail in her footnote, "This poem was printed at the Clarendon Press, Oxford, 1788, and sold by Prince and Cook of that city, and Cadell, Rivington and Faulder, London". Coleridge and Wordsworth both admired this work.

205   The peninsula opposite Weymouth in Dorset is joined to the mainland by a shelf of pebbles that form a chesil bank.

206   A perpendicular cliff.

207   Along the Dorset coast.

208   An Eastern Indonesian Island, one of the Maluku Islands, off the west coast of Halmahera. In the eighteenth century, Ternate was the site of a Dutch East India Company governorship.

209   William Crowe, "Lewesdon Hill" (1788), ll.191–220. Seward has "by the wintry storm" for Crowe's "as, by the wintry storm" and "mid rocks" for "'mong rocks".

210   Seward's infatuation with the music of George Frideric Handel (1685–1759), was fostered by John Saville's regular performance of works by Handel. For further insights, see Robert Manson Myers, *Anna Seward: An Eighteenth Century Handelian* (Williamsburg, VA: The Manson Park Press, 1947) and Gillen D'Arcy Wood, "The Female Penseroso: Anna Seward, Sociable Poetry, and the Handelian Consensus", *Modern Language Quarterly* 67 (2006):451–477. As to Seward's infatuation with Saville, see Mary Alden Hopkins's chapter, "The Saville–Seward Scandal" in her *Dr Johnson's Lichfield*, pp.105–121, and Marion Roberts, "Anna Seward (1742–1809) – The Virgin Muse?", *BMI Insight: The Journal of the Birmingham and Midland Institute and Library* 6 (2005): 12–14.

211   Wind produced music when the instrument was placed in an open window. The Aeolian harp, taking its name from Aeolus, the Greek god of all Winds, became a symbol for the creative process used by poets of the Romantic period. Coleridge produced his first well known lyric poem by this title, published in his *Poems on Various Subjects* (London: C. G. and J. Robinson; Bristol: Joseph Cottle, 1796). The Aeolian Harp owned by Seward's friends, Lady Eleanor Butler and Sarah Ponsonby ("The Ladies of Llangollen"), about which Seward commented in her letters, is on display at their idyllic cottage, Plas Newydd, Llangollen, Wales.

212   Dryden and Pope wrote odes honouring St Cecilia, the patron Saint of music and of the blind who, according to tradition, charmed an angel with her musical skills.

213   According to Dr Darwin, the "pestilential winds of the east are described by various authors under various denominations; as harmattan, samiel, samium, syrocca, kamsin, [and] seravansum" (*Economy of Vegetation*, IV, p.184, note).

214   Sennacherib, the Assyrian King who reigned *c.*705–681 BC. As recorded in II *Kings*: 18–19, Sennacherib captured the fortified cities of Judah, including its capital, Jerusalem. Hezekiah, King of Judah, informed Sennacherib, "I have done wrong. Leave me, and I will pay whatever tribute you impose on me", which he did. An angel of the Lord slew thousands of the Assyrian soldiers. Later, when Sennacherib was worshiping his god Nisroch in Ninevah, his sons Adram-melech and Sharezer slew him with the sword and fled into the land of Ararat, thereby delivering God's judgment upon those who blasphemed him.

215   Darwin used "loud" instead of "dread".

216   Darwin, *Economy of Vegetation*, IV, lines 297–304.

217   John Sargent (1750–1831).

218   John Sergeant's "Mary Queen of Scots: An Ode" (1788), I.2.1–4.

219   In Greek mythology, god of the North Wind.

220   In Greek mythology, god of the East Wind.

221 Darwin, *Economy of Vegetation*, IV, line 318.

222 Chameleon, subject to quick change, a constellation of the Southern sky personifying monstrous characteristics.

223 Zealand being the largest of the isles comprising Denmark.

224 Darwin, *Economy of Vegetation*, IV, line 348, although Darwin's line began with "And" instead of "To" and he used "on" instead of "o'er".

225 Richard Kirwan (1733–1812), Irish natural philosopher.

226 Kirwin's *An Estimate of the Temperature of Different Latitudes* (London: J. Davis for P. Elmsley, 1787).

227 Sir Frederick William Herschel (1738–1822). As Darwin relates, "Herschel has given a very sublime and curious account of the construction of the heavens with his discovery of some thousand nebulae, or clouds of stars; many of which are much larger collections of stars, than all those put together, which are visible to our naked eyes, added to those which form the galaxy, or milky zone, which surrounds us. He observes that in the vicinity of these clusters of stars there are proportionally fewer stars than in other parts of the heavens; and hence he concludes, that they have attracted each other, on the supposition that infinite space was at first equally sprinkled with them; as if it had at the beginning been filled with a fluid mass, which had coagulated. Mr Herschel has further shewn, that the whole sidereal system is gradually moving round some centre, which may be an opake mass of matter, ... If all these Suns are moving round some great central body; they must have had a projectile force, as well as a centripetal one; and may thence be supposed to have emerged or been projected from the material, where they were produced. We can have no idea of a natural power, which could project a Sun out of Chaos, except by comparing it to the explosions or earthquakes owing to the sudden evolution of aqueous or of other more elastic vapours; of the power of which under immeasurable degrees of heat, and compression, we are yet ignorant" (*Economy of Vegetation*, I, p.9, note).

228 Darwin, *Economy of Vegetation*, IV, lines 367–380.

229 Darwin, *Economy of Vegetation*, IV, lines 381–383.

230 The River Indus, a major water supply to Pakistan and areas throughout the Indian subcontinent, is also the derivation for naming the subcontinent "India".

231 Darwin, *Economy of Vegetation*, IV, lines 407–408.

232 Darwin, *Economy of Vegetation*, I, lines 105. 381–383.

233 In *Exodus* 7, we read of Aaron's rod in which God imparted the ability to display miraculous powers. Aaron casts down this rod, as did Pharaoh's sorcerers their own, all of which turned to serpents, but that formed by Aaron's rod consumed the others. This rod was placed, together with the Ten Commandments and the golden pot of hidden manna, in the Ark of the Covenant.

234 *Cypripedium*, a genus of the orchid family, *Orchidaceae*, whose species are commonly known by names including Lady's Slippers, moccasin flowers, and Venus' shoes.

235 Darwin, *Economy of Vegetation*, IV, lines 501–505, though Darwin used the singular "balm" in line 503.

236 Since 2003, the Royal Botanic Gardens, Kew have been officially designated as a UNESCO World Heritage Site. During the reign of George III, these Royal Botanical Gardens just west of London on the River Thames were enhanced by a number of individuals including Sir Joseph Banks (1743–1820), the naturalist who, after attending both Oxford and Cambridge Universities, sailed with Cook and later served as President of the Royal Society.

237 Darwin used "And" instead of "The".

238 Darwin used "tides" instead of "sides".

239 Darwin used "sweets" instead of "scents".

240 Darwin, *Economy of Vegetation*, IV, lines 571–574, though Darwin closed this passage with "his vales" instead of "the vales".

241 Darwin, *Economy of Vegetation*, IV, lines 601–606.

242 In Greek Mythology, the goddess of Health.

243 Darwin, *Economy of Vegetation*, IV, lines 623–628.

244 Darwin, *Economy of Vegetation*, IV, lines 629–640, though he began the last line with the word "Pierce". For further discussion of Dr Darwin's speculation about flying cars, see Desmond King-Hele, "The Air Man", in Smith and Arnott (eds) *The Genius of Erasmus Darwin*, pp.273–288. Darwin (*Economy of Vegetation*, I, lines 289–298) described these flying cars as follows:

> Soon shall thy arm, Unconquer'd Steam! Afar
>
> Drag the slow barge, or drive the rapid car;
>
> Or on wide-waving wings expanded bear
>
> The flying-chariot through the fields of air.
>
> – Fair crews triumphant, learning from above,
>
> Shall wave their fluttering kerchiefs as they move;
>
> Or warrior-bands alarm the gaping crowd,
>
> And armies shrink beneath the shadowy cloud.

Chapter VI

We now come to yet more playful composition in the second part of this Poem, as the floral system is a lighter and less important theme than the elementary properties, however generally gay the robes in which poetic imagination has dressed them both; but let it never be forgotten that the sexual nature of plants has a demonstrated existence.

The Preface to this second part is a compendium of the Linnaean system.[1] The Poem makes lively, yet very modest claims for the succeeding metamorphoses, amid whose lighter graces we meet with passages of intrinsic grandeur and sublimity.

Loves of the Plants.[2]

In which the Poet ordains that the Muse of Botany *(Figure 28)* shall succeed to its ascended Empress, as historian of the scene, and dictatress to its dramatis personae. He introduces her by invoking, in his own person, the attentive silence of the winds, the waters, and the trees, and by requesting the insects to pause upon their wings. Eight different insects are mentioned, and each forms a striking picture of its whole species, by the Poet having seized and exhibited its most characteristic feature. He next apostrophises the Muse who "led the Swedish Sage [3] by her airy hand", intreating her to say how tiny Graces dwell on every leaf, and how the pleasures laugh in the bell of a blossom.

The Ovidian metamorphosis of the flowers then commences. The floral ladies, and their harems, rise to the amused eye in all the glow of poetic colouring. Attentive to diversify them by the varieties of landscape, we generally find this Poet producing contrasted scenery by the introduction of flowers or plants which are indigenous to climates strikingly the reverse of each other. Much of that happy skill has been displayed in the *Economy of Vegetation*, and instances may be selected from this its brilliant precursor. After several plants and flowers have passed before us in the semblance of beautiful women, with their trains of adoring lovers, we find the following sketches of contrasted landscape attached to the history of the social heath-plant, *Anthoxa*,[4] or vernal grass, and the lonely *Osmunda*,[5] which grows on moist rocks and in their caverns.

Figure 28: "Flora at Play with Cupid". Engraving by J. Atkin based upon Emma Crewe's illustration. Darwin used this engraving at the frontispiece of The Loves of the Plants *(1789).*

Two gentle shepherds, and their sister wives,
With thee, Anthoxa, lead ambrosial lives;
Where the wide heath its purple bed extends,
And scatter'd furze its golden lustre blends,
Clos'd in a green recess, unenvied lot!
The blue smoke rises from their turf-built cot;
Bosom'd in fragrance blush their infant train,
Eye the warm sun, and[6] drink the silver rain.
Beauteous[7] Osmunda seeks the silent dell,
The ivy canopy, the[8] dripping cell.[9]

In the description of the *Chondrilla*[10] and her five amicable lovers, we find, in their accordant sympathy with each other, a supposed resemblance to the unison-strings of the Eolian harp; and there is a sweet enumeration of the excellencies of its varied style of tones and expression.

To the picture of the *Lychnis*[11] succeeds that of *Gloriosa Superba*,[12] with her successive train of lovers, the second number rising to maturity when the first perish. This libertine lady of the groves introduces the story of the celebrated female Voluptuary, in the reign of Louis the Fourteenth,[13] Ninon de L'Enclos,[14] whose beauty and graces are recorded to have been triumphant over the power of Time. The story of that passion, so terrible in its consequences, with which she unintentionally inspired her natural son by Lord Jersey of England,[15] is finely told in this part; that son, totally unconscious of his birth and fatal nearness of blood to the charming Madam de L'Enclos! In the first edition of the *Loves of the Plants* this extraordinary woman received both personal and mental injustice from the prelude to that story. She is there represented by the Poet, as wrinkled, grey, and paralytic; circumstances incompatible with the possibility of the attachment, and contrary to the representation of her biographers. Upon their testimony we learn that Ninon retained a large portion of her personal beauty and graces to an almost incredible period; that it was considerable enough to procure her young lovers at the age of eighty, whose passion for her, however inconceivable, could not be interested, as she was not rich, and much too delicate in her sentiments to purchase the attention of the other sex.

When her son, by Lord Jersey, was a young officer about Court, known to her but unknown to himself, Madame de L'Enclos was scarcely forty years old, a period at which a very captivating degree of beauty and grace is sometimes found in the female sex. Of their existence at a considerably later period, the English fashionable circles, at this hour, exhibit some remarkable instances.

In the first edition of this Poem what is here *fatal* smiles was *harlot* smiles, an epithet most injurious to Madame de L'Enclos. Her attentions to her son, however affectionate, must have been purely maternal, though so deplorable in their consequences. The declaration by which she repulses his impious suit, entirely acquits her of the least design to inspire him with passion. Dr Darwin was influenced by the author of this *Memoir* to rescue the form of Ninon from the unreal decrepitude he had imputed to it, and her principles from such unnatural excess of depravity.

If we may credit her historians, Ninon was an exception to a maxim of the Duke de Rochefaucault [sic],[16] which has perhaps very few exceptions, viz. "Generally speaking, the least fault of an unchaste woman is her unchastity". Considering this remark as an axiom, the reason probably is, that chastity being the point of honour, as well as of virtue in women, its violation has a strong tendency to engraft deceit and malignity upon the secret consciousness of self-abasement; a consciousness more fatal to the existence of other good qualities than voluptuousness itself; a consciousness too likely to produce hatred and envy towards people of spotless reputation, together with a desire to reduce others to their own unfortunate level. The great Moralist of the Old Testament,[17] says, "There is no wickedness like the wickedness of a woman";[18] not because the weaker sex are naturally more depraved, but from the improbability that a fallen female should ever, even upon the sincerest repentance, regain the esteem and confidence of society, while it pardons a male libertine the instant he seems disposed to forsake his vice, and too often during its full career.

But the fault of Madam de L'Enclos was single, and surrounded by solid virtues. Truth, sincerity, disinterested friendship, economy, generosity, and strict pecuniary justice, marked her commerce with the world, and secured to her the friendship and countenance of the most eminent people of that epoch, both as to talents and character.

The rigid and pious Madame de Maintenon [19] never ceased to be her avowed and intimate friend, as appears from a most interesting dialogue which passed between them after Maintenon became the wife of Louis the Fourteenth. It will be found in the *Memoirs of Madame de L'Enclos*, which are elegantly translated from the French into our language, and were published by Dodsley [20] in 1761.[21] It is a very brilliant and entertaining work.

After the animation of the *Silene*,[22] or Catch Fly, as an enchantress; after that of the *Amarylis*,[23] illustrated by a beautiful picture of a church vane in the setting sun, the *Ilex*,[24] or Holly, comes forward with her giant lovers, grasping their thousand arrows. With this metamorphosis we find involved a lovely allusion to Needwood Forest, the late pride and glory of Staffordshire, now sacrificing, with all its prostrate honours, to a popular scheme of apprehended utility.

Mr Wright's [25] pictures are here introduced as a simile; but it must be confessed that not the most distant similitude can be traced between them and the *Ilex*, or Holly, which, as enchanters and giants, guard the Forest; but the poetic copy of these unallusive [sic] landscapes is transcendent.

The immense *Kleinhovia*,[26] indigenous to the plains of Orixa,[27] is presented as an amazonian nymph; and as the male parts of the tree are, in nature, supported by the female, she is pourtrayed [sic] in Herculean beauty, bearing in her arms her puny lovers, trembling beneath the consciousness of her superior strength. A grand picture of the Grecian Thalestris,[28] appropriate to the subject, thus illustrates the transformation:

So bright [29] Thalestris shook her plumy crest,
And bound in rigid mail her swelling [30] breast,
Pois'd her long lance amid the walks of war,
And Beauty thunder'd from Bellona's [31] car;
Greece, arm'd in vain; her captive heroes wove
The chains of conquest with the wreaths of love.[32]

The noble landscape of the late and wintered period of Autumn, quoted in an early part of these Memoirs, introduces the personification of the Tulip.[33] The bulbous root of flowers is termed by Linnaeus the *hybernacle*, or winter-lodge of the young plant. He says, "each bulb contains the leaves and flowers in miniature, which are to be expanded in the ensuing spring". The same embryon miniatures are found in the buds of the *Hepatica*,[34] the *Daphne-Mezereon*,[35] and at the base of *Osmunda-Lunaria*. The Tulip, in poetic animation, is a beautiful Matron, flying from the chill and stormy season to a lone cavern. She is then presented as sitting in that retreat, and nursing her infant on her bosom till warmer days shall come. A pretty allusive description of the Dormouse, and its half year's slumber, adorns that passage.

Colchicum Autumnale,[36] or Autumnal-meadow-sweet, ascends amid the troubled air, with her attendant lovers. Thus eminent in beauty is the stella simile for that flower:

> So shines, with silver guards, the Georgian star,
> And drives, on Night's blue arch, his glittering car;
> Hangs o'er the billowy clouds his lucid form,
> Wades through the mist, and dances in the storm.[37]

The *Helianthus*,[38] or sun-flower, becomes a Dervise, and leads his devout trains to worship the rising orb of day. Since the head of that majestic plant always, and by nutation, follows the course of the sun, it properly assumes the name and habits of a Dervise or Bramin. With this and the three succeeding metamorphoses, in themselves full of beauty and grace, the *Drosera*,[39] or sun-dew, the *Lonicera*,[40] or honey-suckle, and the Alpine *Draba*,[41] sweet traits of contrasted landscape are blended; with Helianthus, the warm unshadowed lawns of morning; with Drosera the moist, the rush-enwoven and mossy scenes in which she wantons; with *Draba*, the icy caves and volcanos of Tenerif,[42] amid which she builds her eyry,

> Aspiring Draba builds her eagle nest;[43]

and we are told that,

> Her tall shadow waves o'er the distant land.[44]

When we learn, from the note on this passage, that *Draba* is one of the Alpine grasses, we wonder that so minute and dwarfish a plant should become so vast, commanding, and imperial in her transformation. The poet next exercises his Proteus art upon *Viscum*, Misletoe,[45] which never grows upon the ground, but grafts itself upon the branches of trees. This aerial nymph is shown as an angel of air, seeking amongst its clouds her soaring lovers.

When *Zostera*, Grasswrack,[46] (which grows at the bottom of the ocean, and, rising to its top, covers many leagues with its leaves,) comes forth from beneath the wand of this potent magician, we meet one of the happiest sallies of his sportive pen. She is shown as Queen of the coral groves; her palace in the sea, supported on crystal columns; its turrets roofed with lucid shells, which dart their every-coloured rays afar into the deep; the shadows on its floor, philosophically described from the rising and breaking of the exterior billows; the mermaid-train enweaving orient pearls in her hair; her shooting up to the surface like a meteor; ascending the strand, and summoning, by a loud-struck shell, her sea-born lovers to attend her progress; creative imagination, the high and peculiar province of the genuine Poet, has few more beautiful creations than this marine picture and scene.

That curious plant of the polar regions, the *Barometz*,[47] from its exterior resemblance to a sheep or lamb, is, by poetic magic, transformed into that animal, and to it the whale is compared; surely on no other possible relation, than as both the odd plant and the sea-monster, are natives of the arctic regions. The whale, however, makes a grand poetic picture:

> Since then, the thing itself is rich and rare,
> Exclaim not, "How the d....l came it there!"[48]

Mimosa,[49] Sensitive-plant, becomes a nymph of infinite delicacy. The objects aptly chosen to illustrate the nervous sensibility with which that plant recedes from the approaching hand, are thus described, and surely with no common happiness:

> So sinks, or rises, with the changeful hour,
> The liquid silver in its glassy tower;
> So turns the needle to the pole it loves,
> With fine vibrations quivering as it moves.[50]

The *Anemone*[51] and her modern-life objects of comparison, by no means form one of the gems of this poem, however harmonious the lines. A lady's calash[52] and a landau[53] are out of their place in high heroic numbers. The Anemone and her trivialities, are sublimely contrasted by the rock-born Lichen,[54] both in scenery and accomplishment. She has too much dignity from her surrounding landscape to have, or to want an illustrative simile. Her habitation is on the top of Snowdon,[55] nodding over the tumultuous river Conway;[56] the hour midnight; the stars and cold moon gilding the rifted rocks; the whirlwind and dark thunder-storm rolling and bursting below the summit of the mountain. From its topmost stone the transformation of the Dipsaca[57] conveys us to a valley glowing beneath the long prevalence of the dog-star, when the channel of every rill is dry, and the parched earth gapes. The personification of the plant has every graceful charm of a languid beauty.

The *Rubia*,[58] madder, a plant used for the purpose of making a crimson dye, is compared to Medea bending over her caldron, in which youth was restored by immersion. It is an apt allusion to the faded beauty, who restores her lost bloom by rouge.

Vallisner,[59] a curious aquatic plant of the Rhone, apostrophises, when in her human form, the stars and moon, shining at midnight on the shores of her watery home; and the sea-weed, *Ulva*,[60] with her young family, guarded on the deep by *Halcyons*,[61] serves to introduce the famous *Galatea*[62] in her shelly chariot, drawn by dolphins over the ocean. She has more state and more superb attendants on her maritime progress, than Europa, in the second Canto of the *Economy of Vegetation*, or than the Nereid in the third; though in the picture of Galatea there is perhaps a less degree of originality.

But, upon the transformation of the *Tremella*,[63] star-jelly, (a fungus often found in the state of transparent jelly, after it has been frozen in autumnal mornings,) the Poet has lavished some of the finest effusions of his fancy. It is surely the transcendent passage of this second part of Dr Darwin's poem. No eye has seen, or ever can see a beautiful Nymph frozen into an ice-statue; but admit the possibility, and every circumstance of the gradual petrification is no less natural than it is lovely; nor can any degree of admiration be too high for the beauty and grace of the description. It is superior to the Ovidian Daphne.[64]

This Canto now prepares to close; the muse of Botany perceives a tempest approaching, and she is led by Wood-Nymphs into their most sequestered bowers. They suspend her lyre upon their laurel trees, and bind her brow with myrtles. If she had no other claim, the *Tremella* alone ought to give her wreath unperishable bloom. Symptoms of the impending shower are given with that accuracy with which, on every occasion, this genuine Poet observed the objects of nature, thus:

> Now the light swallow, with her airy brood,
> Skims the green meadow and the dimpled flood.
> Loud shrieks the lone thrush on her [65] leafless thorn;
> Th' alarmed beetle blows [66] his bugle horn;
> Each pendant spider weaves,[67] with fingers fine,
> Her [68] ravell'd clue, and climbs along the line;
> Gay Gnomes, in glittering circles, stand aloof
> Beneath a spreading mushroom's ample [69] roof;
> Swift bees, returning, seek their waxen cells,
> And Sylphs hang [70] quivering in the lily's bells;
> Through the still air descend the genial showers,
> And pearly rain-drops deck the laughing flowers.[71]

An Interlude in prose succeeds this Canto. It is a supposed dialogue between the Poet and his Bookseller, in which the former gives us his ideas of the constitution of true Poetry. His first speech, "I am only a flower-painter, or occasionally attempt a landscape", is neither true, nor did Dr Darwin desire that it should be considered as veritable.

In the course of this Interlude he will be found making much higher claims for himself, and too exclusively limiting poetry to the sphere of picturesque expression; yet his criticism on this line in Pope's *Windsor Forest* [72] is perfectly just,

> And Kennet [73] swift, for silver Eels renown'd.[74]

Since, whenever objects are introduced in verse, which, plainly mentioned, can excite no interest, it is questionless the Poet's duty to awaken interesting remembrance of them by little picturesque touches, such as we find in the Doctor's suggested change of that line, to

> And Kennet swift, where silver graylings play.[75]

His stricture upon Burke's [76] style in prose, as much too ornamented, has surely little justice. Eloquence can only be produced by a strict union of strength and ornament. The Corinthian [77] pillar is not less stable than the Doric;[78] not less firm on account of its flowers. Dr Darwin here seems to wish that prose should be precluded by its plainness from rising into eloquence. He wished to keep prose too plain, and his warmest admirers will surely acknowledge that he insists upon poetry being dressed with too elaborate magnificence. We find him in this Interlude, very ingenious on the subject of allegoric figures, also on that of dreams, and in his comparison of them to the reveries which the true Poet excites in his intelligent readers; but he is greatly indeed mistaken when he represents the art of exciting such rapt and abstracted sensations as solely consisting in picturesque writing. Instruction, pathos, all the grandeur and beauty of moral and religious sentiment, are here turned over to the prose writer, as if they were not equally capable of giving fascinating power to verse, as well as to oratory. The following passages are not picturesque; but no pictures ever presented by the muses, are more potent to impress, thrill, and captivate that mind which is alive to the magic influence of their art:

Some say, that, ever, 'gainst the season comes
At which our Saviour's birth is celebrated,
The bird of dawning singeth all night long;
And then, they say, no spirit walks abroad;
The nights are wholesome; then no planets strike,
No fairy takes, no witch hath power to charm,
So hallow'd and so gracious is the time!

Hamlet.[79]

... I fled, and cried out ... Death;
Hell trembled at the hideous name, and sigh'd
Through all her caves, and back resounded ... Death!

Milton.[80]

... if prayers
Could alter high decrees, I to heaven's throne
Would speed before thee, and be louder heard
That on my head all might be visited,
Thy frailty and infirmer sex forgiven,
By me committed, and by me expos'd.

Milton.[81]

Remember March! the ides of March remember!
Did not great Julius bleed for justice' sake?
What villain touch'd his body, that did stab,
And not for justice? What! shall one of us,
That struck the foremost man in all the world
But for supporting robbers, shall we now

Contaminate our fingers with base bribes,
And sell the mighty space of our large honours
For as much trash as may be grasped thus?
I had rather be a dog, and bay the moon,
Than such a Roman.

Julius Caesar.[82]

Plac'd on this isthmus of a middle state
A Being darkly wise and rudely great;
With too much knowledge for the Sceptic side,
With too much weakness for the Stoic's pride,
He hangs between, in doubt to act or rest,
In doubt to deem himself a god or beast;
In doubt his mind or body to prefer,
Born but to die, and reasoning but to err;
Sole judge of truth, in endless error hurl'd,
The glory, jest, and riddle of the world.

Pope, *On the Construction of Man.*[83]

Not e'en a spot unfought the hero gave,
No! till his foes had earn'd it, not a grave!

Wesley, *Of King William the Third.*[84]

Reflect, that lessen'd fame is ne'er regain'd,
That virgin honour once is always stain'd!
Timely advis'd the growing danger shun,
Better not do the deed than weep it done!
No penance can absolve a guilty flame,
Nor tears, that wash out sin, can wash out shame.

Henry and Emma.[85]

Methought I heard a voice cry, Sleep no more!
Macbeth doth murder sleep! the innocent sleep!
Sleep, that knits up the ravell'd sleeve of care,
The death of each day's grief, sore labour's bath,
Balm of hurt minds, chief nourisher in life's feast!
…
Still it cried, Sleep no more, to all the house,
Glamis hath murder'd sleep, and therefore Cawdor
Shall sleep no more, Macbeth shall sleep no more![86]

Who will call these passages prosaic? Who are they that will not confess them to be poetry, and such poetry as requires no aid from picture to establish its claims? Perhaps Dr Darwin would not have deemed them sufficiently adorned, since all there is to the heart and nothing to the eye. To be consistent with the criticism of this his Interlude, he must have asserted their deficiency, and thus have proved that, while his imagination was so richly exuberant; while sublimity, as well as beauty, attended the commanding march of his Muse, there was a radical defect in his poetic system, which would forever have incapacitated him from being a first-rate Epic or Dramatic writer; but as nature hovered over the cradle of Shakespeare, and gave him her golden keys, to unlock the gates of the Passions, so did Imagination over that of Dr Darwin, and put into his grasp her magic wand, and spread over his form her every-coloured robe.

Second Canto

> Again the Goddess strikes the golden lyre,
> And tunes to wilder notes the warbling wire,
> With soft, suspended step Attention moves,
> And Silence hovers o'er the listening groves.[87]

The second line of this passage is too alliterative, and therefore palls upon the ear. Alliteration is an edge tool in the Poet's hand, improving or injuring his verse, as it is judiciously or injudiciously used. Homer, Virgil, Ovid, Spenser, Milton, and all the best poets, have employed it to admirable effect; and to admirable effect has Dr Darwin frequently employed it, though not in this instance. It often increases, and sometimes entirely constitutes, that power which, by a metaphoric expression that literal terms would neither so concisely nor so well explain, is called *picturesque sound*. To increase the harmony of verse, alliteration must be with the vowels, the liquid letter *l*, or by the sonorous letters *m* and *n*, and even with them its too frequent use in a poem, or too lavish repetition in a single line or couplet, will injure what it is designed to improve, as in the above second line of this second Canto. Dryden, in his noble *Ode on St Cecilia's Day*,[88] has alliterated with the hissing *s*, in two lines, which he meant should be peculiarly musical; thus,

> Softly sweet in Lydian [89] measures
> Soon he sooth'd the soul to pleasures.[90]

A foreign ear would not endure the lines, which, however lively, are certainly not tender, not harmonious; yet the *s* and all the harsher consonants, are capable of producing, by skilful application, that "echo of sound to sense", which is so eminently desirable in poetry. When Milton observes in the *Paradise Lost*,

> So talk'd the spirited sly snake,[91]

the line attains, solely by alliteration, the perfect hiss of the serpent; and Pope, in his Homer, by a masterly intermixture of the vowels and the sonorous consonants with his alliteration of the letter *s*, has nobly conveyed to our ear the peculiar noise of the ocean-waves when they are loud on the beach; thus,

Silent he wander'd by the sounding main.[92]

The murmur of a calm sea has been well expressed by the alliteration of the following line:

Slow on the damp and shelly shore she stray'd.[93]

There is somewhere a line, in which a poetaster, mentioning the violet, says,

Where blue it blooms with balmy breath.[94]

He thought he had hammered out an immensely fine verse, though in fact it is to the ear no whit more agreeable than,

Three blue beans in one blue bladder.[95]

The letters *b* and *p* make miserable alliteration. Milton has used the harsh letter *r*, to very fine effect in the following lines:

Vex'd Scylla,[96] bathing in the sea that parts
Calabria [97] from the hoarse Trinacrian [98] shore.[99]

Dr Beattie,[100] in his charming *Minstrel*,[101] has so used alliteration as to produce two of the most harmonious verses in our language.

Young Edwin, lighted by the evening star,
lingering and listening, wander 'd down the vale.[102]

This digression into general criticism will not be thought irrelevant to the peculiar theme of these pages, when it is considered that, for the presumption of censuring, even in one instance, the eminently harmonious numbers of the *Botanic Garden*, it was requisite to justify such censure by examining the use or abuse of that habit of style, which strengthens or enfeebles, adorns or misbecomes the verse, as the good or bad taste of the writer shall direct its application. Churchill [103] has ridiculed alliteration in a line of singular felicity, for an unworthy purpose, a satirical passage on the beautiful poetry of Mason;[104] thus,

… I, who never pray'd
For apt alliteration's artful aid.[105]

But the ridicule intended for the sweet Swan of the Humber,[106] falls equally on the elder classics of Greece, Rome, and England.

The first transformation of this second Canto is the *Carline* Thistle.[107] We learn, from a note on the passage, that its seeds are furnished with a plume, by which they are borne through the air. Carlina, in human shape, is represented as fabricating Daedalion wings for herself and offspring, with most ingeniously described mechanism, and with happier success than those of the renowned mechanic in ancient fable.

And now succeeds, in happy similitude, a balloon-voyage, exact and accurate to the circumstances of aerial journeying in the first instance, and sublime in the imaginative part, the astronomic allusions: they are thus given:

> Rise, great Mongolfier! urge thy venturous flight
> High o'er the moon's pale, ice-reflected light;
> High o'er the pearly star, whose beamy horn
> Hangs in the east, gay harbinger of morn;
> Leave the red eye of Mars on rapid wing,
> Jove's silver guards, and Saturn's dusky[108] ring;
> Leave the fair beams, that,[109] issuing from afar,
> Play, with new lustre,[110] round the Georgian star;
> Shun, with strong oars, the sun's attractive throne,
> The sparkling zodiac, and the milky zone,
> Where headlong comets, with increasing force
> Through other systems bend their blazing course!
> For thee Cassiope[111] her chair withdraws,
> For thee the Bear[112] retracts his shaggy paws.
> High o'er the north thy golden orb shall roll,
> And blaze eternal round the wondering pole.
> So Argo,[113] rising from the southern main,
> Lights with new stars the blue etherial plain;
> With favouring beams the mariner protects,
> And the bold course, which first it steer'd, directs.[114]

So beautifully does this high priest of Fancy choose to constellate the first adventurous Aeronaut.

In the animation of *Linum* Flax[115] we are presented with the exactest-possible description of the machinery, and the art of weaving; and in that of *Gossipiam*,[116] Cotton Plant, the late Sir Richard Arkwright's[117] apparatus at Matlock,[118] with the whole progress of its operations, is brought distinctly before the eye, recalling them to those by whom they have been examined, and instructing in their progress those who never beheld them.

So, in the personification of *Cyperus Papyrus*,[119] under the name of Papyra, another art, that of printing, passes before us with equal precision. The leaves of this plant were first used in Egypt for paper, and gave the name, which it retains to this day; so, leaf, or folium, for the fold of a book. We have here, in sweet versification, the whole process of that inestimable invention, which paints thoughts, sounds, and numbers, in mystic and imperishable characters; imperishable, at least, during the reign of Time. Yes, it was the encouragement given by that art to the sciences, which enabled this Bard to throw over them all his splendid robe of descriptive poesy. The venerable and celebrated Mrs Delany,[120] sometime deceased, and her miraculous *Hortus Siccus*,[121] are here introduced as a simile to Papyra; but describing a totally different art from hers, even that of a mere artificial flower-maker, this simile, which bears so little resemblance to writing and printing, forms one of the most censurable passages in the whole poem. Mrs Delany, in her representation of plants and flowers, native and exotic, and which fill ten immense folio volumes, used neither the wax, moss, or wire, attributed to her in this entirely false description of her art. She employed no material but paper, which she herself, from her knowledge of chemistry, was enabled to dye of all hues, and in every shade of each; no implement but her scissors, not once her pencil; yet never did painting present a more exact representation of flowers of every colour, size, and cultivation, from the simple hedge and field-flower, to the most complicated foliage that Horticulture has multiplied. This lady, once Mrs Pendarvis, the friend and correspondent of Swift, and in her later years honored by the friendship and frequent visits at Windsor, of the King, Queen, and Princesses, began this her astonishing self-invented work at the age of seventy-four. The Poet here misrepresents her as being assisted by her virgin train. She had no assistant; no hands, but her own, formed one leaf or flower of the ten volumes. Her family were mortified by a description which they justly thought degraded her peculiar art; and remonstrated with Dr Darwin on the occasion, expressing a wish that future editions might contain its more just picture on his poetic page. He said, the description in the note was accurate; but that truth in this, as in many other instances, being less favourable to poetry than fiction, he did not choose to alter the text.

The *Lepsana*,[122] the *Nymphea alba*,[123] and the *Calendula*,[124] whose flowers, as do many other flowers, open and shut at certain hours of the rising and declining day, are transformed into elegant female watchmakers. Linnaeus calls the forty-six flowers of this order, the *Horologe*, or Watch of Flora.[125] This transformation involves an highly poetic description of the art that traces the march of Time. The progressive mechanism which completes a watch, is traced with accuracy, and, in the mention of its ornamental trophies, we meet sublime imagery; such as Time dashing Superstition from its base, and the Hours leading their trains around the wreck; but the Moments are impersonized [sic] with too much quaint prettiness. The whole of this imagery is an imitation, as indeed the author afterwards acknowledges, of the following passage in Young's *Night Thoughts*,

> Each moment has its sickle, emulous
> Of Time's enormous scythe, whose ample sweep
> Strikes empires from the root; each Moment plies
> His little weapon in the narrower sphere
> Of sweet domestic comfort, and cuts down
> Our fairest blooms of sublunary bliss.[126]

The Hours leading their trains around the wrecks their parent had made, and planting amidst them the growth of science and taste, is an original and beautiful addition in Dr Darwin's imitative passage. The moments are obnoxious to his own criticism in the first Interlude; they become unpleasing from being too distinctly described, with their kisses and their baby hands. Perhaps the personified moments are not less distinctly pourtrayed [sic] in the above passage from the *Night Thoughts*; but *there*, a pensive interesting morality casts over them a softening veil; while their gayer appearance and employment on the Darwinian page, brings them into glaring, and perhaps almost ludicrous view.

That unpleasing change, which takes place in the *Helleborus* [127] after impregnation, produces, in its metamorphoses, a fair nymph, suddenly smitten by a loathsome distemper, which utterly destroys her charms. An odd comparison ensues, the supposed actual transformation of Nebuchadnezzar into a beast; whereas the scripture only says, that he dwelt with the beasts of the field, and took their prone habits. His imputed change into their *shape* is ingeniously, but somewhat ludicrously painted; and we are apt to fancy the Euphrates [128] slandered in these lines, which finely describe a river of sluggish and sullied current:

> Lolls his red tongue, and from the reedy side
> Of slow Euphrates laps the muddy tide.[129]

That harmoniously-named river of the East, has too long rolled through our imagination in beautiful and lucid currents, for us to like this reverse picture of its streams. One of our poets, probably Milton, has somewhere said,

> … and by the verdant side
> Of palmy Euphrates.[130]

At last, since the situation of Babylon [131] was certainly flat and marshy, Dr Darwin is probably correct in this instance, however obstinately our sensations may refuse to grant that one of the rivers which encircled Paradise can deserve to be *so* described; but there, as it was nearer its source in the mountain Niphates,[132] it would certainly be more pure; besides, that it may be supposed to have become polluted by its progress through less hallowed earth. The last line of the Nebuchadnezzar-transformation is burlesque, by reason of the epithet *pendant*:

> Nor Flattery's self can pierce his pendant ears.[133]

And the alliterating *p* makes the sound of the line displeasing as is the image it conveys.

The *Menispernum*,[134] Indian-berry, which intoxicates fish, being of the class two females, twelve males, here assumes the form of two Sister Nymphs, scattering their inebriating berries on the waters. The Popish legend of St Anthony preaching to the fish,[135] and converting them to Christianity, forms the whimsical and not very pleasing illustration. Its language violates the third commandment deplorably.

The *Papaver*, Poppy,[136] becomes a drowsy Enchantress of malignant operation; but her somniferous palace is described in their lovely numbers:

> Sopha'd on silk, amid her charm-built towers,
> Her meads of asphodel,[137] and amaranth [138] bowers,

Where Sleep and Silence guard the soft abodes,
In sullen apathy, Papaver nods.
Faint o'er her couch, in scintillating streams,
Pass the light forms of Fancy and of Dreams.[139]

Her enchantments are poetically given from old *Tales of the Genii,*[140] and she is compared to Hermes [141] driving the Ghosts to the shores of Erebus;[142] and again *his* employment to the drawings of Miss Emma Crew,[143] a compliment of very forced introduction.

The *Cistus,*[144] a plant whose transient, but plenteous flowers expand in succession on the first warmth of May, becomes a Nymph, who calls her train to choir the birth of that month. She is obeyed, and a very exquisite song ensues, in which the altered measure relieves the ear. Without any perceivable chain of thought, the sudden death of the fair Cista serves to usher in a fine picture of an hoar-frost landscape, dissolving instantaneously beneath a change of keen to soft wind, accompanied by the emerging sun.

Cinchona,[145] Peruvian bark tree, passes before us as a Peruvian Maid, on her way to the altar, which, in Quito,[146] she had raised to the goddess Hygeia,[147] and of which she is the administrant priestess. Her progress thither, and her ceremonies at the shrine, and her prayer to the Goddess, are beautiful; the personified Diseases sublime, particularly Ague.[148] The accidental manner, in which, it is well known, the medicinal virtues of the bark were first discovered, is here conveyed to the reader with the happiest ingenuity, as a dictate of Hygeia to her Priestess, in answer to the prayer. Cinchona is commanded to yield her sacred forests to the axe, and to strew their bitter foliage on the rivers. She obeys; her lovers fell the trees, and impregnate the waters with the leaves, while pale infected squadrons kneel on the margin, and health and bloom return as they drink. All this forms a complete and charming little drama. It needed no illustration, but it has a very serious one, that of Moses in the Wilderness, striking the rock, "so that the waters flowed out".[149]

To the bark-metamorphosis succeeds that of the *Digitalis,* Fox-glove,[150] of whose now experienced, though not infallible virtue, in dropsical cases, Dr Darwin claims the first discovery. The bloated and cadaverous form of Dropsy appears, and his unquenchable thirst is compared to that of Tantalus in these four admirable lines:

So bends tormented Tantalus [151] to drink,
While from his lips the refluent waters shrink;
Again the rising stream his bosom laves,
And thirst consumes him 'mid circumfluent waves.[152]

Hygeia assumes the form of Digitalis; waves over the diseased her serpent-wreathed wand, "and charms the shapeless monster into man".

To her is compared the good Bishop of Marseilles,[153] when the plague raged in that city; also the generous and active Mayor of London,[154] when London was under similar visitation. From him the Poet slides into a most animated contemplation of the great Howard's [155] virtue, and asserts that the rays of philanthropy

Dart round the globe from Zembla to the Line;
O'er each dark prison plays the cheering light,
As northern lustres o'er the vault of night;
From realm to realm, by [156] cross or crescent crown'd,
Where'er mankind and misery are found,
O'er burning sands, deep waves, or wilds of snow,
Thy Howard, journeying, seeks the house of woe;
Down many a winding step to dungeons dank,
Where anguish wails,[157] and galling [158] fetters clank;
To caves bestrew'd with many a mouldering bone,
And cells, whose echoes only learn to groan;
Where no kind bars a whispering friend disclose,
No sun-beam enters, and no zephyr blows,
He treads, inemulous of fame or wealth,
Profuse of toil, and prodigal of health;
With soft persuasive [159] eloquence expands
Power's rigid heart, and opes his clenching hands;
Leads stern-ey'd Justice to the dark domains,
If not to sever, to relax the chains;
Or guides awaken'd Mercy through the gloom,
And shows the prison sister to the tomb;
Gives to her babes the self-devoted wife,
To her fond husband, liberty and life!

The spirits of the good, who bend from high,
Wide o'er these earthly scenes, their partial eye,
When first, array'd in Virtue's purest robe,
They saw her Howard traversing the globe;
Saw round his brow [160] the sun-bright glory blaze
In arrowy circles of unwearied rays,
Mistook a mortal for an angel guest,
And ask'd what seraph-foot the earth imprest.
Onward he moves, Disease and Death retire,
And murmuring Demons hate him, and admire.[161]

If praise for a single verbal beauty may not degrade the exalted merit of the above quotation, the biographer would observe that its word *inemulous* has a sweet effect, and that, she believes, it is there in first coinage. *Unambitious*, the word in common use for that meaning, is comparatively hard and cumbrous in verse.

This citation constitutes far the sublimest eulogy by which Poetry has immortalized the matchless Howard, Mr Hayley's [162] noble Ode [163] alone excepted. That was the earliest tribute to his high worth, and it is admirable in a degree which only Darwin has equalled [sic], and which perhaps no Poet can excel.

The Gnomes now suspend the again silent lyre on the shrine of Hygeia; the Sylphs slacken the strings, and catch the rain-drops on their shadowy pinions, while a Naiad prepares the tea-urn. The last Canto closed with a shower. That it should rain also in the termination of this, is a sameness which surprises us from an imagination so various. Then surely there is too strong a contrast between the solemn dignified praise of Howard, immediately preceding, and the light and frolic idea which places a Muse, the recent Historian of virtue so truly great, at the tea-table! It is out of keeping, as the painters say.

We meet ingenious and just criticism in the Interlude to this second Canto. Aware of the frequent want of evident resemblance between his subjects and their similies, Dr Darwin shelters himself under the authority of Homer, which perhaps will not entirely secure his practice from censure; since, if Homer's similies do not often touch the object with which they are compared at all points, yet are they never so utterly without connexion [sic] with it, as several which may be found in this poem. That a poetic simile should not be precise in its resemblance is certain, at least that it is the more sublime, or more beautiful, for not quadrating exactly; yet it ought to possess such a degree of affinity with the subject, that when the theme and its illustration are viewed together, we may feel, though we cannot verbally demonstrate the perfect justness of the similitude.

Thus, in general, are the similies of Homer constructed, and thus Milton's, several of which, in the *Paradise Lost*, are grander than most of those in the *Iliad* and *Odyssey*. A deceased modern Poet [164] has given one of extreme beauty, which, from its aptness without precision, bears exactly that relation to the object it illustrates which a poetic simile ought to bear. There is no obvious connexion [sic] between our idea of youthful beauty, paled and shadowed over by death, and a vernal day-spring, which rises cold and rainy:

Her face was like an April morn
Clad in a wintry cloud:[165]

yet when Poetry connects them, we are immediately sensible of their interesting affinity. Death itself cannot at first conceal, however it may shroud the traits of youth, and of what once was loveliness; neither can the dull sky and nipping wind prevent our perceiving the youth of the year, when April has put forth her fresh grass and verdant sprays.

In the course of Dr Darwin's second Interlude, there is fine discrimination between the tragic and the disgustingly horrid; and his censure of the painters for their frequent choice of disagreeable subjects for their pencil, such as torture and carnage, is perfectly just.

Third Canto

From the pensive graces of this exordium result extended ground of censure for the undignified situation of the Muse at the close of the second Canto; since her modern Tea-table is here converted into a grassy throne, bedewed with tears, around which float the thin forms of Sorrows and Apprehensions, of Sighs whispering to the chords of her lyre, and Indignations, half unsheathing their swords. These same *Indignations* are new allegoric personages, and may be of dubious welcome. The Passions, with *swords* by their sides, form imagery which is liable to give a ludicrous impression; yet we should remember, that Milton puts a sword into the hand of the archangel, Michael, in the 6th book of the *Paradise Lost*, and Pope into that of a Ghost in his Elegy to the Memory of an unfortunate Lady;[166] but Milton gives the weapon dignity by investing it with flames, on the authority of Scripture, and Pope, softens off the literality by its imputed indistinctness, and by the epithet *visionary*. "Why dimly gleams the visionary sword"?[167]

Circea, Enchanter's Nightshade,[168] is the first transformation in this Canto. We learn from the note to the passage, that it grows among the mouldering bones and decayed coffins of Sleaford Church, Lincolnshire,[169] and that it was celebrated in the mysteries of witchcraft, and for the purpose of raising the devil.

As the *Tremella* is the most beautiful, so is *Circea* the sublimest transformation of the four Cantos. Her marriage with the two Fiends; its portentous signs which precede the satanic nuptials; the screaming bats, the owls, and the dog of midnight howling the epithalamium;[170] the bursting ground; the ascending Demons; their progress with the grim Bride to the violated temple; those shapeless spectres, which, by glimpses of the moon through the coloured glass, are seen to quiver on the walls, as *Circea* and her horrid bridegrooms pass along the ailes, that dismally echo their steps; the unblessed wine with which they pollute the chalice; their hideous laugh which disturbs the silence of the choir; and the impious mummery of the nuptial rites; all these circumstances were conceived, and are expressed with prodigious strength of fancy.

The *Laura-cerasus*,[171] twenty males, one female, appears next, as the Pythian priestess [172] delivering her oracles. This is her grand portrait:

> Avaunt ye vulgar! from her sacred groves,
> With maniac step, the Pythian Laura moves;
> Full of the God her labouring bosom sighs,
> Foam on her lips, and fury in her eyes,
> Strong writhe her limbs; her wild dishevell'd hair
> Starts from her laurel wreath, and swims in air,
> While twenty priests the gorgeous shrine surround,
> Cinctur'd with epods [173] and with garlands crown'd,
> Contending hosts, and trembling nations wait
> The firm immutable behests of fate;
> She speaks in thunder from her golden throne,
> With words unwill'd, and wisdom not her own.[174]

To the Pythian Laura is compared the distress of a beautiful nymph in slumber, beneath the influence of the night-mare. It is a poetic picture after Fuseli.[175] The squab and grinning Fiend, as he sits on the bosom of the sleeping Maid, and his moon-eyed mare, looking in through the bed curtains, are pictures of ludicrous horror. They are drawn with rival strength by the Poet and Painter; and are contrasted by the lovely form of the agitated slumberer; but the *succession* of her convulsive appearances which the Poet brings to the eye, affords another instance of the superior power of the pen to that of the pencil, when eash [176] are directed by the impulse of true genius.

The personification of the Indian fig-tree [177] is made a vehicle of introduction for the scenery of Dovedale and Ilam,[178] the cave of Thor,[179] the Saxon God, and all the sanguinary sublimities of his druidical rites. The only connexion [sic] between the subject and its illustration is, that "each branch of the large fig-tree of India, emits a slender, flexile, depending appendage from its summit, like a cord, and which roots into the earth, and rises again; and the Hamps and Manifold, rivers of the Dovedale vicinity *(Figure 29)*, in their course over a romantic moor, sink suddenly into the earth, and rise again in Ilam gardens, after their subterranean passage of three miles".[180]

Impatiens,[181] Touch-me-not, from the peculiar nature of the plant, and the elastic motion by which it throws its seeds to a great distance, has, in its transformation, sufficient affinity to the story of Medea,[182] here introduced as its simile. Nowhere is that striking poetic legend so finely told. The passions of jealousy and despair, excited by the mercenary ingratitude of Jason,[183] are here painted in their strongest colours, rising in power and force, till the dire filiacide closes the episode.

Those electrical properties of the *Dictamnus, Fraxinella*,[184] asserted by Dr Darwin as having witnessed them in the still summer nights after long draught, induces him to transform her also into an enchantress, and the hour and season in which she celebrates her magical rites, is thus sweetly specified:

> What time the Eve her gauze pellucid spreads
> O'er the dim flowers, and veils the misty meads,
> Slow o'er the twilight sands and leafy walks,
> In gloomy dignity, Dictamna stalks.[185]

Figure 29: Dove Dale, Derbyshire, north of Ashbourne.

The deleterious tree, the *Mancinella*;[186] the *Urtica*, English nettle,[187] and the *Lobelia longiflora*,[188] a deadly plant of the West Indies, form a continuation of Enchantresses, and their metamorphose is attended by still darker traits of demonism. As the first and last of these three vegetables have life-destroying properties, and the English nettle only inflicts a slight and transient pain, she ought not to have appeared in such company. Her comparative insignificance is that of a wasp between a cobracapella [189] and a rattle-snake. The ruins of Palmira [190] are described as a simile to the mischiefs of the four preceding witches, but why or wherefore defies all poetic guess; however, the fault of utter inconnection is atoned by the grandeur of this sombre picture.

To that succeeds the embrutality of the Upas Tree,[191] now supposed to be of fabulous existence. It is preceded by a beautiful landscape of the Isle of Java, in the centre of which this dreadful tree was asserted to have stood. The seas of glass, the noble rocks, the ever-summered gales, and the sylvan graces which zone that large island, form an exquisite contrast in this passage, to the desolation round the Hydra Tree of Death, as its author sublimely calls it. The Upas Tree becomes a terrific monster under the wand of our potent magician. The enormous dragon is grand, with his unnumbered heads extending over ten square leagues, and with many infant serpents growing out of him, like those of Sin in the *Paradise Lost*; a dragon, that

Looks o'er the clouds, and hisses in the storm.[192]

Into a monster the Upas must be made. This Poet's system of vegetable animality would not permit it to remain in that so much more impressive though quieter horror, with which it is described in the Dutch surgeon's [193] narrative. A lonely tree by the side of a rivulet, in a barren and stony valley, circled round by vast and sterile mountains; no tree but itself! no hedge! no blade of grass! no wing of bird! nothing that breathes to disturb the dreadful silence! dead bodies scattered about the waste in every various stage of putridity; and the tree itself exhaling a visible and poisonous vapor, instantly fatal to every living thing which breathes the air it taints within a diameter of fifteen miles! what furious dragon, even from the pen of Dr Darwin, but loses its terrors before this still, this ghastly desolation!

The prose narration, taken from the *London Magazine*, is inserted in the close of the additional notes to the *Loves of the Plants*. It has such an air of simple veracity, that we do violence to our feelings when, on reflection, we refuse to give it credit. The gum of this tree is there asserted to be of high price, and used to envenom the Indian arrows; that it is procured by Criminals under sentence of death, who redeem their lives if they can bring from the Upas a box of its gum; an experiment of immense hazard, since the possibility of returning depends upon the perpetually veering winds blowing a steady gale towards the tree as the delinquent approaches it, in the [194] progress of at least fifteen miles. The seldomness with which that happens, and the frequency of the attempt, strew the circumjacent plains with the dead. Faith in this wonderful tale has melted away in subsequent inquiry. Many have said that Dr Darwin certainly believed the account. He certainly *writes* as if he believed it; yet that was but to serve a poetic purpose; credulity was not one of his propensities.

The *Orchis Morio*,[195] the parent root of which shrivels up and dies as the young one increases, is transformed into a fond mother, nursing her infant at the expense of her own health and life. This animation is short, and, compared to many of the others, has little interest; but its two illustrations have every interest, and the second forms a very sweet and mournful episode. The first is a lovely picture of a wounded deer, escaping from her ambushed archer, and flying with her fawn to the woodlands, over plains spotted with her blood; and, amid thick shades, hanging over her young, and weeping her life away. Then, in successive simile, comes the thrice interesting story. An Officer's Wife with her infants, watching, from a near hill, the battle of Minden,[196] in which her husband was engaged, is mortally wounded by a random shot. We find this incident related with so much pathos as almost to dissipate the apprehension, that Dr Darwin's rage for the picturesque would, in a subject of genuine interest for the human passions, have proved destructive to his powers of awakening them. The mournful truth of one line in this episode ought to sink deep in every human heart, viz.

The angel Pity shuns the walks of War.[197]

Truly honourable is it to the Poets of this reign, that the best of them have never stimulated, but, on the contrary, have endeavoured to meliorate and abate that belligerent spirit, always injurious to the true interest of this country, and fruitful in the extreme of human misery. A spirit, by which Britain looks over the Atlantic, shorn of her continental beams; a spirit, to whose unwarned and persisting violence in later years, the lives of the soldiery, and the comforts of millions of families, were lavished in defiance of the Gospel, which preaches peace on earth, and good-will towards men.

But to return to the episode; the lisping boy, on his father's approach.

Speak low, he cries, and gives his little hand;
Eliza [198] sleeps upon the dew-cold sand;
Poor weeping babe, with bloody fingers press'd,
And tried, with pouting lips, the milkless breast.
Alas! we both with cold and hunger quake,
Why do you weep? Mamma will soon awake!
She'll wake no more! the hapless mourner said![199]

Nothing can be more natural and more affecting than the ideas in this speech of the child, only that *dew-cold* and *milkless* are not infantine expressions.

The *Cuscuta*, Dodder,[200] four males two females. It does not root itself in the earth, but ascends the vegetables in its neighbourhood, and ultimately destroys the plant on which it had grown to maturity. In this system of animality it is represented as two treacherous coquets, smiling to betray; and, from the circumstance of the plant twining round the shrub or tree, which it finally kills, the ungrateful beauties are compared to the serpents, which strangled Laocoon [201] and his sons. That story here forms a faithful poetic picture of the celebrated statue.[202]

In the transformation of the Vine into a Bacchanalian Female, the Doctor introduces, and enforces his just and favourite system, of considering the free use of vinous fluid, in all its stages, as the source of our most fatal chronic diseases.[203] They are very poetically impersonised

[sic] as they hover round the seductive nymph, *Vitis*,[204] while Chemia [205] mingles poison in her bowl. This fell group is admirably illustrated by an image of Prometheus [206] chained to a rock, with a vulture devouring his liver. The many disorders of the liver, so torturing and so fatal, which ebriety causes, are nobly allegorized in this fable of him, who is represented as being thus punished for having stolen fire from heaven. Dr Darwin's note to this passage deserves to be engraven on every man's memory, since it is the attestation of a great Physician, founded on an extensive practice of nearly half a century.

The *Cyclamen*, Shewbread or Sowbread,[207] which, "when its seeds are ripe, gradually twists its stalk spirally downward, till it touches the earth, and there inserts its offspring", is changed into a tender matron, resigning her departed infants to the grave, and breathing a pious hope of their resurrection. The simile on this occasion is perhaps the sublimest passage in the whole work; its real, and, in former ages, often existing horrors, transcend in strength all Imagination has formed, or can form, with her train of spectres, witches, and demons:

> So when the Plague, o'er London's [208] gasping crowds,
> Shook her dank wing, and steer'd her murky clouds;
> When o'er the friendless bier no rites were read,
> No dirge slow chanted,[209] and no pall outspread;
> While Death and Night pil'd up the naked throng,
> And Silence drove their ebon cars along,
> Six [210] lovely daughters, and their father, swept
> To the throng'd grave, *Cleone* [211] saw, and wept.
> Her tender mind, with meek religion fraught,
> Drank, all-resign'd, Affliction's bitter draught;
> Alive, and listening to the whisper'd groan
> Of other's woes, unmindful [212] of her own.
> One smiling boy, her last sweet hope, she warms,
> Hush'd on her bosom, cradled [213] in her arms.
> Daughter of woe! ere morn, in vain caress'd,
> Clung the cold babe upon thy milkless breast;
> With feeble cries thy last sad aid requir'd,
> Stretch'd it's stiff limbs, and on thy lap expir'd!
> Long, with wide eye-lids, on her child she gaz'd,
> And long to Heav'n their tearless orbs she rais'd;
> Then, with quick foot and throbbing heart, she found
> Where Chartreuse [214] open'd deep his holy ground;
> Bore her last treasure through the midnight gloom,
> And kneeling dropp'd it in the mighty tomb.
> "I follow next!" the frantic mourner said,
> And living plung'd amid the festering dead.[215]

It appears to the author of this memoir, that, in the above solemn, great, and impressive episode, only two words, an epithet and its substantive, "ebon cars", could be changed to advantage. Ebony has a glossy and polished black, and is therefore of unsuitable resemblance to that vehicle of horror. Then amid the dreadful truths of the description, the dead cart should have been called by its simple name; *car*, has a fine triumphant sound, which somewhat disturbs the awful horror of the impression. Surely the vehicle without nominal alteration, and with a stronger epithet prefixed, that should not specify its complexion, would be better,

> While Death and Night pil'd up the naked throng,
> And Silence drove their ghastly carts along.[216]

From the banks of the Ontario we have the *Cassia*.[217] It is one of those American fruits which are annually thrown on the coast of Norway, in wonderful emigration. Dr Darwin accounts for it by a supposed existence of under currents in the depth of the ocean, or from vortexes of water passing from one country to another through caverns of the earth. The *Cassia*, ten males one female, is represented as a fair American matron, who, alarmed by the rising tempest, trusts her children to the floods. The Scripture tradition of Moses, committed to the Nile by his Hebrew mother, is here told with aptness to the subject, with picturesque beauty, and with pathetic sweetness.[218] This child, rescued from the flood, and rising into an ambassador of Heaven, a mighty Prophet, that wrested the scourge from the oppressor's hand, and broke the iron bonds of his nation's slavery, nobly and religiously closes the passage; and in that close awfully contrasts the tenderness of the opening. From thence the Poet passes into another sublime philippic on the plague-spot in the moral and religious health of Britain, her cruel Slave Trade, and makes this striking appeal to our senators:

> E'en now, e'en now, on yonder western shores,
> Weeps pale Despair, and writhing anguish roars:
> E'en now in Afric's groves, with hideous yell,
> Fierce Slavery stalks, and slips the dogs of hell;
> From vale to vale the gathering cries rebound,
> And sable nations tremble at the sound!

> Ye bands of senators, whose suffrage sways
> Britannia's realms; whom either Ind obeys;
> Who right the injur'd, and reward the brave,
> Stretch your strong arm, for ye have power to save!
> Thron'd in the vaulted heart, his dread resort,
> Inexorable Conscience holds his court;
> With still small voice the plots of guilt alarms,
> Bears his mask'd brow, his lifted hands disarms;
> But wrapp'd in night, with terrors all his own,
> He speaks in thunder when the deed is done.
> Hear him, ye senates! hear this truth sublime,
> He who allows oppression, shares the crime.

No radiant pearl, which crested Fortune wears,
No gem, that sparkling [219] hangs from Beauty's ears;
Not the bright stars which night's blue arch adorn
Not rising suns that gild the vernal morn,
Shine with such lustre as the tear, that breaks
For other's woe, down Virtue's manly cheeks.[220]

So admirably does this Bard drop the curtain of moral truth and humanity over the tissues of his fancy, in this the grandest of his second-part Cantos.

The Muse of Botany now retires with much more serious grace from her choir than she had done in the preceding Cantos, and it becomes her well, from the more sombre nature of its recent themes.

Alike ingenious and just are the critical observations with which this third Interlude commences; they are on the relation between the arts of Poetry and Painting. In the *progress* of its strictures Dr Darwin has not succeeded so well. When he would establish affinity between the measures of metrical and musical composition, it was owing to his total want of knowledge in musical science that he is visionary, abstruse, and incomprehensible. The instances he gives of fancied triple and common time in our verse, by no means support his theory, after all the pains which can be taken to comprehend it by those who understand both the arts. His suggested possibility of luminous harmony, accordant to that which is vocal, seems metaphysical in as wild extreme as the supposed analogy between the measures of poetry, and the time of music, had been unsuccessfully mathematical.

A pleasing instance of paternal eulogy occurs in this Interlude concerning the ingenious discovery on the harmony of colours, by Dr Darwin of Shrewsbury. The demonstrated existence of that harmony gives, as our Poet justly observes, Music and Painting undoubted right to borrow metaphors from each other; "Musicians, to speak of the brilliancy of sounds, and the light and shade of a concerto; and Painters, of the harmony of colours and the tone of a picture";[221] but, when he seeks to extend in our sensorium these real affinities between the nature of colours and of musical sounds, into an equal relationship between the poetical and the musical measures, he becomes incomprehensible to those who know the nature of each too well to believe it possible that the mechanical divisions of musical time have their corresponding rules in the formation of English verse, whether blank or in rhyme. Perhaps the system may, as he asserts, extend to the possibility of setting pictures, as well as verbal expressions, to music, but not, surely, as Dr Darwin supposes, with better effect than when music is adapted to the sentiments or the imagery of verse. The love of novelty only could have induced such a preference. It is conceivable that a picture, whether historic or scenic, might be exhibited while such harmonic strains are played by a band, as should well express the passions and feelings of the historic group before us, or the particular character of the landscape; but as the picture has only its moment, so must the corresponding melody and harmony of instruments have only one strain; no successive and contrasted movements. Poetry and Music are both progressive, Painting is stationary, therefore the natural union is between the two first; and pictures can be worth nothing to the musician in his imitative art, in comparison with poetry, whose passions and scenes are changeful, often contrasted, and always proceeding.

Again, the poetic Critic emerges into truth and day-light, when he compares the nature and privileges of the Greek and Latin languages with those of our own. Silent about the tones of each, where superiority is universally confessed to be with the two former, he proves that the constitution of the English language is, from its power of more variously compounding its terms, and from its greater facility in producing personifications, better calculated for poetry than the Greek and Latin. Accordingly our poetry has more imagery than that of either of those languages. From this comparison the author slides into the subject of plagiarism from the Ancients, and from former Bards of this nation. He distinguishes well what is, and what is not amenable to that censure, and acknowledges the few passages of borrowed ideas in the three preceding Cantos. He says, "Where the sentiment and expression are taken from other writers without due acknowledgment, an author is guilty of plagiarism, but not on the testimony of single words and casual phrases"; and adds, "they are lawful game, wild by nature, the property of all who can capture them. Perhaps a few common flowers of speech may be gathered as we pass over our neighbour's ground, but we must not plunder his cultivated fruit".[222] Dr Darwin forgot that just restraint when he took, unacknowledged, forty-six entire lines, the published verses of his friend, for the exordium of the first part of his work. That extraordinary, and in a Poet of so much genius, unprecedented instance of plagiarism excepted, not one great Poet in England is more original than Darwin. His design, his ideas, his style, his manner, are wholly his own.

> Bright forms that glitter in the Muse's ray,
> With orient hues, unborrow'd of the sun.[223]

Fourth Canto

Opens with a sun-rise and a rain-bow, each of Homeric excellence. The Muse of Botany gazes enchanted on the scene, and swells the song of Paphos to softer chords. Her poet adds:

> Long ailes of oak return'd the silver sound,
> And amorous Echoes talk'd along the ground.[224]

This is almost verbatim from Pope's line,

And more than Echoes talk along the walls.[225]

Plagiarism is atoned when it improves upon its original, and that is always to be expected from genius rich as Dr Darwin's; but in the present instance we are disappointed. This generally so very accurate describer, here indolently sacrifices the verisimilitude of the circumstance, rather than change his rhymes. Echoes talk in the air and along walls, but we never hear their voice at our feet. They are there in double inaccuracy, since if the oaken vistas returned the sound, that sound is echo; so we have first a literal echo, and, immediately after, a plurality of personified echoes creeping on all four, and telling their imitative tales where no "Nymph of the airy cell",[226] as Milton beautifully terms the echo, ever deigned even to whisper.

Suppose,

Long ailes of oak the silver sounds retain,
And all their echoes breath'd the amorous strain.[227]

Dr Darwin proceeds to recall his readers to the local situation of his Muse:

Pleas'd Lichfield listen'd from her sacred bowers,
Bow'd her tall groves, and shook her stately towers.[228]

The first transformation of this Canto is the *Cereus grandiflora*,[229] of Jamaica, twenty males one female. It flowers and becomes odoriferous during a few hours in the night, and then closes to open no more. The *Cerea* becomes a Maid of Night, contemplating, it's "stellar suns"; and she is compared to the Fairy Queen of Mr Mundy's [230] Poem, *Needwood Forest*, in a lovely strain, descriptive of the Elfin Sovereign. Of such a pleasing personage a second portrait is welcome. The reader may be gratified by comparing on this page the pictures of *Titania* [231] from two Poets of whom Staffordshire may be proud.

Needwood Forest

Hark the soft lute! along the green
Moves, with majestic step, the Queen.
Attendant Fays around her throng,
And trace the dance, or raise the song;
Or touch the shrill reed as they trip,
With finger light and ruby lip.

High on her brow sublime is borne
One scarlet woodbine's tremulous horn;
A gaudy bee-bird's ample plume
Sheds o'er her neck it's wavy gloom;
With silvery gossamer entwin'd,
Stream the luxuriant locks behind.
Thin folds of tangled net-work break,
In airy waves adorn her neck;
Warp'd in his loom, the spider spread
The far diverging rays of thread.
One rose-leaf forms her crimson vest,
The loose edge crosses o'er her breast,
And one translucent fold, which fell
From a tall lily's ample bell,

Forms, with sweet grace, her snowy train,
Flows, as she steps, and sweeps the plain.
Silence and Night enchanted gaze,
And Hesper [232] hides his vanquish'd rays.[233]

Botanic Garden

Thus, when old Needwood's hoary scenes the Night
Paints with blue shadow, and with milky light;
Where Mundy [234] pour'd, the listening nymphs among,
Loud to the echoing vales his parting song,
With measur'd step the Fairy Sovereign treads,
Shakes her high plume, and glitters o'er the meads;
Round each green holly leads her sportive train,
And little footsteps mark the circled plain;
Each haunted rill with silver voices rings,
And Night's sweet bird in livelier accent, sings.

The next floral animation, the *Tropoeolum Majus*,[235] Garden Nasturtion, eight males one female, is introduced by these lovely lines:

Ere the bright Star which leads the morning sky
Hangs o'er the milky [236] East its [237] diamond eye,
The chaste Tropoeo leaves her secret bed:
And saint-like glory trembles round her head;[238]

alluding to the "electric flashes, which Miss E. C. Linnaeus first observed about this flower in a summer morning, before sun-rise". A plenty and pomp of illustration is allotted to this flower; first the fire-fly of the tropics; next the ignis-fatuus, Dr Darwin had deemed fabulous; and last the intrepid Youths of Judea, condemned by Nebuchadnezzar to the burning fiery furnace.

With sublime simplicity has the Prophet Daniel told that story.[239] Beneath every remembrance in favor of the inspired historian, we are here impressed and charmed anew by grandeur of imagery and picture, suited to the miraculous greatness of the scene. We again behold the blazing deluge, the fiery cavern, white with seven-fold heat; the three Heroes in the midst:

And now a fourth, with Seraph-beauty [240] bright,
Descends; accosts them; and outshines the light.
Fierce flames innocuous, as they step, retire,
And slow they move amid a world of fire![241]

How beautiful is the latter part of the second line!

The *Avena*,[242] Oat, three males two females, becomes a pair of musical nymphs, alluding to the oaten pipes of early times, perhaps the first invented instrument of the harmonious science. The sister Avenas sing a lovely pastoral ballad, whose shorter measure again, as twice before, in the course of this poem, agreeably relieves the ear.

Cannabis,[243] Chinese Hemp, is introduced by this fine appropriate landscape, where China,

> O'er desert sands, deep gulfs, and hills sublime
> Extends her many [244] wall from clime to clime;
> With bells and dragons crests her Pagod-bowers,[245]
> Her silken palaces, and porcelain towers;
> With long canals a thousand nations laves,
> Plants all her wilds, and peoples all her waves;
> Slow treads fair Cannabis the breezy strand,
> The distaff streams dishevell'd in her hand.[246]

The female form is always attractive from the poetic pencil of Darwin. Even the homely distaff [247] becomes elegant, as in the hand of a fair Nymph, its flax is buoyant on the gales of morning. *Cannabis* proceeds in her spinning, and the Graces [248] hover around her wheel; yet to her is "stern Clotho" compared, who weaves the web of Human Destiny, the cradle and the coffin binding its ends; but the Lady is here in her kindest mood, auspicious Fortune turning the giddy wheel;

> But if sweet Love, with baby-fingers, twines,
> And wets, with dewy lips, the lengthening lines,
> Skein after skein celestial tints unfold,
> And all the silken tissue shines with gold.[249]

Galanthus Nivalis,[250] Snow-drop, six males one female, is introduced as a delicate and sprightly lady, playing amidst a wintery scene of silent floods, white hills and glittering meadows. She chides the tardy Spring, and commands the West Wind to stretch his folded pinions. She awakens the hoarse Cuckow [251] in his gloomy cavern, calls the wondering Dormouse [252] from his temporary grave; bids the mute Redbreast enliven the budding groves, and the plighted Ringdove [253] coo. The Redbreast,[254] however, is not mute amid the hybernal silence of nature, he warbles on the hoary spray.

Bellis Prolifera,[255] Hen and Chicken Daisy, next becomes an affectionate matron, surrounded by her happy infants. Their childish sports, with the insects of the advanced Spring, and with the harebells [256] and primroses,[257] form a domestic scene of tender and lively interest. In the course of it a compound epithet for the Snail brings that reptile instantly to the eye:

> Admire his eye-tipp'd horns and painted mail;[258]

also, by the adverb, pausing, "the pausing butterfly", is that gay insect recalled to us on its airy evolutions. Venus and her Loves making arrows for Cupid in Vulcan's forge, is given as a simile to that scene; if simile it may be called which similitude has none. However, the mechanism of bow and arrow-making is presented with very amusing precision.

Evidently to support a splendid preclusive description of Matlock, and the theory of the warmth of its fountain proceeding from internal volcano, is the aquatic plant, the *Fucus*,[259] introduced, which, we are told, soon appears in all basins that contain water. The *Fucus* is represented as a beauteous youth, who bathes his fair forehead in the streaming fountain. The scriptural Angel who shook his plumes over the pool of Bethesda,[260] illustrates the *Fucus*, presiding over the salubrious springs of Matlock. This simile has much propriety, since Dr Priestley informs us that "great quantities of pure dephlogisticated air are given up in water at the points of the Fucus, particularly in the sunshine, and that hence it contributes to preserve the water in reservoirs from becoming putrid".[261]

Trapa,[262] four males one female, another aquatic plant, comes before us; thus,

Amphibious Nymph, from Nile's prolific bed
Emerging *Trapa*, lifts her pearly head.
Fair glows her virgin cheek and modest breast,
A panoply of scales deforms the rest;
Her quivering fins and panting gills she hides,
But spreads her silver arms upon the tides;
Slow as she sails, her ivory neck she laves,
And shakes her golden tresses o'er the waves.
Charm'd round the Nymph, in circling gambols glide
Four Nereid forms, or shoot along the tide;
Now, all as one, they rise with frolic spring,
And beat the wondering air on humid wing;
Now all descending plunge beneath the main,
And lash its [263] foam with undulating train;
Above, below, they wheel, retreat, advance,
In air and ocean weave the mazy dance;
Bow their quick heads, and point their diamond eyes,
And twinkle to the sun with ever changing dyes.[264]

By this picture we are reminded of the figure of Sin at the gates of hell.

The one seem'd woman to the waist, and fair,
But ended foul in many a scaly fold,
Voluminous and vast!

Milton's *Paradise Lost* [265]

The ensuing transformation conveys us from the flat shores of the Nile to the base of the Andes. The plant is the *Ocymum Salinum*,[266] Saline Basil, two males two females. She is complimented with chastity as having but one lover. Her situation presents a fine landscape, and her form is arrayed in every feminine and modest attraction. The spray of ocean bathes

217

her delicate limbs, uncurls her amber-hued tresses, and encrusts her person with saline films, through which, as from, amidst a shrine of chrystal, her beauty beams. To this saline plant belongs a note extremely worth the attention of the reader,[267] since it contains an opinion of universal medical importance, from one of the most discerning physicians which perhaps the world has produced. It relates, by him, to the supposed pernicious effect of too frequent indulgence in that most agreeable of all the artificial tastes, the love of salt with our food. The transformation of the *Ocymum Salinum* brought to the Poet's memory the unfortunate wife of Lot, whose story is here told with great and pathetic beauty. Herself and husband are compared to Orpheus and Eurydice,[268] to Aeneas and Creusa.[269] The story concludes with a fine versification of the scriptural picture of the ruins of Sodom and Gomorrah.[270] Perhaps it will be found somewhat inferior to Mason's [271] paraphrase of the desolation of Babylon. The reader will compare the passages, and judge for himself.

Botanic Garden

Oft the lone Pilgrim, that his road forsakes,
Marks the wide ruins and the sulphur'd lakes;
On mouldering piles, amid asphaltic mud,
Hears the hoarse Bittern where Gomorrah stood;
Recalls th' unhappy pair, with lifted eye,
Leans on the crystal tomb, and breathes the silent sigh.[272]

Mason's *Ode on the Fate of Tyranny* [273]

Where yon proud City stood
Now spreads the stagnant mud;
And there the Bittern in the sedge shall lurk,
Moaning with sullen strain,
While sweeping o'er the plain,
Destruction ends her work.[274]

Arum,[275] of the class Gynandria, or masculine ladies, becomes an Amazon, in the modern military garb, and its appendages. *Dejanira* [276] exchanging her distaff for the lion-spoils of her mighty lover, illustrates the Haram in a beautiful poetic picture.

The mule-flower, produced from the union of the *Dianthus Superbus*,[277] Proud Pink, and the *Caryophillus*,[278] Clove, produces, in the transformation of its parent flowers, a whimsical but highly ingenious comparison to the Persian fable of the amours of the Nightingale and the Rose.[279] With romantic, but exquisite fancy is this amour, and its beautifully-monstered offspring, made out. That curious plant, the *Chundali Borrum*,[280] whose history and strange habits are described in a note to the passage, is preceded by an African landscape of sublime features, beneath the rage of the Summer Solstice,[281] and the poisonous breath of the Harmattan,[282] the only gale that flits over the tawny hills. Gasping panthers are rolling in the dust, and dying serpents are writhing in foamy folds; the woods on Atlas,[283] blasted by the heats, and the waters of the Gambia [284] shrinking in their channels; Ocean rolling to land his sick shoals, and Contagion stalking along the shore. Amid the sultry waste rises the graceful nymph, Chunda,[285] with her brow unturbaned, and with loosened zone. Her ten lovers are employed in mitigating for their fair mistress the ardours of the climate, with the umbrella and the fan.

Of equal excellence, a Greenland picture contrasts, in the utmost possible extreme, the preceding landscape. A dayless horizon, streaming with the milky light of the Aurora Borealis,[286] and all the white mountains gleaming to the moon; Bears stalking slowly over the printed snows; and vast ribs of ice, bursting with the noise of loudest thunder. Then is shown the vernal dissolution of this scene, beneath the rising of the pale, six-months day; and the *Muschus*,[287] Coral-Moss, in the form of an Arctic-regioned lover, awakens his Fair One, and describes the symptoms of returning Spring.

The lake and sea-plant, Aega, *Conserva Aegagropila*,[288] is next introduced by this beautiful line,

Night's tinsel beams on smooth Loch-Lomond[289] dance.[290]

Where the charms of poetic sound are felt, *that* is one of the lines which, after perusal, takes possession of the memory, and lingers on the ear. We are told, in a note, that this vegetable is found loose in many lakes; that it is of a globular form, from the size of a walnut to that of a melon; does not adhere to any thing, but rolls from one part of the lake to the other. Here it becomes a fair maid, sitting on the banks of Loch-Lomond, expecting her lover to swim to her from the centre of the water, and exploring, with anxious eyes, every passing wave. Since a number of aquatic plants had been previously humanized, it is probable *this* is indebted for such distinction to the inclination of the Poet to retell the celebrated story of Hero and Leander, after Ovid. As a simile it is perfectly comparative to the described situation and solicitude of Aega. Dr Darwin was conscious of his rarely-equalled talent in descriptive story; of his power to bring objects full and distinct on the reader's eye, by attitudes, looks, and employments, peculiar to their situation. Ovid says, Hero hung her lamp in a tower which overlooked the Hellespont, that her lover, as he swam across the flood, might see to steer his course by its light. The art of glass-making, unknown in those times, the danger of the lamp being blown out must have been imminent. It is therefore natural that Hero should assiduously strive to guard it from the wind. Of that picturesque circumstance Ovid did not avail himself. Our modern Bard [291] has been happier.

So, on her sea-girt tower, fair Hero stood
At parting day, and mark'd the dashing flood,
While high in air, the glimmering rocks above,
Shone the bright lamp, the pilot-star of love.
With robe out-spread, the waving [292] flame behind,
She kneels, and guards it from the rising [293] wind;
Breathes to her Goddess [294] all her vows, and guides
Her bold Leander o'er the dusky tides;[295]
Wrings his wet hair, his briny bosom warms,
And clasps her daring lover in her arms.[296]

The charm of appropriation, as evinced in the third couplet of the above passage, exists only with the genuine Poet. Mere tuneful versifiers know nothing of it, they rest in general description, and general description has been long since exhausted. Genius knows this; he seizes the peculiar circumstance of the situation; pours all his strength and light upon that, and leaves to the reader to conceive the *whole* by that distinct and luminous *part*; but for which, the scene would pass unimpressive over the mind of the examiner, and probably in no hour of recollection return to it again.

The Truffle,[297] a well known fungus, which never appears above ground, now meets our attention as a fine lady, married to a Gnome, stretched on beds of silvery asbestos,[298] beneath a grand subterranean palace; soothed by the music of the Eolian strings, which make love to tender Echoes in the circumjacent caves; while Cupids hover round and shake celestial day from their bright lamps. It must be confessed that the Empress of this proud palace has not the claim of birthright to her splendour.

This personification is succeeded by that of *Caprifica*,[299] Wild Fig, as a Nymph who slumbers away her life on a downy couch. She is betrothed to a Sylph. Her awakening is compared to that of the insect in a nut, and to a young linnet [300] on the instant of its first flight from the nest. *Caprifica* strikes a talisman, and her airy husband flies to her on the wings of a gnat. This flight is painted with lavish play of fancy; its swiftness is compared to that of the electric aura; its impatient constancy to that of the polar needle. The *Byssus* [301] of the northern shores, which floats on their seas by day, and is found in their caverns, we see ushered to our notice by a sublime poetic picture of Fingall's Cave,[302] of which Pennant's *Tour to the Hebrides* [303] contains an engraving. The male and female of this vegetable become a Youth and Maid of those regions, pursuing their amorous voyage by night, in a boat with green sails, and lighted to their cave by the star of Venus.

Conserva Polymorpha,[304] found on the English shores, from the changeful appearance of the substance, is termed a Proteus Lover, and is represented after that fable. Beneath this fancy we see him a Dolphin, a spotted Pard,[305] a Swan; and traits of the manners of each of those animals give poetic value to the transformations.

Adonis, many males many females in the same flower. Here is the final metamorphosis of this great work of Imagination. The multifarious florets in each individual flower of that species, are made to assume the human figure, and to become a band of libertine lovers, who plight their promiscuous hymeneals. To them is compared that licentious institution, the Areoi of Otaheite,[306] as recorded in Cook's *Voyages*.[307]

And now the Muse of Botany dismisses her ministers, and closes her inchantments [sic], thus:

Here ceas'd the Goddess. O'er the silent strings
Applauding Zephyrs swept their fluttering wings;
Enraptur'd Sylphs arose in murmuring crowds,
To air-wove canopies and pillowy clouds;
Each Gnome, reluctant sought his earthly cell,
And each bright floret cloth'd her velvet bell.
Then, on soft tiptoe, Night, approaching near,
Hung o'er the tuneless lyre his sable ear;

Gemm'd with bright stars the still, etherial plain,
And bade his nightingales repeat the strain.[308]

These last verses drop the curtain, with serene dignity, over a brilliant little world of Genius and its creations. The passage may not possess the spirit and sublimity which attach to a number of others in this division. Probably the Poet remembered the plainness with which Homer, Virgil, and Milton, closed their Epics, and chose to diffuse over his farewell lines an emulous sobriety. Perhaps the whole Canto, with all its mass of picturesque elegance, has more sameness, less grandeur, less sublimity, than any of its predecessors in either part of this magnificent Poem. It seems to bear that species and degree of inferiority to the three former Cantos, as the *Loves of the Plants*, considered as an whole, bears to the sublimer first part, the *Economy of Vegetation*; where we find impersonised [sic] each various elementary property of Creation, as a race of ministrant Beings, endowed with scientific intelligence and benevolent powers. They rise before us, the Handmaids of Nature, ordained to watch over all her operations and productions, on earth and beneath it; in air and in ocean; as Nature herself appears in the semblance of the Goddess of Botany.

Perhaps it would have been better if her proper and general name, Nature, had been assigned to her in the *Economy of Vegetation*, and the botanic title been reserved exclusively for the Muse in the Second Part, who records the transformations and the loves of the Plants and Flowers. In that case, to her also would have been resigned the floral car and its gay descent, and a vehicle of graver magnificence supplied its place to the "Mighty mother", immortal Nature. Nymph, or Goddess of Botany, implies empire only over the vegetable part of creation; while, in the *Economy of Vegetation*, she presides over the astronomic, electric, aerial, and mineralogic properties. Into so wide a field has the union of Philosophy with Poetry conducted this daring Bard. The light of his imagination will shine with increasing lustre in the eyes of future generations, so long as discerning Taste shall be the Vestal to watch and support its fires.

Nor let it once be thought that any error in Dr Darwin's poetic system; any occasional deviation from perfection in the plan, arrangement, or execution of this his complicated work, ought to prevent its being considered as one of the richest effusions of the poetic mind, that has shed lustre over Europe in the eighteenth century.

Human ability never did, and probably never will, produce an absolutely perfect composition. The author of this memoir has, from infancy, sedulously studied and compared the writings of the distinguished Bards of her nation, together with the best translations of those of Greece, Rome, and modern Italy. She has presumed to descant upon what appeared to her the graces and defects of the *Botanic Garden*; induced by a conviction that the unbiassed mixture of candid objection with due praise, better serves the interest of every science than blind unqualified encomium upon its professors. Hence, rising genius may be guarded against the betraying influence of enthusiastic homage; which charmed by general excellence, melts down particular defect in its shining mass. So doing, the inexperienced and ardent fancy is full as liable to adopt the faults as to attain the merits of the author it emulates.

By unprejudiced investigation, that sickly, partial, and fastidious taste which confines its attention and its praise to a few chosen and darling writers, may be induced to reflect, that if, after a just balance of beauty and defect, the first outweighs the latter in immense degree, then attention, love, and applause is due to that work as an whole, in which such preponderance is found.

Posterity, if not always, yet generally acts upon that fair principle in the measure of fame it allots, when the mists of prejudice, from causes foreign to the intrinsic claims of an author, shall disperse. Those compositions which, with a considerable degree of genius, are yet level to the comprehension of ordinary minds, immediately attain their full measure of celebration; but it is seldom that poetry of the higher orders is exempt from those mists; it must struggle through them into full and universal day.

The slowly-accumulating suffrages of those discerning and generous readers who delight in fertile and daring Genius, will accumulate for the *Botanic Garden*, as they have for many other poems, whose early appreciation was dubious; whose celebration, during the life of their authors, was far from being uncontroverted. When that time shall come, the querulous and disdainful tones of peevish prejudice will not venture to assail the ear of an admiring Nation, proud of its distinguished Sons. Then, however imperfection may still be perceived in this as in all other works of bold imagination, it will be observed without acrimony, and with grateful delight in its plenteous atonement.

No eminent Poet has so many passages which are every way exceptionable, as the *most* eminent Poet that this, or perhaps any other nation has produced from the morning of Time, our great, our glorious Shakespeare.

Notes

1   This Linnaean overview by Dr Darwin begins as follows: "Linnaeus has divided the vegetable world into 24 Classes; these Classes into about 120 Orders; these Orders contain about 2000 Families, or Genera; and these Families about 20,000 Species; besides the innumerable Varieties, which the accidents of climate or cultivation have added to these Species. The Classes are distinguished from each other in this ingenious system, by the number, situation, adhesion, or reciprocal proportion of the males in each flower. The Orders, in many of these Classes, are distinguished by the number, or other circumstances of the females. The Families, or Genera, are characterized by the analogy of all the parts of the flower or fructification. The Species are distinguished by the foliage of the plant; and the Varieties by any accidental circumstance of colour, taste, or odour; the seeds of these do not always produce plants similar to the parent; as in our numerous fruit-trees and garden flowers; which are propagated by grafts or layers. The first eleven Classes include the plants, in whose flowers both the sexes reside; and in which the Males or Stamens are neither united, nor unequal in height when at maturity; and are therefore distinguished from each other simply by the number of males in each flower" (*Loves of the Plants*, preface, p.i). For a more complete appreciation of Linnaean methodology, see H.K. Svenson, "On the Descriptive Method of Linnaeus", *Rhodora* 47 (1945): 273–302, 363–388.

2   Footnote citations are drawn from the 3rd edition of this book, published in 1791 by J. Johnson in London. This edition was also reprinted as part of Priestman's edited *Collected Writings of Erasmus Darwin* (Bristol: Thoemmes Continuum, 2004) Vol.2.

3   Linnaeus.

4   *Anthoxanthum odoratum*.

5   Ancient ferns of the genus *Osmunda*, family *Osmundaceae*.

6   Darwin used "or" instead of "and".

7   Darwin used "The fair" instead of "Beauteous".

8   Darwin used "and" instead of "the".

9   Darwin, *Loves of the Plants*, I, lines 85–94.

10 Plants of the genus *Chondrilla* of which the rush skeleton weed (*C. juncea*) is quite common.

11 Plants of the genus *Lychnis*, commonly known by names including campion and catchfly.

12 Plants of the family *Liliaceae* (lily), commonly known as glory lily or tiger claw.

13 Louis XIV (1638–1715), also known as Louis the Great and The Sun King.

14 Anne "Ninon" de l'Enclos (1620–1705), French courtesan, author, and patron of the arts, known for her wit and her beauty. For an enduring overview of this era, see that by C.S. Lewis's (1898–1963) brother, W.H. Lewis, *The Splendid Century: Some Aspects of French Life in the Reign of Louis XIV* (London: Eyre & Spottiswoode, 1953).

15 Edward Villiers, 1st Earl of Jersey (*c.*1656–1711), Knight-Marshal to the Royal Household, Master of the Horse to Queen Mary, and Lord Chamberlain to William III and Queen Anne. In 1696, he represented Great Britain at the Congress of Ryswick. He also served as a Lord Justice of England and as Ambassador to Paris.

16 François VI, Duke de La Rochefoucauld (1613–1680), French classical author and prime supporter of the *maxime*, an epigram that expresses truths with brevity, as described in his *Réflexions ou Sentences et Maximes Morales* (Paris: Claude Barbin, 1665).

17 Solomon (*c.*1000 BC), son of King David and Bathsheba, served as King of Israel 971–931 BC.

18 *Ecclesiastics* 25:19.

19 Françoise d'Aubigné Scarron (1636–1711) titled, in 1674, Madame de Maintenon by Louis XIV, whom she secretly married in 1683 following the death of Queen Marie-Thérèse (1638–1683).

20 Robert Dodsley (1703–1764).

21 Elizabeth Griffith (*c.*1727–1793), Irish dramatist, author and essayist, translated Charles-Louis-Sulpice Lepeigné Douxménil's work as *The Memoirs of Ninon de L'Enclos; With Her Letters to the Marquis de Sevigné and Mons. de St Evremond*.

22 Genus of plants of the family *Caryophyllaceae*, commonly known, as are plants of the genus *Lychnis*, as campion and catchfly.

23 Plants of the single species, *Amaryllis belladonna*, commonly known as the Belladonna Lily or naked ladies.

24 *Ilex* is the genus of hundreds of species of the family *Aquifoliaceae*, commonly known as Holly.

25 Joseph Wright, of Derby.

26 *Kleinhovia hospital*, an evergreen, also known as the Guest Tree.

27 Province near Bengal, nourished by the River Ganges.

28 Amazonian Queen who, according to legend, procured hundreds of Amazonian women to breed with Alexander the Great in hopes of creating a new race of strong, intelligent individuals.

29 Darwin used "fair" instead of "bright".

30 Darwin used "jutting" instead of "swelling".

31 In Roman mythology, a goddess of War. Eighteenth-century landscape gardens frequently contained a Temple of Bellona.

32 Darwin, *Loves of the Plants*, I, lines 193–198.

33 *Tulipa*, the genus name of many species of the family *Liliaceae*. Their bulbous flowers were thought to represent turbans. In their native Turkey, these flowers were given the Turkish name for the gauze with which turbans are made. For more on the excessive popularity of this plant in Europe, see Mike Dash, *Tulipomania. The Story of the World's Most Coveted Flower & the Extraordinary Passions It Aroused* (New York: Three Rivers Press, 1999) and Anne Goldgar, *Tulipmania: Money, Honor, and Knowledge in the Dutch Golden Age* (Chicago: University of Chicago Press, 2007).

34   Genus of plants belonging to the family *Ranunculaceae*, commonly known as buttercups, liverleaf, or liverwort.

35   A large shrub, with spicy pink flowers, commonly known as the Spurge Olive or the Female Bay.

36   Commonly known as autumn crocus, meadow saffron or naked lady.

37   Darwin, *Loves of the Plants*, I, lines 219–222.

38   Genus of scores of species belonging to the family *Asteraceae*.

39   *Drosera rotundifolia*, one of several carnivorous species of sundew, commonly known as the common sundew or the round-leaved sundew.

40   Honeysuckles, plants of the genus *Lonicera* of the family *Caprifoliaceae*, are also commonly known as woodbine or eglantine.

41   *Draba*, the genus of cruciferous plants of the family *Brassicaceae* commonly known as Whitlow-grasses. *Draba alpina* is known as alpine whitlow-grass.

42   Tenerife is one of the several volcanic Canary Islands off the coast of Africa. In July 1795, the British attacked the capital, Santa Cruz de Tenerife. Their forces were repelled by the Spanish, during which Horatio Nelson (1758–1805), the Rear Admiral of the Blue, received the wound that cost him his right arm.

43   Darwin, *Loves of the Plants*, I, line 252.

44   Darwin, *Loves of the Plants*, I, line 258, though Darwin used "on" instead of "o'er" and did not use the word "the".

45   *Viscum*, the genus of a various species of the family *Loranthaceae*, commonly known as Mistletoe.

46   *Zostera*, the genus of several species of the family *Zosteraceae*, commonly found along the shores and in salt water, and known as grass wrack, sea wrack, eel grass, or grass weed.

47   *Agnus scythicus* or *Planta Tartarica Barometz*, a legendary Asian plant reputed to grow sheep as its fruit, Barometz derived from the Russian *baran*, meaning ram. Supposedly, the sheep, connected to and supported by the plant, would graze upon the vegetation surrounding it. Plants do exist, such as the fern, *Cibotium barometz*, that produce a cotton-like, wooly mass.

48   Seward's own footnote, "Parody of Pope's lines on the Amber". This passage was not taken from *The Botanic Garden*. Pope, *An Epistle from Mr Pope to Dr Arbuthnot* (1735), ll. 171–72. The original lines are: "The things we know are neither rich nor rare/But wonder how the devil they got there".

49   The genus of hundreds of species of the subfamily *Mimosoideae* (family *Fabaceae*), including the Venus Fly Trap, all known for their capability of motion. The plant Dr Darwin mentioned, the *Mimosa pudica*, also known as the sensitive plant, enfolds its leaves when touched, though many other Mimosa species enfold their leaves with changes in temperature. For further insight into the literary symbolism of this plant, see Robert M. Maniquis, "The Puzzling Mimosa: Sensitivity and Plant Symbols in Romanticism", *Studies in Romanticism* 8 (1969): 129–155.

50   Darwin, *Loves of the Plants*, I, lines 313–316, though Darwin used the word "librations" rather than "vibrations".

51   A genus of many species of buttercups of the family *Ranunculaceae*.

52   Darwin was likely referring to a lady's bonnet to wear outdoors which, when carried, would collapse like a fan. Calash was also a type of carriage with a folding top that was popular during this period.

53   A closed carriage, originating in Landau, Germany, with seats facing each other. Drop windows and a foldable top allowed this carriage to be opened in good weather.

54   Lichens exist as a symbiotic arrangement of a parasitic fungus with either algae or cyanobacteria as its partner. To overcome competition with plants for sunlight, they have adapted the ability to grow where plants have difficulty becoming established, such as on rocks.

55   *Yr Wyddfa* in Welsh, it is the predominant mountain in Wales.

56   The River Conwy (*Afon Conwy* in Welsh) flows for twenty seven miles at the base of Snowdon from Migneint moor to the mediaeval town of Conwy.

57   *Dipsacus sylvestris*, of the family *Dipsacaceae*, known as Common Teasel. As Darwin adds, "There is a cup around every joint of the stem of this plant, which contains from a spoonful to half a pint of water; and serves both for the nutriment of the plant in dry seasons, and to prevent insects from creeping up to devour its seed" (*Loves of the Plants*, I, p.37, note).

58   Genus of several species of plants of the madder family, *Rubiaceae*.

59   *Vallisneria*, the genus of several species of aquatic plants of the family *Hydrocharitaceae*, commonly known as eel grass or tape grass.

60   The genus of several species of plants of the family *Ulvaceae*, commonly known as sea lettuce.

61   *Halcyon Hosta*, of the family *Liliaceae*, commonly known as the Plantain lily.

62   Galatea, the ivory statue with which King Pygmalion fell in love and which, by the goodness of Aphrodite, was brought to life and became his queen.

63   Genus of several species of fungus of the family *Tremellaceae*, commonly known as yellow brain fungus, golden jelly fungus, or Witch's butter.

64   Anna Seward's "Daphne's Coyness Accounted For" appears in her *Poetical Works*, Vol.2, pp.306–307.

65   Darwin used "from his" instead of "on her".

66   Darwin used "sounds" instead of "blows".

67   Darwin used "winds" instead of "weaves".

68   Darwin used "His" instead of "Her".

69   Darwin used "fretted" instead of "ample".

70   Darwin used "cling" instead of "hang".

71   Darwin, *Loves of the Plants*, I, lines 473–481.

72   Alexander Pope, *Windsor Forest* (London: B. Lintott, 1713). The Forest, in Berkshire, contained the Royal Hunting Ground.

73   The River Kennet joins the River Thames at Reading.

74   Darwin had quoted Pope's *Windsor Forest* (1713), l. 339.

75   Darwin, *Loves of the Plants*, Interlude, p.48. Graylings are freshwater fish related to salmon.

76   Edmund Burke (1729–1797).

77   The Corinthian style columns, common in Rome, had the most ornate of the architectural capitals which were decorated with acanthus leaves and rosettes.

78   Doric columns, the oldest of the Greek style of columns, were simple in design in that they stood on the bare floor and were topped by a plain capital.

79   Shakespeare, *Hamlet* I.i.158–64. Seward has "walks abroad" for Shakespeare's "dare stir abroad".

80   Milton, *Paradise Lost*, II.787–89. Seward has "Through all her caves" for Milton's "From all her caves".

81   Milton, *Paradise Lost*, X.952–57. Seward has "heaven's throne" for Milton's "that place" and "By me committed" for "To me committed".

82   Shakespeare, *Julius Caesar*, I, ii, 18–28. Seward has "all the world" where Shakespeare has "all this world".

83   Pope, *An Essay on Man* (1733–34), Epistle II, ll.3–10, 17–18. Seward omits lines 11–16.

84   John Wesley (1703–1791) "To the Memory of the Right Revd. Francis Gastrell, D. D., Lord Bishop of Chester", *A Collection of Moral and Sacred Poems from the Most Celebrated English Authors* (1744), ll. 233–34.

85   Matthew Prior, *Henry and Emma. A Poem, Upon the Model of The Nut-brown Maid* (London: J. Tonson, 1709). ll. 308–13. Where Seward has "flame" Prior has "fame".

86   Shakespeare, *Macbeth*, II.ii.32–37, 38–40. Seward substitutes "each day's grief" for Shakespeare's "each day's life" and drops the phrase "great nature's second course" from l. 37. Macbeth is Thane of Cawdor and Thane of Glamis.

87 Darwin, *Loves of the Plants*, II, lines 1–4.

88 John Dryden (1631–1700), *A Song for St Cecilia's Day* (London: T. Dring, 1687).

89 A mode of Greek music composition named after the ancient kingdom of Lydia in Anatolia.

90 Dryden, *A Song for St. Cecilia's Day*, V.5–6.

91 Milton, *Paradise Lost*, IX.613.

92 Pope, *The Iliad*, I.50.

93 Song CCXXVII from *The Bull-Finch. Being a Choice Collection of the Newest and Most Favourite English Songs Most of which have been Sett to Music and Sung at the Public Theatres & Gardens* (London: I. Hinton, 1746), l. 2.

94 Untraced.

95 Prior, *Alma, or the Progress of the Mind* (1721), I.26.

96 One of two grotesque sea monsters (the other being Charybdis) that lived on either side of a narrow straight through which Odysseus had to sail.

97 The narrow peninsula south of Naples that extends into the Mediterranean Sea.

98 Ancient name for Sicily.

99 Milton, *Paradise Lost*, II.660–61.

100 James Beattie (1735–1803), a Scottish poet, essayist, and philosopher. He matriculated at Marischal College, Aberdeen, where he later served as Professor of Moral Philosophy.

101 *The Minstrel, or, Progress of Genius. A Poem* (London: E. & C. Dilley, 1771), a work in Spenserian stanza form that traces the development of a poet's mind according to the influence of nature and its beauty.

102 James Beattie, *The Minstrel, or, a Progress of Genius, A Poem* (1771), XXXII.3–4.

103 Charles Churchill (1731–1764).

104 William Mason (1724–1797).

105 Charles Churchill (1731–1764), *The Prophecy of Famine. A Scots Pastoral* (1763), l. 86.

106 The Humber Estuary, formed by the River Trent and River Ouse, flows into the North Sea. Just as Seward was known as the "Swan of Lichfield", Mason was known as the "Swan of the Humber". For more discussion of this title, "Swan", see Norma Clarke, "Anna Seward: Swan, Duckling, or Goose?" in Jennie Batchelor and Cora Kaplan (eds) *British Women's Writing in the Long Eighteenth Century* (Basingstoke, Hampshire: Palgrave Macmillan, 2005), pp.34–47.

107 *Carlina*, the genus of many species of thistles of the family *Asteraceae*.

108 Darwin used "crystal" instead of "dusky".

109 Darwin used "which" instead of "that".

110 Darwin used the plural, "lustres".

111 A constellation, in Greek mythology, Andromeda's daughter.

112 A constellation, Ursa Major, the Great Bear.

113 A Southern hemisphere constellation. In Greek mythology, the ship in which Jason sailed on his search for the Golden Fleece.

114 Darwin, *Loves of the Plants*, II, lines 47–66.

115 The genus of many species of flowering plants of the family *Linaceae*, one of which, Common Flax, is used in producing linen.

116 The genus of many shrubs of the family *Malvaceae*, which include the plants producing cotton.

117 Arkwright (1732–1792), inventor and textile industrialist whose factory, as King-Hele (*Doctor of Revolution*, p.166) reminds us, has regularly been viewed as the 'take off' point of the Industrial Revolution. Fortunately for posterity, he "stimulated" the painter Joseph Wright to "bequeath to us a series of views of the area where [Arkwright] built up his industrial empire" (Nicholson, *Wright*, p.164).

118 Matlock, Derbyshire, near Worksworth on the edge of the River Derwent. As to the apparatus, in 1769, Arkwright patented a water-driven frame for spinning cotton yarn of suitable strength, thereby improving James Hargreaves's (bap.1721–1778) spinning jenny of 1767. According to Dr Darwin, Arkwright "has created his curious and magnificent machinery for spinning cotton; which had been in vain attempted by many ingenious artists before him. The cotton-wool is first picked from the pods and seeds by women. It is then carded by *cylindrical cards*, which move against each other, with different velocities. It is taken from these by an *iron-hand* or comb, which has a motion similar to that of scratching, and takes the wool off the cards longitudinally in respect to the fibres or staple, producing a continued line loosely cohering, called the *Rove* or *Roving*. This Rove, yet very loosely twisted, is then received or drawn into a *whirling canister*, and is rolled by the centrifugal force in spiral lines within it; being yet too tender for the spindle. It is then passed between *two pairs of rollers*; the second pair moving faster than the first elongate the thread with greater equality than can be done by the hand; and is then twisted on spoles [sic] or bobbins" (*Loves of the Plants*, II, p.161, note).

119 *Cyperus papyrus*, of the sedge family *Cyperaceae*, known as Papyrus sedge or paper reed.

120 Mrs Mary Delany (1700–1788).

121 According to Dr Darwin, Mrs Delany finished "nine hundred and seventy accurate and elegant representations of different vegetables with the parts of their flowers, fructification, &c. according with the classification of Linnaeus, in what she terms paper-mosaic". Her "curious *Hortus siccus* … I suppose contains a greater number of plants than were ever before drawn from the life by any one person. Her method consisted in placing the leaves of each plant with the petals, and all the other parts of the flowers, on coloured paper, and cutting them with scissars [sic] accurately to the natural size and form, and then parting them on a dark ground; the effect of which is wonderful, and their accuracy less liable to fallacy than drawings" (*Loves of the Plants*, I, pp.65–66, note).

122 *Lapsana communi*, the only species of this genus of the family *Asteraceae*, and it is commonly known as Nipplewort.

123 *Nymphaea alba*, the aquatic flowering plant of the family *Nymphaeaceae*, commonly known as the White Water lily or White Lotus.

124 *Calendula*, the genus of several species of the daisy family *Asteraceae*, which are commonly known as marigolds.

125 This great Swedish botanist invented a *Horologium Florae* (or flower clock), "whose wheels were the sun and earth and whose index-figures were flowers". For a recent construction of such a flower clock in the United States, see the Gaber Solar Clock Garden, designed under the direction of Professor Steven B. Carroll, outside of Magruder Hall at Truman State University, Kirksville, Missouri (www.solarclockgarden.truman.edu). Carroll also co-authored (with Steven D. Salt) a modern-day practical approach to botany and agricultural science ala Dr Darwin, *Ecology for Gardeners* (Cambridge, MA: Timber Press, 2004).

126 Young, *The Complaint, or, Night-Thoughts on Life, Death, and Immortality*, I.193–98.

127 Hellebores are from a genus of several species in the family *Ranunculaceae*, commonly known by the somewhat misleading name Christmas Rose or Lenten Rose, though not truly of the rose family, *Rosaceae*. Hellebore has frequently been featured in history and literature throughout the ages.

128 A river of significant importance since ancient times flowing from Turkey through Syria and Iraq to join the River Tigris.

129 Darwin, *Loves of the Plants*, II, lines 217–218.

130 John Dyer (bap.1699, *d*.1757) uses the phrase "palmy Euphrates" in *The Ruins of Rome* (1740), l. 46. The lines are not found in Milton's verse.

131 Ancient city in Babylonia, south of Baghdad, near the Euphrates River.

132 A mountain chain in the Taurus range of Armenia where John Milton, in *Paradise Lost*, envisioned Satan encountering Earth.

133 Darwin, *Loves of the Plants*, II, line 228.

134 *Menispermum*, a genus of a few species of woody vines of the family *Menispermaceae*, whose crescent-shaped seeds give them the common name, moonseed. Their poisonous fruit is commonly known as *Cocculus Indicus* or Indian Berry.

135 Upon being ridiculed by heretics, St Anthony of Padua once went to a river's edge where, filled with the Holy Spirit, he began to preach to the fish, pointing out the God-given beauties of being a fish. Reputedly, they began to gather together, listening to his speech, and they did not disperse until receiving his blessing.

136 A genus of many species of poppies of the family *Papaveraceae*. Seward composed a sonnet "To the Poppy", Sonnet LXXI in *Original Sonnets on Various Subjects; And Odes Paraphrased from Horace* (London: G. Sael, 1799).

137 *Asphodelus*, a genus of many species of the family *Asphodelaceae*.

138 *Amaranthus*, a genus of herbs of the family *Amaranthaceae*, commonly known as amaranth or pigweed.

139 Darwin, *Loves of the Plants*, II, lines 267–272.

140 Sir Charles Morell (pseudonym of Revd. James Ridley, 1736–1765), *The Tales of the Genii; or, The Delightful Lessons of Horam, the Son of Asmar. Faithfully Translated from the Persian Manuscript; and Compared with the French and Spanish Editions published at Paris and Madrid* (London: J. Wilkie 1764).

141 In Greek mythology, Hermes was messenger of the gods.

142 In Greek mythology, the place of darkness in the underworld enroute to Hades.

143 Emma Crewe (*c.*1768–1850), daughter of the Cheshire magistrate, John Crewe, 1st Baron Crewe (1742–1829). Emma was a key designer of images that Josiah Wedgwood used as medallions in his brooches, teapots, and vases.

144 Genus with a few species of the family *Cistaceae*, commonly known as rockrose.

145 Genus of a few species of the family *Rubiaceae*, commonly known as Jesuit's Bark or Peruvian Bark, which were widely used among physicians of Dr Darwin's era for treatment of fevers, especially malarial fevers. For an historical context of this therapeutic agent, see Saul Jarcho, *Quinine's Predecessor: Francesco Torti and the Early History of Cinchona* (Baltimore: The Johns Hopkins University Press; 1993).

146 San Francisco de Quito, the capital of Ecuador.

147 In Greek mythology, Hygieia, a daughter of Asclepius, was goddess of health.

148 A fever, like that induced by malaria, marked by paroxysms of regularly recurring chills, fever, and sweats, though generally used to denote intermittent fevers of all kinds.

149 *Exodus* 17:1–7, a story captured by many artists including William Blake (1757–1827) in his engraving, "Moses Striking the Rock".

150 A genus of a few species of the family *Plantaginaceae*, commonly known as foxglove. Given Dr Darwin's role in discovering its medicinal effects, his quotation in *Loves of the Plants* (II, p.83, note) is included in full. "The effect of this plant in that kind of Dropsy, which is termed anasarca, where the legs and thighs are much swelled, attended with great difficulty of breathing, is truly astonishing. In the ascites accompanied with anasarca of people past the meridian of life it will also sometimes succeed. The method of administering it requires some caution, as it is liable, in greater doses, to induce very violent and debilitating sickness, which continues one or two days, during which time the dropsical collection however disappears. One large spoonful, or half an ounce, of the following decoction, given twice a day, will generally succeed in a few days. But in more robust people, one large spoonful every two hours, till four spoonfuls are taken, or till sickness occurs, will evacuate the dropsical swellings with greater certainty, but is liable to operate more violently. Boil four ounces of the fresh leaves of purple Foxglove (which leaves may be had at all seasons of the year) from two pints of water to twelve ounces; add to the strained liquor, while yet warm, three ounces of rectified spirit of wine. A theory of the effects of this medicine, with many successful cases, may be seen in a pamphlet, called, *Experiments on Mucilaginous and Purulent Matter*, published by Dr Darwin in 1780.

Sold by Cadell, London". For further insight into the contemporary popularity of this medicinal plant, see G.C. Cook, "Erasmus Darwin FRS (1731–1802) and the Foxglove Controversy"; T.W. Peck and K.D. Wilkinson, *William Withering of Birmingham*; P. Sheldon, *The Life and Times of William Withering*; and J. Worth Estes, *Hall Jackson and the Purple Foxglove: Medical Practice and Research in Revolutionary America, 1760–1820* (Hanover, NH: University Press of New England, 1979).

151 In Greek mythology, son of Zeus, father of Niobe. As punishment for divulging divine secrets to humans, Tantalus was tormented by always having food and drink in sight, but always finding it just beyond reach.

152 Darwin, *Loves of the Plants*, II, lines 419–422.

153 Henri François Xavier de Belsunce de Castelmoron (1671–1755).

154 Dr Darwin, drawing upon Daniel Defoe's *Journal of a Plague Year* (London: E. Nutt, 1722) relates that Sir John Lawrence (d.1692), as Lord Mayor, "continued the whole time [of the plague's ravage] in the city; heard complaints, and redressed them; enforced the wisest regulations then known, and saw them executed. The day after the disease was known with certainty to be the Plague, above 40,000 servants were dismissed, and turned into the streets to perish, for no one would receive them into their houses; and the villages near London drove them away with pitch-forks and fire-arms. Sir John Lawrence supported them all, as well as the needy who were sick, at first by expending his own fortune, till subscriptions could be solicited and received from all parts of the nation" (*Loves of the Plants*, II, p.84, note).

155 John Howard (1726–1790).

156 Darwin used "with" instead of "by".

157 Darwin added the word "aloud" following "wails".

158 Darwin did not include the word "galling".

159 Darwin used "assuasive" instead of "persuasive".

160 Darwin used the plural, "brows".

161 Darwin, *Loves of the Plants*, II, lines 440–472.

162 William Hayley (1745–1820).

163 Hayley's *Ode, Inscribed to John Howard, Esq. F.R.S., Author of 'The State of English and Foreign Prisons'* (London: J. Dodsley, 1780), was also included in John Aiken and William Hayley, *View of the Life, Travels and Philanthropic Labors of the Late John Howard* (Philadelphia: W.W. Woodward for John Ormrod, 1794). Robert Southey was John Howard's literary executor.

164 David Mallet (*c*.1702–1765).

165 Mallet, *Margaret and William: A Ballad* (1723), ll. 5–6.

166 Pope's *Elegy to the Memory of an Unfortunate Lady*, first published in his *Works* (London: W. Bowyer for Bernard Lintot, 1717).

167 Pope, "Elegy to the Memory of an Unfortunate Lady" (1717), l.4.

168 *Circaea lutetiana*, of the Evening Primrose family, *Onagraceae*, commonly known as Enchanter's Nightshade. In folklore, it has often been used in sorcery and witchcraft.

169 St Denys, the church on the market in Sleaford, some 14 miles from Lincoln.

170 A type of poem written for a bride and, in ancient days, sung at the door of her nuptial chamber.

171 *Laurocerasus*, species of the genus *Prunus*, family *Rosaceae*, commonly known as the Cherry Laurel.

172 Seward's own footnote, "The Pythian priestess is supposed to have been made drunk with the effusion of laurel leaves, when she delivered her oracles. The intoxication, or inspiration, is finely described by Virgil".

173 Darwin used "ephods" instead of "epods".

174 Darwin, *Loves of the Plants*, III, lines 39–50.

175   Henry Fuseli (1741–1825).

176   Correctly printed as "each" in the 1804 version of Seward's *Life* published in Philadelphia.

177   East Indian fig tree (*Ficus bengalensis*, of the family *Moraceae*), which extends its aerial shoots downward, forming additional trunks which can actually move the tree over time. Commonly known as the banyan tree or walking tree, it is greatly respected in India.

178   Village in Staffordshire on the River Manifold, 4 miles to the northwest of Ashbourne, close to Dovedale valley.

179   A cave in Staffordshire's Manifold valley, inhabited in the Stone Age as well as in the Roman era. As Dr Darwin relates, "Near the village of Wetton, a mile or two above Dove-Dale, near Ashburn in Derbyshire, there is a spacious cavern about the middle of the ascent of the mountain, which still retains the Name of Thor's house; below is an extensive and romantic common, where the rivers Hamps and Manifold sink into the earth, and rise again in Ham gardens, the seat of John Port, Esq. about three miles below. Where these rivers rise again there are impressions resembling Fish, which appear to be of Jasper bedded in Limestone. Calcareous Spars, Shells converted into a kind of Agate, corallines in Marble, ores of Lead, Copper, and Zinc, and many strata of Flint, or Chert, and of Toadstone, or Lava, abound in this part of the country. The Druids are said to have offered human sacrifices inclosed in wicker idols to Thor" (*Loves of the Plants*, III, p.100, note).

180   Seward combines sections of two of Darwin's notes, *Loves of the Plants*, III, Ficus indica p.99, note, and Gigantic Thor p.100, note.

181   The genus of hundreds of species of flowering plants of the family *Balsaminaceae*, commonly known as Balsam, Jewelweed, or "touch-me-not", the last derived from the plant's seed pods which, when mature, "explode" when touched, thereby dispersing their seeds.

182   In Greek mythology, the Sorceress who assisted Jason, her husband, in acquiring the Golden Fleece.

183   In Greek mythology, the son of Alson and Alkimeda who became a hero when, with the Argonauts, he fetched the Golden Fleece.

184   *Dictamnus albus*, the only species of this genus of the family *Rutaceae*, its flowers give it the common name, Burning-bush. Also known as Fraxinella and the Gas Plant.

185   Darwin, *Loves of the Plants*, III, lines 181–184, though Darwin began the last line with the word "With" instead of "In".

186   *Hippomane mancinella*, a species of the spurge family *Euphorbiaceae*, known as the Manchineel Tree, from Spanish *manzanilla* ("little apple"), *manzanilla de la muerte* ("little apple of death"), in reference to the highly poisonous sap of this tree that has commonly been used for centuries on arrow tips and blowgun darts.

187   Genus of several species of the family *Urticaceae*, nettle being the common name, or frequently, stinging nettle, given the stinging hairs present on many of these plants.

188   *Lobelia*, the genus of hundreds of species of flowering plants of the family *Campanulaceae*, known by common names including Asthma Weed, Indian Tobacco, Pukeweed and Vomitwort. The particular plant, of the same family, to which Dr Darwin referred is *Hippobroma longiflora*.

189   One of the most common, yet most poisonous, snakes in India.

190   Dr Darwin is referring to the ancient Syrian city.

191   *Antiaris toxicaria*, an evergreen of the family *Moraceae*, that produces a toxic latex is commonly known as the Upas Tree. In its native Java, "Upas" means "poison". For further account of Dr Darwin's popularization of the legend surrounding this tree, see Richard F. Gustafson, "The Upas Tree: Pushkin and Erasmus Darwin", *Proceedings of the Modern Language Association* 75 (1960): 101–109.

192   Darwin, *Loves of the Plants*, III, line 244.

193   N.P. Foersch.

194   The word "a" appears instead of "the" in the 1804 version of Seward's *Life of Dr Darwin* published in Philadelphia.

195 *Anacamptis morio*, of the orchid family, *Orchidaceae*, commonly known as the Green-winged Orchid.

196 Key British/Hanoverian victory over the French during the Seven Years' War (1756–1763). It was during this Battle that Colonel Edward Pole was wounded when a bullet entered his left eye, coming out through the back of his head. He survived this injury, living until 1780.

197 Darwin, *Loves of the Plants*, III, line 297.

198 Elizabeth Pole, Dr Darwin's second wife.

199 Darwin, *Loves of the Plants*, III, lines 313–319, though Darwin closed this line with "the hopeless mourner cried" instead of "the hapless mourner said!".

200 *Cuscuta* is a genus of many species of the family *Convolvulaceae*, commonly known as Dodder, as well as devil's hair, goldthread, love vine, strangleweed, and witch's hair.

201 Laocoön, a Trojan priest, warned the Trojans to "Beware of Greeks bearing gifts", for which he was subsequently killed, with his sons, by two serpents sent to Troy by the Greeks.

202 Pliny the Elder (23–79) informs us that the Rhodian sculptors Agesander, Athenodoros, and Polydorus created the famous and much copied "Laocoön and His Sons", a marble statue currently displayed in the Vatican Museums.

203 In an "Ode to the Grape and its Vine", Darwin exclaimed:

> "Drink deep, sweet youths", Vitis [Vine] cries,
> The maudlin tear-drop glittering in her eyes;
> Green leaves and purple clusters crown her head,
> And the tall Thyrsus stays her tottering tread.
> – Five hapless swains [male aspects of the vine] with soft assuasive smiles
> The harlot meshes in her deathful toils;
> "Drink deep", she carols, as she waves in air
> The mantling goblet, "and forget your care". –
> O'er the dread feast malignant Chemia scowls,
> And mingles poison in her nectar'd bowls;
> Fell Gout peeps grinning through the slimy scene,
> And bloated Dropsy pants behind unseen;
> Wrapp'd in his robe white Lepra hides his stains,
> And silent Frenzy writhing bites his chains.

Loves of the Plants, lines 357–370.

204 *Vitis vinifera* of the family *Vitaceae* is known as the Common Grape Vine.

205 Chymia, the personification of alchemy.

206 In Greek mythology, Prometheus was the Titan punished as such for bringing culture and fire to humankind.

207 *Cyclamen*, the genus of several species of flowering plants of the family *Myrsinaceae*, commonly known as sowbread and shrewbread.

208 The Plague devastated London in 1665–1666 and spread throughout Britain. Some communities, notably Anna Seward's birthplace, the village of Eyam in Derbyshire, imposed a self-quarantine which, although impeding its spread, led to the death of 75% of the village. For more on the London plague encounter, see Daniel Defoe's graphic narrative, long thought to be history, but partly fictitious, *A Journal of The Plague Year* (1722) and a recent best-selling fictionalized historical account of the village of Eyam, Geraldine Brooks, *Year of Wonders* (New York: Penguin, 2002).

209 Darwin used "chaunted" rather than "chanted".

210 Seward's own footnote, "During the last great plague in London, one pit, to receive the dead, was dug in the Charter House, forty feet long, sixteen feet wide, and twenty feet deep, and in two weeks received 1114 bodies. During this dire calamity there were instances of mothers carrying their own children to those public graves; and of people delirious, or in despair for the loss of friends, who threw themselves alive into these pits. See [Defoe's] *Journal of the Plague in 1665*, printed for E. Nutt, Royal Exchange".

211 *Cleome* is a genus of many species of flowering plants, traditionally classed within the family *Capparaceae*, but more recently some of which are classed in the family *Cleomaceae*, among the most common being *Cleome hassleriana* also known as the spider flower.

212 Darwin used "unconscious" instead of "unmindful".

213 Darwin used "circled" instead of "cradled".

214 Charterhouse. See Seward's own footnote just above, regarding the plague.

215 Darwin, *Loves of the Plants*, III, lines 387–412.

216 Seward rewrites Darwin's *Loves of the Plants* III.391–92, substituting "ghastly" for his "ebon".

217 The genus of hundreds of species of the family *Fabaceae*. In Darwin's era, this genus (now reclassified under the genus *Senna*), included the plants whose sun dried leaves produced senna and the fruits or pods produced pectin. *Cinnamomum aromaticum*, also classed as *Cinnamomum cassia*, of the family *Lauraceae*, commonly known as Chinese Cinnamon, is closely related to "true" cinnamon.

218 *Exodus* 2:1–10.

219 Darwin used "twinkling" instead of "sparkling".

220 Darwin, *Loves of the Plants*, III, lines 441–462.

221 Darwin, *Loves of the Plants*, III, Interlude, pp.136–137.

222 Darwin, *Loves of the Plants*, III, Interlude, p.139, though Darwin used "both borrowed" instead of "taken from other writers". For further discussion of plagiarism of this era, see Tilar J. Mazzeo, *Plagiarism and Literary Property in the Romantic Period* (Philadelphia: University of Pennsylvania Press, 2007).

223 Thomas Gray (1716–1771), "The Progress of Poetry: A Pindaric Ode" (1757), ll. 119–20.

224 Darwin, *Loves of the Plants*, IV, lines 9–10, though Darwin used the plural, "oaks" in line 9.

225 Pope, *Eloisa to Abelard*, l. 306.

226 Milton, *Comus* (1637), ll. 230–30. Milton's lines are: "Sweet Echo, sweetest nymph, that liv'st unseen/Within thy airy cell".

227 This is Seward's own contribution.

228 Darwin, *Loves of the Plants*, IV, lines 11–12.

229 *Selenicereus grandiflora*, the plant belonging to the cactus family *Cactaceae*, commonly referred to as the Night Blooming Cereus or Queen of the Night, noting the time of its bloom.

230 Francis Noel Clarke Mundy (1739–1815).

231 Wife of Oberon and Queen of the Fairies in Shakespeare's (1564–1616) *A Midsummer Night's Dream*.

232 The evening star.

233 Francis Mundy, *Needwood Forest* (1776), ll. 57–82. "Disafforestation and inclosure came at the beginning of the 19th century. In spite of an organized opposition in favour of regulated pasturing, an Inclosure Act was passed in 1801 which provided that Needwood should cease to be a forest from Christmas Day 1802 ....The dismemberment of Needwood was greeted with mixed feelings. It was hoped that the morals of the people would benefit: 'An extensive forest is not favourable to the virtue and industry of its poorer inhabitants; it affords temptations to idleness and dishonesty. On the other hand, the destruction of the forest scenery was lamented by Francis Mundy in his *Fall of Needwood*'", as recorded in M.W. Greenslade and J.G. Jenkins (eds) *The Victoria History of the County of Stafford* (London: University of London Institute for Historical Research, 1967), Vol.2, p.354.

234 Francis Noel Clarke Mundy (1739–1815).

235 *Tropaeolum majus* of the family *Tropaeolaceae*, commonly known as the Garden Nasturtium or Indian Cress.

236 Darwin used "blushing" instead of "milky".

237 Darwin used "his" instead of "its".

238 Darwin, *Loves of the Plants*, IV, lines 43–46.

239 *Daniel 2*.

240 In Christian tradition, the Seraphim are the highest rank of Angels.

241 Darwin, *Loves of the Plants*, IV, lines 67–70.

242 A genus of several species of true grasses of the family *Poaceae*, commonly known as oats.

243 A genus of a few species of flowering plants of the family *Cannabaceae*, from which hemp is produced. In more recent times, it has most widely been cultivated for the psychoactive effects produced by its cannabinoid content. For more insight, see Martin Booth, *Cannabis: A History* (New York: Picador, 2005).

244 Darwin used "massy" instead of "many".

245 A multi-storied Buddhist tower, erected as a shrine or memorial.

246 Darwin, *Loves of the Plants*, lines 109–116.

247 A spinning tool.

248 In Greek mythology, the three goddesses of fertility, charm, and beauty: namely Aglaia (Brightness), Thalia (Bloom), and Euphrosyne (Joyfulness).

249 Darwin, *Loves of the Plants*, IV, lines 133–136.

250 One of a few species of this genus in the family *Amaryllidaceae*. Known as the common snowdrop, it is, in many climates, among the first blooms of spring.

251 The common cuckoo (*Cuculus canorus*).

252 Rodents in the family *Gliridae*.

253 Ringneck or Ring Dove (*Streptopelia risoria*).

254 Robin redbreast (*Erithacus rubecula*).

255 Species of the *Prolifera*, or English Daisy, of the family *Compositae*, most commonly known as "Hens and Chickens".

256 Common name of *Campanula rotundifolia*, a bellflower of the family *Campanulaceae*.

257 Common name of *Primula vulgaris*, of the family of flowering plants *Primulaceae*, commonly known as the Primrose, the Common Primrose, or the English Primrose.

258 Darwin, *Loves of the Plants*, IV, line 152.

259 The genus of brown alga of the family *Fucacea*, commonly called pondweed.

260 *John 5:1–16* relates the miracle performed at the Pool of Bethesda. In 1736, William Hogarth (1697–1764) commemorated this healing miracle in a mural of the same name in the staircase entrance to the Great Hall of St Bartholomew's Hospital in London.

261 Basing his account upon Priestley's *Vegetable Respiration*, Darwin encourages his readers to see his "Vegetable Respiration", in *Economy of Vegetation*, pp.101–105, Note 37. He also informs his readers that Priestley "found that great quantities of pure dephlogisticated air were given up in water at the points of this vegetable, particularly in the sunshine, and that hence it contributed to preserve the water in reservoirs from becoming putrid. The minute divisions of the leaves of subaquatic plants, as mentioned in the note on Trapa, and of the gills of fish, seem to serve another purpose besides that of increasing their surface, which has not, I believe, been attended to, and that is to facilitate the separation of the air, which is mechanically mixed or chemically dissolved in water by their points or edges; this appears on immersing a dry hairy leaf in water fresh from a pump; innumerable globules like quicksilver appear on almost every point; for the extremities of these points attract the particles of water less forcibly than those

particles attract each other; hence the contained air, whose elasticity was but just balanced by the attractive power of the surrounding particles of water to each other, finds at the point of each fibre a place where the resistance to its expansion is less; and in consequence it there expands, and becomes a bubble of air. It is easy to foresee that the rays of the sunshine, by being refracted and in part relieved by the two surfaces of these minute air-bubbles, must impart to them much more heat than to the transparent water; and thus facilitate their ascent by further expanding them; that the points of vegetables attract the particles of water less than they attract each other, is seen by the spherical form of dew-drops on the points of grass" (*Loves of the Plants*, I, p.156, note).

262 The genus of two species of floating aquatic plants of the family *Trapaceae*, commonly known as water chestnuts or water caltrops.

263 Darwin used "the" instead of "its".

264 Darwin, *Loves of the Plants*, IV, lines 203–220.

265 Milton, *Paradise Lost*, II.650–52.

266 The Abbe Juan Ignacio Molina (1740–1829) mentioned this species in *The Geographical, Natural, and Civil History of Chili* (London, Longman, Hurst, Rees, and Orme, 1809), although this species of basil is now identified as *Ocymum basilium* of the family *Labiatae*. For a review of this modification, see Helen Noyes Webster, "A Correction: Notes on the True Identity of *Ocymum salinum*, the so-called 'Saline Basil' of Chile", *The Herbarist* 3 (1937): 40–41.

267 Thus, we draw it to your attention here: In Dr Darwin's words, as "an article of diet, salt seems to act simply as a stimulus, not containing any nourishment, and is the only fossil substance which the caprice of mankind has yet taken into their stomachs along with their food; and, like all other unnatural stimuli, is not necessary to people in health, and contributes to weaken our system; though it may be useful as a medicine. It seems to be the immediate cause of the sea-scurvy, as those patients quickly recover by the use of fresh provisions; and is probably a remote cause of scrophula (which consists in the want of irritability in the absorbent vessels), and is therefore serviceable to these patients; as wine is necessary to those whose stomachs have been weakened by its use. The universality of the use of salt with our food, and in our cookery, has rendered it difficult to prove the truth of these observations. I suspect that flesh-meat cut into thin slices, either raw or boiled, might be preserved in coarse sugar or treacle; and thus a very nourishing and salutary diet might be presented to our seamen" (*Loves of the Plants*, IV, p.159, note).

268 In Greek mythology, musical god and husband of Eurydice, whose lyre held the power to charm.

269 In Greek mythology, Aneas, the son of Anchises and Aphrodite, was a Trojan hero who married Creusa, the daughter of Priam and Hecuba.

270 *Genesis* 19 describes how God employed "brimstone and fire" to destroy these cities for the impenitent sins of their inhabitants.

271 Revd. William Mason (1724–1797).

272 Darwin, *Loves of the Plants*, IV, lines 277–282.

273 Included in William Mason, *Odes* (Cambridge: J. Bentham, 1756).

274 William Mason (1725–1797), "Ode on the Fate of Tyranny" (1756), III.3.4–9. Seward's second line differs from Mason's, which he writes in God's voice: "I'll spread the stagnant flood".

275 A genus of several species of flowering plants of the family *Araceae*.

276 In Greek mythology, Dejanira was the daughter of Oeneus, King of Calydon, who was given to Hercules in marriage. She eventually gave Hercules a tunic – the Tunic of Nessus – which she knew would disclose his infidelity. Disfigured by the tunic, Hercules laid himself on a funeral pyre on Mount Oeta. Handel, who had become an English citizen and composer for the Chapel Royal, featured this tale as part of his 1745 musical drama, *Hercules*.

277 Flowering plant of the family *Caryophyllaceae*, known as Proud Pink.

278 *Dianthus caryophyllus* a species of the family *Caryophyllaceae,* commonly known as Clove Pink.

279 This fable was a favorite of Sir William "Persian" Jones (1746–1794).

280 According to Dr Darwin, this is "the name which the natives give to this plant; it is the *Hedylarum gyrans*, or moving plant; its class is two brotherhoods, ten males. Its leaves are continually in spontaneous motion; some rising and others falling; and others whirling circularly by twisting their stems; this spontaneous movement of the leaves, when the air is quite still and very warm, seems to be necessary to the plant, as perpetual respiration is to animal life" (*Loves of the Plants*. IV, p.168, note).

281 The summer solstice marks the official first day of the season of summer in the northern hemisphere where it is also the longest day (and the beginning of winter and shortest day in the southern hemisphere). The declination of the Sun on the (northern hemisphere) summer solstice is known as the Tropic of Cancer.

282 The dusty wind on the Atlantic coast of Africa.

283 The Atlas Mountain range in northwest Africa which runs from Morocco to Tunisia.

284 The river in western Africa flowing through Senegal into the Atlantic.

285 Chunda, *Solanum torvum*, is a hardwood shrub of the family *Solanaceae*, commonly known as Turkey berry or Devil's Fig.

286 The arches of light that appear along the earth's magnetic field lines in the Northern Hemisphere.

287 According to Dr Darwin, "*Corallinus*, or *lichen rangiferinus*" also Coral-moss. This moss "vegetates beneath the snow, where the degree of heat is always about 40; that is, in the middle between the freezing point, and the common heat of the earth; and is for many months of the winter the sole food of the rain-deer, who digs furrows in the snow to find it: and as the milk and flesh of this animal is almost the only sustenance which can be procured during the long winters of the higher latitudes, this moss may be said to support some millions of mankind. The quick vegetation that occurs on the solution of the snows in high latitudes appears very astonishing; it seems to arise from two causes, 1. the long continuance of the approaching sun above the horizon; 2. the increased irritability of plants which have been long exposed to the cold" (*Loves of the Plants*, IV, pp.169–170, note).

288 Linnaeus identified several species of the alga *Conferva aegagropila*.

289 The largest lake in Scotland.

290 Darwin, *Loves of the Plants*, IV, line 367.

291 Dr Darwin is the bard in reference.

292 Darwin used "wavering" instead of "waving".

293 Darwin used "shifting" instead of "rising".

294 Seward's own footnote, "Hero was a Priestess of Venus".

295 Darwin used the singular, "tide".

296 Darwin, *Loves of the Plants*, IV, lines 385–394.

297 The edible fruiting body of the subterranean plant of the genus *Tuber*, family *Tuberaceae*.

298 Minerals, including chrysotile, that separate into long flexible fibers.

299 *Ficus carica caprifica*, of the family *Moraceae*, known as caprifigs or wild figs.

300 The common small brown finch.

301 A long filament excreted by mussels and other mollusks by which they attach themselves to rocks along the sea bed.

302 Fingal's Cave, the sea cave in Western Scotland off Staffa Island which Sir Joseph Banks found in 1772 and which became named after the hero of James Macpherson's epic poem. Felix Mendelssohn-Bartholdy's (1809–1847) visit to this cave in 1829 was the inspiration behind his Opus 26 "Hebrides (also called 'Fingal's Cave') Overture" of 1830.

303 Thomas Pennant (1726–1798) *A Tour in Scotland 1769 [with] A Tour in Scotland and Voyage to the Hebrides* (Warrington, Chester: Eyres, Monk, 1774).

304 A green alga of the family *Scarabaeoidea*.

305 Leopard.

306 Society of Tahiti.

307 James Cook, *An Account of the Voyages for Making Discoveries in the Southern Hemisphere. A Voyage Towards the South Pole, and A Voyage to the Pacific Ocean*, First Voyage (1768–1771), three volumes (London: W. Strahan, 1773); Second Voyage (1772–1775), two volumes and atlas (London: W. Strahan, 1777); Third Voyage (1776–1780), three volumes and atlas (London: G. Nicol, 1784). Upon hearing of the death of Captain Cook on the shore of the Sandwich Islands, Anna Seward composed *An Elegy on Captain Cook; To Which is Added an Ode to the Sun* (London: J. Dodsley, 1780), a work which became widely known and which served to establish Seward's reputation as a poet. Darwin who, some claim, contributed much to the particular writing of this work of Seward, cites two lines from this *Elegy* in *Loves of the Plants*, Interlude III, p.138. David Samwell (1751–1798), a Welsh poet and naval surgeon, who served on Captain Cook's Third Voyage and witnessed Cook's death, was a correspondent of Anna Seward's. Seward's writing on Cook is still discussed in many works and exhibits regarding Cook, including, among others, Bernard Smith, "Cook's Posthumous Reputation", in R. Fisher and H. Johnston (eds) *Captain James Cook and His Times* (Vancouver: Douglas and McIntyre, 1979), p.167, Bernard Smith, *European Vision and the South Pacific* (New Haven, CT: Yale University Press, 1985), and Dan O'Sullivan *In Search of Captain Cook: Exploring the Man Through his own Words* (London: I.B. Tauris, 2008). Lord Carlisle, to whom Seward dedicated her *Life of Dr Darwin*, also held great interest in Cook's voyages, and he purchased Joshua Reynolds's 1779 portrait of "Omai" for Castle Howard in 1796. Cook had transported Omai from Tahiti to England on his Second Voyage where Britain's natural philosophers wished to evaluate this "savage's" responses to "civilized" Western virtues. In turn, Omai hoped to gain British support that would allow him to confront those who had driven him from his native island, Raiatea. Omai returned to Tahiti on Cook's Third Voyage. For an overview of this encounter between two worlds, see Richard Connaughton, *Omai: The Prince Who Never Was* (London: Timewell Press, 2005).

308 Darwin, *Loves of the Plants*, IV, lines 491–500.

Chapter VII

Before Dr Darwin stood forth a candidate for the Delphic laurels,[1] he was extremely alive to the beauties of poetic literature, as it rose and expanded around him. No person could be more ready to discern and to praise its graces; but, from the commencement of the *Botanic Garden*, the jealous spirit of authorism darkened his candor. When, with avowed delight in the poetic powers of Cowper's *Task*, the writer of these strictures, in conversation with Dr Darwin and Sir Brooke Boothby, asked their opinion of that poem, each declared they could not read it through; each taxed it with egotism, with prosaicism, with a rough and slovenly style, and with utter want of regular design. Perhaps those censures, unbalanced by just praise, should not, however, be imputed solely to unworthy jealousy in either of those gentlemen; certainly not to Sir Brooke, at any rate, who, with all his native brilliance of fancy, was never tenacious of the Muses' favors. Both had always preferred rhyme to blank verse, asserting that it better suited the nature of our language. Dr Darwin had ever maintained a preference of Akenside's blank verse to Milton's; declared that it was of higher polish, of more classic purity, and more dignified construction. This preference may fairly allow us to place his blindness to the charms of the *Task* to the score of taste somewhat enervated by too much refinement, rather than to soreness under rival reputation. A still more scrupulous attachment to classic elegance attaches to the opinions of Sir Brooke, respecting Poetry. It was thence, doubtless, that he became disgusted by the planless wanderings of Cowper's Muse, in her principal work, and by the occasional roughness and prosaicism of its style. Another prejudice in the minds of each was likely to have operated in producing this injustice to Cowper. Previous to the *Task* he had published poems in rhyme, into which they had probably looked. In those poems, whatever strength of thought may be found, the poetic essentials certainly are not, inharmonious as is their versification; barren as they are of landscape and picture, metaphor and imagery.

The author of the *Task* was more just to Darwin than he had been to that spirited, that interesting, that often sublime, though not faultless composition. About the year 1792, Mr Cowper sent Dr Darwin a lively and pleasing encomium in verse upon the *Botanic Garden*.[2] This agreeable eulogy justly says, no Poet who can refuse to bestow a wreath on Darwin deserves to obtain one for himself. It was accompanied by another poetic tribute from Mr Hayley, of yet warmer praise and more brilliant grace.[3]

Mr Polwhele [4] also addressed a fine sonnet to Dr Darwin on his *Botanic Garden*,[5] who, by inserting it in his work, proved that he thought highly of its merit, and that he considered such praise as genuine fame. The neglect of Mr Polwhele's poetic writings is a disgrace to the present period of English literature.

Our botanic Poet had in general no taste for Sonnets, and particularly disliked Milton's. The characteristic beauties of the legitimate sonnet, its nervous condensation of idea, the graceful undulation of its varied pause, which blends with the sweetness of rhyme the dignity of blank verse, were all lost on Dr Darwin, at least from the time in which he entertained the design of becoming a professed poet. Absorbed in the resolve of bringing the couplet-measure to a degree of sonorous perfection, which should transcend the numbers of Dryden and Pope, he sought to confine poetic excellence exclusively to that style.

> "Desiring much the letter'd world might own
> The countless forms of beauty only one".[6]

From the time at which Dr Darwin left Lichfield to reside at Derby *(Figure 30)*, on the irresistible injunction of Love, the author of these memoirs will not attempt to trace more than the outline of his destiny, not possessing the means of giving its interior parts with sufficient precision.

The pen which on these leaves has pursued him through his ascending day to its meridian, may yet remark that Dr Darwin's reputation as a poet first emanated from Derby, though his Delphic *inspirations* commenced at Lichfield; that as a physician his renown still increased as time rolled on, and his mortal life declined from its noon. Patients resorted to him, more and more from every part of the kingdom, and often from the Continent. All ranks, all orders of society, all religions leaned upon his power to ameliorate disease, and to prolong existence. The rigid and sternly pious, who had attempted to renounce his aid from a supposition that no blessing would attend the prescriptions of a sceptic, sacrificed, after a time, their superstitious scruples to their involuntary consciousness of his mighty skill.

Wealth must have flowed in rapidly beneath employment of unprecedented extent, at least in any country practitioner; and from the large sums for which he sold the copy-right of his writings, poetic and philosophic. The sweet temper and benevolence of that long adored wife,[7] for whose sake he had changed his sphere of action; the numerous young family which rose and bloomed around him, rendered the Lares [8] of his hearth not less

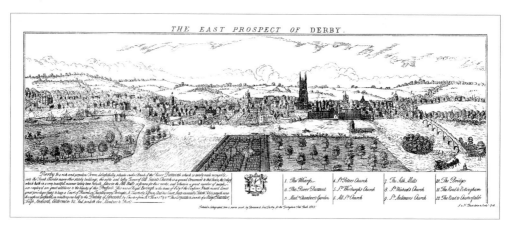

Figure 30: The East Prospect of Derby. Courtesy of Archives and Heritage, Birmingham Central Library.

auspicious to Darwin than he had found the gifts of fortune and the voice of Renown. His son Erasmus, by the former wife, had settled at Derby nearly as soon as himself went thither, and in the profession of the law obtained considerable practice, with a fair reputation.[9] The talents and virtues of his youngest son, by the first marriage, were making every promise of that prosperity which has since been amply fulfilled.

The *Zoonomia*, of so much elder birth than the *Botanic Garden*,[10] suffered her poetic younger sister to precede her on their entrance into the world of letters, and did not herself appear till the year 1794. Of the *Zoonomia* sufficient has been said in the former part of this biography, considering the writer's limited powers to speak of its excellences and defects.

About thirteen or fourteen years after Dr Darwin's second marriage, the Miss Parkers, his relations,[11] opened a female boarding-school at Ashbourne in Derbyshire *(Figure 31).*[12] To the education of those ingenious and good young women he had paid some general attention, and had sedulously and warmly, by recommendation and by other means, exerted himself to serve them. To promote the success of their undertaking he published, on its commencement, a small tract on Female Education.[13] The precise time of its appearance is not recollected. The composition was by no means worthy of Dr Darwin's exalted abilities. Its subject cannot be supposed to have employed much of his consideration.

The system of his whole life on that theme had been at war with all sorts of restraint on the time, the amusements, and the diet of children. Irony was the only corrective weapon he had ever used to his own. The docility of them all, and the talents and good qualities of

Figure 31: View of the Grounds from Ashbourne Hall from the Vantage point of the Miss Parkers' Boarding School.

his three eldest sons, one, alas! cut off in the dawn of manhood and of fame, and the happy prospects of the other two, had confirmed his disdain of incessant attention to young people. He always said, "If you would not have your children arrogant, conceited, and hypocritical, do not let them perceive that you are continually watching and attending to them; nor can you keep that perpetual watch without their perceiving it. Inspire them with a disdain of meanness, falsehood, and promise-breaking; but do not try to effect this purpose by precept and declamation, but as occasion arises, by expressed contempt of such as commit those faults, whether it be themselves or others. Teach them benevolence and industry by your own example, for children are emulous to acquire the habits of advanced life, and attach to them an idea of dignity and importance".[14]

Perhaps, if Dr Darwin had to this incomplicate [sic] and so easily practicable system, added the inspiration of religion by the same means, viz. expressed contempt for impiety, and daily example of grateful devotion, it would better answer the end of making wise and good men and women, than all the laboured Treatises on Education which have, of late years, been poured from the press; Treatises so universally read, so seldom, if ever, even in the slightest degree, reduced to practice! In truth they must be found impracticable, inconsistent as they are with the established habits of society. Obedience to their directions must devote every present generation, at least the maternal part of every present generation, to preparing the future. Every mother must be wholly absorbed in word-watching, and look-watching, and all this by *book*.

Yet was Dr Darwin aware that these voluminous receipts to make human angels, or to make practical philosophers of every boy and girl in the higher and middle classes of life, were too popular for him, without sacrificing the design of his Tract, to bring against them his own conciser plan; which, if rational, does away the utility of them all. His little work could not serve Miss Parkers if it combated the educating metaphysicians and their unobeying admirers. Avoiding such combat, his Treatise would certainly call the attention of the neighbourhood to the seminary for which it was written. Some good rules for promoting the health of growing children will be found on its pages, and they promised unseed [sic] attention from its author to the diseased in that school. On the whole, however, it is a meagre work, of little general interest, those rules excepted, and with an odd recommendation of certain novels, of no eminence, to the perusal of young people. That was one of those follies of the wise, which daily present themselves to our surprised attention.

In the year 1791 a splendid archery-meeting [15] was held at Drakelow in Staffordshire,[16] the seat of Sir Nigel Gresley.[17] Miss Susan Sneyd,[18] of Belmont, was distinguished by her skill and success in the contest of that day. Honoured by Dr Darwin's celebration, her name and her unerring arrow, are on permanent record. The verses he wrote on that occasion appeared in the Derby paper anonymously.[19] There were people who pretended to be judges of verse, and yet were in doubt concerning their author. Before Dr Darwin acknowledged them, they were attributed to various versifiers; and when the writer of this Tract, who saw the Darwinian stamp on the lines at one glance, declared they must be his, her assertion was repeatedly combated, as if the peculiar style and manner of his muse were not instantly apparent.

On a Target at Drakelow

With sylvan bow, on Drakelow's shadowy green,
Arm'd like Diana,[20] trod the Cyprian Queen;[21]
O'er her fair brow the beamy crescent shone,
And starry spangles glitter'd round her zone;
Love's golden shafts her snow-white shoulders press'd,
And the fring'd ribbon cross'd upon her breaft.

With careless eye she view'd the central ring,
Stretch'd her white arms, and drew the silken string!
Mute wonder gaz'd the brazen studs betwixt;
Full in the boss the flying arrow fix'd!
Admiring circles greet the victor fair,
And shouts of triumph rend the breezy air;
Trent, with loud echoes thrills the flowery grounds,
And Burton's [22] towers return applausive sounds.

The graceful Huntress eyes the gaudy grove,
And bends again th' unerring bow of Love.
Now guard your hearts, with playful malice cries,
And wing'd with smiles the shining arrow flies;
With random aim the dazzled crowd she wounds,
The quiver'd heroes strow the velvet grounds;
Beau after beau expiring, prints the plain,
And Beauty triumphs o'er the archer train.

Now, with light bound, she mounts her wreathed car,
Rolls her blue eyes, and waves her golden hair.
Fond youths bow homage as the wheels proceed,
Sigh as they gaze, and call the goddess, SNEYD![23]

There are beautiful lines in this little composition, but it is not faultless. The fourth and fifth couplets form the most striking and elegant picture which poetry can exhibit of a graceful young woman employed in arrow-shooting. The epithet *careless* has the accustomed felicity of this author, in giving character to his portraits; since it implies that perfect consciousness of skill which precludes all strain and effort of attitude, so prejudicial to grace! In these verses Miss Sneyd is described as sending the arrow from the yew, as Dryden [24] makes Cleopatra [25] cast from her eyes the darts of Love, on her voyage down the Cydnus;[26]

As if secure of all Beholders' hearts,
Neglecting she might take them.[27]

The metaphoric shooting which succeeds to acclamations for the fair-one's victory, had perhaps better have been omitted. "Beau after beau", sounds equivocally to the *ear*, in a scene thronged with bows and arrows; besides, beau is in itself an effeminate and uncharacteristic title for a number of young men in the uniform of Woodmen, and in manly sport with a weapon, dignified by its ancientry [sic], and by which Britons of old not only slew the wild boar and the stag, but repelled their foes when warriors cried aloud in the battle,

Draw, Archers, draw your arrows to the head![28]

There is also somewhat too much splendour in the departure of the Conqueress, for why should her vehicle be wreathed? A silver arrow, and not a garland, is the costume of archery reward. However, the final couplet is elegant; the eulogy closing with the name of its subject has an happy effect.

Soon after the death of that variously-charming Poet, Mason, Dr Darwin wrote an Epitaph which he designed should be engraven on his monument. We may be certain, however, that it has not there been inscribed. As an inscription for an urn in a garden or grove, alter a few of the lines for that purpose, and the verses are excellent, though, from being utterly without religious hope or trust, they are improper for a tomb-stone.[29]

For the Monument of The Revd. W. Mason, by Dr Darwin

These awful mansions of the honor'd Dead
Oft shall the Muse of Melancholy tread;
The wreck of Virtue and of Genius mourn,
And point, with pallid hand, to Mason's urn.
Oft shall she gather from his garden bowers [30]
Fictitious foliage and ideal flowers;
Weave the bright wreath, to worth departed just,
And hang unfading chaplets on his bust;
While pale Elfrida,[31] bending o'er his bier,
Breathes the soft sigh and sheds the graceful tear;
And stern Caractacus,[32] with brow depress'd,
Clasps the cold marble to his mailed breast.
In lucid troops shall choral Virgins throng,
With voice alternate chaunt their Poet's song,
And, O! in golden characters record
Each firm, immutable, immortal word!

Those last two lines from the final chorus of *Elfrida*, admirably close this tribute to the memory of him who stands second to Gray as a lyric Poet; whose *English Garden* is one of the happiest efforts of didactic verse; containing the purest elements of horticultural taste; dignified by sentiments of freedom and virtue; rendered interesting by episode, and given in those energetic and undulating measures which render blank verse excellent; whose unowned satires, yet certainly his, the *Heroic Epistle to Sir William Chambers*,[33] and its Postscript, are at once original in their style, harmonious in their numbers, and pointed in their ridicule; whose Tragedies [34] are the only pathetic Tragedies which have been written in our language upon the severe Greek model. The *Samson Agonistes* [35] bears marks of a stronger, but also of an heavier hand, and is unquestionably less touching than the sweet Elfrida, and the sublime Caractacus.

Since these pages were in the press, an *Epitaph on General Wolfe* [36] first met their author's eye in a collection of manuscript poetry; and it bears Dr Darwin's signature. Perfectly in his manner, she cannot doubt its authenticity; else the names of deceased people, of eminence are so often affixed to compositions they never framed, that we ought to look jealously at all which do not carry to the mind of the reader internal evidence of their imputed origin. But for such evidence the ensuing lines had found no place on these pages.

On the Death of General Wolfe

Thy trembling hills, Quebec, when Victory trod,
Shook her high plume, and wav'd her banner broad;
Saw Wolfe advance; heard the dire din of War,
And Gallia's [37] genius shrieking from afar,
With fatal haste th' astonish'd Goddess flew,
To weave th' immortal chaplet for his brow.
Cypress she gather'd with the sacred bays,
And weav'd the asp of Death among the sprays.
They fly! they fly! th' expiring Hero cried,
Hung his wreath'd head; thank'd the kind Gods, and died.[38]

Will the reader again extend indulgence to the spirit of authorism, tenacious beneath a sense of recent injury? As in the course of this little work its writer has claimed her own verses from the splendid poem she analysed, so will he now permit her to disclaim other verses, that, by singular effrontery (her existence considered) have been printed since, with her name affixed. In the Spring 1803, she sent these memoirs to Mr Johnson [39] for publication; she now, January 1804, but first discovered an illegitimate Sonnet in one of the *Gentleman's Magazines* for August or September last,[40] with her signature at full length. It is addressed to Mr Dimond,[41] of whose poetic existence she had never heard, and it praises a poem of his which she has never seen. One line of the forged sonnet begins, "Bright Dimond", thus making a miserable pun from an unfortunate name; and the writer's ear was defective enough to induce his alliterating with the harsh *th* thus,

Young joys awake in many a *th*rilling *th*rong[42]

which last words form completely the Gander's hiss.

She finds also that these alternately – rhyming stanzas, which call themselves *sonnet*, are interpolated, and given as her's [sic], in the 6th Vol. of *Public Characters*,[43] recently published, see page 554 of that Vol. They close anecdotes of her, that have been chiefly collected from previous tracts in the monthly publications. All are of much too partial description; and strangely indeed is the talent of singing agreeably attributed to her, who, conscious of total want of voice, never attempted to sing in her whole life. Amid these latest anecdotes a stanza is quoted from her [44] "Ode to General Elliot on his return from Gibraltar",[45] and the quotation has two gross misprints, "*industrious* soldier" for *illustrious* soldier, and "honour *to* the lap of peace", instead of, honour *on* the lap of peace.

When this sonnet–forgery was contrived, its writer forgot that she, whose name was affixed to it, had, in her Preface to the *Centenary of Legitimate Sonnets*,[46] which she published in 1798, denied to three alternately rhyming stanzas, closing with a couplet, all right to the name of that peculiar and strict order of verse. It was therefore most unlikely that she should herself assume it for fourteen lines, written on the feeble model which she had reprobated.

But it is time to resume a more interesting subject.

The close of the year 1799 brought a severe trial to the stoical fortitude of Dr Darwin. From the period of his second marriage all had been sunshine in his fortune, his fame, and domestic connexions [sic]; but then a storm descended upon his peace; unforeseen, sudden, dreadful! His eldest son, Mr Darwin *(Figure 32)*,[47] so prosperously situated, without one adequate cause for even transient affliction, became the victim of secret and utter despair. It had often been observed that any more than ordinary recurrence of professional business perplexed and oppressed him. A demand was made that he should arrange and settle some complicated accounts, which a disposition to procrastinate had too long delayed. A disposition

Figure 32: Dr Erasmus Darwin (right) playing chess with his son, Erasmus Darwin (1790s), used with Permission of Erasmus Darwin House.

which is always, in a greater or less degree, punished by its consequences. Though a remote, it is the most frequent cause of suicide, accumulating debts till their entanglement becomes inextricable, their weights too heavy to be borne. But in this case it had produced only an accumulation of business. From the necessity of entering upon it Mr Darwin had seemed to shrink with so much dejection of spirit as to induce his partner to intreat that he would leave the inspection solely to his management. He declined the proposal, saying, in a faint voice, that it was impossible.

This was on a December evening,[48] cold and stormy. The river Derwent, which ran at the bottom of his garden, was partially frozen. About seven o'clock he sent his partner out of the way on business, real or pretended. Mr Darwin was on the couch complaining of the head-ach. Soon after eight his partner returning found the parlour vacant. He went to Mr D.'s upstair apartment, vacant also, inquired of the servants; they had not seen their master since this gentleman went out, an hour before. He waited a few minutes expecting his friend's return from the garden. Not appearing, a degree of apprehension seized his mind. He ran thither, and in the walk which leads to the river, he found Mr Darwin's hat and neckcloth. Alarm was immediately given, and boats were sent out. Dr Darwin had been summoned. He staid [sic] a long time on the brink of the water, apparently calm and collected, but doubtless suffering the most torturing anxiety. The body could not be found till the next day. When the Doctor received information that it was found, he exclaimed in a low voice, "Poor insane coward!" and it is said never afterwards mentioned the subject.

Mr Darwin died in very good circumstances, leaving an untainted reputation for probity and benevolence; beloved, respected, and mourned by all who knew him. He never married; had purchased a pretty estate near Derby,[49] which, with all his other effects, he left to his father. The accounts, whose apprehended embarrassment had proved fatal to him, were settled after his death to the satisfaction of all parties.

Though this unfortunate victim of causeless despondency had a gentle, ingenuous, and affectionate heart, he attained middle life without any known or suspected attachment of the impassioned kind. There seemed a want of energy in his character, and too extreme a delicacy of feeling on the occurrence of every thing which was in the slightest degree repulsive. He had never loved business, and his attention to it appeared a force upon his inclinations. While his profession was undetermined, he expressed a wish to go into the Church rather than the Law. That preference was repulsed by paternal sarcasms upon its indolence and imputed effeminacy. From infancy to his last day, Mr Darwin had shrunk, with pained sensibility, from his father's irony. Probably from the less active, less scientific disposition of Erasmus, in comparison with that of his brothers Charles and Robert, Dr Darwin had always appeared colder towards him than to his other children. Doubtless it was that inferior degree of attachment which made the lesson of stoicism somewhat more practicable on this trying, this dire occasion. It excited, however, universal surprise to see him walking along the streets of Derby the day after the funeral of his son,[50] with a serene countenance and his usual cheerfulness of address. This self-command enabled him to take immediate possession of the premises bequeathed to him; to lay plans for their improvement; to take pleasure in describing those plans to his acquaintance, and to determine to make it his future residence; and all this without seeming to recollect to how sad an event he owed their possession!

The folly of suffering our imagination to dwell on past and irretrievable misfortunes, and of indulging fruitless grief, he often pointed out, and always censured. He relied much on self-discipline in that respect, and disdained, from deference to what he termed the prejudices of mankind, to display the outward semblance of unavailing sorrow, since he thought it wisdom to combat its reality. On occasions and subjects which he considered trivial, he professed to indulge human prejudice; but whenever, by mock assent, he extended that indulgence, a slight satiric laugh and a gay disdain lurking in his eye, counteracted the assumed coincidence. On circumstances which touched him nearly, he acted steadily upon his own principles.

And there were subjects out of himself on which he was always seriously and earnestly ingenuous. Politics was one. He hated war, and thought the motives few indeed, which could vindicate its homicide, especially in this commercial and sea-defended country. That of forcing America into internal, unrepresented taxation, and of interfering, through jealousy of her principles, with the internal government of France, he utterly disapproved. The event of both those contests accomplished his prophecies, and justified his disapprobation.

Early in the year, 1800, Dr Darwin published another large quarto volume, entitled, *Phytologia, or the Philosophy of Agriculture and Gardening*.[51] The writer of these pages does not presume to speak her opinion of this production as an whole; the subject did not induce her to read it regularly. Incompetent therefore to declared opinion as her perusal may have been, it has yet convinced her that in parts, at least, it is highly ingenious. Dr Darwin's conviction that vegetables are remote links in the chain of sentient existence, often hinted in the notes to the *Botanic Garden*, is here avowed as a regular system. The *Phytologia* insists that plants have vital organization, sensation, and even volition; and a number of instances are adduced, which seem firmly to support the theory. Certainly those appear to sleep which close their petals at sun-set, and unfold them in the rising day. Dr Darwin tells us that plants possess low heat and cold blood, like winter-sleeping animals, and like them continue the descending scale of existence. From this theory of vegetable sensation some good may proceed, and no evil can flow. If the affluent improver of his paternal or purchased domain, shall be impressed with its belief, such impression must augment his pleasure in attending to the sustenance, the growth, and comfort of his trees, his grain, his shrubs, and his flowers. He will say to himself, "It is I who enable this little world of vegetation, by my care, attention, and kindness, to smile upon the sun, and bask delighted in its rays". The labourer in the field and garden, assured that the grain and the plants he is cultivating will not only nurture his fellow creatures but are *themselves* capable of receiving comfort or discomfort while yet they grow on the earth, will thence feel an additional motive to become worthy of his hire. Every honest heart is gratified by the idea of contributing to the common stock of happiness. It is an idea which produces self-respect in the mind, which, when founded in benevolence, and not in haughtiness, is the fairest and most productive soil in which the virtues can grow, whether those virtues be lowly and plain in ignorance and poverty, or heightened and refined by knowledge and affluence.

Of this theory, however, Dr Darwin is neither the source, nor the first who drew the scattered hints of former philosophers concerning it, into a regular system. The ingenious and excellent Dr Percival,[52] of Manchester, preceded him in maintaining that system from the press. Congeniality on its subject between a mild, a temperate, and religious sage, and a bold philosopher of the modern school, who possessed the eye of a lynx for nature's arcana, leave us little reason to doubt that it is veritable. Why should we suppose the chain of existence broken at the last, inert class of animals, since its continuity is perfectly consonant to the order of creation?

> The chain that leads from infinite to man,
> From man to nothing.
>
> *Night Thoughts.*[53]

The nourishment of plants is next considered with a view to their health and increase; and ingenious experiments are stated. The decomposition of water is asserted to be one of the most important discoveries of modern science.[54] Thence was demonstrated the immense proportion of oxygene or vital air, with which water is impregnated, in comparison with air which is less pure. A plentiful supply of water absolutely necessary to fertilize soil. The wisdom asserted, and the means pointed out, of giving artificial and salutary moisture to arid situations. On the contrary, where the ground is naturally too wet and swampy, the necessity of subterranean and superficial drains is enforced. Sudden and violent showers extremely detrimental, from their washing down the diffusable and soluble parts of the soil into muddy rivers. It is observed, that every such shower conveys through those channels into the sea, many thousand pounds-worth of fertilizing matter, thus considerably diminishing the food of terrestrial animals, however it may add to the sustenance of the aqueous tribes. Great attention is necessary to counteract the mischief of these impetuous and impelling rains, equally noxious to the dry soil and situation, as to those which are irriguous. To such end we are informed that all hills should be ploughed horizontally, and not in ascending and descending furrows; also, that sloping fields of pasture-land might be laid in transverse ridges and depressions. Thus the water of these partial inundations would remain some hours in the horizontal furrows of the ploughed hills, and in the transverse hollows of inclined plains, that are grass-land. These little detaining reservoirs must be a great advantage in parched situations, while in those which are wet and spongy, they might be opened into each other by the spade so as to prevent that loss of soil which must result from the downward rush and speedy passing away of the temporary deluge.

The great waste in towns and cities, of substances capable of being converted into manure, is observed and deplored; and in that respect the better police of China held up to imitation.[55] The author alleges, that similar practice in Europe would at once promote the purity and consequent health of towns, and contribute to the economy and fertility of their surrounding countries. He explains the means of accomplishing purposes so desirable.

Here let the biographic pen arrest its course, nor attempt to follow this penetrating and excursive mind through the wide and complicated mazes of agricultural dissertation. Returning back to the verge of this vast field of treasured observation and scientific literature, the memorialist may be allowed to observe what never-slumbering attention to the operations of nature and the present state of cultivation; what unwearied research into the records of other philosophers, this book evinces! A man of such immense professional engagements as Dr Darwin, composing and publishing this work only, had built his lettered reputation upon no narrow or unstable basis. But when we consider it as a brother-production to the *Zoonomia*, two large quartos, as bulky, as small a type, and as crowded writing as the *Phytologia*; when we consider also his splendid poetic work, with its host of philosophic notes; there is surely no partiality to him, no want of candour to others, in maintaining that it can only be from native littleness or acquired warp of mind, where the greatness and energy of Dr Darwin's genius and knowledge are denied. Yet let it be remembered, that it is poetic eminence, not pre-eminence, which has here been demanded for his muse. Superlative epithets have found no place in his eulogium on these pages; for their author remembers and reveres the exalted claims of his poetic predecessors and contemporaries of the eighteenth century. Incomparable, unrivalled, matchless, are terms of applause which can only be, with truth, applied to three men of genius in times past; to Shakespeare as a dramatic poet;[56] to Newton as a philosopher; to Handel as a musician; not to Homer, not to Milton, since they stand abreast with each other, and divide the epic palm. Perhaps, without trespass on literary truth, Gray might also be termed peerless, as a lyric poet, since he equals Pindar in the dignity of his language, in the sublimity of his imagery, and in the interwoven morality, alternately aweful and tender; and since he chose subjects so much more exalted than the Pindaric [57] themes, for those two great Odes which place him first at the goal of the Lyric Muse. Their measures are magnificent and harmonious to the utmost power of the English tongue. Pindar could not carry that excellence higher in the Greek language; therefore if any superiority remains to the ancient classic, respecting his metre, it must result from the more sonorous tones of the Greek, not from transcendence of genius in its great lyrist, compared with the British poet. Whatever importance the fashion of that period might attach to Pindar's themes, however mythologic and historic allusion might give them auxiliar elevation, yet the foot-races of children, though the sons of princes, and the chariot-races of youthful heroes, possess no eternity of attraction compared to the subject of Gray's *Progress of Poesy*,[58] and of his Bard. For the first, the physical and moral powers of the muses; their universal influence, in different degrees, in every clime; the three great seats of their empire, Greece, Italy, and England, Dramatic, Epic, and Lyric Poetry, supported in Britain by Shakespeare, Milton, and Dryden.

For the second, and still greater Ode, the sanguinary crime against the Muses committed by an otherwise illustrious monarch, the supposed consequences of that crime, a train of misfortunes to the remaining line of the Plantagenets;[59] its regal sons,

Another and another gold-bound brow,[60]

passing before us in the awful obscurity, the "darkness visible" of poetic prophecy; the accession of another royal house, in which the rival roses were entwined; the brilliant reign of its virgin queen, who was to carry the prosperity and the renown of a great nation to its utmost line; the day of poesy, sunk in eclipse from the period of the massacre, rising again with redoubled splendour in that epoch; the exultation of the Cambrian Bard[61] who thus foresees the restored glory of his art in the genius of him who sung the fairy region, and by that of the mighty master of the sock and buskin; the continuance of that glory through future times by the Song of Eden,[62] and the strains of successive warblers; the exultation closing by the plunge of the injured Bard amid Conway's[63] deep and tumultuous flood! Can pedestrian speed, and the dexterity of the whip and rein, by any effort of talent, be raised to the intrinsic grandeur of themes like these? Ah! when will our schools and universities, exchange classical partiality for patriotism, and become just to the exalted merits of the English Poets? To that sincere and ardent patriotism the author of these memoirs hopes will be remitted her tributary digression to the fame of Gray.

Sunday, the eighteenth of April, 1802, deprived Derby and its vicinity, and the encircling counties, of Dr Darwin; the lettered world of his genius. During a few preceding years he had been subject to sudden and alarming disorders of the chest, in which he always applied the lancet instantly and freely; he had repeatedly risen in the night and bled himself. It was said that he suspected *angina pectoris* to be the cause of those his sudden paroxysms, and that it would produce sudden death. The conversation which he held with Mrs Darwin and her friend,[64] the night before he died, gave colour to the report. In the preceding year he had a very dangerous illness.[65] It originated from a severe cold caught by obeying the summons of a patient in Derby, after he had himself taken strong medicine. His skill, his courage, his exertion, struggled vehemently with his disease. Repeated and daring use of the lancet at length subdued it, but, in all likelihood, irreparably weakened the system. He never looked so well after as before his seizure; increased debility of step, and, a certain wanness of countenance, awakened those fears for him which great numbers felt who calculated upon his assistance when hours of pain and danger might come. It was said, that during his illness he reproved the sensibility and tears of Mrs Darwin, and bid her remember that she was the wife of a philosopher.

The public papers and magazines recorded, with tolerable accuracy, the nature of his final seizure; the conversation he held in the garden of his new residence *(Figure 33)*, the Priory,[66] with Mrs Darwin and her female friend;[67] the idea which he communicated to them, that he was not likely to live to see the effect of those improvements he had planned; Mrs Darwin affectionately combating that idea by observing, that he looked remarkably well that evening; his reply that he had generally found himself in his best health a few days preceding his attacks; the spirits and strength with which he arose the next morning at six to write letters; the large draught of cold butter-milk, which, according to his usual custom, he had swallowed. All these circumstances early met the public eye; and, in the

Figure 33: Breadsall Priory, near Derby. The house Erasmus Darwin, Jr. had purchased just before his death. Dr and Mrs Darwin moved here in March 1802, and it was here that Dr Darwin died the following month.

imperfect sketches of his life which accompanied them, a strange habit was imputed to Dr Darwin, which presents such an exterior of idiot-seeming indelicacy that the author of this tract is tempted to express her entire disbelief of its truth; viz. that his tongue was generally hanging out of his mouth as he walked along. She has often, of late years, met him in the streets of Lichfield, alone and musing, and never witnessed a custom so indecent. From the early loss of his teeth he looked much older than he was. That loss exposes the tongue to view while speaking, and Dr Darwin's mouth certainly thus disclosed the ravages of time, but by no means in any offensive degree.

It was the general opinion that a glass of brandy might have saved him for that time. Its effects would have been more powerful from his utter disuse of spirits; but such was the abhorrence in which he held them, that it is probable no intreaties could have induced him to have swallowed a dram, though surely, on any sudden chill of the blood, its effects, so injurious on habitual application, might have proved restoring.

On that last morning, he had written one page of a very sprightly letter to Mr Edgeworth, describing the Priory, and his purposed alterations there, when the fatal signal was given.[68] He rang the bell, and ordered his servant to send Mrs Darwin up to him. She came immediately, with his daughter, Miss Emma Darwin. They saw him shivering and pale. He desired them to send directly to Derby for his surgeon, Mr Hadley.[69] They did so; but it was all over before he could arrive.

It was reported at Lichfield, that, perceiving himself growing rapidly worse, he said to Mrs Darwin, "My dear, you must bleed me instantly". "Alas, I dare not, lest…". "Emma, will you? There is no time to be lost". "Yes, my dear father, if you will direct me". At that moment he sunk into his chair, and expired!

The body was opened,[70] but it was said the surgeons found no traces of peculiar disease; that the state of the viscera indicated a much more protracted existence; yet thus, in one hour, was extinguished that vital light which the preceding hour had shone in flattering brightness, promising duration; such is often the "cunning flattery of nature"; that light, which, through half a century, had diffused its radiance and its warmth so widely; that light, in which penury had been cheered, in which science had expanded; to whose orb Poetry had brought all her images; before whose influence Disease had continually retreated, and Death so often turned aside his levelled dart!

Awful is the lesson of such an extinction; trebly awful in its suddenness. Let no one say that it is not more awful than the similar destiny of ordinary human beings; for the impression made by unexpected, immediate, and everlasting absence, will be diffusive, will be strong, in proportion to the abilities and usefulness of those who vanish at once from society. We feel the solemn lesson sink deep into our hearts, when minds, so largely endowed and adorned, evince, in their fate, the truths uttered by that sublime Poet,[71] who made the threats and the promises of the Gospel the theme of his midnight strains; and thus they admonish,

By nature's law, what must be, may be *now*;
There's no prerogative in human hours.
In human hearts what bolder thought can rise

Than man's presumption on to-morrow's dawn?
Where is to-morrow?.... In another world!
For numbers this is certain, the reverse
Is sure to none; and yet, on this perhaps,
This peradventure, infamous for lies,
As on a rock of adamant, we build;
Though every dial warns us as we pass,
Portentous as the written wall, that turn'd,
O'er midnight bowls, the proud Assyrian pale![72]

Another, and the last poetic work of Dr Darwin, is now in the press. The *Temple of Nature*.[73] His memorialist, on these pages, has not seen a line of the composition. The curiosity of the ingenious must be ardently excited to view the setting emanation of this brilliant day-star; they must hope that neither age, disease, nor the dread calamity he had endured, in December 1799, shed mist or cloud upon its rays.

Dr Darwin died in his sixty-ninth year.

This Tract is presented to the Public beneath its author's idea, that it may probably displease two classes of readers, should it attract their notice; the dazzled idolaters of the late Dr Darwin, who will not allow that there were any spots in his sun; and that much larger class, who, from party prejudice, religious zeal, or literary envy, or a combination of all those motives, are unjust to his [74] claims; at least as a Philosopher and Poet. There is another class of readers, who, if these faithful records shall be honoured by their perusal, will feel gratified to see one distinguished character of these times, neither varnished by partiality, nor darkened by prejudice. They must be conscious that human beings, whatever may have been their talents, whatever their good qualities, are seldom found perfect, except on the pages of their eulogists; conscious also, that, while the intellectual powers of the wise and the renowned, excite admiration, their errors may not less usefully be contemplated as warnings, than their virtues as examples.

Lichfield,
April 13, 1803.[75]

The End.

Notes

1   A laurel wreath was awarded to the winners of the Panhellenic Pythian games at Delphi. A similar award, though myrtle rather than laurel, was bestowed upon the winner of the original poetry read before Lady Anne Miller's (1741–1781) fortnightly assemblies in Batheaston.

2   To Dr Darwin

Two Poets, (poets, by report,

Not oft so well agree)

Sweet harmonist of Flora's court!

Conspire to honour thee.

They best can judge a Poet's worth,
Who oft themselves have known
The pangs of a poetic birth,
By labours of their own.

We, therefore pleased, extol thy song,
Though various yet complete,
Rich in embellishment, as strong
And learn'd as it is sweet.

No envy mingles with our praise,
Though could our hearts repine
At any Poet's happier lays,
They would, they must, at thine.

But we in mutual bondage knit
Of friendship's closest tie,
Can gaze on even Darwin's wit
With an unjaundiced eye;

And deem the bard, whoe'er he be,
And howsoever known,
Who would not twine a wreath for thee,
Unworthy of his own.

> W. Cowper, Weston Underwood, Olney, Bucks, June 23, 1793.

3   To Dr Darwin
     As Nature lovely Science led
     Through all her flowery maze,
     The volume she before her spread
     Of Darwin's radiant lays.

     Coy Science starts – so started Eve
     At beauties yet unknown:
     "The figure that you there perceive
     "(Said Nature) is your own".

     "My own? It is:– but half so fair
     "I never seem'd till now:
     "And here, too, with a soften'd air,
     "Sweet Nature! here art thou".

"Yes – in this mirror of the Bard

"We both embellish'd shine;

"And grateful will unite to guard

"An artist so divine".

Thus Nature and thus Science spake

In Flora's friendly bower;

While Darwin's glory seem'd to wake

New life in every flower.

This with delight two poets heard;

Time verifies it daily;

Trust it, dear Darwin, on the word

Of Cowper and of Hayley!

W. Haley. Eartham, near Chichester, June 27, 1792.

For the sake of completeness, it should be noted that The Revd. William Bagshaw Stevens (1756–1800) also addressed a poetic contribution to *The Botanic Garden*, which was published in the preface of several editions.

To The Author of the Poem on the Loves of the Plants

Oft tho' thy genius, D—! amply fraught

With native wealth, explore new worlds of mind;

Whence the bright ores of drossless wisdom brought,

Stampt by the Muse's hand, enrich mankind;

Tho' willing Nature to thy curious eye,

Involved in night, her mazy depths betray;

Till at their source thy piercing search descry

The streams, that bathe with Life our mortal clay;

Tho', boldly soaring in sublimer mood

Through trackless skies on metaphysic wings,

Thou darest to scan the approachless Cause of Good,

And weigh with steadfast hand the Sum of Things;

Yet wilt thou, charm'd amid his whispering bowers

Oft with lone step by glittering Derwent stray,

Mark his green foliage, count his musky flowers,

That blush or tremble to the rising ray;

While FANCY, seated in her rock-roof'd dell,

Listening the secrets of the vernal grove,

Breathes sweetest strains to thy symphonious shell,

And gives new echoes to the throne of Love.

Repton, Nov. 28, 1788

4   Richard Polwhele (1760–1838), divine, poet, and topographer. In response to Polwhele's poem, *The Influence of Local Attachment with Respect to Home. A Poem. In Seven Books* (London: J. Johnson, 1796), Seward issued a sympathetic poem entitled, "Sonnet, to the Revd. Richard Polwhele, On his Poem upon the Influence of Local Attachment", in her *Poetical Works*, Vol.3, 50–52, is as follows:

Polwhele, whose genius, in the colours clear

Of poesy and philosophic art,

Traces the sweetest impulse of the heart,

Scorn, for thy Muse, the envy-sharpen'd spear,

In darkness thrown, when shielded by desert

She seeks the lyric fane. To virtue dear

Thy verse esteeming, feeling minds impart

Their vital smile, their consecrating tear.

Fancy and judgment view with gracious eyes

Its kindred tints, that paint the silent power

Of local objects, deeds of high emprize

To prompt; while their delightful spells restore

The precious vanish'd days of former joys,

By Love, or Fame, enwreath'd with many a flower.

5   To Dr Darwin

While Sargent winds with fond and curious eyes,

Through every mazy region of "the mine –"

While, as entrancing forms around him rise,

With magic light the mineral kingdoms shine;

Behold! amid the vegetable bloom,

O Darwin, thy ambrosial rivers flow,

And suns more pure the fragrant earth illume,

As all the vivid plants with passion glow.

Yes! – and, where'er with life creation teems,

I trace thy spirit through the kindling whole;

As with new radiance to the genial beams

Of Science, isles emerge, or oceans roll,

And Nature, in primordial beauty, seems

To breathe, inspired by thee, the Philosophic Soul!

R. Polwhele Kenton, near Exeter, April 18, 1792.

6   These lines echo William Hayley's *An Essay on Epic Poetry: in five epistles to the Revd. Mr Mason* (London: J. Dodsley, 1782): "Yet if the Bard to glory must aspire … That Beauty's countless forms are only one" (I.387–94).

7   Mrs Elizabeth Darwin, Dr Darwin's second wife.

8   Household.

9   Erasmus Darwin, Jr., had, for a time, been Thomas Day's protégé, as P. Rowland noted in *Life of Thomas Day*, p.107. Erasmus, Jr., was admitted to Middle Temple on 26 April 1776, having previously worked under the watch of his uncle, the lawyer, William Alvey Darwin (1726–1783). As a solicitor, Erasmus, Jr., had a number of respectable clients, among them, he "acted on behalf of the Wedgwood firm" (B. Dolan, *Wedgwood*, p.329).

10 Darwin began working on *Zoonomia* in 1770–1771, soon after Polly Darwin's death. Ashmun, *Singing Swan*, pp.65–66.

11 E. Posner provided a brief overview of these daughters of Darwin in "Erasmus Darwin and the Sisters Parker", *History of Medicine* 6 (1975): 39–43.

12 Dr Darwin's granddaughter, Elizabeth Anne Galton (1808–1906) claimed that her mother, Frances Ann Violetta Darwin (1783–1874), her aunts the Sitwells, and "Most of the young girls in Derbyshire" were educated there. Andrew Moilliet, *Elizabeth Anne Galton (1808–1906): A Well Connected Gentlewoman* (Northwich, Cheshire: Léonie Press, 2003), p.14. For further insights into contemporary education in the West Midlands, see W.H.G. Armytage, "The Lunar Society and Its Contributions to Education", *University of Birmingham Historical Journal* 11 (1967): 65–78, and Jenny Uglow, "But What About the Women? The Lunar Society's Attitude to Women and Science, and to Education of Girls", in Smith and Arnott (eds) *Genius of Erasmus Darwin*, pp, 83–88. See also Malcolm McKinnon Dick and Ruth Watts's guest edited special issue of *History of Education* devoted to "Eighteenth-Century Education: Discourses and Informal Agencies" 37 (208): 509–631.

13 *A Plan for the Conduct of Female Education in Boarding Schools* (Derby: J. Drewry, for J. Johnson, London, 1797; Dublin: J. Chambers, 1798, Philadelphia: John Ormrod, 1798).

14 Most likely drawn from Seward's own recollections of her talks with Dr Darwin. This passage does not appear to be a direct quotation of a written text, although it summarizes aspects of Darwin's pedagogical recommendations in his tract on *Female Education,* particularly the chapter on Compassion.

15 Lichfield was also known as a center for archery, including women's archery, in the decades following the publication of Seward's *Life of Dr Darwin*. See, for example, Walter Michael Moseley, *An Essay of Archery: Describing the Practice of that Art in All Ages and Nations* (Worcester: J. and J. Holl, 1792); M.W. Greenslade (ed) *A History of the County of Stafford* (Oxford: Oxford University Press, 1990), Vol.14 ("Lichfield"), p.162; and *Laws and Regulations of the Society of Lichfield Archers Established 1846* (Lichfield: Thomas George Lomax, 1850), the last of which includes a list of members. The editors are grateful to David Tucker of Lichfield for sharing his knowledge of this sport and its history.

16 An area of woodland and heath, together with sandstone cliffs, along the southern part of Kinver Edge forming the Staffordshire-Worcestershire border, five miles north of Kidderminster.

17 Sir Nigel Gresley, 6th Baron Gresley (*c.*1727–1787), who served as High Sheriff of Staffordshire in 1759. For an historical overview, see Falconer Madan's *The Gresley's of Drakelow: An Account of the Family, and Notes of its Connexions by Marriage and Descent from the Norman Conquest to the Present Day* (Oxford: H. Hart, 1899).

18 Seward's own footnote, "Now Mrs Broughton". Susan Sneyd Broughton (*b.*1768).

19 The *Derby Mercury*.

20 Roman goddess of the hunt.

21 Venus, who arose fully formed from the sea at Cyprus, as captured in the painting by Alessandro di Mariano di Vanni Filipepi, better known as Sandro Botticelli (1445–1510).

22 Burton-upon-Trent, Staffordshire, known for its massive multi-arched long bridge.

23 Darwin's "Early Poems": "On the Drakelow Target". p.66. UCL. Pearson Papers 577.

24 Dryden features the story of Antony and Cleopatra in his play, *All for Love: or, The World Well Lost. A Tragedy, As it is Acted at the Theatre-Royal; And Written in Imitation of Shakespeare's Stile.* (London: T. Newcomb for H. Herringman, 1678).

25 Cleopatra VII Philopator (69–30 BC), the last Pharaoh of Ancient Egypt.

26 The River Cydnus (or Kydnos) originated in the Tarsos Mountains along the Kilikian border of Syria, from which it flowed into the Mediterranean Sea near Tarsos.

27 Dryden, *All for Love or the World Well Lost: A Tragedy* (1678), III.190–91. Seward has "might" where Dryden has "could".

28 Shakespeare, *The Tragedy of Richard the Third* (1592–93), V.iii.339.

29 There are monuments erected to Revd. William Mason (1725–1797) at Westminster Abbey, a cenotaph in the gardens at Nuneham, near Abingdon, Oxfordshire, and in Aston Church, near Rotherham, Yorkshire, though none of these include these lines by Darwin.

30 Seward's own footnote, "Alluding to the Poem, *English Garden*". Mason's *The English Garden: A Poem in Four Books* (York: A. Ward, 1781).

31 Mason's *Elfrida. A Dramatic Poem. Written On the Model of The Ancient Greek Tragedy* (London: J. and P. Knapton, 1752).

32 Mason's *Caractacus. A Dramatic Poem. Written on the Model of the Ancient Greek Tragedy* (London: J. Knapton, R. and J. Dodsley, 1759).

33 Mason's *An Heroic Epistle to Sir William Chambers, Knight, Comptroller General of His Majesty's Works, and Author of a Late Dissertation on Oriental Gardening* (London: J. Almon, 1773), based on the life of Sir William Chambers (1722–1796), the Scottish architect who oversaw the building of Royal households in London and at Kew Gardens and whose publications on Chinese architecture greatly influenced public taste for Chinese design. Mason's *Epistle to Chambers* actually supported the views of Chambers' rival, Lancelot "Capability" Brown (bap.1716–1783).

34 *Elfrida* and *Caractacus*.

35 John Milton first published this as *Paradise Regain'd. A Poem. In IV Books. To which is added Samson Agonistes* (London: Printed by J. Macock for John Starkey, 1671).

36 James Wolfe (1727–1759).

37 Gaul, that part of Western Europe south and west of the Rhine, west of the Alps, and north of the Pyrenees which, in Ancient times, served under provincial Roman rule.

38 Seward prints this poem for the first time, though it was printed in the same year also in a brief biographical account of Darwin by Francis William Blagdon, "Biographical Sketches: Dr Erasmus Darwin" *Flowers of Literature for 1803* (1804): 15–23. Blagdon remarks: "The following epitaph has never been printed, and has met his biographer's eye in a collection of manuscript poetry: it bears Dr Darwin's signature". The poem was eventually printed in *The Poetical Register, and Repository of Fugitive Poetry for 1810–11* (London: F.C. and J. Rivington, 1814). See also Darwin's "Early Poems": "Death of General Wolf" P.16. UCL. Pearson Papers 577.

39 Joseph Johnson (1738–1809) had previously published Seward's *Elegy on Captain Cook* (4th and 5th eds, 1784), *Monody on Major André* (1st and 2nd eds, 1781), and *Louisa: A Poetical Novel, In Four Epistles* (1st–4th eds, 1784).

40 The illegitimate sonnet appeared in *Gentleman's Magazine* ixiiii (1803): 762. It reads as follows:
Sonnet, Addressed to W. Dimond, Esq. written after perusing his "Hero of the North".

> Hail to the Bard, with native genius blest,
> Who breathes *new* impulse to our British choir;
> Who roves through Fancy's maze, with soul possest,

And twines with roses the historic lyre!

Bright Dimond! as I trace thy glowing page,

Young joys awake in many a thrilling throng;

In thee the minstrels of an happier age

New voice assume, and swell their boldest song!

The Sister Muses with contending love

Thy favour'd Harp of mingled notes inspire,

And bid its sounding strings alternate move,

With Otway's softness, and with Dryden's fire.

Proceed, thou gifted Youth, and o'er thy way

A Nation's hand shall wave its *greenest bay*.

Anna Seward

41   William Dimond (*c*.1784–1837), playwright and author.

42   Seward quotes from the illegitimate sonnet.

43   *Public Characters of 1803–1804* (London: Richard Phillips, 1804), the 6th volume, which is a continuation of the five volumes of *Public Characters of 1798–9. A New Edition. Enlarged and Corrected to the 25th of March, 1799. [of 1799–1800; 1800–1801; 1801–1802; 1802–1803.] To Be Continued Annually.* (London: Richard Phillips, 1799–1803).

44   Anna Seward's.

45   Seward, *Ode to General Elliot on His Return from Gibraltar* (London: T. Cadell, 1787), and reprinted in Felix Farley's *Bristol Journal* (30 June 1787).

46   Seward, *Original Sonnets on Various Subjects; And Odes Paraphrased from Horace* (London: G. Sael, 1798). In the preface, Seward refers to "minute Elegies of twelve alternate rhimes, closing with a couplet, which assume the name of Sonnet, without any other resemblance to that order of Verse, except their limitation to fourteen lines". This work was also cited in Seward's *Llangollen Vale, With Other Poems* (London: G. Sael, 1796), p.43.

47   His eldest living son, Erasmus, Jr.

48   29 December 1799. The Revd. William Bagshaw Stevens, who occasionally dined with Dr Darwin, noted in his journal in response to hearing that Erasmus, Jr. had thrown himself into the river, *Causa latet* (no one knows why). G. Galbraith (ed) *Journal of Revd. William Bagshaw Stevens*, p.503.

49   Breadsall Priory, four miles northeast of Derby. According to Whitbread PLC archivist, Nicolas Redman (*Dr Erasmus Darwin and Breadsall Prior, Derbyshire*, Privately Printed), Erasmus, Jr. paid £3,500 for this house, what his father viewed as "a very cheap purchase". He planned to move into the Priory on 25 March, Lady Day, 1800, by which time he thought it would be "completely habitable". Alas, such a move was never to be made.

50   Erasmus, Jr., was buried in All Saints Church, Breadsall, on 2 January 1800.

51   *Phytologia; or, The Philosophy of Agriculture and Gardening With the Theory of Draining Morasses, and With an Improved Construction of the Drill Plough* (London: J. Johnson, 1800). Darwin's work is mentioned, albeit briefly, in Sir E. John Russell, *A History of Agricultural Science in Great Britain, 1620–1954* (London: George Allen & Unwin, 1966). See also, Mark Overton, *Agricultural Revolution in England: The Transformation of the Agrarian Economy 1500–1850* (Cambridge: Cambridge University Press, 1996).

52   Thomas Percival (1740–1804).

53   Edward Young, *The Complaint; or, Night-thoughts*, I.74–75: "Distinguished link in being's endless chain! / Midway from nothing, to the Deity!"

54   We have been unable to trace information about the particular experiment.

55   Darwin explained the usefulness of manures as the "Food of Plants" in *Phytologia; or, The Philosophy of Agriculture and Gardening, With the Theory of Draining Morasses and with an Improved Construction of the Drill Plough* (London: J. Johnson, 1800), pp.184–256. As to the benefits provided by the Chinese, Darwin noted their methods of flooding lands for irrigation and of planting their grain on even surfaces rather than in ridges or furrows. He noted, drawing upon Sir George Leonard Staunton's (1737–1801) *An Authentic Account of an Embassy from the King of Great Britain to the Emperor of China; Including Cursory Observations made, and Information Obtained, in Travelling through that Ancient Empire, and a Small Part of Chinese Tartary* (W. Bulmer and Co. for G. Nicol,1798), that "In China, it is said that they spawn of fish in the proper season brought to market, and purchased for the purpose of peopling the floods on their rice grounds with fish, part of which becomes large enough to be fried and eaten by the land cultivator; and the rest serve the purpose of fertilizing the soil, when the floods are drawn off, by their death and consequent decomposition" (Darwin, *Phytologia*, pp.240–241). As to the policing of manure handling, he again draws upon Staunton, noting that the manure in town and cities "which are all now left buried in deep ells, or carried away by soughs into the rivers, should be removed by a police, which is said to exist in China; and carries out of towns at stated intervals of time for the purposes of agriculture; which might be performed in the night, as is done in Edinburgh; or by means of large basons [sic] or reservoirs at the extremities of the common shores, or soughs for the reception of the manure, before it is washed into the rivers" (Darwin, *Phytologia*, p.242). For more on the agricultural value of manure, see Richard Kirwan's (1733–1812) *The Manures Most Advantageously Applicable to the Various Sorts of Soils and the Causes of their Beneficial Effect in each Particular Instance* (London: Vermor & Hood, 1796), and the recent, more general and popular work, Ralph A. Lewin, *Merde: Excursions in Scientific, Cultural, and Socio-Historical Coprology* (New York: Random House, 1999).

56   The word "or" is inserted here in the 1804 version of Seward's *Life* published in Philadelphia.

57   Pindar (*c*.518–*c*.438 BC), an accomplished lyric poet of Ancient Greece, known particularly for his odes celebrating victories at the Panhellenic festivals and games.

58   Thomas Gray, *The Progress of Poesy. A Pindaric Ode* (Strawberry-Hill: R. and J. Dodsley, 1757).

59   House of Plantagenet (or Anjou), the dynastic royal household of England from 1154–1485. It came to an end when the York King, Richard III, was defeated at Bosworth Field, Leicestershire, by the Lancastrian, Henry Tudor (later Henry VIII), thus initiating the rule of the House of Tudor.

60   Shakespeare, *Macbeth*, IV.i.112–15: "Though art too like the spirit of Banquo; down!/The crown does sear mine eyeballs. And thy hair,/Thou other gold-bound brow, is like the first./A third is like the former".

61   Thomas Gray, "The Bard. A Pindaric Ode", *Odes by Mr Gray* (Strawberry Hill: J. Dodsley, 1757).

62   "Gales from blooming Eden bear", in Gray's "The Bard", l. 132.

63   "Frowns o'er old Conways foaming flood", in Gray's "The Bard", l. 16.

64   Mrs Mary Manwaring (1728–*c*.1810).

65   Pneumonia, according to King-Hele (*Doctor of Revolution*, p.282), from which he never regained his previous vigour.

66   The Darwins moved into Breadsall Priory, previously owned by Erasmus, Jr., on 25 March 1802. Elizabeth Darwin continued to reside there until her death on 5 February 1832, at which time it was passed along to her son, Sir Francis Sacheveral Darwin (1786–1859) who retained it until his death in 1859. Currently the Priory, a Marriott hotel and country club, is owned and managed by the Whitbread Hotel Company.

67   Mrs Mary Manwaring, Elizabeth Darwin's foster mother, according to Uglow, *Lunar Men*, p.489.

68   E. Darwin to R.L. Edgeworth, "Priory, near Derby, April 17, 1802

Dear Edgeworth.

I am glad to find, that you still amuse yourself with mechanism, in spite of the troubles in Ireland.

The use of turning aside, or downwards, the claw of a table, I don't see; as it must then be reared against the wall, for it will not stand alone. If use be for carriage, the feet may be shut up, like the usual brass feet of a reflective telescope.

We have all been removed from Derby about a fortnight, to the Priory, and all of us like our change of situation. We have a pleasant house, a good garden, ponds full of fish, and a pleasing valley somewhat like [the poet and landscape gardener William] Shenstone's [(1714–1763)] – deep, umbrageous, and with a talkative stream running down it. Our house is near the top of the valley, well screened by hills from the east, and north, and open to the south, where, at four miles distance, we see Derby tower.

Four or more strong springs rise near the house, and have formed the valley, which, like that of Petrarch, may be called *Val chinsa*, as it begins, or is shut, at the situation of the house. I hope you like the description, and hope farther, that yourself and any part of your family will sometime do us the pleasure of a visit.

Pray tell the authoress [Maria Edgeworth], that the water-nymphs of our valley will be happy to assist her next novel.

My bookseller, Mr Johnson, will not begin to print the Temple of Nature, till the price of paper is fixed by Parliament. I suppose the present duty is paid ... ". Edgeworth goes on to say, "At these words Dr Darwin's pen stopped". Edgeworth, *Memoirs*, Vol.2, pp.241–242.

69 Henry Hadley (1762/63–1830), surgeon whom Susanna Parker (1772–1856) married.

70 Dr Francis Fox (1759–1833) and Mr Henry Hadley (1762/63–1830) performed the autopsy on Dr Darwin.

71 Seward's own footnote, "Dr Young".

72 Young, *The Complaint, or, Night-Thoughts on Life, Death, and Immortality*, the first 9 lines are from Night I. ll. 371–379, the last 3 lines are from Night II, ll. 405–407.

73 *The Temple of Nature; or, The Origin of Society* (London: J. Johnson, 1803).

74 The word "high" inserted here in the 1804 version of Seward's *Life* published in Philadelphia.

75 Seward's book was published in February 1804.

Biographical Register

Joseph Addison (1672-1719), the eldest son of Lancelot Addison (1632-1703), Dean of Lichfield Cathedral beginning 1683, and Archdeacon of Coventry in 1684. Joseph, who began his education at Lichfield Free Grammar School, matriculated at Queen's College, Oxford, later becoming a noted essayist, poet, and dramatist. Together with his fellow Whig Kit-Kat Club companion, Richard Steele (1672-1729), Addison was a major contributor to the thrice weekly gossip publication, *Tatler*, from 1709-1711 and to *The Spectator*, a daily from 1711-1714, in a style greatly admired by Samuel Johnson.

John André (1750-1780) was born in Geneva, Switzerland. His lasting memory rests primarily upon his military plights during much of the War of Independence (1775-1783). In September and October 1775, American troops laid siege to the fort at St Johns, Quebec, where his regiment lodged. André was captured during the capitulation of St Johns and transferred to Lancaster, Pennsylvania, where his severe treatment turned him against the American cause. Released in a prisoner exchange of 1776, he became known to Sir William Howe (1729-1814), the British commander-in-chief, who grew interested to know what André had learned while in prison. During the following year, André became *aide de camp* to Sir Henry Clinton (1730-1795), the new British commander-in-chief. In 1779, as Howe's head of British Secret Intelligence, André tracked considerable information for British forces and prompted the Commander of West Point, Benedict Arnold's (1741-1801) turn of allegiance, an act for which André was promoted to adjutant general. With the arrival of the British in Philadelphia, André was quartered in Benjamin Franklin's house which had been abandoned by Franklin's daughter, Sarah Bache (1743-1808). There, he enjoyed what leisure hours he had perusing Franklin's library, from which he reputedly appropriated some choice volumes, as noted by Harry Stanton Tillotson, *The Beloved Spy: The Life and Loves of Major John André* (Caldwell, Idaho: Caxton Printers, 1948), pp.44, 66.

On 20 September 1780, André boarded *The Vulture*, a British sloop in the Hudson River off of Teller's Point, from which he would be picked up by an American vessel and delivered to Arnold. During their meeting in the Joshua Hett Smith House in Haverstraw, New York, Arnold handed André papers that detailed West Point's defense strategy. Upon returning to the Hudson, André found himself stranded, for *The Vulture* had been forced to move upriver after being fired upon. Thus, André was forced to head back over land. Equipped with passes from Arnold that identified André as "John Anderson", he was captured near Tarrytown, New York, by John Paulding (1758-1818), David Williams (1754-1831), and Isaac Van Wart (c. 1759-1828) while holding compromising information. Arnold and George Washington (1732-1799), who were both headquartered nearby, were alerted. Arnold received his letter first, fled for *The Vulture*, and escaped. Washington organized a Court of Inquiry to review André's case, and they found him guilty of spying. Although many, including Washington, sought to imprison André or to offer him as an exchange for Arnold, the imposed punishment for such actions was death. André was hanged at Tappan, New York, on 2 Oct 1780. Though unbeknownst to him at the time, Honora Sneyd – who had become enamoured with André in Lichfield in 1769 – had died on 30 April earlier that year. The night before his execution, André wrote letters to his mother, his sisters, and to Anna Seward.

Anna Seward received a letter from her friend, André, written 3 November 1775, shortly after he had been taken prisoner at the capitulation of St John's. In it, he claimed that he was "stripped of everything except the picture of Honora, which I concealed in my mouth. Preserving this yet think myself fortunate". She later addressed André's ultimate fate in her *Monody on Major Andre* [sic] ... ; *To Which are Added Letters Addressed to Her by Major Andre, [sic] in the Year 1769* (Lichfield: J. Jackson, 1781). Seward's "severe reflections on Washington for his conduct" provided a response from the "Father of the late great Republic" who, after the war, sent a military agent to Seward in Lichfield with "copies of the correspondence which followed upon the Major's arrest, to prove that he had endeavoured to save André's life" (*Memoirs of Dr Whalley*, vol. 1, p.13). For additional accounts on André, see, among others, Joshua Hett Smith, *An Authentic Narrative of the Causes Which Led to the Death of Major André, Adjutant-General of his Majesty's Forces in North-America.*(New York: Evert Duyckinck, 1809); Winthrop Sargent, *The Life and Career of Major John André, Adjutant-General of the British Army in America* (Boston: Ticknor and Fields, 1861); and John Evangelist Walsh, *The Execution of Major André* (New York: Palgrave, 2001).

Marriot Arbuthnot (1711-1794) was a nephew of the physician and satirist, John Arbuthnot (1667-1735). Despite concern over his tactical and administrative know-how, following a long career at sea, Arbuthnot gained sequential control of the British Royal Navy during the War of Independence, first as Vice Admiral of the Blue and Commander of the Atlantic Station in 1779, Vice Admiral of the White in 1780, and ultimately, Admiral of the Blue in 1793. He worked, albeit uncooperatively, with General Clinton in the siege and capture of Charleston, South Carolina in 1780.

Sir Richard Arkwright (1732-1792), inventor and textile industrialist whose factory, as King-Hele (*Doctor of Revolution*, p.166) reminds us, has regularly been viewed as the 'take off' point of the Industrial Revolution. In 1769, Arkwright patented a water-driven frame for spinning cotton yarn of suitable strength, thereby improving James Hargreaves's (bap.1721-1778) spinning jenny of 1767. Fortunately for posterity, he "stimulated" the painter Joseph Wright to "bequeath to us a series of views of the area where [Arkwright] built up his industrial empire" (Nicholson, *Wright*, p.164). Many works have explored the importance of cotton. Among works contemporary to the period, see particularly Sir Edward Baines, *History of the Cotton Manufacture in Great Britain: With a Notice of its Early History in the East, and in All the Quarters of the Globe; A Description of the Great Mechanical Inventions, which have Caused its Unexampled Extension in Britain; And a View of the Present State of the Manufacture, and the Condition of the Classes Engaged in its Several Departments* (London: H. Fisher, R. Fisher, and P. Jackson, 1835), and for a modern historical telling, see Stephen Yafa, *Big Cotton: How a Humble Fiber Created Fortunes, Wrecked Civilizations, and Put America on the Map* (New York: Viking, 2004). In 1979, the Arkwright

Society purchased Sir Richard Arkwright's Cromford Mill site and began restoring the listed buildings, In 2001, UNESCO inscribed this Cromford area as a World Heritage site.

Anna Letitia Barbauld (née Aikin) (1743-1825) was the daughter of John Aikin (1713-1780), a tutor of languages and *belles lettres* at Warrington Academy, the dissenting school at Warrington, then part of the manufacturing-centered Lancashire, where Joseph Priestley (1733-1804) joined as a tutor in September 1761. Anna Barbauld's close friend, Mary Wilkinson (*c.*1744-1796) became Mrs Joseph Priestley in 1762. For an overview of the Academy, see John Fulton, "The Warrington Academy (1757-1786) and its Influence upon Medicine and Science", *Bulletin of the History of Medicine* 1 (1933): 50-80, and H. McLachlan, *Warrington Academy: Its History and Influence*, Volume 107, new series (Manchester: Printed for the Chetham Society, 1943). Anna Barbauld's brother, John Aikin (1747-1822), a physician, encouraged and helped her prepare a number of poems and hymns, thematically ranging from religion, politics, friendship, and love to the abolition of slavery. The most famous of these poems continues to be her abolitionist verse satire *Epistle to William Wilberforce* (1791). Later, she wrote a number of books for the children of the boarding school she and her husband, Rochemont Barbauld (d. 1808), created. Several of her works for children enjoyed an audience far beyond the boarding school: *Lessons for Children* (1778-1779), *Hymns in Prose for Children* (1781), and *Evenings at Home* (1792-1796), co-authored with her brother. The piece that Seward cited, frequently reprinted, first appeared in *Miscellaneous Pieces in Prose* (London: J. Johnson, 1773). In it, the author begins with the idea that "most of the unhappiness of the world arises rather from disappointed desires than from positive evil". She further remarks that "Men of merit and integrity often censure the dispositions of Providence for suffering characters they despise to run away with advantages which, they yet know, are purchased by such means as a high and noble spirit could never submit to. If you refuse to pay the price, why expect the purchase?" Anna Barbauld was featured in Richard Samuel's 1779 painting as one of "The Nine Living Muses of Great Britain", a work imitating the nine muses of Ancient Greece, each of whom was associated with a particular contribution to literature and the arts. For further reading, see William McCarthy, *Anna Letitia Barbauld: Voice of the Enlightenment* (Baltimore: The Johns Hopkins University Press, 2008).

James Beattie (1735-1803), a poet and philosopher, lectured on moral philosophy and logic at Marischal College, and is best known for his *Essay on the Nature and Immutability of Truth* (Edinburgh: A. Kinkaid & J. Bell; London: E & C Dilly, 1770), an attack on David Hume, and for his poetic autobiography *The Minstrel*, written in Spenserian stanzas and published in two books (London: Edward and Charles Dilly; Edinburgh: William Creech 1771; London: Edward and Charles Dilly; Edinburgh: A. Kinkaid, W. Creech, and J. Bell, 1774).

Frances Anne Beaufort (1769-1865), daughter of the Church of Ireland Rector of Navan, Co. Meath, and "foundation" member of the Royal Irish Academy, Daniel Augustus Beaufort (1739-1821), best known as the cartographer of the 1792 "Civil and Ecclesiastical Map of Ireland". Frances was the sister of Francis Beaufort (1774-1857), a prominent naval hydrographer who developed the 13-point wind strength measurement scale now known as the Beaufort Scale. He later arranged for Erasmus's grandson, the naturalist Charles Darwin, to sail aboard *The Beagle*, a voyage spanning 1831-1836, during which he uncovered findings that eventually led him to posit the theory of natural selection as the driving force underlying evolutionary change. For an accessible work on Beaufort, see Scott Huler, *Defining the Wind: The Beaufort Scale and How a 19th-Century Admiral Turned Science into Poetry* (New York: Crown, 2004).

Dewhurst Bilsborrow (alternatively spelled Bilsboro, b. 1776), the son of the Derby solicitor, George Bilsborrow (b. 1747) served as a physician at Derbyshire General Infirmary, a model institution which Erasmus Darwin helped design. From J. A. Venn, *Alumni Cantabrigienses: A Biographical List of All Known Students, Graduates and Holders of Office at the University of Cambridge* (Cambridge: Cambridge University Press, 1922), we learn that Bilsborrow matriculated at Trinity College, Cambridge, in 1792, from which he received his BA in 1797 and a Licentiate in Medicine in 1803. He had once been a pupil and later, a friend, of Erasmus Darwin. For further information, see V. M. Leveaux, *History of the Derbyshire General Infirmary 1810-1894* (Cromford: Scarthin Books, 1999) as well as Paul Elliott's brief mention of Bilsborrow and his Infirmary connection in "The Derbyshire 'Darwins': The Persistence of Erasmus Darwin's Influence on a British Provincial Literary and Scientific Community, *c.* 1780-1850", in C.U.M. Smith and Robert Arnott (eds) *The Genius of Erasmus Darwin* (Aldershot, Hampshire: Ashgate, 2005), p.187. While studying at Trinity, Bilsborrow composed a poem summarizing the virtues he saw in *Zoonomia*, a work Darwin published between 1794-1796. King-Hele notes that Bilsborrow's biography of Darwin "was never published" and that the manuscript "has been lost". *Erasmus Darwin: Life of Unequalled Achievement*, p.288.

Sir Brooke Boothby (1744-1824), 6th Baronet of Broadlow, lived at Ashbourne Hall, Derbyshire. Boothby was among the leading intellectuals of the Midlands who imbibed Rousseau's enlightened ideals of nature. Although not scientific-minded enough to become a Lunar Society man, he frequently associated with these individuals. He published a number of political tracts, translations, and the poetry collection *Sorrows Sacred to the Memory of Penelope* (1796), dedicated to his deceased daughter. For further discussion, see Frederick Cumming's "Boothby, Rousseau, and the Romantic Malady", *The Burlington Magazine* 110 (1968): 659-667, and Jacques Zonneveld, *Sir Brooke Boothby: Rousseau's Roving Baronet Friend* (Uitgeverij: De Nieuwe Haagsche, 2003).

James Boswell (1740-1795), while staying at the Bishop's Palace in Lichfield, approached Seward for anecdotes – among other things – regarding all that he had on his mind at the time. For Boswell's *The Life of Samuel Johnson, LL.D* (London: H. Baldwin for C. Dilly, 1791), Seward provided anecdotes. For his other repeated requests, she replied with a lock of her hair and this rebuff:

> With spotless lilies cull'd from friendship's bowers,
> That hide no thorns beneath their snowy flowers,
> By Boswell's hand be this light lock enwove,
> But never with the dangerous rose of love.
> Anna Seward to James Boswell, 20 June 1784

Seward scholar Teresa Barnard recounts this story in, "Anna Seward and the Battle for Authorship", CW3 Journal: Corvey Women Writers on the Web www2.shu.ac.uk/ corvey/CW3journa/Issue%20one/barnard.html 15 September 2008. This lock of hair, tied with pink ribbon, was found in Boswell's private papers after his death. 1 YUB (Yale University Bodleian Library) "Letters of Anna Seward" MSC2469 fol.767. Seward "Letter to James Boswell.22.May.1784". Boswell had previously published insights into Samuel Johnson (1709-1784) in *The Journal of a Tour to the Hebrides, with Samuel Johnson, LL.D.* (London: H. Baldwin for C. Dilly, 1785). Seward's views of Johnson are included in Adam Sisman's accessible *Boswell's Presumptuous Task: The Making of the Life of Johnson* (New York: Farrar, Strauss and Giroux, 2000).

Matthew Boulton (1728-1809), a leader among the entrepreneurs of the Industrial Revolution, established a considerable reputation and fortune as a manufacturer of metal goods including buckles, buttons, "Sheffield" plate, and the gilded decorative metal, ormolu, in Birmingham, the "toy shop" of Europe. Soho Manufactory, the site of his enterprise, including his joint venture with James Watt (1736-1819) in steam engine production, as well as a coining mint, also included his residence, Soho House. His house, at Handsworth Heath, two miles north of Birmingham, served as the site of many Lunar Society meetings. Dr Darwin first met Boulton around the time Erasmus moved to Lichfield, and the two remained close friends throughout Darwin's life, particularly in their mutual pursuits of experimentation and invention. Boulton had Lichfield connections, for it was there, in 1760, that he married Anne Robinson (1733-1783), daughter of Lichfield mercer Luke Robinson (1683-1749), and the coheiress of her maternal grandfather, John Babington's (d. 1710) Curborough Hall Farm. For further glimpses into Boulton's contributions, see H.W. Dickinson's *Matthew Boulton* (Cambridge: Cambridge University Press, 1936); Nicholas Goodison, *Ormolu: The Work of Matthew Boulton* (London: Phaidon, 1974); Maxwell Craven, *John Whitehurst of Derby: Clockmaker & Scientist 1731-1788* (Mayfield, Ashbourne: Mayfield Books 1996); Jenny Uglow, *The Lunar Men: The Friends Who Made the Future* (London: Faber and Faber, 2002); Shena Mason, *The Hardware Man's Daughter: Matthew Boulton and His 'Dear Girl'* (Chichester: Phillimore & Co Ltd, 2005); Gavin Weightman, *The Industrial Revolutionaries: The Creators of the Modern World 1776-1914* (London: Atlantic, 2007); and Peter Jones, *Industrial Enlightenment in Birmingham and the West Midlands, 1760-1820: Science, Technology and Culture* (Manchester: Manchester University Press, 2009). Information on Boulton's residence is available from Soho House, Soho Avenue, Handsworth, Birmingham B18 5LB, United Kingdom. William Hutton (1723-1815) produced the standard contemporary historical account of Birmingham in *An History of Birmingham, to the End of the Year 1780* (Birmingham: Pearson and Rollason, 1781). He provided additional regional information in his autobiography, *The Life of William Hutton, F.A.S.S. Including a Particular Account of the Riots at Birmingham in 1791*, 2nd ed (London: Baldwin, Cradock, and Joy, and Birmingham: Beilby and Knotts, 1816.

Robert Boyle (1627-1691), prominent Irish experimental natural philosopher involved with the "Invisible College" meetings at Oxford, the organization which became the Royal Society of London for the Improvement of Natural Knowledge in 1662, with Boyle on the

Council. With the assistance of Robert Hooke (1635-1703), Boyle devised an improved air pump in 1659 with which he experimentally determined many properties of air. A century later, in 1768, Joseph Wright's oil paining, "An Experiment on a Bird in the Air Pump" reminds us of the enduring popularity of this experimental tool.

James Brindley (1716-1772), a patient of Dr Darwin's, was a Staffordshire millwright who became one of England's most prominent "Inland Navigation" (i.e., canal) surveyors and engineers. His Trent and Mersey (Grand Turk) Canal, England's first major canal, built between 1766 and 1777 and opened May 1777, formed a network of over 350 miles of canals, joining the Mersey to the Thames and the Trent to the Severn, Britain's longest river. These major jointures were then linked together with four major ports: London, Liverpool, Bristol and Hull, forming the "Grand Cross", all of which greatly improved the transportation needs of the Industrial Revolution. Brindley's 1758 plan to construct a 20 mile canal from Lichfield to the Trent, despite Erasmus Darwin's backing, never secured the requisite funding. For a contemporary overview, see John Phillips, *A General History of Inland Navigation, Foreign and Domestic: Containing a Complete Account of the Canals Already Executed in England, With Considerations on those Projected, to which are Added, Practical Observations* (London, I. and J. Taylor at the Architectural Library, 1792), and for a later historical appreciation, see Jean Lindsay, *The Trent and Mersey Canal* (Newton Abbot, Devon: David & Charles, 1979).

Edmund Burke (1729/30-1797), a Dubliner who served as a Whig British parliamentarian from Bristol (1774) and later from Malton, a pocket borough of the Prime Minister, Charles Watson-Wentworth, 2nd Marquess of Rockingham (1730-1782). Burke edited the *Annual Register* for thirty years beginning in 1758. He expressed hostile opposition to the French Revolution in his *Reflections on the Revolution in France* (London: J. Dodsley, 1790). This work prompted counter arguments in England, including those of Boothby and Wollstonecraft, as well as in the American colonies, chiefly that of Thomas Paine (1737-1809) in *The Rights of Man: Being an Answer to Mr Burke's Attack on the French Revolution* (London: J. S. Jordan, 1791). He also gained notice on the Continent for his treatise on aesthetics, *A Philosophical Enquiry into the Origin of Our Ideas of the Sublime and Beautiful* (London, R. and J. Dodsley, 1757), a work which influenced the taste of connoisseurs for the remainder of the century. Through these and other writings, Burke became viewed historically as the "Father of Modern British Conservatism".

The Reverend Charles Burney (1757-1817), a classical scholar and clergyman, brother of the novelist whom Johnson admired, Francis 'Fanny' Burney (1752-1840) and of Admiral James Burney (1750-1821) who sailed with Captain James Cook on his Second and Third Voyages. These Burneys were children of the renowned organist, composer, music historian, and Shrewsbury native, Dr Charles Burney (1726-1814), whose 4-volume *General History of Music* (London: Bremner, 1776-89) escalated both the author's fame as well as that of England's position within musical history. Dr Burney, a regular in the small London salon of Mrs Thrale, once contemplated writing a life of his friend Dr Samuel Johnson, but abandoned that idea for others to take up. The Reverend Charles Burney established an

Academy at Greenwich in 1793, after which he educated a number of eminent naval and military officers. As a curious happenstance, Thomas Day's friend and poetical coauthor, John Bicknell had (under the *nom-de-plume* Joel Collier), previously infuriated the musical historian, Dr Burney, in his satire (*Musical Travels Through England by the Late Joel Collier. Licentiate in Music*, London: G. Kearsly, London, 1776) based upon Burney's *The Present State of Music in France and Italy: Or, The Journal of a Tour Through those Countries, Undertaken to Collect Materials for A General History of Music* (London: T. Becket and Co., J. Robson and G. Robinson, 1773).

Lady Eleanor Butler (1739-1829) was, with Sarah Ponsonby, known as The Ladies of Llangollen. Seward became a friend and occasional visitor of The Ladies at their idyllic cottage, Plas Newydd, Llangollen, Wales. John Brewer noted that The Ladies lead a "life of rustic isolation, intellectual refinement and ardent female friendship [which] fascinated fashionable society", in a chapter titled, "'Queen Muse of Britain': Anna Seward of Lichfield and the Literary Provinces", in his *The Pleasures of the Imagination: English Culture in the Eighteenth Century* (New York: Farrar Straus Giroux, 1997), p.591. Seward's admiration of The Ladies is apparent through her poem, *Llangollen Vale* (1796), and her close association with The Ladies is recounted in Elizabeth Mavor, *The Ladies of Llangollen* (Harmondsworth, Middlesex: Penguin, 1973) and in Paula R. Backsheider, *Eighteenth-Century Women Poets and their Poetry: Inventing Agency, Inventing Genre* (Baltimore: The Johns Hopkins University Press, 2005), esp. pp.291-313. At the time of her demise, Seward remembered The Ladies with a mourning ring (Wickham, Journals *and Correspondence of Thomas Sedgewick Whalley*, vol. 2, p.440, note).

Lady Mary Anne Carnegie (d. 1798). Carnegie's brother, William (1756-1831), who became the 7th Earl of Northesk, was a Vice-Admiral who commanded, together with Vice-Admiral Horatio Nelson, 1st Viscount Nelson (1758-1805) at the Battle of Trafalgar in 1805. Seward's "Sonnet LIX To the Right Honourable Lady Marianne Carnegie" appeared in her *Poetical Works*, vol. 3, p.180.

Sir William Chambers (1723-1796) had traveled to China as part of the Swedish East India Company during the 1740s. He established an architectural practice in London in 1755, and, the following year, he became architectural tutor to the Prince of Wales, later George III (1738–1820). In 1757 he published *Designs of Chinese Buildings, Furniture, Dresses, Machines, and Utensils: To which is Annexed a Description of their Temples, Houses, Gardens, &c* (London: William Chambers). This work became the standard source for realistic Chinese architecture of the era, expanding the earlier 18th-century fashion for Chinoiserie. His *Chinese Influences on British Gardening. A Dissertation on Oriental Gardening. The Second Edition, with Additions. To Which is Annexed, An Explanatory Discourse by Tan Chet-qua, of Quang-chew-fu, Gent.* (London, W. Griffin & T. Davies, 1773) also greatly influenced public taste for Chinese design. For further information, see John Harris and Michael Snodin, *Sir William Chambers: Architect to George III* (New Haven: Yale University Press in association with the Courtauld Galley, Courtauld Institute of Art, London, 1996), and David Beevers (ed) *Chinese Whispers: Chinoiserie in Britain 1650-1930* (Brighton House: The Royal Pavilion and Museums, 2008).

Charles Churchill (1731-1764), Curate of Westminster parish (1758-1762), friend of the radical journalist and Parliamentary friend of liberty, John Wilkes (1725-1797), was also known for his poetry in which he incorporated polemical satires in the form of heroic couplets.

Sir Henry Clinton (1730-1795) replaced William Howe as Commander-in-Chief of the British Army in North America following the British defeat at the Saratoga Campaign in 1777. Clinton, one of the British field commanders at Battle of Bunker Hill in 1775, was replaced as Commander-in-Chief in 1782 by Sir Guy Carleton, 1st Baron Dorchester (1724-1808).

Samuel Taylor Coleridge (1772-1834), matriculated at Jesus College, Cambridge, became a close friend of Josiah Wedgwood's son, Thomas Wedgwood (1771-1805), and held differing opinions of Dr Darwin. In recounting his 1796 meeting with Dr Darwin in Derby, Coleridge, a Unitarian, acknowledged that Darwin "possesses, perhaps, a greater range of knowledge than any other person in Europe. He thinks in a *new* train on all subjects except religion". Religion, Darwin argued, was "unworthy of a philosopher's investigation". In short, Darwin was "the everything, except the Christian!", as cited in Earl Leslie Griggs, *Collected Letters of Samuel Taylor Coleridge* (Oxford: Oxford University Press, 1956-1959), vol. 1, p.99. Despite the criticism that Coleridge later heaped upon Darwin, many writers, including King-Hele, have noted considerable direct influences of Darwin upon Coleridge's writing, including his famed *Rime of the Ancient Mariner*, first published in *Lyrical Ballads, With A Few Other Poems* (London: For J. & J. Arch, T. Longman & O. Rees, 1798-1800). See King-Hele, *Life of Unequalled Achievement*, pp.318-319 as well as his lengthier treatment in *Erasmus Darwin and the Romantic Poets* (New York: Macmillan, 1986). Trevor H. Levere provides further context for appreciating Coleridge in his *Poetry Realized in Nature: Samuel Taylor Coleridge and Early Nineteenth-Century Science* (Cambridge: Cambridge University Press, 1981). For excellent literary and biographical insights into the shaping of Coleridge's early work, see Richard Holmes, *Coleridge: Early Visions* (London: Hodder & Stoughton, 1989).

Captain Thomas Coram (*c.* 1668-1751), philanthropist and Trustee for the Colony of Georgia, who was granted a charter by George II in 1739 to establish a hospital for the care and education of abandoned children. He oversaw the building of the Foundling Hospital in Lambs Conduit Fields, London. The Foundling Hospital became a cultural centre with many notables contributing to the cause. Regarding Anna Seward's musical interests, it should be remembered that George Frideric Handel (1685-1759) donated the rights of *The Messiah* to Coram's Hospital and personally held fund-raising concerts in its chapel. Supportive of the cause, Thomas Day became a Governor of the Foundling Hospital in London. (P. Rowland, *Life of Day*, p.18). Ruth K. McClure provided an insightful overview of the development of the Foundling Hospital in *Coram's Children: The London Foundling Hospital in the Eighteenth Century* (New Haven, CT: Yale University Press, 1981). Elsewhere, McClure noted that not everyone agreed with Foundling Hospital ideals. See her "Johnson's Criticism of the Foundling Hospital and Its Consequences", *Review of English Studies*, New Series, 27 (1976): 17-26. See also John Brown, *Memoranda; or, Chronicles of The Foundling Hospital, including Memoirs of Captain Coram, &c.* (London: Sampson Low, 1847).

Charles Cornwallis, 1st Marquis and 2nd Earl, Viscount Brome, Baron Cornwallis (1738-1805). Following his education at Clare College, Cambridge, and the Scuola di Applicazione Militare (the military academy of Turin), he entered the Army, fighting in the Seven Years' War, including the Battle of Minden. During the War of Independence, he served directly under both Howe and Clinton, but is most frequently remembered as the British Army Commander who, upon facing the tremendous assault of General Washington's American forces and General Jean-Baptiste Donatien de Vimeur, Comte de Rochambeau's (1725-1807) French forces at Yorktown, was forced to surrender. This capitulation spurred the negotiations to end the War. Cornwallis later served as Britain's Governor-General of India (1786-1793, and 1780), and Viceroy of Ireland (1798-1801). His relations were well known within Lichfield. Frederick Cornwallis (1713-1783), who had matriculated at Christ's College, Cambridge, and had once served as Chaplain to George II, was uncle to the General. Frederick Cornwallis served as Bishop of Lichfield and Coventry (1750-1768), after which time he was elected to the See of Canterbury, appointed by the Crown as Archbishop, the "Primate of All England" until his death. James Cornwallis, 4th Earl Cornwallis (1743-1824), brother of the General, held a succession of clerical leadership roles before he was consecrated as Bishop of Lichfield and Coventry by his uncle, the Archbishop of Canterbury.

William Cowper (1731-1800) a poet, hymn-writer, letter-writer, and translator who became known for his letters on everyday life in Olney and Weston Underwood, Buckinghamshire, as well as for his writings on various political and literary events. In Olney, Cowper worked closely with John Newton (1725-1807), the cleric and previous slave ship captain known for the hymn, "Amazing Grace" – one of the "Olney Hymns" on which Newton and Cowper collaborated. For further insight into Newton, see Jonathan Aitken, *John Newton: From Disgrace to Amazing Grace* (Wheaton, IL: Crossway Books, 2007). Seward's "Remonstrance Addressed to William Cowper, Esq in 1788 On the Sarcasm Levelled at National Gratitude in *The Task*" appeared in her *Poetical Works*, vol. 3, pp.5-14.

Thomas Day (1748-1789) studied classics at Corpus Christi, Oxford, from 1764-67, slightly after Edgeworth's time there. Although little had been written about Day before Anna Seward's *Life of Dr Darwin* appeared, he has received considerable biographical attention in recent years. Two works that appeared before Seward's *Life of Dr Darwin* were James Keir, *An Account of the Life and Writings of Thomas Day, Esq* (London: John Stockdale, 1791), and Johann Jacob Carl Timaeus, *Thomas Day, Esq; Das Leben eines der edelsten Männer unsers Jahrhunderts* (Leipzig, 1798). Among the works that appeared later, see John Blackman, *A Memoir of the Life and Writings of Thomas Day, Author of 'Sandford and Merton'* (London: John Bedford Leno, 1862); George Warren Gignilliat, Jr., *The Author of Sandford and Merton: A Life of Thomas Day, Esq.* (New York: Columbia University Press, 1932); S.H Scott, *The Exemplary Mr Day, 1748-1789, Author of Sandford and Merton, A Philosopher in Search of the Life of Virtue and of a Paragon Among Women* (London: Faber and Faber Ltd., [1935]); and Peter Rowland, *The Life and Times of Thomas Day, 1748-1789: English Philanthropist and Author, Virtue Almost Personified* (Lewiston: E. Mellen Press, 1996). For Day's Lunar Men associations, see especially Sandra Burr, "Inspiring Lunatics: Biographical Portraits of the Lunar Society's Erasmus Darwin, Thomas Day, and Joseph Priestley", *Eighteenth-Century Life* 24 (2000): 111-127.

Mrs Mary Delany (1700-1788), daughter of Colonel Bernard Granville, Lord Lansdowne (1671-1723), married Alexander Pendarves (d. 1724), then Patrick Delany (*c.* 1686-1768). Delany had matriculated at Trinity College Dublin, served as Dean of Downpatrick, and was an intimate of Jonathan Swift (1667-1745). Mrs Delany was an accomplished oil painter, embroiderer, and designer of shell work within the interior of Delville, the Delany's Dublin home. In her late years, Mrs Delany introduced her own art form, a "new way of imitating flowers" in the form of "paper mosaicks", a construction of elegantly decorated compositions of coloured paper in an imitation of her *hortus siccus* (dried flower collection). Mrs Delany's botanical interests were stimulated when she resided with the Duchess of Portland at Bulstrode. There, in 1771, she met with Joseph Banks and Daniel Solander (1733-1782) – both of whom had sailed as Cook's naturalists, collecting botanical specimens along the way. The Portland's family chaplain, the Revd. John Lightfoot (1735-1788), was an accomplished botanist, as was the botanical artist, George Dionysius Ehret (1708-1770), whose wife, Susannah Kennet, was sister-in-law to the famed author and Gardener at Chelsea Physic Garden, Philip Miller (1691-1771). Mrs Delany's elder brother, Bernard Granville, 2nd Duke of Albemarle, (1700-1776), lived at Calwich, close to Wootton, while Rousseau was there making his own botanical ramblings. Bernard was also a favourite friend of Handel, whose music Seward adored. For an illustrative overview of Mrs Delany, please see her descendant, Ruth Hayden's *Mrs Delany: Her Life and Her Flowers* (London: Colonade, 1980).

William Dimond (*c.* 1784-1837), playwright and author of *The Hero of the North: A Historical Play* (1803), also went by the names James Dimond and William Driver, particularly when he encountered legal problems. In addition to writing approximately 30 pieces for the stage, Dimond contributed Della Cruscan poetry to the *Morning Herald* under the pseudonym "Castilio." He took over the management of the Bath and Bristol theatres from his father William Wyatt Dimond in 1812, but gave up control of the Bath theatre in 1823 and thereafter seems to have been accused of a number of crimes.

Robert Dodsley (1703-1764), author, bookseller and publisher of authors including Samuel Johnson, Alexander Pope, and Thomas Gray. He prepared a three-volume widely reprinted multi-edition work of what were seen to be significant miscellaneous poems (including Thomas Seward's influential "The Female Right to Literature, in a Letter to a Young Lady from Florence") entitled, *A Collection of Poems by Several Hands* (London: R. and J. Dodsley, 1748). Dodsley also founded the *Annual Register* in 1758 with Edmund Burke as the editor. For further information, see Harry M. Solomon, *The Rise of Robert Dodsley: Creating the New Age of Print* (Carbondale, Illinois: Southern Illinois University Press, 1996).

Henry Essex Edgeworth (1745-1807), later The Abbé Edgeworth de Firmont, gained particular notice at the other end of the French Revolution. He converted to Catholicism, left Co. Longford, was educated by Jesuits in Toulouse and Paris, was ordained at the Seminaire des Trente Trois, Paris, became Confessor to Louis XVI and attended him on the scaffold (21 July 1793). It was at the point of regicide that the people of France lost considerable sympathy and support from many abroad. For an overview of this Edgeworth, see Vivienne Abbot, *An Irishman's Revolution: The Abbé Edgeworth and Louis XVI* (Dublin: Kavanagh Press, 1989).

Maria Edgeworth (1768-1849), the daughter of Richard Lovell Edgeworth and his first wife, Anna Marie Elers (1743-1773). Among her many works on childhood education were *The Parent's Assistant; or, Stories for Children* (London: J. Johnson, 1796), and the five-volume *Moral Tales for Young People* (London: J. Johnson, 1801). Her major modern biographer, Marilyn Butler, claimed that Edgeworth was "easily the most celebrated and successful of practising English novelists of her day" publishing more than a dozen novels, including her first and most famous *Castle Rackrent* (1800) (*Maria Edgeworth: A Literary Biography*, Oxford: Oxford University Press, 1971, p.1). For more background on Edgeworth, see the introductory essays in the 12 volumes of *The Works of Maria Edgeworth*, Gen. Ed. Marilyn Butler (Pickering and Chatto, 2003), and the numerous and insightful published essays on Edgeworth written by Mitzi Myers.

Richard Lovell Edgeworth (1744-1817) matriculated at Trinity College, Dublin, but after "uproarious living", he went on to Corpus Christi, Oxford, where, as one of the College's sixteen students, he lodged with the family friend and Oxford solicitor at nearby Black Bourton, Paul Elers (d. 1781), son of the Dutch Burselm, Staffordshire, potter, John Philip Elers (1664-1738). Edgeworth eloped with Paul's daughter, Anna Marie Elers (1743-1773) in 1763, and they were married a year later. In later years, Edgeworth spent considerable time in London where he met with a loosely organized group of influential men with natural philosophical interests including Captain James Cook (1728-1779), the exploring naturalists, Sir Joseph Banks (1743-1820) and Daniel Solander (1733-1782), the engineers John Smeaton (1724-1792) and Jesse Ramsden (1735-1800), the surgeon, John Hunter (1728-93), physicians Sir Charles Blagden (bap.1748-1820) and Dr George Fordyce (1736-1802), and the Astronomer Royal, Nevil Maskelyne (1732-1811). For more on Edgeworth, see R. L Edgeworth and M. Edgeworth, *Memoirs of Richard Lovell Edgeworth, Esq.*, 2nd ed (London: Hunter, Baldwin, Cradock, and Joy, 1821); D. Clarke, *The Ingenious Mr Edgeworth* (London: Oldbourne, 1965); and Uglow, *The Lunar Men*.

George Augustus Eliott, 1st Baron Heathfield of Gibraltar (1717-1790) who had distinguished himself at the Battle of Minden, is best known for his work both as a British General and as Governor of Gibraltar in withstanding the long siege of Gibraltar by French and Spanish forces 1779 to 1783. This event is captured in George Carter's (bap.1737-1794) 1784 painting, "The Siege of Gibraltar, 1782". As Ashmun noted (*Singing Swan*, p.155), Lord Heathfield visited Anna Seward in Lichfield in the summer of 1787, during his triumphal tour of England, in recognition of the encomiums Seward had placed upon him in her *Ode*.

Robert Fellowes (1771-1847) was editor of the *Critical Review, or, Annals of Literature* and had become quite well known for his many religious writings that were "tinged with the ideas of practical philanthropy", according to The Reverend Alexander Gordon, "Robert Fellowes", *Dictionary of National Biography* (London: Smith, Elder, and Co, 1889), vol. 18, pp.300-301. By 1804, Fellowes had published *A Picture of Christian Philosophy: or, A Theological, Philosophical, and Practical Illustration of the Character of Jesus* (London: H. Sharpe for John White, 1798), *The Anti-Calvinist:, or, Two Plain Discourses on Redemption and Faith*

(Warwick: H. Sharpe for White and Cooke, 1800), *Religion Without Cant; or, A Preservative Against Lukewarmness and Intolerance, Fanaticism, Superstition, and Impiety* (London: J. White, 1801), and *The Guide to Immortality; Or, Memoirs of the Life and Doctrine of the Four Evangelists: Digested into One Continued Narrative* (London: J. White, 1804). Fellowes gained further notice as a promoter of the University of London, established in the early 19th century.

Sir John Floyer, MD (1649-1734), physician in Lichfield, "arranged for the funding and construction of St Chad's Bath at Unite's Well, Abnalls, a mile southwest of Lichfield". In a series of writings, Floyer resurrected the medicinal value of cold bathing, invoking both ancient wisdom and his own experience in Lichfield. He envisioned that "many afflictions of the time had resulted from a dietary hot regimen, which had become popular since the opening up of trade with the Indies, and which was unsuited to English constitutions", as summarized by Denis Gibbs and Philip K. Wilson (eds), *'Advice to a Young Physician' and Other Essays by Sir John Floyer (1649-1734) of Lichfield in Staffordshire* (York, England: Sessions, 2007), esp. pp. 8-10.

Henry Fuseli (1741-1825), formerly Johann Heinrich Füssli, Swiss-born painter of exotic, sensual art, working in London (and Italy) beginning 1764, becoming Professor of Painting at the Royal Academy in 1799. Noted for his macabre image, "The Nightmare" (1781), a painting Sir Brooke Boothby purchased for Ashbourne Hall, Fuseli's oeuvre greatly influenced William Blake, among others. Fuseli's support of several radical causes was noted in his writings in the *Analytical Review*. An engraving of "The Nightmare" was also included in *The Poetical Works of Erasmus Darwin, Containing the Botanical Garden, In Two Parts; And the Temple of Nature* (London: For J. Johnson by T. Bensley, 1806), vol. II, facing p. 126. In his early years in Switzerland, Fuseli was a friend and classmate of the Swiss poet and physiognomist, Johann Kaspar Lavater (1741-1801). Donald Reiman (Introduction, *The Botanic Garden*, p.xii) noted that Darwin's poetry "strongly influence[d] Blake's later art, especially in [Blake's] own engraved poetry, where human figures regularly emerge from vegetation". For more on Fuseli and Dr Darwin, see Asia Haut, "Reading Flora: Erasmus Darwin's *The Botanic Garden*, Henry Fuseli's Illustrations, and Various Literary Responses", *Word & Image* 20 (2004): 240-256, and on Fuseli in general, see Frederick Antal, *Fuseli Studies* (London: Routledge & Kegan Paul, 1956). Alan E. Boulton is currently working on a doctoral dissertation at the Barber Institute of Fine Art at the University of Birmingham that is provisionally entitled, "The Embodiment of Sublimity: Discourses Between Visual, Literary, and Philosophical Conceptions of Sentience in the Drawings of Henry Fuseli, 1770-78". For more on Blake and Darwin, see Matthew Green, "Blake, Darwin and the Promiscuity of Knowing: Rethinking Blake's Relationship to the Midlands Enlightenment", *British Journal for Eighteenth-Century Studies* 30 (2007): 193-208.

John Gisborne (1770-1851), husband of Millicent Pole with whom he had eleven children. The Gisborne's lived at Holly Bush, at Newborough, Staffordshire, in the heart of the ancient Needwood Forest, just a mile from the Gisborne family estate, Yoxall Lodge. They became close friends of Jane Austen's (1775-1817) cousin, their neighbour Edward

Cooper (1770-1835) and his wife, Carolina Isabella Powys (1775-1838). The men shared an evangelical passion as well as a strong interest in botany. For a contemporary account of Gisborne, see the work of his daughter, Emma Nixon, *A Brief Memoir of the Life of John Gisborne, Esq., To which are Added, Extracts from his Diary* (London, 1852).

Revd. Thomas Gisborne (1758-1846), divine, poet, writer, and drawing and musical companion of Joseph Wright of Derby. Thomas had been at St John's, Cambridge, with William Wilberforce (1759-1833) who, in turn, spent considerable time with the Gisbornes at their home, Yoxall Lodge, Staffordshire, in Needwood Forest, while pursuing his abolition of slavery work.

Thomas Gray (1716-1771), the Eton educated poet, later matriculated at Peterhouse College, Cambridge, and remains best known for *An Elegy Written in a Country Church Yard* (London: R. Dodsley, 1751). He later became Professor of History and Modern Languages at Cambridge in 1768.

Richard Greene (1716-1793), a Lichfield apothecary who had established both his shops and a collection of curiosities displayed in a museum within his Market Street shop. Annette French delivered a paper on "Mr Greene's Museum of Curiosities" at the Annual General Meeting of the Johnson Society of Lichfield on 22 March 2006. This paper was published in *The Transactions of the Johnson Society* 2006 (Lichfield: The Johnson Society, 2007), pp.19-28, and is also available online at: www.lichfieldrambler.co.uk/famous_argument.htm.

William Hayley (1745-1820) a poet and biographer, friend of William Cowper and one-time employer of William Blake who frequently corresponded with Anna Seward, first visiting her in Lichfield for a fortnight in December 1781. He was known as the "Bard of Eartham" after his home in Sussex, where Seward visited him for six weeks during the summer of 1782. Seward's biographer, Ashmun, claimed that Hayley "lived for some years in the possession of unrivalled popularity" (*The Singing Swan*, p.9).

Frederick Howard, the Fifth Earl of Carlisle (1748-1825). In 1778, Lord Carlisle was sent to America by Britain's Prime Minister, Frederick North, 2nd Earl of Guilford (1732-1792) to "treat, consult and agree upon the means of quieting the disorders" in the American colonies. Alas, he was too late to "talk peace" and to block France's alliance with the colonies. A liberal patron of the fine arts, and one whom Anna Seward regarded as "Professedly a disciple of the Muses", Lord Carlisle was later appointed as the guardian of his first cousin, George Gordon, Lord Byron (1788-1824). The Prime Minister's brother, Brownlow North (1741-1820) served as Bishop of Lichfield and Coventry from 1771-1774. Lord Carlisle married Lady Margaret Caroline Leveson-Gower (1753-1824), daughter of Sir Granville Leveson-Gower, the First Marquis of Stafford (1721-1803), in 1770. Their son, Henry Edward John Howard (1795-1868), was appointed Dean of Lichfield Cathedral in 1833.

William Howe, 5th Viscount Howe (1729-1814), was Commander-in-Chief of the British Army in North America from 1776-1778, during which time his troops won the Battle of Brandywine and the Battle of Germantown, but failed to conquer General Washington's troops which were encamped at Valley Forge.

Joseph Johnson (1738-1809) a Unitarian, gained considerable fame for his publication of the more radical, progressive thinkers of the day, including Dr Joseph Priestley (1733-1804), Anna Barbauld (1743-1825), Henry Fuseli (1741-1825), Mary Wollstonecraft (1759-1797), and Maria Edgeworth (1767-1849). For overviews of his publishing career, see Gerald P. Tyson, *Joseph Johnson, A Liberal Publisher* (Iowa City: University of Iowa Press, 1979) and Helen Braithwaite, *Romanticism, Publishing and Dissent: Joseph Johnson and the Cause of Liberty* (Gordonsville, Virginia: Palgrave Macmillan, 2003).

Samuel Johnson (1709-1784), born in Lichfield, was influenced by the many books that his father, a Lichfield-based book publisher and book seller, produced. He matriculated at Pembroke College, Oxford, but insufficient finances did not allow him to complete a degree. He returned to Lichfield and, after a short stint as a grammar school teacher, he famously left Lichfield for London to seek his fortune. There, he turned to writing for a living, producing a number of significant poems, essays, book reviews, and derivative biographies. In 1755, he produced his monumental *A Dictionary of the English Language: In Which the Words are Deduced from their Originals, and Illustrated in their Different Significations by Examples from the Best Writers* (London: Printed by W. Strahan for J. and P. Knapton, T. and T. Longman, C. Hitch. L. Hawes, A. Millar, and R. and J. Dodsley, 1755). Seward published several sonnets on Dr Johnson, including "On Doctor Johnson's Unjust Criticism in his *Lives of the Poets*" (Sonnet LXVII), "On the Posthumous Fame of Doctor Johnson" (Sonnet LXVIII), and "The Critics of Dr Johnson's School" (Sonnet LXXVI) in *Original Sonnets on Various Subjects; And Odes Paraphrased from Horace* (London: G. Sael, 1799). Further information about Johnson's life, and in particular his early years in Lichfield, is available from The Samuel Johnson Birthplace Museum, Breadmarket Street, Lichfield, Staffordshire WS13 6LG, United Kingdom or online at: www.samueljohnsonbirthplace.org.uk/index.asp.

Sir William "Persian" Jones (1746-1794), a graduate of University College, Oxford, who became an accomplished linguist and friend of Samuel Johnson and Edmund Burke and, for a period, shared rooms in the Lamb's Building of Middle Temple with Thomas Day, as noted by P. Rowland, *Thomas Day*, p.53. For a thorough overview of Jones' travels and scholarship, see Garland Cannon, *The Life and Mind of Oriental Jones: Sir William Jones, The Father of Modern Linguistics* (Cambridge: Cambridge University Press, 2006). Seward's "Eastern Ode, Translated from the Prose of Sir William Jones", appeared in her *Poetical Works*, vol. 2, pp.300-304, and her "Invocation to the Shade of Petrarch, and to the Spirits of the Persian Poets, on their Compositions being Translated into English, by Sir William Jones" appeared in her *Poetical Works*, vol. 1, pp.113-114.

James Keir (1735-1820) initially studied medicine at the University of Edinburgh but temporarily abandoned academic studies for Army service during The Seven Years' War

(1756-1763). This war between France and England was linked to the French and Indian War which had erupted in the American colonies two years previously. The Treaty of Paris, which ended this warfare, awarded England the country of Canada and all its territory east of the Mississippi River (from France) and Florida (from Spain). However, England's success was costly, and its attempts to cover debts and to pay for a sustained military presence in America by taxing the colonists in America considerably strained relations between England and her American colonies. Keir later returned to his pursuits in chemistry. Combining chemistry and industrialism, he pursued successful ventures in glass manufacturing, alkali manufacturing (i.e., producing caustic soda from salt), and, most profitably, soap manufacturing. His writings and discussions as part of the Lunar Society added further support to Joseph Priestley's promotion of the phlogiston theory as an account of why things burn. According to this theory, combustible substances and metals contain phlogiston. Although undetectable to our senses, phlogiston is released from combustible substances upon burning as was "caloric" (heat). For further insight into Keir's chemical investigations, see Barbara M.D. Smith and J.L. Moilliet, "James Keir of the Lunar Society", *Notes and Records of the Royal Society of London* 22 (1967): 144-154.

Richard Kirwan (1733-1812), Irish natural philosopher who contributed to meteorology, chemistry, geology, magnetism, and philology and who, in 1799, became President of the Royal Irish Academy. A friend of Priestley and other Lunar Men, Kirwan was one of the last supporters of the phlogiston theory. For an overview of his contributions, see R. Reilly and N. O'Flynn, "Richard Kirwan, an Irish Chemist of the Eighteenth Century", *Isis* 13 (1930): 298-319.

William Mason (1724/25-1797), poet and cleric, matriculated at St John's College, Cambridge, and published an account of Thomas Gray, whose poems greatly influenced his own work, as "Memoirs of the Life and Writings of Mr Gray" in his edited *The Poems of Mr Gray* (York: A. Ward, 1775). Mason was a friend of Dr Darwin's Chesterfield School Headmaster, William Burrow (1683-1758).

John Michell (1724-1793) generally noted for his skill in the geological sciences, for which he briefly held the Woodwardian Professorship in Geology at Cambridge, as well as in astronomy and in the study of magnets. Dr Darwin had come to know Michell when the latter was a tutor at Queens College, Cambridge. Following his service as Woodwardian Professor, Michell turned to a different calling, serving as Rector of Thornhill, Yorkshire, near Leeds. For a time, Michell lived at Park Hall, Alcester, part of the Ragley Estate. It was there that Anna Seward and John Saville visited him in 1780. For further insight into Michell's contributions, see A. Geikie, *Memoirs of John Michell* (Cambridge: Cambridge University Press, 1918), and Clyde L. Hardin, "The Scientific Work of the Reverend John Michell", *Annals of Science* 22 (1966): 27-47.

Lady Anna Miller (1741-1781), the "Sappho of the Batheaston Literati" from 1774-1781. These assemblies, which Anna Seward attended, attracted a number of notables, including William Mason, Frederick Howard, the Fifth Earl of Carlisle, Lady Georgina Spencer, the

Duchess of Devonshire, the dramatist and poet, Edward Jerningham (1737-1812), the poet, novelist and Rector of Claverton, Richard Graves (1715-1804), the Prebendary of Wells Cathedral, Thomas Sedgwick Whalley (1746-1828), the Lichfield-born divine, George Butt (1741-1795), Christopher Anstey (1724-1805), the author of *The New Bath Guide* (1766), and the Lichfield-educated London actor, David Garrick (1717-1779). Upon Lady Miller's death, Seward composed a *Poem to the Memory of Lady Miller* (London: G. Robinson, 1782) as well as the epitaph in verse for John Bacon the Elder's (1740-1799) sculpted monument in the Abbey Church of St Peter, Bath. According to Seward, Lady Miller "rendered this Meeting a Poetical Institution, giving out Subjects at each Assembly for Poems to be read on the ensuing one. The Verses were deposited in an antique Etruscan Vase and were drawn out by Gentlemen appointed to read them aloud and to judge of their rival Merits. These Gentlemen, ignorant of the Authors, selected three Poems from the Collection which they thought most worthy of the three Myrtle Wreaths, decreed as the Rewards and Honours of the Day. The Names of the Persons who had obtained the Prizes were then announced by Lady Miller. Once a Year the most ingenious of these Productions were published" (A. Seward, *Poem to the Memory of Lady Miller*, Preface). Four volumes were published. For more on this literary salon, see R.A. Hesselgrave, *Lady Miller and the Batheaston Literary Circle* (New Haven: Yale University Press, 1927).

Esther Milnes (1753-1792) spent her formative years in Mrs Dennis' Female Boarding School, Queen's Square, Bloomsbury, London. She inherited the Wakefield, Yorkshire estate of her merchant father, Richard Milnes (1705-1757). Richard had gained a monopoly over cotton manufacturing in the area, amassing great wealth with which he acquired, among other things, one of the largest collections of Joseph Wright's landscape paintings. (B. Nicholson, *Wright*, p.159).

Lady Mary Wortley Montagu (1689-1762) observed first-hand the practise of inoculating against smallpox (actually the practise of variolation or engrafting) in Constantinople, where her husband, Sir Edward Wortley Montagu (1678-1761), served as England's Ambassador to the Ottoman Empire (1716-1718). Shortly after her return to London, that city experienced yet another severe smallpox epidemic in 1721, during which, after the successful inoculation of six condemned prisoners at Newgate Prison, the Royal Family acquiesced to having their children inoculated, whereupon the procedure gained wide public support. For further discussion, see Isabel Grundy, *Lady Mary Wortley Montagu: Comet of the Enlightenment* (Oxford: Oxford University Press, 1999). At the western end of the north aisle of Lichfield Cathedral, one finds the monument noting Lady Mary's contribution that, in 1789, Henrietta (née Wrottesley) Inge (b. 1715), wife of Theodore William Inge (1711-1753), and herself a relative of Lady Mary, had erected. This cenotaph, with Beauty weeping over the loss of her preserver, reads, "Sacred to the Memory of The Right Honourable Lady Mary Wortley Montague [sic] Who happily introduc'd from Turkey into this country, The Salutary Art of inoculating the Small-Pox. Convinc'd of its Efficacy She first tried it with Success On her own Children; And then recommended the practice of it To her fellow-Citizens. Thus by her Example and Advice, We have soften'd the Virulence, And escaped the danger of this malignant Disease, To perpetuate the Memory of such Benevolence; And to express her Gratitude For the benefit She herself has receiv'd From the alleviating Art". This remains the only such memorial tribute to Lady Mary's efforts against smallpox. For an historical context of smallpox, see Jennifer Lee Carrell, *The Speckled Monster: A Historical Tale of Battling Smallpox* (New York: Dutton, 2003), Ian and Jennifer Glynn, *The Life and Death of Smallpox* (London: Profile Books, 2004), and in relation to literature, David E. Shuttleton, *Smallpox and the Literary Imagination 1660-1820* (Cambridge: Cambridge University Press, 2007). Lady Mary was also a writer of both ambition and renown, publishing *Poetical Works* (1768), and *Letters Written During her Travels* (1763), among other volumes. Although her complete literary output is yet to be discovered, twentieth-century scholars have identified her as the author of the novella *Princess Docile* and the political periodical *The Nonsense of Common Sense*.

Francis Noel Clarke Mundy (1739-1815), matriculated at New College, Oxford, in 1757, then returned to Markeaton Hall, Derbyshire. A sportsman and poet, he remains known particularly for his Lichfield-published work, *Needwood Forest* (Lichfield: John Jackson, 1776). This work, published anonymously, also included poems written by Anna Seward and Dr Darwin. Mundy followed this work with *The Fall of Needwood* (Derby: J. Drewry, 1808). Seward's "Epistle to F.C.R. Mundy, Esq." appeared in her *Poetical Works*, vol. 2, pp.199-206, and her "To F.N.C. Mundy, Esq on his Poem, *The Fall of Needwood Forest*", appeared in her *Poetical Works*, vol. 3, pp.394-397.

Mary Parker (1753-1820) was initially employed as Robert Darwin's nursemaid during which time Dr Darwin's sister, Susannah (1729-1789) had come to live with her brother as his housekeeper when his wife died. Her two daughters, Mary Parker (1774–1859) and Susanna Parker (1772–1856) were both natural daughters of Dr Darwin. Parker married Joseph Day (1745-1811) in 1782 and moved to Birmingham, as noted by King-Hele (ed) *Collected Letters of Erasmus Darwin*, p.240, note 1.

Thomas Percival (1740-1804), began his education at Warrington Academy and later received an MD from Edinburgh. He subsequently became a major public health reformer. He founded the Manchester Literary and Philosophical Society in 1781, over which he presided until his death. He is often noted as the "Father" of English medical ethics for his publication, *Medical Ethics; or, A Code of Institutes and Precepts, Adapted to the Professional Conduct of Physicians and Surgeons. To Which is Added an Appendix; Containing a Discourse on Hospital Duties* (Manchester: S. Russell for J. Johnson, 1803). For further discussion of Percival's many contributions, see Lisbeth Haakonssen, *Medicine and Morals in the Enlightenment. John Gregory, Thomas Percival and Benjamin Rush* (Amsterdam and Atlanta: Rodopi, 1997). Percival's Manchester was well known to John Aikin who gained notice for his historical *Description of the Country from Thirty to Forty Miles Round Manchester* (1795) reprinted in facsimile by (Newton Abbot: David & Charles, 1968).

Francesco Petrarca (1304-1374), the Italian poet and founding Renaissance humanist. By 1336, Petrarch began to compile *Rerum vulgarium fragmenta*, better known as *Il Canzoniere*, or *The Song Book* which, at the time of his death, contained 366 poems. Most of these poems were sonnets written to and about Laura, most likely Laure de Noves (1310-1348) – if "Laura" actually existed all – the love of his life who always remained unreachable. At a public coronation in 1341, Petrarch received the title and the laurel crown of Poet Laureate of Rome. He travelled considerably, adopted Parma, the residence of princes, as his home, but frequently returned to Vaucluse, that celebrated valley near Avignon, for solitude and enjoyment of the rural surrounds.

Richard Polwhele (1760-1838), divine, poet, and topographer, matriculated at Christ Church, Oxford, and became known for many poetical works as well as for his topographical histories of Devonshire and Cornwall. Polwhele's *The Unsex'd Females: A Poem, Addressed to the Author of the Pursuits of Literature* (London: Cadell and Davies, 1798) raised considerable ire. During the revolutionary era when freedom and equality were common themes for radical writers, women, too, joined the fray of those seeking an equal voice. Among the most prominent female voices in England during this time was that of Mary Wollstonecraft (1759-1797). Polwhele, a conservative Anglican, opposed Wollstonecraft's belief in free love relationships as well as her arguments for women's equal access to education. However, Polwhele admired "Bluestocking" authors, women including Seward, who showed what he deemed proper femininity and morality in their works. Curiously, though Polwhele noted Dr Darwin's *Botanic Garden* as a work of merit, he typically despised the growth of amateur pursuits of botany for women as an area in which they were exposed to the improper teachings of reproduction – what he interpreted as a sign of the moral decay of society.

Sarah Ponsonby (*c.* 1755-1831) with Lady Eleanor Butler, was known as The Ladies of Llangollen. Seward became a friend and occasional visitor of The Ladies at their idyllic cottage, Plas Newydd, Llangollen, Wales. John Brewer noted that The Ladies lead a "life of rustic isolation, intellectual refinement and ardent female friendship [which] fascinated fashionable society", in a chapter titled, "'Queen Muse of Britain': Anna Seward of Lichfield and the Literary Provinces", in his *The Pleasures of the Imagination: English Culture in the Eighteenth Century* (New York: Farrar Straus Giroux, 1997), p.591. Seward's admiration of The Ladies is apparent through her poem, *Llangollen Vale* (1796), and her close association with The Ladies is recounted in Elizabeth Mavor, *The Ladies of Llangollen* (Harmondsworth, Middlesex: Penguin, 1973) and in Paula R. Backscheider, *Eighteenth-Century Women Poets and their Poetry: Inventing Agency, Inventing Genre* (Baltimore: The Johns Hopkins University Press, 2005), esp. pp.291-313. At the time of her demise, Seward remembered The Ladies with a mourning ring (Wickham, Journals *and Correspondence of Thomas Sedgewick Whalley*, vol. 2, p.440, note).

Margaret Cavendish Bentinck, Duchess of Portland (1715-1785) from whose estate, William Henry Cavendish-Bentinck, 3rd Duke of Portland (1738-1809) purchased the vase. The Duke, who eventually served as Chancellor of the University of Oxford and as Prime Minister, loaned Wedgwood the vase to be copied. For an interesting cultural history of this vase, see Robin Brook's *The Portland Vase. The Extraordinary Odyssey of a Mysterious Roman Treasure* (New York: HarperCollins: 2004). See, in addition, D.E.L. Hayes, *The Portland Vase*

(London: The British Museum, 1964), and Milo Keynes, "The Portland Vase: Sir William Hamilton, Josiah Wedgwood and the Darwins", *Notes and Records of the Royal Society of London* 52 (1998): 237-249. After three years of work, Wedgwood produced what he deemed his first perfect copy of this black jasper vase with white cameo reliefs in Autumn 1789, and he sent it to Dr Darwin. Since 1963, the vase that Wedgwood sent to Darwin has resided in Cambridge University's Fitzwilliam Museum. Darwin celebrated this vase – Wedgwood's production of a lifetime – in his *Botanic Garden* together with accompanying engravings of four different aspects of the vase prepared by William Blake. (Mona Wilson, *The Life of William Blake*, Oxford: Oxford University Press, 1971, p.46. See also David Worrall, "William Blake and Erasmus Darwin's *Botanic Garden*", *Bulletin of the New York Public Library* 78 (1975): 397-417). Dr Darwin noted that the cameos on the vase depicted initiation rites into the Greek Eleusian Mysteries, central to which lay the belief that natural organic matter could not be destroyed, but merely transformed. He corroborated this view of a universal cycle of life in his *Botanic Garden*. Among Darwin and Wedgwood's contemporaries, William Warburton (1698-1779), Bishop of Gloucester during much of Darwin's residence in Lichfield, devoted serious attention to the Eleusian Mysteries in his *Divine Legation of Moses Demonstrated on the Principles of a Religious Deist* (London: Fletcher Gyles,1737-1741). For an historical reflection, see Irwin Primer, "Erasmus Darwin's *Temple of Nature*: Progress, Evolution, and the Eleusian Mysteries", *Journal of the History of Ideas* 25 (1964): 58-76. The Duchess of Portland was a generous patron to the arts and sciences. A botanical enthusiast, she was instrumental in creating the herbarium, now at Kew Gardens, and with her close friend Mary Delany created a shell grotto in Bulstrode.

Joseph Priestley (1733-1804) joined Warrington Academy as a tutor in September 1761. He is best known for promoting the phlogiston theory as an account of why things burn. According to this theory, combustible substances and metals contain phlogiston. Although undetectable to our senses, phlogiston is released from combustible substances upon burning as was "caloric" (heat). Notably, in 1774 while working at Bowood House, near Chippenham, Wiltshire, the home of William Petty, 2nd Earl of Shelburne, later 1st Marquis of Lansdowne (1737–1805), Priestley found that unlike the other gases he had tested, one gas had the unique ability to enhance a candle's burning within a sealed glass apparatus. Based upon the phlogiston theory, he called this special gas that he had discovered dephlogisticated air; the gas we have come to know as oxygen. For further recently published insights into Priestley's multifaceted pursuits, see Robert E. Schofield, *The Enlightenment of Joseph Priestley: A Study of His Life and Work from 1733-1773* (University Park, Pennsylvania: Penn State Press, 1997); Robert E. Schofield, *The Enlightened Joseph Priestley: A Study of His Life and Work from 1773-1804* (University Park, Pennsylvania: Penn State University Press, 2004); Malcolm Dick (ed) *Joseph Priestley and Birmingham* (Studley, Warwickshire: Brewin, 2005), Joe Jackson, *A World On Fire: A Heretic, An Aristocrat, and the Race to Discover Oxygen* (New York: Viking, 2005), and Steven Johnson, *The Invention of Air: A Story of Science, Faith, Revolution, and the Birth of America* (New York: Riverhead Books, 2008). For a broader discussion of oxygen, see Nick Lane, *Oxygen: The Molecule that Made the World* (Oxford: Oxford University Press, 2002) and Carl Djerassi and Roald Hoffman, *Oxygen: A Play in Two Acts* (New York: Wiley, 2001). In something of a self-exile, Priestley relocated to Pennsylvania, USA following the destruction of his home during the 1791 Birmingham Riots. Particulars about his American home and life are available at Joseph Priestley House, 472 Priestley Avenue, Northumberland, Pennsylvania, 17857 USA, via its website, www.josephpriestleyhouse.org/links.html, as well as in Alison Duncan Hirsch, *Joseph Priestley House: Pennsylvania Trail of History Guide* (Mechanicsburg, PA: Stackpole Books: 2003).

Matthew Prior (1664-1721), studied at St John's, Cambridge, wrote poetry and held various Tory diplomatic posts, including Britain's Ambassadorship to Paris. Prior was perhaps best known for *Alma; or, The Progress of the Mind* (1715). This work, included in his *Poems on Several Occasions* (London: J. Tonson, and J. Barber, 1725), was a humorous speculative piece on the relations between the body and the soul. For more on Prior see, for example, Charles Eves, *Matthew Prior: Poet and Diplomatist* (New York: Octagon Books, 1973).

Samuel Richardson (1689-1761), an English novelist known for composing novels that extensively used letters, a form known as the epistolary novel which served as a model for Jane Austen. Major novels include *Pamela* (1740), *Clarissa* (1748), and *The History of Sir Charles Grandison* (1753). He gained his experience through apprenticeship in the Stationers' Company, the guild of printers and of the book trade, and he eventually became a close friend of Samuel Johnson.

Jean-Jacques Rousseau (1712-1778), a Swiss-born philosopher, educational theorist, and introspective autobiographer who, in his early works, envisioned humans as "noble savages" when in their natural state (i.e., before the corrupting influence of civilization and society). Later, in his *Du Contract Social; Ou Principes du Droit Politique* (Amsterdam: Marc Michel Rey, 1762), he reversed his earlier views, arguing that goodness in humanity is only derived from one's mutual interaction with society. Dr Darwin met Rousseau in 1766, while the philosopher was composing the first portion of his fully revealing autobiography, *The Confessions of J.-J. Rousseau: With the Reveries of the Solitary Walker* (London: J. Bew, 1783, translated from first French edition, Geneva: 1782), as a guest of the Cheshire merchant, Richard Davenport (*c.*1706-1771) at Wootton Hall, Staffordshire, in the parish of Ellastone, near Ashbourne. Knowing that Rousseau despised being interrupted, Darwin sauntered by the entrance of a cave on the terrace of Wootton Hall, where he "Minutely examined a plant growing in front of it". This action "drew forth Rousseau, who was very interested in botany, and they conversed together, and afterwards corresponded for years" (C. Darwin, *Life of Erasmus Darwin*, p.47). Alexandra Cook recounts some of Rousseau's England experiences with botany in "Botanical Exchanges: Jean-Jacques Rousseau and the Duchess of Portland", *History of European Ideas* 33 (2007): 142-156. Rousseau composed a popular botanical treatise, *Letters on the Elements of Botany. Addressed to a Lady. [Madame Madeleine-Catherine Delessert (1747-1816)] Translated into English, with Notes, and Twenty-Four Additional Letters, Fully Explaining the System of Linnaeus* (London: B. White and Sons, 1785), which went through several editions in French and in English translation. The translator, Thomas Martyn (1735-1825), was appointed Professor of Botany at Cambridge University in 1762. For overviews of Rousseau's time in England, see J.H. Broome, "Jean-Jacques Rousseau in Staffordshire 1766-1767", *North Staffordshire Journal of Field Studies* 6 (1966): 47-60, and David Edmonds and John Eidinow, *Rousseau's Dog: Two Great Thinkers at War in the Age of the Enlightenment* (New York: Ecco/HarperCollins, 2006), as well as Leo Damrosch, *Jean-Jacques Rousseau: Restless Genius* (New York: Houghton Mifflin, 2005).

David Samwell (1751-1798), a Welsh poet and naval surgeon, who served on Captain Cook's Third Voyage and witnessed Cook's death, corresponded with Anna Seward and, upon visiting her in Lichfield, presented her with a number of natural curiosities that had been collected on the voyage. Seward later presented them to Richard Greene (1716-1793), an apothecary who had established both his shop and a collection of curiosities displayed in a museum within his Market Street shop. Seward later expressed her disgruntlement to Samwell at not being presented with a commemorative medal of Cook that had been prepared by the Society for Arts and Sciences. In a 16 August 1790 letter to Samwell, Seward wrote, "So little value did the society ... set upon my poem on his death, that, while they avowedly presented one to every person, who had taken public interest in his fate and his virtues; while they gave Mr Greene of this town a medal, merely for having displayed, in his museum, some relics of those illustrious voyages, they took no notice on me". She expressed further regret in the following year (15 May), "It is curious that your bounty to me enabled Mr Greene to display in his museum those Otaheitean curiosities, whose exhibition obtained him a medal. I presented him with a part of your present, and was doubly glad that I had done so, when I found his displaying them rewarded by a distinction which cheered and delighted his honest benevolent heart". Through his good offices, Samwell was able to have Seward invested as an "*ovat*" (3rd degree) of the Welsh Bards at a *gorsedd* on Primrose Hill, London in 1793. Samwell contributed his own perspective on the death of Cook in *A Narrative of the Death of Captain James Cook. To Which are Added Some Particulars Concerning his Life and Character and Observations Respecting the Introduction of the Venereal Disease into the Sandwich Islands* (London: G.G.J. and J. Robinson, 1786). For more on Samwell, see William Ll. Davies, David Samwell (1751-1798): Surgeon of the 'Discovery', London-Welshman and Poet", *The Transactions of the Honourable Society of Cymmrodorion*, Session 1926-27 (1928): 69-133; E.G. Bowen, *David Samwell (Dafydd Ddu Feddyg) 1751-1798* (Cardiff: University of Wales Press, 1974); and Nicholas Thomas, Martin Fitzpatrick and Jenny Newell, *The Death of Captain Cook and other writings by David Samwell* (Cardiff: University of Wales Press, 2007).

John Sargent (1750-1831), Etonian who matriculated at St John's, Cambridge, and later became a director of the Bank of England. He was primarily known for his dramatic poem, *The Mine* (1785). The *Ode* Seward cited focused on Mary Queen of Scots and was included with the 3rd edition of this dramatic poem, published by T. Cadell and W. Davies in London in 1796.

Thomas Seward (1708-1790) was Rector of Eyam (pronounced ēēm), a village in the High Peak district of Derbyshire, at the time of his daughter Anna's birth. Seward was the protégé of Charles FitzRoy, 2nd Duke of Grafton (1690–1757), who had obtained for him the livings of Eyam as well as of Kinglsey, Staffordshire, both of which he continued to hold after his appointment in Lichfield. Joseph Wright painted Canon Seward's portrait (which was later engraved by Robert Hartley Cromek, 1770-1812) in the early 1780s. Anna composed the following words of gratitude as part of her "Verses to the Celebrated Painter, Mr Wright of Derby":

> Now, ardent Wright, from thy creative hand,
> With outline bold, and mellowest colouring warm,
> Rival of life, before the canvas stands
> My Father's lov'd and venerable form!
>
> O! when his urn shall drink my falling tears,
> Thy faithful tints shall shed a bless'd relief,
> Glow with mild luster through my darken'd years,
> And gild the gathering shades of filial grief!

These lines, the last two stanzas of her poem, appeared in *The Poetical Works of Anna Seward*, vol. 2, p, 142. Lunar Man John Whitehurst designed his most sophisticated sundial for the wall of Eyam Church where it was placed while Seward was Rector. The dial shows the parallel of the sun's declination for every month of the year, the scale of the sun's meridian altitude, and the scale of the azimuth as well as the points of the compass and a number of other meridians (Craven, *John Whitehurst*, pp.33-34).

Algernon Sidney (1622/23-1683), an aristocratic, libertarian republican Parliamentarian, supporter of Cromwell and enemy of Charles II. He adamantly opposed the divine right of kings and was executed in 1683 for plotting against the English monarchy. Sidney's *Discourses Concerning Government* (London: John Toland, 1698) was influential in the American colonies. Thomas Jefferson, for example, regarded Sidney's works as among the most influential philosophical voice for the foundations of liberty and human rights.

William Small (1734-1775), a Scot, received his MA (1755) and his MD (1765) from Marischal College, Aberdeen. Prior to meeting Dr Darwin, Small had taught natural philosophy, ethics, rhetoric, and *belles lettres* for six years at William and Mary College in the American colony of Virginia where among his students was the young Thomas Jefferson. Small also befriended Benjamin Franklin (1706-1790) when he visited the College in 1763. Returning to England in 1764, Small soon met Matthew Boulton and became one of the founding members of the Lunar Society, established a substantial medical practice in Birmingham, and contributed to many scientific developments in ceramics, chemistry, geology, gunnery, horology, mechanics, metallurgy, and optics. Indicative of his generous nature, Dr Small spent part of his career in a clinic with Dr John Ash (1723-1798) with whom he shared a house and practice at No. 9, Temple Row, in Birmingham, near the cathedral. There, they devoted considerable time to treating the poor. For further information, see Uglow *The Lunar Men*; King-Hele, *A Life of Unequalled Achievement*; Herbert L. Ganter, "William Small, Jefferson's Beloved Teacher", *William and Mary Quarterly* 41 (1947): 505-511; Gillian Hull, "William Small

1734-1775: No Publications, Much Influence", *Journal of the Royal Society of Medicine* 90 (1997):102-105; and Marion Roberts, "Dr William Small: Friend of Mankind and the Ingenious Arts", *Aesculapius* (Summer 2007): 17-20. Jonathan Reinarz has explored much of the Birmingham medical scene of this era. See, for example, his *The Birth of a Provincial Hospital: The Early Years of the General Hospital, Birmingham, 1765-1790* (Stratford: Shakespeare Birthplace Trust, 2003), Jonathan Reinarz, "Towards a History of Provincial Medical Education", *Medical Historian* 17 (2006): 30-37, and his edited *Medicine and the Midlands, 1750-1950.* Special Edition of *Midland History* (Birmingham: Midland History Society, 2007).

Honora Sneyd (*c.* 1751-1780), daughter of Edward Sneyd (1711-1795), a Major in the Royal Horse Guards (The Blues) who lived at Byrkley Lodge, near Lichfield, became a ward of The Reverend Thomas Seward *c.*1755, when she was five years old. Upon the death of his wife, Major Sneyd placed Honora and her four sisters in the care of relatives and friends. The Major later removed Honora from the Seward's care in 1771. Richard Lovell Edgeworth then married Honora in Lichfield Cathedral on 17 July 1773. Honora, a patient of Dr Darwin, died of consumption (tuberculosis) at Beighterton, near Shifnal, Shropshire, on 30 April 1780 and was buried in the parish church at King's Weston.

Robert Southey (1774-1843), an English poet and prose writer, attended Balliol, Oxford, and later befriended Coleridge and Wordsworth, also meeting Seward in Lichfield in 1808. Southey was Poet Laureate beginning in 1813, a position he held for thirty years. Southey was included, along with other "radicals" such as Dr Darwin and Joseph Priestley, presenting their revolutionary ideas before an altar presided over by Justice, Philanthropy, and Sensibility in James Gillray's (1756/57-1815) satirical etching, "New morality; or, The Promis'd Installment of the High-Priest of the Theophilanthropes, with the Homage of Leviathan and his Suite", that was published to accompany George Canning's verses in *The Anti-Jacobin* in 1798.

Edmund Spenser (*c.*1552-1599) published the first three books of his epic poem, *The Faerie Queene* (London: J. Wolfe for W. Ponsonbie, 1590), with the rest to follow in 1596. Spencer used allegory to glorify England and Protestantism as well as the dominance of good over evil in nine-line (Spenserian) stanzas, a style that was imitated by many poets of the eighteenth and nineteenth centuries.

Richard Vyse (1746-1824/25), son of William Vyse (1709/10-1770), one-time beau of Anna Seward, later General Vyse. He married Ann Howard (1754-1784), daughter of Field Marshal Sir George Howard (1718-1796) and Lady Lucy Wentworth (d. 1771). Seward's "Elegy Addressed to Coronet V___ in the Autumn 1765" appeared in her *Poetical Works*, vol. 1, pp.15-18, and her "Monody on Mrs Vyse" appeared in the same volume, pp.104-107. As Colonel of the 3rd Dragoon Guards, Richard Vyse commanded a brigade at Flanders under the Prince Frederick, Duke of York and Albany (1763-1827), and, in 1799, he began his service as Comptroller of the Household of Ernest Augustus, the Duke of Cumberland and Teviotdale (1771-1851). His son, Richard William Howard-Vyse (1784-1853), followed a military career and, with John Shae Perring (1813-1869) in 1837, began exploring and excavating the Egyptian pyramids at Giza. Dr William Vyse (1742-1816), brother to Richard, senior, was Rector of Newington and of Brasted, Kent, Rector of St Mary's, Lambeth and of Sundridge, Kent, and of Coventry 1777, where he also served as Chaplain to Archbishop Cornwallis, Archdeacon of Coventry. In 1774, Dr Vyse was appointed Archdeacon of Shropshire, and later, in 1798, he was installed as Canon residentiary at Lichfield, subsequently becoming Chancellor of the Diocese.

William Vyse (1709/10-1770), matriculated at Pembroke College, Oxford, where he was a contemporary of Samuel Johnson. Vyse became Rector of St Philip's Cathedral, Birmingham, then Canon Residentiary of Lichfield Cathedral beginning in 1734, Treasurer of Lichfield Cathedral and Archdeacon of Salop. He married Catherine Smalbrooke (*c*.1715-1790), daughter of Richard Smalbrooke (1672-1749), Bishop of Lichfield Cathedral from 1731-1749. One of their children was Richard Vyse (1746-1824/25).

James Watt (1736-1819) initially turned his talents to instrument making in Glasgow where he was a member of the Literary Society of Glasgow. In 1768, he visited Dr Darwin in Lichfield to discuss his improvements upon the steam engine, a topic he shared with Boulton in Birmingham in the following year. They collaborated between Glasgow and Birmingham until Watt was lured to Birmingham in 1774, and the Boulton-Watt partnership commenced in earnest in 1776. On Watt, see J.P. Muirhead, *The Life of Watt, With Selections from His Correspondence* (London: John Murray, 1858); H.W. Dickinson, *James Watt, Craftsman and Engineer* (Cambridge: Cambridge University Press, 1935); L.T.C. Rolt, *James Watt* (London: T. Batsford, 1962); and R.V. Jones, "The 'Plain Story' of James Watt", *Proceedings of the Royal Society of London. Series A, Mathematical and Physical Sciences* 316 (1970): 449-471.

William Wilberforce (1759-1833), the parliamentarian and abolitionist, spent considerable time with the Thomas Gisbornes at their home, Yoxall Lodge, Staffordshire, in Needwood Forest. There, he took "advantage of Gisborne's quiet haven in the forest where he and Mrs Gisborne's brother worked on the vast quantity of evidence on the slave trade so as to become fully conversant with it and thereby strengthen their arguments. For much of the day they would work uninterrupted in an upper room, eating little, only coming down to walk in the forest for a half hour before dinner", as cited by Gaye King, "Jane Austen's Staffordshire Cousin: Edward Cooper and His Circle", *Persuasions* 15 (1993):252-259. On one such visit, Wilberforce accompanied Gisborne to Etruria to meet Wedgwood who had manufactured a jasper-ware cameo depicting a slave in chains and the motto, "Am I not a man and a brother". For further insight into the Lunar Men's views on abolition, see Uglow, *Lunar Men*; Brian Dolan, *Wedgwood: The First Tycoon* (New York: Viking, 2004); and Malcolm Dick, "Joseph Priestley, the Lunar Society and Anti-Slavery", in Malcolm Dick (ed) *Joseph Priestley and Birmingham* (Studley: Brewin Books, 2005), pp.65-80. On Wilberforce's passionate campaign for abolition, see Gareth Lean, *God's Politician: William Wilberforce's Struggle* (Colorado Springs: Helmers & Howard, 1987); Kevin Belmonte, *William Wilberforce: A Hero for Humanity* (Colorado Springs, Colo.: NavPress, 2002); Clifford Hill, *The Wilberforce Connection* (London, Monarch Books, 2004); Christopher Leslie Brown, *Moral Capital: Foundations of British Abolitionism* (Chapel Hill, North Carolina: University of North Carolina Press, 2006); Eric Metaxas, *Amazing Grace: William Wilberforce and the Heroic*

Campaign to End Slavery (Wheaton, Illinois: Crossway, 2006); William Hague, *William Wilberforce: The Life of the Great Anti-Slave Trade Campaigner* (London: HarperPress, 2007); and Stephen Tomkins, *William Wilberforce: A Biography* (Grand Rapids, Michigan: William B. Eerdmans, 2007).

Richard Wilkes (1691-1760) of Willenhall had, after study at St John's College, Cambridge, established a considerable medical practice, covering all of Staffordshire and large parts of Shropshire and Warwickshire. Denis Gibbs commented upon Wilkes's career in "Physicians and Physic in Seventeenth- and Eighteenth-Century Lichfield", in Smith and Arnott (eds) *The Genius of Erasmus Darwin*, pp.40-45. See also N. Tildsley, "Dr Richard Wilkes of Willenhall, Staffs: An Eighteenth Century Country Doctor", *Transactions of the Lichfield and South Staffordshire Archaeological Society* 7 (1965): 1-10.

James Wolfe (1727-1759) fought during the Jacobite uprising to defeat Prince Charles Edward Stuart (1720-1788) in the Battles of Falkirk and Culloden. Later, he served as the Major General in command of the British Army in capturing Quebec from the French at the Battle of the Plains of Abraham. On 18 September 1759, Wolfe fell mortally wounded, but learned of Britain's conquest before his death. Louis-Joseph de Montcalm-Gozon, Marquis de Saint-Veran (1712-1759), the commander of the French forces in North America during the Seven Years' War, also fell mortally wounded in this Battle. This conquest led to Britain's rule over all of Canada. Among the many commemorations to Wolfe is the Anglo-American historical painter, Benjamin West's (1738-1820) heroic painting, "The Death of General Wolfe" (1770), from which William Woollet's (1735-1785) engraving was widely disseminated.

Joseph Wright (1734-1797) became an unofficial associate of the Lunar Society, having depicted many of its members in portrait. Apart from those mentioned elsewhere in this volume, Wright also painted the portrait of the renowned clockmaker, geologist, and Lunar Society member, John Whitehurst (1713-1788), around 1782-83. In addition, Wright's artistic talents were turned to capturing scenes of scientific investigation in the Midlands as well as of this region's industrial landscape. Many of his original paintings remain in this region, being displayed in the Derby Museum and Art Gallery. For more on the scientific and industrial works of Wright, see David Fraser, "'Fields of Radiance': The Scientific and Industrial Scenes of Joseph Wright", in Denis Cosgrove and Stephen Daniels (eds) *The Iconography of Landscape: Essays on the Symbolic Representation, Design and Use of Past Environments* (Cambridge: Cambridge University Press, 1988), pp.119-141, and David Fraser, "Joseph Wright and the Lunar Society", in Judy Egerton (ed), *Wright of Derby* (London: Tate Gallery Publications, 1990), pp.15-24. See also William Bemrose, *The Life and Works of Joseph Wright ARA, Commonly Called 'Wright of Derby'* (London: Bemrose & Sons, 1885), and B. Nicholson, *Joseph Wright of Derby*, 1968. Wright became a patient of Dr Darwin in Derby.

Appendix I:
Erasmus Darwin's Writings

By Desmond King-Hele, Updated and Extended by Janice Wilson. Used with Permission from www.erasmusdarwin.org/libraryfm.htm

Chief Publications

"The Death of Prince Frederick", in *Academiae Cantabrigiensis Luctus in Obitum Frederici Celsissimi Walliae Principis* (Cambridge: Joseph Bentham, 1751). Republished in *European Magazine* 27 (1795): 75–6.

"Remarks on the Opinion of Henry Eeles, Esq., Concerning the Ascent of Vapour", *Phil. Trans. Roy. Soc.* 50 (1757): 240–54.

"An Uncommon Case of an Haemoptysis", *Phil. Trans. Roy. Soc.* 51 (1760): 526–9.

[Anonymous] *A View of the Advantages of Inland Navigations; With a Plan of a Navigable Canal* (sold by Becket and De Hondt, 1765).

"Experiments on Animal Fluids in the Exhausted Receiver", *Phil. Trans. Roy. Soc.* 64 (1774): 344–9.

"A New Case in Squinting" *Phil. Trans. Roy. Soc.* 68 (1778): 86–96.

[Anonymous] *An Elegy on the Much-Lamented Death of a Most Ingenious Young Gentleman* (London: G. Robinson; sold by M. Morgan, Lichfield, 1778).

Experiments Establishing a Criterion Between Mucaginous and Purulent Matter. And an Account of the Retrograde Motions of the Absorbent Vessels of Animal Bodies in Some Diseases (Lichfield: J. Jackson; London: T. Cadell, and Edinburgh: W. Creech, 1780) [Written by Charles Darwin (1758–1778), Erasmus Darwin's son; edited, with a life, by Erasmus Darwin].

A System of Vegetables According to Their Classes Orders Genera Species with their Characters and Differences, Trans. from the Thirteenth Edition of the *Systema Vegetabilium* of the late Professor Linnaeus (as published by Dr. Murray) by a Botanical Society at Lichfield, 2 vols. (Lichfield: J. Jackson, for Leigh and Sotheby, London, 1783).

"An Account of an Artificial Spring of Water", *Phil. Trans. Roy. Soc.* 75 (1785): 1–7.

"An Account of the Successful Use of Foxglove in Some Dropsies, and in the Pulmonary Consumption", *Medical Transactions* 3 (1785): 255–86.

The Families of Plants, Trans. from Reichard's edition of the *Genera Plantarum* and the *Mantissae Plantarum* of the elder Linnaeus; and the *Supplementum Plantarum* of the younger Linnaeus by a Botanical Society at Lichfield, 2 vols. (Lichfield: J. Jackson for J Johnson, London; T. Byrne, Dublin; and J. Balfour, Edinburgh, 1787). "Key of the Sexual System" section reprinted in Judith Hawley (ed) *Literature and Science, 1660–1834* (London: Pickering & Chatto, 2002), Vol. 4, "Flora".

"Frigorific Experiments on the Mechanical Expansion of Air", *Phil. Trans. Roy. Soc.* 78 (1788): 43–52. Translated into German in *Journal der Physik* (1790): 73–82.

"Of the Medicinal Waters of Buxton and Matlock", in James Pilkington's *A View of the present State of Derbyshire* (Derby: J. Drewry for J. Johnson and J. Deighton, London, 1789), pp.256–75.

[Anonymous in first edition], *The Botanic Garden; a Poem, in Two Parts.*

Part I, *The Economy of Vegetation* (London, J. Johnson, 1791 [actually 1792]).

Part II, *The Loves of the Plants* (Lichfield: J. Jackson, for J. Johnson, London, 1789).

Later English editions:

Part I. 2nd ed. (London: J. Johnson, 1791); 3rd ed. (London: J. Johnson, 1795); 4th ed. (London: J. Johnson, 1799); 5th ed. (London: J. Johnson, 1806); 6th ed. (London: Jones & Company, 1824); [Another edition] (London: Jones & Company, 1825).

Part II. 2nd ed. (London: J. Johnson, 1790); 3rd ed. (London: J. Johnson, 1791); 4th ed (London: J. Johnson, 1794); [5th ed.] (London: J. Johnson, 1799); [6th ed.] (London: J. Johnson, 1806); [7th ed.] (London: Jones & Company, 1824).

Irish editions:

Part I (Dublin: J. Moore, 1793); Part II, 3rd ed. (Dublin: J. Moore, 1790), 4th ed. (Dudlin [sic]: J. Moore, 1796).

American editions:

(New York: T. & J. Swords, 1798) [Part I is from the 3rd, Part II from the 4th London edition]. 2nd ed. (New York: T. and J. Swords, 1807).

Abridged version

Beauties of the Botanic Garden. [selections]:

(London: T. Cadell, 1805); (New York: D. Longworth, 1805).

Translations:

Part I: Portuguese, by V. P. N. da Cunha (Lisbon: Regia Officina Typografica, 1803–4), 2 vols.

Part II: French, by J. P. F. Deleuze (Paris: Digeon, 1800).

Part II: Italian, by G. Gherardini (Milan: Pirotta e Maspero, 1805); (Naples: Luca Marotta, 1817); 2nd ed. milanese (Milan: P. E. Giusti, 1818); 3rd ed. (Milan: Paolo Emilio Giusti, 1830); 3 ed. milanese/riveduta dal traduttore (Milan: Paolo Andrea Molina, 1844).

Facsimile reprints of *The Botanic Garden*:

(Menston: Scolar Press, 1973). Facsimile reprint of 1st ed., originally published in 2 vols. Vol.1 originally published (London: J. Johnson, 1791). Vol.2 originally published (London: J. Johnson, 1789); ([St. Clair Shores, MI]: Scholarly Press, 1977); (New York: Garland, 1978), Reprint of the 1791 ed. of pt. 1 (J. Johnson: London) and the 1790 ed. of pt. 2 (J. Nichols for J. Johnson, London); (Oxford: Woodstock Books, 1991), Part II, 1789 only; (Bristol: Thoemmes Continuum, 2004), 2 vols; and in Judith Hawley (ed) *Literature and Science, 1660–1834* (London: Pickering & Chatto, 2002), Vol.4, "Flora".

Electronic editions (Parts I and II) include:

www.gutenberg.org/browse/authors/d; www.echo–library.com; Kindle Edition; www.kessinger.net

Zoonomia; or, The Laws of Organic Life.

Part I (London: J. Johnson, 1794).

Parts II and III (London: J. Johnson, 1796). With 2nd ed. of Part I, corrected, 2 vols.
Later English edition:
3rd ed (London: J. Johnson, 1801), 4 vols.
Irish editions:
(Dublin: P. Byrne and W. Jones, 1794), Vol. 2 dated 1796; (Dublin: P. Byrne, 1800), Vol. 2
bears the imprint (printed for P. Byrne, and W. Jones, 1796), 2 vols.; (Dublin: printed
for Gilbert and Hodges, 1803), 2 vols.
American editions:
Part I (New York: T. and J. Swords, 1796); Parts II and III (Philadelphia: T. Dobson, 1797),
2 vols.; 2nd American from the 3rd London ed. (Boston: D. Carlisle for Thomas and
Andrews, 1803), 2 vols.; [Boston, 1806 (ed S. L. Mitchill)]; 3rd American ed. (Boston:
Thomas and Andrews, 1809), 2 vols.; 4th ed. (Philadelphia: Edward Earle, 1818), 2 vols.
Translations:
German, by J. D. Brandis (Hannover: Hahn, 1795–9), 5 vols.; (Pesth: Joseph. Leyrer,
1801), 4 vols.
Italian by G. Rasori (Milan: Pirotta e Maspero, 1803–5), 6 vols. [placed on the Papal Index,
22 December 1817]; (Naples: Porcelli, 1820), 6 vols.); by G. Rasori, 2nd ed. Milanese
(Milan: P. A. Molina, 1834–36), 4 vols. in 2; by Giovanni Rasori, (Rome: n.p., 1885).
Portuguese, by H[enrique] X[avier] Baeta (Lisboa: Joao Rodrigues Neves, 1806)
[Summary of Pts I & II; Part III in full].
French, by J. F. Klyskens (Ghent: P –F. de Geosin-Verhaeghe, 1810–11), 4 vols.
Facsimile reprints:
(New York: A. M. S. Press, 1974), 2 vols. Reprint of (London: J. Johnson, 1794–96); ([St.
Clair Shores, MI]: Scholarly Press, 1977); (Bristol: Thoemmes Continuum, 2004).
Electronic editions include:
www.gutenberg.org/browse/authors/d; www.echo-library.com (Vol. 1 only); Kindle Edition.
A Plan for the Conduct of Female Education in Boarding Schools. (Derby: J. Drewry, for J. Johnson,
London, 1797).
Irish edition:
(Dublin: J. Chambers, 1798).
American edition:
(Philadelphia: John Ormrod, 1798).
Translations:
German, by C[hristoph] W[ilhelm] Hufeland (Leipzig: F. A. Brockhaus, 1822); 2nd ed.,
by Friedrich August von Ammon (Leipzig: F. A. Brockhaus, 1852).
Dutch, by G. Bakker (Groningen: W. van Boekeren, 1824).
Facsimile reprints:
(New York: Johnson Reprint Corp., 1968); (East Ardsley, Wakefield, Yorkshire: S. R.
Publishers Ltd., 1968); (London: Routledge/Thoemmes, 1996), in *History of British
Educational Theory*, [Vol. 5]; (Otley, West Yorkshire: Woodstock Books, 2001); (Bristol:
Thoemmes Continuum, 2004).
Electronic editions include:
www.kessinger.net

Phytologia: or the Philosophy of Agriculture and Gardening With the Theory of Draining Morasses, and With an Improved Construction of the Drill Plough (London: J. Johnson, 1800).
Irish edition:
> (Dublin: P. Byrne, 1800).

Translation:
> German, by E[rnst]. B[enjamin] G[ottlieb] Hebenstreit (Leipzig: Wolf, 1801), 2 vols.

Facsimile reprint:
> (Bristol: Thoemmes Continuum, 2004).

The Temple of Nature; or, The Origin of Society. (London, J. Johnson, 1803).
Later English editions:
> 2nd ed. (London: J. Johnson, 1806) [as part of *Poetical Works*]; 3rd ed. (London: Jones & Company, 1825).

American editions:
> (New York: T. and J. Swords, 1804); (Baltimore: John W. Butler and Bonsal & Niles, 1804).

German edition:
> (Brunswick: L. Lucius, 1808).

Translations:
> Russian: by N. A. Kholodkovskii, in *Journal of Ministry of National Education* (1911); in book form (Moscow: Izd-vo Akademii nauk SSSR, 1954); 2nd ed. (Moscow: Izd-vo Akademii nauk SSSR, 1960).

Facsimile reprints:
> (Menston: Scolar Press, 1973); ([St. Clair Shores, MI]: Scholarly Press, 1977); ([Lichfield]: The Erasmus Darwin Foundation, 2003); (Bristol: Thoemmes Continuum, 2004).

Electronic editions include:
> www.rc.umd.edu/editions/darwin_temple (edited by Martin Priestman, August 2006); www.english.upenn.edu/Projects/knarf/Darwin/templetp.html (undated); www.echo-library.com; Kindle Edition; www.kessinger.net

The Poetical Works of Erasmus Darwin, M.D. F.R.S.: Containing The Botanic Garden, in Two Parts; and The Temple of Nature. With Philosophical Notes and Plates, 3 vols. (London: printed for J. Johnson by T. Bensley, 1806).

Other Printed Sources of Primary Writings

All of Erasmus Darwin's book-length writings are available via electronic resources through many research libraries.

Desmond King-Hele (ed) *Essential Writings of Erasmus Darwin* (London: McGibbon & Kee, 1968).

Desmond King-Hele (ed) *The Letters of Erasmus Darwin* (Cambridge: Cambridge University Press, 1981) prints the 272 letters known at that time, with notes.

Desmond King-Hele (ed) *The Collected Letters of Erasmus Darwin* (Cambridge: Cambridge University Press, 2006) prints the 460 letters now known, with notes.

Martin Priestman (ed) *The Collected Writings of Erasmus Darwin*, 9 volumes (Bristol: Thoemmes Continuum, 2004).

A Concordance to Erasmus Darwin's Poem "The Botanic Garden", compiled by D. King-Hele, (London: Wellcome Institute for the History of Medicine, 1994).

Concordance to "The Temple of Nature" [1803] by Erasmus Darwin, compiled by Stuart Harris, (Sheffield: Stuart Harris, 2006).

Stuart Harris (ed) *Cosmologia: A Sequence of Epic Poems in Three Parts comprising Part One: The Economy of Vegetation (1791) Part Two: The Loves of the Plants (1789) Part Three: The Temple of Nature (1803) by Erasmus Darwin (1731–1802)* (Sheffield: S. Harris, 2002).

Paper about the mortality of horned cattle, the Derby *Weekly Entertainer* for 29 September 1783, pp.301–301.

The Pussey Cats' Love Letters: Persian Snow, Po Felina (by Erasmus Darwin and Anna Seward) (Collingswood, N.J.: Private Press of William Lewis Washburn, 1934).

Some of Darwin's shorter poems have appeared in print:

The poem on Gurney's shorthand was printed in the *London Magazine* 20 (1751): 325, and in the third edition of T. Gurney's *Brachygraphy* (1752).

Seven poems written as letters appear in *The Collected Letters of Erasmus Darwin*: a schoolboy letter to Susannah his sister (60 lines); a Christmas letter-in-verse in 1749 (48 lines); to Miss Howard with Dodsley's miscellaneous Collection of Poems (26 lines); the "Speech of a Wood-Nymph" (16 lines); the "Tea-Vase" poem (36 lines); the "Platonic Epistle to a married Lady" (96 lines); and the poem to Anna Seward's cat (16 lines). *Collected Letters,* letters 47–1, 49–6, 57–2, 75–7, 77–7, 78–12 and 80–5 respectively.

Six poems, including the epitaph to William Small and the "Dread Dream" poem, are printed in Anna Seward's *Memoirs*.

The "Address to the Swilcar Oak" was published at the end of F.N.C. Mundy's poem *Needwood Forest* (Lichfield: Printed by John Jackson, 1776).

The "Ode to the river Derwent" is in *Gent. Mag.* 55 (1785): 641; and 'Idyllium, a Prison' in *Monthly Mag.* 1 (1796): 54.

Typescript copies of some early poems and those to Elizabeth Pole are in University College London Library, Pearson papers 577.

Manuscripts

Most of Darwin's known manuscript letters are held in 40 public or institutional archives, which are listed on pages xxi–xxiii of *The Collected Letters*. Of these manuscripts, 216 are at Cambridge University Library, mostly in the archives DAR 227, DAR 218, and DAR 267. There are 65 manuscript letters at Birmingham City Archives; 15 at Keele University Library; 10 at the Fitzwilliam Museum Library, Cambridge; and 10 at the William Salt Library, Stafford. The rest are at 35 other repositories in Britain, the USA and Sweden.

Darwin's manuscript "Commonplace Book" is at present on loan at Erasmus Darwin House, Lichfield, and a photocopy is available to visitors. A manuscript poem "To Peter Pindar", of doubtful authorship, is also at the Erasmus Darwin House, Lichfield. Other autograph papers are at Cambridge University Library, mostly in DAR 227: these include early drafts of *The Temple of Nature* and a guide to shorthand. Other 18th-century family manuscripts at Cambridge fill most of the 67 notebooks in DAR 267: these include about 1,000 lines of unpublished early verse by Erasmus Darwin (copied out by his father). The autograph manuscript of Darwin's canal pamphlet is at University College London Library.

Appendix II:
Anna Seward's Writings

Chief Publications

Elegy of Captain Cook. To Which is Added, An Ode to the Sun (London: J. Dodsley, 1780); 2nd ed (London: J. Dodsley, 1780; 3rd ed (London: J. Dodsley, 1781); 4th ed (Lichfield: J. Jackson and London: J. Dodsley); 5th ed (Lichfield: J. Jackson and London: J. Dodsley).

Monody on Major André. To Which are Added Letters Addressed to her by Major André, in the Year 1769 (Lichfield: J. Jackson, also sold by London: Robinson: London: Cadell and Evans, Oxford: Prince, Cambridge: Merrill, and Bath: Pratt and Clinch); [another edition] (New York: James Rivington, 1781); 2nd ed (Lichfield: J. Jackson, also sold by London: Robinson: London: Cadell and Evans, Oxford: Prince, Cambridge: Merrill, and Bath: Pratt and Clinch, 1781); [another edition, edited by E.C.G. (Penzance: T. Virgus, 1806)]. *Monody on Major André, (Who was Executed at Tappan, November − 1780). To Which are Added Major André Letters Addressed to Miss Seward When at His 18th Year* (New York: Harrison and Purdy for T. Allen, 1788); 2nd edition (New York: T. Allen); [another edition] (Philadelphia: Enoch Story, [1788?]); 4th American ed (Boson: W. Spotswood and C.P. Wayne, 1798). *Monody on the Unfortunate Major André, Who was Executed at Tappan, November − 1780). To Which are Added Major André Letters Addressed to Miss Seward When at His 18th Year.* (Hanover, New Hampshire: J. Dunham, 1794).

Poem to the Memory of Lady Miller (London: G. Robinson, 1782); www.kessinger.net.

Louisa, A Poetical Novel, In Four Epistles (Lichfield: J. Jackson, London: G. Robinson, 1784); [another edition] (Dublin: J.M. Davies for Jenkins, White, Byrne, Burton, Cash, and Davis, 1784); 2nd ed (Lichfield: J. Jackson, London: G. Robinson, 1784); 3rd ed (Lichfield: J. Jackson, London: G. Robinson, 1784), 4th ed (Lichfield: J. Jackson, London: G. Robinson, 1784); 5th ed (New Haven: Abel Morse, 1789); 5th ed (London: T. Cadell, Lichfield: Morgan, 1792); www.kessinger.net.

Ode on General Eliott's Return from Gibraltar (London: T. Cadell, 1787).

Humphrey Repton, *Variety: A Collection of Essays. Written in the Year 1787* [By Anna Seward] (London: T. Cadell, 1788).

Llangollen Vale, With Other Poems (London: G. Sael, 1796); 2nd ed (London: G. Sael, 1796); 3rd ed (London: G. Sael, 1796); www.kessinger.net.

Original Sonnets on Various Subjects; And Odes Paraphrased from Horace (London: G. Sael, Birmingham: Swinney, Lichfield: Morgan, 1799); 2nd ed (London: G. Sael, Birmingham: Swinney, Lichfield: Morgan, 1799); 3rd ed (London: G. Sael, Birmingham: Swinney, Lichfield: Morgan, 1799); Kindle Edition.

Memoirs of the Life of Dr Darwin, Chiefly During His Residence at Lichfield, With Anecdotes of His Friends, and Criticisms of His Writings (London: Printed for J. Johnson by T. Bensley, 1804); [another edition] (Philadelphia: Classic Press for W. Poyntell and Co., 1804); www.kessinger.net; www.archive.org; http://books.google.com.

Blindness, A Poem (Sheffield: J. Montgomery, 1806).

Sir Brooke Boothby, Bart. and Anna Seward, *Monumental Inscriptions in Ashbourn Church, Derbyshire* (Ashbourn: Parkes [*c.*1806]).

Other Printed Sources of Primary Writings

Miss C. Short, *Dramas for the Use of Young Ladies. With a Prologue and Epilogue to the First Drama by Miss Seward* (Birmingham, n.p., 1792).

William Haley, *Amelia; or, The Faithless Briton. An Original American Novel, Founded Upon Recent Facts, To Which is Added, Amelia; or, Malevolence Defeated; and, Miss Seward's Monody on Major André* (Boston: W. Spotswood and C.P. Wayne, 1798).

John Hughes, Petrus Abelardus, *Memoirs of the Lives, Amours, and Misfortunes of Abelard and Eloisa; With Poems on Their Fate by Pope and Mrs Madan; Also Anecdotes and Memoirs of Those Unfortunate Characters by Miss Seward* (Newcastle-on-Tyne: J. Mitchell, 1805).

Joshua Hett Smith, *An Authentic Narrative of the Causes Which Led to the Death of Major André, Adjutant-General of His Majesty's Forces in North America. To Which is Added a Monody on the Death of Major André. By Miss Seward* (London: Mathews and Leigh, 1808); [another edition] (New York: Evert Duyckinnck, 1809).

Walter Scott, (ed) *The Poetical Works of Anna Seward; With Extracts from Her Literary Correspondence*, 3 vols (Edinburgh: J. Ballantyne and Co., 1810); www.kessinger.net.

A[rchibald] Constable, (ed) *Letters of Anna Seward; Written Between the Years 1784 and 1807*, 6 vols (Edinburgh: A. Constable and Co., 1811). The letters from which those included in this publication were drawn are in the collection of the National Library of Scotland: Millgate Union, MSS 845, 865, 870, 910, 1750, 1753, 2223, 2521, 3652, 3874–5, 3877, 9609, Catalogue of Walter Scott Correspondence; www.kessinger.net.

W.C. Oulton, *The Beauties of Anna Seward, Carefully Selected and Alphabetically Arranged, Under Appropriate Heads* (London: C. Chapple, 1813).

Miss Seward's *Monody on Major André; and Elegy on Captain Cook. Also Mr Pratt's Sympathy, A Poem*, 10th ed (London: Longman, Hurst, Rees, Orme, and Brown, 1817), and a new edition (London: Otridge and Rackham, 1821).

Miss Seward's Enigma (London: R. Theobald, 1855).

Benson John Lossing. *The Two Spies: Nathan Hale and John André. Illustrated with Pen-and-Ink Sketches by H. Ross. Anna Seward's Monody on Major André* (New York: D. Appleton and Co., 1886), reprinted in 1897, 1904, 1907, 1909, 1910, and 1914.

Hesketh Pearson, (ed) *The Swan of Lichfield; Being a Selection from the Correspondence of Anna Seward* (London: H. Hamilton, 1936); [another edition] (New York: Oxford University Press, 1937).

Anna Seward in Jennifer Kelley, (ed) *Bluestocking Feminism: Writings of the Bluestocking Circle 1738–1785*, Vol.4. (London: Pickering & Chatto, 1999).

Appendix III:
An "Ode Formerly Dedicated to Camerarius" in Latin translated into English by John Martyn

To sing new Loves, and new Desires,
Of am'rous Plants, before unheard,
As yet untrac'd by any Bard,
My wond'ring Muse aspires;

You that admire the Lyrick Strain,
And Joys of Venus love to sing,
Give Ear; thy Succours, Flora, bring,
I sing thy flow'ry Reign:

And ye, O Lovers, and ye Herds
Of am'rous Animals, attend;
Your chaste, melodious Voices lend,
You tuneful Choir of Birds.

When Winter's gone, and Spring succeeds,
With gentle blasts Favonius blows,
The opening Flow'rs each Sex disclose,
And promise future Seeds.

The Stamina with Meal abound,
And when the gentle Zephyrs blow,
They from their double Summits throw
The Golden Dust around.

Which born by the propitious Winds,
About the Female-Vessels spreads,
And round the Pointal's hollow Beds,
A glad Reception finds.

No anxious Thoughts their Love destroys,
They want no suble Night, to hide
The Blushes of the yielding Bride,
Fill'd with tumultuous Joys.

Hither the beauteous Lillies bring,
And the luxuriant Charms disclose,
Of the too soon declining Rose,
The Glory of the Spring.

There the Farina we may see,
Down from th'aspiring Summits flow,
The greatest part of Flow'rs we know
Hermaphrodites to be.

Now let us leave the flow'ry Plain,
And to the shady Woods retire,
The Catkins of the Nuts admire,
Which pour down sulph'rous Rain:

Let us behold the lofty Pine,
That part whereon the Fruit appears,
Is Female; that which Flowers bears
In male, both Sexes join;

As Shell-Fish in the briny Main,
At the same Time from one part give,
What with the other they receive,
Both sexes they contain.

Not thus the verdant Laurel fares,
The noble Palm and Juniper,
For on those Trees which flowers bear,
No shining Fruit appears.

And those, upon whose Boughs we find
The Fruit, no tender Flow'r can shew;
Thus we the different sexes know,
Of Beasts, and all Mankind.

If any farther Doubt appears,
Those, who to Bacchus bow,
The twining Hops with Pleasure know,
Which ease them of their Cares.

The Mecury both Sexes shews;
And Hemp, which pays with double Gains,
The Labours of the weary Swains,
Both Male and Female knows.

Thus when her Eggs a Hen conceives,
If the fierce Cock his Female treads,
A living Off-spring then succeeds,
No fruitless Egg she grieves.

But if her absent Lord she mourns,
A fruitless Egg the Widow bears,
No living Off-spring then appears,
Till her lov'd Spouse returns.

So Fish, that haunt the stormy Main,
By bounteous Nature taught, o'erspread
The Female's Eggs with genial Seed,
Nor can the Waves restrain.

So when the Pointal's hollow Beds
Are cover'd o'er with Golden Meal,
With growing Fruit the Caverns swell,
And promise future seeds.

On the same Plain each Sex is found,
The ready Wife conceives the Seeds,
When the propitious Zephyr spreads
The gen'rous Dust around.

But if the Apex you remove,
Or ravish from the Husband's Arms,
The Virgin Bride's unspotted Charms,
The Flowers will fruitless prove.

Sometimes the Female strives in vain,
To form th' abortive Seeds, why should
The double Flowers then be proud,
Since they no Seeds obtain.

Oh! with what Joys my Eyes behold
The wond'rous Frame of Nature's Laws!
How my aspiring Thoughts rejoice,
These Mysteries to unfold!

Great Man, thy glorious Theme pursue,
Whilst thee th' attentive World admires;
All other Breasts thy Glory fires,
To trace what former Ages never knew.

Almighty God, who did'st the World create,
And from an empty nothing form us all,
Preserve this glorious Order we entreat,
Until the World decays, and Stars from their
     exalted Seats shall fall.

Appendix IV:
Review of Anna Seward's
Memoirs of the Life of Dr Darwin in
Edinburgh Review 4 No.7 (April 1804): 230–241

ART. XVIII. *Memoirs of the Life of Dr Darwin, chiefly during his residence at Lichfield; with Anecdotes of his Friends, and Criticisms on his Writings.* By Anna Seward. London. 1804. 8 vo. pp.430.

It has been long held, on high critical authority, that history must always please, independently of the particular mode, and even in spite of the defects, of its execution: and unquestionably even that moderate portion of fact which may be reasonably expected in the life of every eminent individual, can scarcely be presented under any disguise so perversely absurd, as entirely to divest it of interest. Under the influence of stubborn curiosity, we have been accordingly carried through a faithful perusal of these Memoirs of the celebrated author of *The Botanic Garden*: and although we are bound to admit that our labour has not been entirely unrewarded, yet Miss Seward must forgive us, if we add, that the most striking lesson we have derived from her volume, has been the truly wonderful extent of that tolerant maxim to which we have alluded. The share which she appears to have long enjoyed of the intimate society of Dr Darwin, and her opportunities of accurate information relative at least to a considerable portion of his life, had given to Miss Seward some peculiar advantages in becoming, as she terms it, "the recorder of vanished genius". It is therefore the more to be regretted that she should not have been restrained, by some visitations of a better taste, from clothing her narrative in a garb so injudicious and fantastic. But it would appear that Miss Anna Seward has been too long accustomed to soar into the high and giddy regions of verse, to be able to tread with sober step and becoming gravity of air in the humbler pathway of prose.

Of the matter and arrangement of these *Memoirs*, the Preface gives us the following notice: "My work consists of the following particulars: – the person, the mind, the temper of Dr Darwin; his powers as a Physician, Philosopher, and Poet; the peculiar traits of his manners; his excellences and faults; the Petrarchan attachment of his middle life, more happy in its result than was that of the Bard of Vaucluse; the beautiful poetic testimonies of its fervor, while yet it remained hopeless; an investigation of the constituent excellences and defects of his magnificent poem, *The Botanic Garden*; remarks upon his philosophic prose writings; the characters and talents of those who formed the circle of his friends while he resided in Lichfield; and the very singular and interesting history of one of them, well known in the lettered world, [Mr Thomas Day] whose domestic history, remarkable as it is, has been unaccountably omitted by the gentleman who wrote his life". Pref. p.v. vi.

After perusing this table of contents, the reader will have himself alone to blame if he expects in this volume any exact or orderly deduction of the facts of Dr Darwin's life. Miss Seward apparently spurns the fetters of vulgar, chronological narration; and has chosen rather to expatiate, free and at large, under the impulse of her own spontaneous feelings, or accidental associations. After having followed her with patience through her eccentric and capricious evolutions, we are unable to say that our progress has been rendered more pleasing by this irregular variety, or that it has afforded us any tolerable compensation for the want of a distinct and intelligible narrative. An analysis of the first chapter of the work may serve sufficiently to justify these remarks, and may furnish a sufficient specimen of its plan and execution.

On the birth, parentage, and education of her hero, Miss Seward has not deigned to bestow a single line. We are abruptly introduced to him at the age of twenty-four, when he first came to practise physic at Lichfield in the autumn of the year 1756; and even then, instead of proceeding directly in her narrative, she stops on the threshold to give us a "sketch of his character and manners", such as they had appeared to her in the subsequent course of Dr Darwin's life. This inversion of the usual arrangement in biographical writing may be perfectly consonant to the desultory plan of these memoirs; but, in itself, it is so palpably injudicious, that there is very little hazard of its adoption as a model. Within these few years, a similar innovation was attempted by a Scottish historian, who, at the commencement of every reign, introduced that general delineation of the character of the sovereign, which has usually found a place at the close: but, if we may judge from our own feelings, the example of Mr Pinkerton will not probably prove more seducing than that of Miss Seward.

Of this "sketch of the character and manners of Dr Darwin", we can only say, that it leaves no very distinct impression on the mind; and that impression, such as it is, has not, in our own case at least, been extremely favourable. But Miss Seward does not stand forth as the indiscriminating panegyrist of her deceased friend; nor does she appear to have been withheld, by any violent or undue partialities, from discharging those "sacred duties of biography", – "beneath the ever present consciousness" of which she would be understood to have proceeded. Of the justice of her claims to the praise of rigid impartiality, those only can be competent judges, to whom Dr Darwin was personally known; but it is perhaps less difficult to discover that Miss Seward was not altogether equal to the task of delineating with truth the various parts of his character, or of appreciating the qualities of which it was composed. In this preliminary sketch, and in other parts of her work, we are, indeed, presented with a number of striking traits of temper and of manners, such as must have been obvious to common observation; but in her attempts to mark the extent, the limitations, and the peculiar character and complexion of those higher powers of mind, by which alone the possessor becomes an object of serious interest – her description becomes feeble and indistinct, and she takes refuge in vague, general, or exaggerated statement. Thus, we are informed, that "beauty and symmetry had not been propitious to his exterior"; that "he stammered extremely"; that he was "sore upon opposition", and overbearing and sarcastic in conversation; but whether from the "consciousness of great native elevation above the general standard of intellect", we may be permitted to doubt. Moreover, we are told, that "extreme was his scepticism of human truth"; – that habits of distrust tinctured his conversation with an apparent want of confidence in mankind; – and that "perhaps this proneness to suspicion mingled too much of art in his wisdom". Farther, we are told that he abstained from "vinous fluid"; that he had "an absolute horror of spirits of all sorts"; that his only tolerance was in favour of home-made wines; that "acid fruits, with sugar, and all sort of creams and butter, were his luxuries"; but that "he always ate plentifully of animal food". Of his virtues and talents, we learn that "professional generosity distinguished Dr Darwin's medical practice"; that "his was the cheerful board of open-housed hospitality"; and that "generosity, wit and science were his household gods"; that nature had bestowed on him "the seducing and often dangerous gift of a highly poetic imagination"; but that "through the first twenty-three years of his practice as a physician, Dr Darwin, with the wisdom of Ulysses, bound himself to the medical mast, that he might not follow those delusive syrens, the muses, or be considered as their avowed votary"; nor was it till then, that "the impregnable rock on which his medicinal and philosophical reputation were placed, induced him to contend for that species of fame which should entwine the Parnassian laurel with the balm of Pharmacy".

Such, we can assure our readers, is the amount of the information respecting the character and manners of Dr Darwin, for which we are indebted to his biographer. It may perhaps serve to moderate the expectations of those who may have unwarily looked only to the enviable opportunities of observation which she appears to have enjoyed.

On "returning to the dawn of Dr Darwin's professional establishment", we are informed by Miss Seward of the sudden fame he acquired by his success in a desperate case of fever, and of the imputations of rashness which were ignorantly attached to his practice. Mrs Darwin is then introduced on the scene; and from the account given by Miss Seward, she appears to have been an interesting and accomplished woman: but we must be forgiven if we are not greatly charmed with the felicity of a long oration which is put into her mouth while on her deathbed.

Soon after this lady's death, Dr Darwin purchased an old house in the city of Lichfield, on the lilliputian improvements of which Miss Seward has lavished all her powers of picturesque description.

"To this *rus in urbe*, of Darwinian creation, resorted, from its early rising, a knot of philosophic friends in frequent visitation. The Revd. Mr Mitchell, many years deceased. He was skilled in astronomic science, modest and wise. The ingenious Mr Kier [sic] of West Bromwich, then Captain Kier [sic]. Mr Boulton, known and respected wherever mechanic philosophy is understood. Mr Watt, the celebrated improver of the steam engine. And, above all others in Dr Darwin's personal regard, the accomplished Dr Small of Birmingham, who bore the blushing honours of his talents and virtues to an untimely grave".

Tired already of her proper subject, Miss Seward again digresses into the private history of those who moved in "the Darwinian sphere"; – of Mr Edgworth and his wives; of Dr Small, and the elegies and epitaphs written by his friends; and particularly of Mr Thomas

Day, the author of the popular little volumes of *Sandford and Merton*. Of the last of these gentlemen, a very full and disproportioned account is given, and a great many anecdotes are told, which we shall not attempt to retail [sic], but which, in their proper place, might serve to illustrate the singularly romantic and hair-brained character of this modern philosopher. With the history of Dr Darwin's life they have no intimate connexion: And so ends the first chapter.

On "resuming the recollected circumstances of Dr Darwin's life", Miss Seward is unable for a moment to withstand her wayward propensity to digression; and our attention is instantly drawn aside to the contemplation of new groups of visitors and friends who made their appearance at Lichfield "after Dr Small and Mr Michell had vanished from the earth, and Mr Day and Mr Edgeworth, in the year 1772, had left the Darwinian sphere". But it would be vain to follow this lady in her meandering course; and by attempting it, we should equally fatigue our readers and ourselves. Throughout the whole of that portion of the work which bears the semblance of narrative, it is only for a moment that we catch a glimpse of the principal figure; and even then, our gratification is too often dashed by the frivolity of the information which is conveyed. The reader may look in vain for any thing which merits the name of just biographical narrative. Even when Dr Darwin is the subject, little else is to be found than an inflated translation of the tea-table talk of Lichfield; nor will all the good things which have been uttered on sundry occasions by the choice spirits of the place, be felt as any adequate compensation for this radical defect.

"In the year 1768", we are told, "Dr Darwin met with an accident of irretrievable injury in the human frame": he was thrown from a whimsical carriage of his own invention, and broke the patella of his right knee. For the edification of the curious reader, we extract a philosophical observation suggested to Miss Seward by this occurrence.

"It is remarkable, that this uncommon accident happened to three of the inhabitants of Lichfield in the course of one year; first, to the author of these memoirs in the prime of her youth; next, to Dr Darwin; and, lastly, to the late Mr Levett, a gentleman of wealth and consequence in the town. No such misfortune was previously remembered in that city, nor has it once recurred through all the years which have since elapsed". p.62.

While Dr Darwin resided at Lichfield, Dr Johnson was repeatedly there on his visitations to Miss Lucy Porter. Miss Seward informs us, that "they had one or two interviews, but never afterwards sought each other. Mutual and strong dislike subsisted between them". Miss Seward goes on to remark as curious, that in Johnson's correspondence, "the name of Darwin should not be found, nor indeed that of any of the ingenious and lettered people who lived there; while of its more common-life characters there is frequent mention, with many hints of Lichfield's intellectual barrenness, while it could boast a Darwin and other men of classical learning, poetic talents, and liberal information". Of these ingenious and lettered persons, Miss Seward here gives the reader a farther enumeration, accompanied with specimens of their poetic and colloquial talents, which we shall not presume to injure by a mutilated extract. That Dr Johnson's colloquial despotism should have alarmed the self-importance of a man like Darwin, who was ambitious of being himself a despot in his own "sphere", and who is described as "sore upon opposition, whether in argument or conduct", can hardly be matter of much surprise. The colloquial intrepidity of Johnson was unquestionably too firm to have suffered him to shrink from the society of any man; but if he was avoided by Darwin and the Lichfield coterie, as Miss Seward seems to admit, his silence cannot well be accused of injustice to their talents and accomplishments.

"About the year 1771 commenced that great work, the *Zoonomia*, first published in 1794; the gathered wisdom of three and twenty years". With somewhat more hardihood than prudence, his biographer has attempted to define the character of this work as a philosophical composition, and to appreciate its speculative merits and its practical utility. It cannot be disputed that the work is enriched with a vast variety of curious, though too often doubtful and incautious statements of fact, and that it everywhere displays uncommon powers of ingenious combination; but we are by no means prepared, with Miss Seward, to extol it as a model of philosophical investigation, or to recommend it to the daily and nightly medication of the youthful student.

Before he quitted his residence at Lichfield, Dr Darwin formed a botanical society, consisting of three persons, – which, we believe, is held to be the minimum of a body corporate. The two other members were Sir Brooke Boothby and a proctor of the name of Jackson, whom Miss Seward has characterised as "a would-be philosopher, a turgid and solemn coxcomb"; but who was the chief operator in the translation of the *Linnaean System of Vegetation*, which was published in the name of this society. "His illustrious coadjutors exacted of him fidelity to the sense of the author, and they corrected Jackson's inelegant English, weeding it of its pompous coarseness".

It was about this time also that Dr Darwin first became acquainted with Mrs Pole of Radburn, who was the object of what Miss Seward has called "the Petrarchan attachment of his middle life, more happy in its result than was that of the bard of Vaucluse". It was in consequence of his marriage to this lady in 1781 that he removed from Lichfield to Derby; and it was to her, in married or widowed state, that he addressed several copies of verses, which have since been circulated in periodical publications. But these, with the whole history of this tender attachment, and various other matters of more digressive and extraneous nature, we are compelled to leave without further notice.

From the period of his quitting Lichfield, Miss Seward does not attempt to give more than a slight outline of the domestic history of Dr Darwin. The completion of the task is reserved, we are told, for "his some time pupil, and late years friend, the ingenious Mr Dewhurst Bilsborrow, who is now writing, or has written his life at large". Her information relative to this latter period is avowedly imperfect; and it is to be regretted, that, with better opportunities within her reach, she should have suffered herself to be misled by erroneous report. In the year 1799, Dr Darwin had the misfortune to lose his eldest son, in circumstances extremely distressing. On first perusing the account given by Miss Seward, of the "stoical fortitude" of the father, we were certainly much shocked, and could have pardoned his biographer for a less rigid adherence to the duty of speaking the whole truth. We are pleased now to find, that the statement is partly erroneous, and are happy to afford Miss Seward the present opportunity of correcting it.[1] We now turn to the account which she has given of the poem of *The Botanic Garden*, of which an elaborate analysis and criticism occupies nearly a half of the volume.

About the year 1777, Dr Darwin had purchased "a little, wild, umbrageous valley", in the neighborhood of Lichfield, which he cultivated with great taste; aiming, as Miss Seward expresses it, "to unite the Linnaean science with the charm of landscape". On her first solitary visit to "this luxuriant retreat, with her tablets and pencil, and seated on a flower bank", Miss Seward wrote a little poem of about fifty lines, addressed to Dr Darwin, under the character of the genius of the place; in praise of which, it is enough to say, that, with some alterations, it was afterwards adopted, without acknowledgement, as the introduction to the first canto of *The Botanic Garden*. This we consider as the most curious anecdote in the volume before us; and the correctness of the statement is placed beyond a doubt, by the appearance of her verses as such in the periodical publications of the year in which they were written.

According to Miss Seward's account, it was the perusal of her lines that suggested the idea of a great poem "on the Linnaean system". The composition of it was begun very soon afterwards, but advanced so slowly, that ten years elapsed before the date of publication. By "an inversion of all custom", the second part was first given to the world in 1789; from a consciousness, as Miss Seward supposes, that, in a new and unusual style of poetry, "the loves of the plants" would be more likely to secure immediate popularity, than the bolder conceptions, and still more splendid imagery of *The Economy of Vegetation*.

The long and elaborate analyses of these poems, which Miss Seward has thought fit to give, will, by many readers, be considered as prolix and uninteresting. They are certainly disproportioned to the bulk and nature of her work, if a work so immethodical and desultory can be tried by ordinary rules; but at the same time they will be found interspersed with many critical remarks, which display great justness of poetical taste and feeling.

We have [2] formerly had occasion, at sufficient length, to state our conceptions of the peculiar character and merit of Dr Darwin's poetry; and at present it is not our intention to resume the subject in the point of view under which it was then considered. In truth, the opinions entertained by his biographer, and by those whose criticisms she has adopted, coincide so nearly with those which we had expressed, that there is nothing to justify or provoke a farther discussion. In one respect, however, we feel ourselves compelled to dissent from an opinion entertained by most of the admirers of Dr Darwin, and by none more firmly than Miss Seward. "One extraordinary, and in a poet of so much genius, unprecedented, instance of plagiarism excepted", says Miss Seward, "not one great poet of England is more original than Darwin. His design, his ideas, his style, his manner, are wholly his own".

If it were asked in what chiefly consists the originality of manner which is supposed to characterise the new Darwinian school of English poetry, it would probably be answered, in the first place, that the general design of clothing the philosophy of natural history in the gay attire, and with all the higher graces of poetry, was novel, at least in any English poet; in the second place, that his picturesque style of poetical description, sustained by bold personifications and metaphors, addressed exclusively to the eye, is, in a great degree at least, his own; and, lastly, that, in the loftiness of his laboured and inverted diction, and in the stately march of his highly polished versification, there are peculiarities of manner which it may be difficult to describe, but which must at once be felt as distinguishing him widely from his great predecessors in English poetry.

It is not our intention to arraign Dr Darwin of literary depredation on the property of others, of the felonious kind complained of so justly by Miss Seward; nor shall we venture dogmatically to assert that this peculiar manner to which he has bequeathed his name, was formed on a servile imitation of any existing model. It is true, notwithstanding, that for nearly seventy years there has existed, in obscurity and neglect, a philosophical poem in the English language, stamped incontrovertibly with all those peculiar characters of the Darwinian school to which we have alluded. It is that obscurity and neglect alone which could have exempted Dr Darwin from the charge of having imitated an unsuccessful original; and although it may possibly be true that the poem in question was unknown to him, it will at least become necessary hereafter to date the origin of the school at an earlier period.

The poem was published [3] anonymously in the year 1735; and of its author we have not obtained any information. It is entitled *Universal Beauty*; and its general object is an exposition of whatever is beautiful in the plan and economy of the universe in all its parts. In the prosecution of this object, the author takes a very wide compass; and the general laws which bind the planetary system, the physical laws which peculiarly regulate the globe which we inhabit, the phenomena and provisions of the mineral, the vegetable and the animal kingdoms, are all brought under poetical review; and the more remote and fanciful allusions of the text are illustrated by a series of philosophical notes. That the resemblance does not stop here; but extends still more strikingly to the other characteristic peculiarities of "the Darwinian manner", may be most effectually illustrated by a few extracts, taken at random.

In the third part, which contains a "survey of vegetable nature", after tracing the analogy of animal and vegetable life, we have the following lines, in illustration of "the various provisions of nature, for protecting and supporting the indigent, as the strawberry, cinque-foil, &c.; and supporting the feeble, as the vine, bryony, ivy, &c.; and thus equally propagating and spreading a universality of delights, pleasures, and enjoyments".

'Thus mantling snug beneath a verdant veil,
The creepers draw their horizontal trail;
Wide o'er the bank, the plantal reptile bends;
Adown its stem, the rooty fringe depends,
The feeble boughs with anch'ring safety binds,
Nor leaves precarious to insulting winds;
The tendrils next of slender, helpless size,
Ascendant thro' luxurious pamp'ring rise;
Kind nature soothes their innocence of pride,
While buoy'd aloft the flow'ring wantons ride,
With fond adhesion round the cedar cling,
And wreathing, circulate their am'rous ring,
Sublime, with winding maturation grow,
And clench'd retentive gripe the topmost bough;
Here climb direct, the ministerial rock,
And clasping firm, its steepy fragments lock;
Or various, with agglutinating guile,

Cement tenacious to some neighb'ring pile;
Investing green, some fabric here ascend,
And clust'ring, o'er its pinnacles depend.'

Part III. 1. 271–290.

In allusion to those plants which are supposed to obey the influence of the sun and moon, we find the following lines:

'Here, winding to the Sun's magnetic ray,
The solar plants adore the Lord of Day;
With Persian rites idolatrous incline,
And worship towards his consecrated shrine;
By south, from east to west, obsequious turn,
And mov'd with sympathetic ardours burn.
To these adverse, the Lunar sects dissent,
With convolution of opposed bent;
From west to east by equal influence tend,
And towards the Moon's attractive crescence bend;
There nightly worship with Sidonian zeal,
And Queen of Heaven, Astarte's idol hail.'

Part III. 1. 313–324.

We regret that our limits do not admit of the author's description (Part IV. 1. 120–204) of the circulation of the blood in animals, illustrated by a picturesque analogy of the motions to the fluid parts of the globe. The following lines, taken from Part V., refer to that species of insects which, like the beetle, "by a surprising machinery of little springs and hinges, erect the smooth covering of their backs, and unfolding their wings that were most neatly disposed within their cases, prepare for flight".

'Or who a twofold apparatus share,
Natives of earth, and habitants of air,
Like warriors stride oppressed with shining mail,
But furl'd beneath, their silken pennons veil.
Deceived our fellow reptile we admire
His bright endorsement and compact attire,
When lo! The latent springs of motion play,
And rising lids disclose the rich inlay;
The tissu'd wing its folded membrane frees,
And with blyth quavers fans the gathering breeze;
Elate tow'rds heav'n the beauteous wonder flies,
And leaves the mortal wrapt in deep surprise.

303

So when the guide led Tobit's youthful heir,
Elect, to win the sev'n times widow'd fair,
Th'angelic form, conceal'd in human guise,
Deceiv'd the search of his associate's eyes;
swift each charm bursts forth like issuing flame,
And circling rays confess his heavenly frame;
The zodiac round his waste divinely turns,
And waving radiance o'er his plumage burns;
In awful transports rapt, the youth admires,
While light from earth and dazzling shape aspires.'

Part V. 1. 127–148.

We cannot refrain from giving a part of this writer's description of the creation of those planetary systems of which the universe is composed. It is a favourite topic with both poets.

'Swift roll'd the spheres to their appointed place,
Jocund through heaven to run the various race;
Orb within orb in living circlets turn,
And central suns through every system burn;
Revolving planets on their gods attend,
And towards each sun with awful reverence bend;
Still towards the loved, enlivening beam they wheel,
And pant, and tremble like the amorous steel.
They spring, they revel in the blaze of day,
Bathe in the golden stream, and drink the orient ray;
Their blithe satellites with lively glance
(Celestial equipage) around them dance;
All, distance due, and beauteous order keep,
And spinning soft, upon their centres sleep.'

Part I. 1. 94–104.

Similar passages might easily be accumulated, but these may serve as a specimen of the peculiar manner of this forgotten poet. Of its resemblance to that of Dr Darwin, we shall leave our readers to judge. That there are obvious shades of difference, we have no hesitation to admit; nor do we call in question the decided superiority of the latter. The poem of *Universal Beauty* is indeed extremely unequal: passages occur which are worthy of Sir Richard Blackmore; and in others there may be discovered an unsuccessful effort to imitate the fashionable antithetic manner of Pope. Whether or not the poetry of Darwin would, in the age of Pope, have incurred the same hazard of neglect with that of the writer whom we have ventured to exhibit as his prototype, we shall not presume to conjecture.

Notes

1   The following note has been communicated to the Editor of this *Review*. "The author of the *Memoirs of Dr Darwin*, since they were published, has discovered, on the attestation of his family, and of the other persons present at the juncture, that the statement given of his exclamation, page 406, on the death of Mr Erasmus Darwin, is entirely without foundation, and that the Doctor, on the melancholy event, gave, amongst his own family, proofs of strong sensibility at the time, and of succeeding regard to the memory of his son, which he seemed to have a pride in concealing from the world. In justice to his memory, she is desirous to correct the misinformation she had received, and will therefore be obliged to the Editor of the *Edinburgh Review* to notice the circumstance in the criticisms of the book, since, unless a second edition should be called for, she has no means so effectual of counteracting the mistake".

2   *Review*, No. IV. Art. XX.

3   *Universal Beauty, a Poem* (London: J. Wolcox. 1735). Folio. It consists of six parts, published successively, containing each about 400 lines.

Index